Expert Microsoft Teams Solutions

A guide to Teams architecture and integration for advanced end users and administrators

Aaron Guilmette

Yura Lee

Grant Oliasani

Angel Aviles

BIRMINGHAM—MUMBAI

Expert Microsoft Teams Solutions

Group Product Manager: Ashwin Nair
Publishing Product Manager: Pavan Ramchandani
Senior Editor: Hayden Edwards
Content Development Editor: Aamir Ahmed
Technical Editor: Joseph Aloocaran
Copy Editor: Safis Editing
Project Coordinator: Rashika BA
Proofreader: Safis Editing
Indexer: Hemangini Bari
Production Designer: Shankar Kalbhor

First published: April 2022

Production reference: 1080422

Published by Packt Publishing Ltd.
Livery Place
35 Livery Street
Birmingham
B3 2PB, UK.

ISBN 978-1-80107-555-8

www.packt.com

This book is dedicated to everyone who wants to be more productive.
While many people say that the best technology is invisible, we like to
think that the best technology is that which lets you spend less time with
technology and more time with the people you care about.

– Aaron, Yura, Angel, and Grant

Contributors

About the authors

Aaron Guilmette is a senior program manager at Microsoft, helping customers adopt the Microsoft 365 platform. He primarily focuses on collaborative technologies, including Microsoft Teams, Exchange Online, and Azure Active Directory.

Aaron lives in the Michigan area of Detroit with his five children. When he's not busy solving technical problems, writing, or running his children to events, he's likely making a pizza.

> *I would like to thank my children and my long-suffering partner, Christine, for understanding while I skipped game and date nights to work on this project. I also want to thank the staff at Packt Publishing, including Aamir Ahmed, Divij Kotian, Pavan Ramchandani, and Hayden Edwards. Some of them have endured through seven books with me. I'm not sure which of us is more a glutton for punishment!*

Yura Lee is a security program manager at Microsoft, focusing on cloud data security for her customers. She has years of experience as a Microsoft 365 and Azure consultant and technical specialist in the field.

Yura lives in New Jersey with her husband.

> *I would like to thank my co-authors, Aaron, Angel, and Grant, for this wonderfully collaborative experience. And a shout out to the entire Packt team for this rewarding opportunity and for polishing my work!*

Grant Oliasani is a senior customer success manager at Microsoft, helping customers realize the value in Microsoft Teams and Power Platform.

Grant currently resides in Tennessee with his wife.

> *I would like to thank my Microsoft family and my wife, Lauren,*
> *for supporting me in this project and throughout my career.*

Angel Aviles is a seasoned unified communications and telecommunications engineer with over 20 years of experience in the field. He is passionate about bleeding-edge technology and integrating voice, video, and collaboration systems. He has worked for Microsoft for over 7 years as an Office 365 deployment consultant and voice technology specialist and is currently a Modern Communications Customer Success Manager.

> *I would like to thank my family, especially my wife, Meredith, my parents,*
> *and my wonderful work family for their support in developing me into the*
> *person I am today.*

About the reviewers

Aaron Steele is a 20+ year IT veteran who now works at Microsoft as a technical program manager overseeing meetings and events of Microsoft Teams. He lives "where the Midwest vacations" in the "Cherry Capital of the World" as they call it, with his amazing wife of more than 18 years, two wonderful children, two cats, and one standard poodle named Molly.

Aaron has helped customers implement Teams-powered events solutions during the growth period that Microsoft saw with Microsoft Teams during the Covid pandemic. Before his current role, he was on a team of some of the best in the company at helping customers understand their Teams and Skype for Business setups and problems and helping them to fix them. He took that role after being a solutions architect inside the Microsoft Consulting services team.

Before his current 11+ year career at Microsoft, Aaron spent time working with Teams in the publishing, media, and entertainment sectors, as well as with two higher education institutions in the city of Chicago, along with a start up consulting firm where he led projects to design and implement Microsoft voice solutions for customers from the time when this was first possible in OCS 2007 R2.

In his time away from work, he enjoys baking bread and cooking dinner with, and for, his family, as well as curing and smoking meats. Being near the fresh water of Lake Michigan has always brought him and his family pleasure, playing in and on the water and enjoying its bounties.

Denzil Fernandes is a Teams technical specialist at Microsoft, based in Toronto, Canada. Specializing in modern work, he has guided large financial and manufacturing organizations in deploying Microsoft workloads in the cloud. He is enthusiastic about learning and sharing knowledge, tips, and tricks about digital transformation.

Table of Contents

3
Task Management in Teams

4
Bookings in Teams

Part 2: Meetings

5
Conducting Teams Meetings

Part 3: Bots and Development

8
Power Apps in Teams

9
Workflow Integration

10
Power Virtual Agents in Teams

Part 4: Voice

11
Planning for Teams Phone

12
Deploying Teams Phone

13
Configuring Advanced Teams Phone Features

14

Teams Devices

Part 5: Administration

15

Planning and Adoption

16

Governance

17

Integration with Exchange Server

18

Security and Data Protection

19

Reporting in Teams

Appendix A

Direct Routing and Operator Connect

Index

Other Books You May Enjoy

Preface

Microsoft Teams is the new hub for collaboration in the modern and hybrid workplace! Teams brings together familiar parts of the Microsoft 365 platform, including instant messaging and file sharing. It also introduces telephony, development, and platform tools, helping businesses and end users create an environment that helps them to do more in the same space without switching between applications.

Who this book is for

This book is for individuals who will be responsible for deploying and managing Microsoft Teams-based solutions. Assuming no prior knowledge, this book will equip you with the knowledge and skills to plan and deploy Microsoft Teams for your organizations.

What this book covers

This book has 19 chapters, covering all aspects of Microsoft Teams. It starts by explaining the basic organizational structure and architecture behind Microsoft Teams and then dives into exploring features, including a deep dive on planning and deploying Teams Phone solutions. Finally, it concludes with planning and adoption, governance, and reporting:

Chapter 1, *Taking a Tour of Microsoft Teams*, introduces the Microsoft Teams product, features, architecture, and terminology.

Chapter 2, *Approvals*, provides an overview of how the Approvals app can be used in Microsoft Teams to create approval workflows.

Chapter 3, *Task Management in Teams*, brings together Planner, To Do, and the Tasks app for managing personal and group tasks.

Chapter 4, *Bookings in Teams*, introduces the Bookings app and how it can be used to allow external customers the ability to book appointments.

Chapter 5, *Conducting Teams Meetings*, walks through conducting scheduled, channel, and ad hoc meetings in Teams.

Chapter 6, Microsoft Teams Rooms, introduces Microsoft Teams Rooms—dedicated devices for presenting content in meetings.

Chapter 7, Live Events, provides information on conducting broadcast-style meetings for internal and external attendees.

Chapter 8, Power Apps in Teams, introduces Teams as a development and application integration platform.

Chapter 9, Workflow Integration, shows how Teams can be used to bring users, applications, and business processes together through workflows.

Chapter 10, Power Virtual Agents in Teams, demonstrates how Power Virtual Agents and chatbots can be used to add interactive applications to the Microsoft Teams environment.

Chapter 11, Planning for Teams Phone, is a deep-dive into the Teams Phone architecture, providing guidance on how to design a Microsoft Teams-based telephony solution.

Chapter 12, Deploying Teams Phone, builds on the knowledge acquired in *Chapter 11, Planning for Teams Phone*, and demonstrates how to successfully deploy a Teams Phone system.

Chapter 13, Configuring Advanced Teams Phone Features, provides guidance on configuring advanced features such as auto attendants and call queues.

Chapter 14, Teams Devices, gives an overview of devices specifically designed for the Teams environment, including headsets, desk phones, and Surface Hub devices.

Chapter 15, Planning and Adoption, outlines the Microsoft Adoption Framework for helping organizations generate excitement and scale Teams deployments.

Chapter 16, Governance, introduces concepts regarding the overall life cycle planning for Microsoft Teams.

Chapter 17, Integration with Exchange Server, shows how Teams works with Microsoft Exchange Server and Exchange Online.

Chapter 18, Security and Data Protection, demonstrates the security, data protection, and compliance controls that are available to protect organizational data and Teams users.

Chapter 19, Reporting in Teams, introduces the reports and dashboards that can be used to review Teams usage.

Appendix A, Direct Routing and Operator Connect, provides an overview of Operator Connect and Direct Routing, as well as general configuration guidance.

To get the most out of this book

To follow along with the examples in this book, you should have a Microsoft 365 subscription that includes licenses for Microsoft Teams, Exchange Online, SharePoint Online, and Azure AD Premium P1. Configuring Teams Phone solutions in *Chapter 12, Deploying Teams Phone*, and *Chapter 13, Configuring Advanced Teams Phone Features*, will require enterprise voice features, including a Phone System license and calling plans.

You can obtain a free 30-day trial of Microsoft 365 E5, which includes all licenses and software necessary, from `https://go.microsoft.com/fwlink/ p/?LinkID=698279`. After signing up for an Office 365 E5 trial, you can add either an Azure AD Premium P1 or Microsoft 365 E5 trial from the admin center under **Purchase Services**.

Alternatively, you can sign up for a free developer account at `https://developer. microsoft.com/en-us/microsoft-365/dev-program`, which will give you access to the Microsoft 365 platform for 90 days.

Software/hardware covered in the book	Link
Microsoft Teams PowerShell	`https://docs.microsoft.com/en-us/ MicrosoftTeams/teams-powershell- managing-teams`

Download the example code files

You can download the image files for this book from GitHub at `https://github. com/PacktPublishing/Expert-Microsoft-Teams-Solutions`. If there's an update to the code, it will be updated in the GitHub repository.

We also have other code bundles from our rich catalog of books and videos available at `https://github.com/PacktPublishing/`. Check them out!

Download the color images

We also provide a PDF file that has color images of the screenshots and diagrams used in this book. You can download it here: `https://static.packt-cdn.com/ downloads/9781801075558_ColorImages.pdf`.

Conventions used

There are a number of text conventions used throughout this book.

`Code in text`: Indicates code words in the text, database table names, folder names, filenames, file extensions, pathnames, dummy URLs, user input, and Twitter handles. Here is an example: "You can use the `Get-MsolAccountSku` cmdlet to retrieve a list of SKUs."

A block of code is set as follows:

```
If (!(Get-Module -ListAvailable MSOnline)) { Install-Module
MSOnline}
Connect-MsolService -Credential (Get-Credential)
```

When we wish to draw your attention to a particular part of a code block, the relevant lines or items are set in bold:

```
Set-MsolUser -UserPrincipalName NewYorkMTR01@advancedmsteams.
com -UsageLocation [region]
Set-MsolUserLicense -UserPrincipalName NewYorkMTR01@
advancedmsteams.com -AddLicenses "advancedmsteams:MEETING_ROOM"
```

Any command-line input or output is written as follows:

```
Set-MsolUserLicense -UserPrincipalName NewYorkMTR01@
advancedmsteams.com -AddLicenses "advancedmsteams:MEETING_ROOM"
```

Bold: Indicates a new term, an important word, or words that you see on screen. For instance, words in menus or dialog boxes appear in **bold**. Here is an example: "Search for and select **Power Virtual Agents**."

> **Tips or Important Notes**
> Appear like this.

Get in touch

Feedback from our readers is always welcome.

General feedback: If you have questions about any aspect of this book, email us at `customercare@packtpub.com` and mention the book title in the subject of your message.

Errata: Although we have taken every care to ensure the accuracy of our content, mistakes do happen. If you have found a mistake in this book, we would be grateful if you would report this to us. Please visit www.packtpub.com/support/errata and fill in the form.

Piracy: If you come across any illegal copies of our works in any form on the internet, we would be grateful if you would provide us with the location address or website name. Please contact us at copyright@packt.com with a link to the material.

If you are interested in becoming an author: If there is a topic that you have expertise in and you are interested in either writing or contributing to a book, please visit authors.packtpub.com.

Share Your Thoughts

Once you've read *Expert Microsoft Teams Solutions*, we'd love to hear your thoughts! Scan the QR code below to go straight to the Amazon review page for this book and share your feedback.

https://packt.link/r/1-801-07555-7

Your review is important to us and the tech community and will help us make sure we're delivering excellent quality content.

Part 1: Collaboration and Apps

This part of the book focuses on the native features and built-in apps of the Microsoft Teams platform, as well as some of the underlying technology components.

This part comprises the following chapters:

- *Chapter 1, Taking a Tour of Microsoft Teams*
- *Chapter 2, Approvals*
- *Chapter 3, Task Management in Teams*
- *Chapter 4, Bookings in Teams*

1

Taking a Tour of Microsoft Teams

Welcome to **Microsoft Teams** – the new hub for collaboration in the modern workplace! Microsoft Teams is part revolutionary and part evolutionary – a whole new way to connect and integrate data, applications, and communications by bringing together familiar pieces of the Microsoft 365 ecosystem (and introducing some new ones).

Microsoft Teams is a collaboration and communications tool as well as a development platform. As a collaborative tool, it allows users to natively leverage existing applications such as Exchange calendaring or SharePoint document management. As a communications tool, it replaces the instant messaging and telephony capabilities of Skype for Business. And, as a platform, it provides internal and external developers ways to integrate data in third-party external applications (such as Salesforce or Adobe Document Cloud) as well as use Microsoft-based tools to connect to cloud-based services and applications (such as Dynamics 365, Power BI, or Planner).

In this chapter, we're going to review the foundational concepts of Microsoft Teams, including:

- Architecture
- User interface

Once you have those basics under your belt, we'll be getting into the more advanced features and capabilities.

Let's get going!

Architecture

Microsoft Teams is a collaboration and communications tool as well as an application development platform built on several existing cloud services. While it may present a simple **User Interface** (**UI**) on the surface, Teams brings an enormous number of technologies to bear, all unified under a single experience. These diverse components and services make up the Microsoft Teams architecture.

The core object in Microsoft Teams is a **team**, which is based on a Microsoft 365 group. A Microsoft 365 group is comprised of an Exchange group mailbox, a SharePoint site collection, and a OneNote notebook. Microsoft Teams adds additional features, structures, and extensibility to that Microsoft 365 group.

From an implementation perspective, any Microsoft 365 group can be converted or extended into a Microsoft Teams object (some authors and articles may use the term **teamify** to communicate the idea of converting a standard Microsoft 365 group into a team).

You might think of a team as a sort of container object that can be used to group related conversations and resources. Inside the team, channels can be used to further organize content around topics, departments, projects, or other categories. *Figure 1.1* shows the Microsoft Teams user interface and how these concepts of teams and channels are presented:

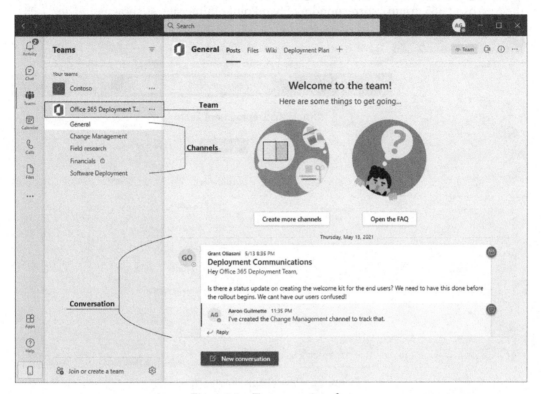

Figure 1.1 – Teams user interface

Different content types such as files and messages are stored and managed inside the team. While a Microsoft 365 group by itself is somewhat of a flat object, teamifying a group creates structures and linkages inside that object. *Figure 1.1* shows both the team channels (such as subfolders). Each of those channels maps to a unique subfolder inside the Microsoft 365 group's corresponding SharePoint Online site, as shown in *Figure 1.2*:

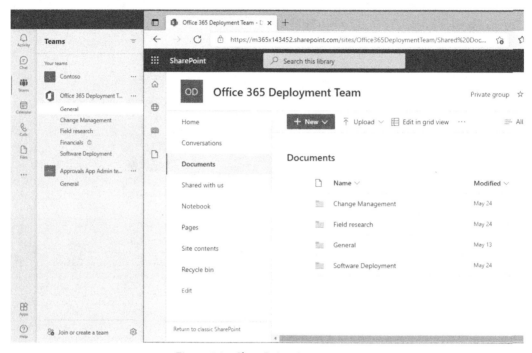

Figure 1.2 – SharePoint site structure

The exception to this is a private channel. Private channels are used to restrict information to a smaller subset of users in the team. Private channels have their own membership list. In *Figure 1.2*, the **Financials** channel is identified as a private channel by the lock icon next to its name. Private channels show up in the team channel hierarchy, but the channel's file content is actually stored in a separate SharePoint site with a different set of permissions. This prevents users who are members of the team (but not the private channel) from gaining access to the data stored in that channel.

The following diagram shows a deeper look at the connection points between services, applications, and storage inside the Microsoft Teams ecosystem:

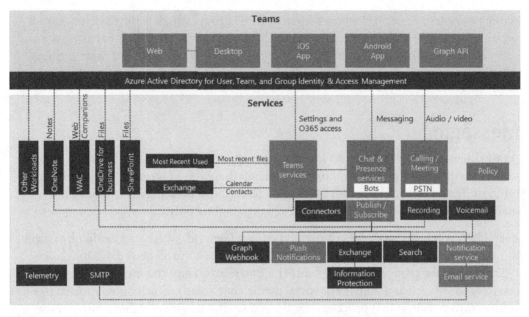

Figure 1.3 – Teams architecture overview

The following list highlights some of the core features and components:

- Identity
- Messaging
- Files
- Voicemail
- Recording
- Calendars and meetings
- Contacts

Let's expand further on some of these.

Identity

It should come as no surprise that identity is the core of everything in the Microsoft 365 ecosystem. Microsoft has emphasized the phrase "identity is the security boundary" as part of its **zero trust** design principles. **Azure Active Directory** (**Azure AD** or **AAD**) provides the identity storage and authentication functionality for all Microsoft 365-based workloads.

As we just noted, Azure AD stores a Microsoft 365 group, which is the directory object on which a team is built. Azure AD also holds other security principals (such as user and guest accounts), which can be added to Microsoft 365 group (and team) memberships. All of these identity components provide the infrastructure and security for all Microsoft workloads.

Messaging

As we discussed a few paragraphs ago, a Microsoft 365 group (and by extension, a team) also includes a group mailbox component. There is no corresponding Exchange on-premises "team" or "Microsoft 365 group" feature and no capability to move the mailbox component on-premises – it is Exchange Online only.

Each Microsoft team has a default channel named **General**, which can neither be deleted nor renamed. *Figure 1.1* depicts a team and how channels are displayed. Channels are typically used for group-related content. The **Posts** tab on any channel contains text conversations (such as a bulletin or social media chat board). Chat content posted in a team's conversation is first processed by the Azure chat service and then stored in the team's corresponding Exchange Online group mailbox to enable compliance features (such as retention and eDiscovery). Chat or instant messaging content transmitted during a chat transaction is ingested into the participating users' mailboxes.

Files

Each team is connected to a SharePoint site. Files can be uploaded directly to the team's SharePoint site, to a particular channel's **Files** tab, or posted in a channel's **Posts** tab. Any file posted to a channel's **Posts** tab will automatically be uploaded to the team's SharePoint site, and a link to the actual file will be placed in the conversation.

Voicemail

If a user is configured for telephony features, any voicemails they receive are stored as audio files in the individual user's mailbox.

Recording

Call or meeting recordings were originally processed by Azure Media services and then encoded for long-term storage in Microsoft Stream. Microsoft has recently updated the architecture and individual user recordings are stored in the user's OneDrive, while recordings of channel meetings stay with the team in SharePoint.

Calendars and meetings

Scheduling objects rely on a user's Microsoft Exchange mailbox. The user's mailbox can be located in Exchange Online or on-premises (though using on-premises deployment will require an Exchange hybrid configuration to work successfully).

You can read more about configuring an Exchange hybrid for Microsoft Teams in *Chapter 17, Integration with Exchange Server*.

Contacts

Like calendars and meeting objects, contacts are also stored in an individual user's Exchange mailbox (online or on-premises). Connecting to an on-premises mailbox requires an Exchange hybrid, as detailed in *Chapter 17, Integration with Exchange Server*.

As you've seen, there are a lot of familiar components in Teams architecture. As a general rule of thumb, *communications* content is stored in a mailbox (either in the team's group mailbox or the user's mailbox) while *file* content is stored in SharePoint Online. Other services may interact with and process data streams, but they will typically store communications or file content in one of those locations. It's important to note that the primary Teams data and artifact storage locations are Exchange and SharePoint Online – both of which can be governed by Microsoft 365 data retention policies.

Other Microsoft 365 applications (such as Power BI, Power Automate, or Tasks by Planner and To Do) have their own primary data storage locations. While these applications and services store data elsewhere in the Microsoft 365 ecosystem, they have very tight API integration with Microsoft Teams.

Architecture deep dive

Now that you have a basic understanding of the components at a high level, let's go a little bit deeper into both the Microsoft 365 and Microsoft Teams architectures.

First, we'll look at the Microsoft 365 group architecture.

Microsoft 365 Groups

As we mentioned earlier in the chapter, the foundation of a team is a Microsoft 365 group. The Microsoft 365 group is an Azure AD object that has an Exchange group mailbox, a SharePoint site collection, and a OneNote notebook. Their relationships are shown in *Figure 1.4*:

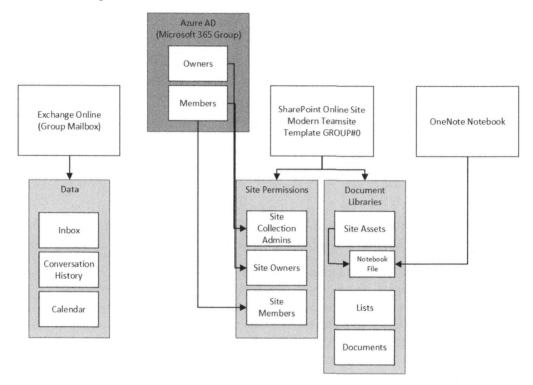

Figure 1.4 – Microsoft 365 Groups

A Microsoft 365 group can be provisioned in many ways, including the following:

- Microsoft 365 admin center
- Azure AD admin center
- Planner
- Yammer
- Exchange Online
- Outlook
- PowerShell
- Dynamics CRM
- Graph API
- SharePoint Online
- Client Side Object Model for SharePoint Online

Microsoft 365 groups provisioned through any of these applications, services, or interfaces will all have the same underlying components (a group mailbox, a site, and a notebook). The provisioning service or application will use the Microsoft 365 Groups membership for its administration and security.

A Microsoft 365 group has the concept of owners (those who can administer the membership or other aspects of the group) and members (those who participate in group messages but cannot control the membership or features of the group). Microsoft 365 group owners are mapped to the SharePoint site collection administrators and site owners groups while the members are mapped to the SharePoint site members group.

The OneNote notebook is stored inside the site assets document library. Files sent to the group are stored in the default document library.

Teams

Building on the Microsoft 365 group, *Figure 1.5* shows where the Microsoft Teams components fit in:

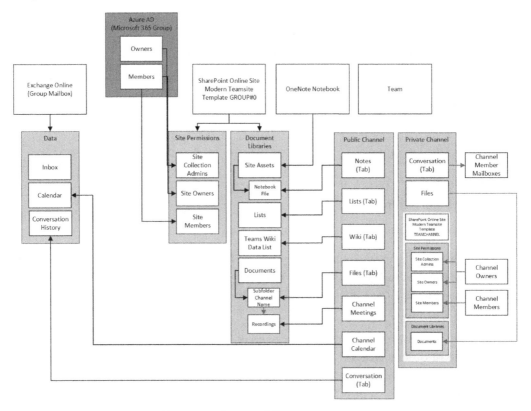

Figure 1.5 – Microsoft Teams components

As you can see, a Microsoft Teams team builds on the foundation of the Microsoft 365 group:

- The **Wiki** data for a team is stored in a new SharePoint list called **Teams Wiki Data**.
- Channel meeting recordings are stored in the **Recordings** subfolder of the corresponding channel's folder in the default document library.
- Conversations are stored in the mailbox's **Conversation History** folder.
- The **Channel Calendar** data is stored in the group mailbox calendar.

You'll also notice that data and permissions for a private channel are handled differently:

- The file storage location is a new site. The permissions of the site are mapped from the private channel owners and members lists.
- The chat on the conversation tab is stored in the **Conversation History** folder of the private channel team members (as opposed to the team's group mailbox **Conversation History** folder).
- Private channel SharePoint sites are linked to their parent site by storing the parent site's object GUID in the `RelatedGroupID` property of the private channel site.

You may want to bookmark this section so that you can refer to it as you progress throughout the book and move on to both Teams administration tasks and troubleshooting. There are a lot of moving pieces in the Teams architecture, and it's easy to forget where they fit in.

Next, we'll look deeper into navigating the Microsoft Teams user interface and some of its features.

User Interface

While we've already seen a little bit of the user interface, in this section, we're going to explore more of it and how the pieces work. We'll start off with a reference image to remind you where things are in general, and then drill down into each of the main areas:

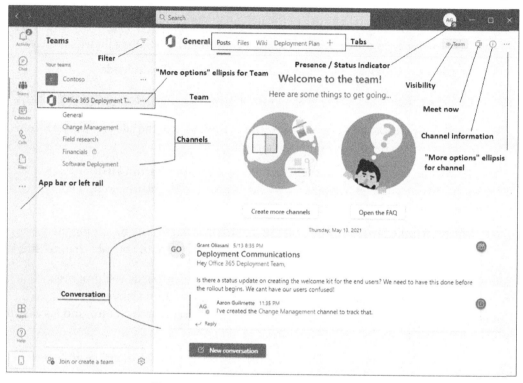

Figure 1.6 – Annotated Teams user interface

There are myriad clickable action buttons and areas in the Teams interface. Here's a quick rundown of the main areas:

- **Menu bar**: This area, along the top of the user interface, has both new and familiar buttons. If you're familiar with Windows applications, you'll instantly recognize the **Minimize, Restore Up/Down**, and **Exit** buttons at the far right of the bar. New to the Teams interface, the **Menu** bar also displays **Forward** and **Back** navigation buttons and hosts a **Search** bar, which can be used to search across all Teams areas. The **Menu** bar also displays the logged-in user's avatar (either their initials or an image if they choose to upload one), along with a small bubble indicating their **presence** (sometimes referred to as **status**) information.

- **App bar (or left rail)**: This is the area on the far-left side of the screen where icons such as **Activity, Chat, Teams, Calendar, Calls**, and **Files** appear. Administrators can manage the icons that appear here, and users can edit the order of the icons.

- **List pane**: This is the middle area of the Teams user interface and displays the items that correspond to the view selected in the left rail. For example, in *Figure 1.6*, the Teams view is selected, so the list pane shows all of the user's currently joined teams. The list pane also features a **Filter** button at the top of the column, which allows you to search and filter items in the list pane to locate things more quickly, and a **Join or create a team** button at the bottom.

- **Main content area**: This is the area on the far-right side of the Teams interface. This area will change to display the content of whatever item is selected in the list pane. For example, in *Figure 1.6*, the Office 365 Deployment Team is selected, and the main content area is displaying data from the **Posts** tab.

Now that you're familiar with the overall structure and layout of the Teams user interface, let's expand upon each of the items on the left rail.

Activity

If you're familiar with modern applications (social media apps, modern mobile phones, or desktop apps), you're probably familiar with the concept of activity and notifications. Like those modern applications that have notifications, Microsoft Teams also uses notification bubbles to highlight new items.

The **Activity** view is used to draw your attention to things specifically targeted to either you, a team you're in, or a channel you're in. For example, in the following **Activity** view example, you can see a few items:

- The user Grant has assigned the logged-in user some tasks.

- The user Grant has modified the priority of these tasks.

- The user Isiah has made the logged-in user the owner of the Contoso group:

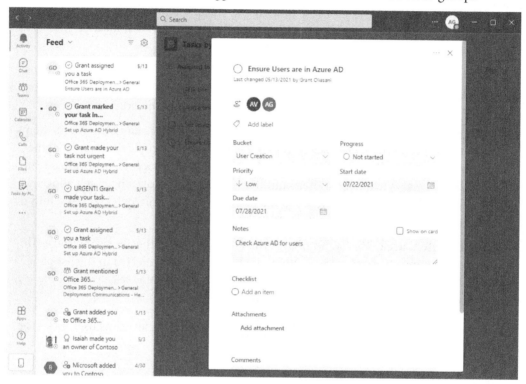

Figure 1.7 – Teams Activity view

As with popular social media platforms, you can use the @ symbol to **mention** an individual, channel, or team. These *mentions* will show up in the **Activity** view for the individual user mentioned (or for each member of a channel or team mentioned), similar to how mentions work in the **To** line of Outlook. In addition to other users mentioning you or your teammates, apps can also generate notifications that will show up in your activity feed.

Chat and presence

By selecting the **Chat** view, you can initiate one-to-one or one-to-many (also known as group) conversations. Chat is an essential part of the Microsoft Teams experience. You can search for users from the address book and add them to conversations.

User avatars (both yourself and others you invite) have a presence indicator in the form of a bubble, which lets others know the status of the user. Broad status categories include the following:

- **Available**
- **Busy**
- **Do not disturb**
- **Away**
- **Offline**

Each status has a corresponding color. Some statuses may include additional detail (such as *Focusing, Presenting,* or *In a Call*). **Do not disturb** statuses are special in that others cannot contact you during this time (with the exception of people you place on a special list called **priority access**).

Teams

You should already be familiar with the **Teams** view, which was displayed previously in *Figure 1.6*. The **Teams** view shows all the teams to which you're currently joined and gives you a way to navigate the various teams and channels.

Calendar

The **Calendar** view shows the entries on your current calendar (whether Exchange Online or on-premises) and allows you to create both impromptu and scheduled meetings:

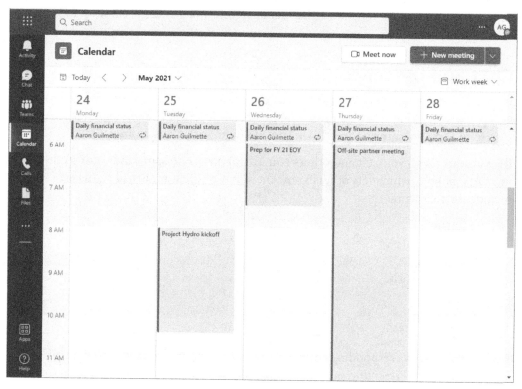

Figure 1.8 – Teams Calendar view

Creating a meeting through the **Calendar** view automatically adds a Teams meeting link if the meeting has attendees.

Calls

The **Calls** view shows a mix of information, depending on what features are enabled. The view will show various calling items, such as a call log and voicemail history, as well as the option to view contacts stored in the user's Outlook mailbox. If the user has a voice plan included, then the screen will display a dial pad:

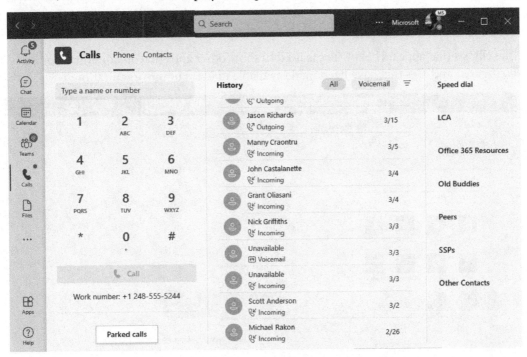

Figure 1.9 – Calls view

As seen in *Figure 1.9*, call directionality (whether incoming or outbound) is included. There is also a status icon, indicating whether an inbound caller left a voicemail.

Files

The **Files** view displays files that the user has stored in the OneDrive for Business site, as well as files they have access to through the Teams interface. Additionally, users can configure external storage services (such as Box, Dropbox, or Google Workspace) to make their data visible in Teams.

More added apps

The ellipsis that appears below files is used to show other apps that an administrator has configured and files that have been made available to users in the organization:

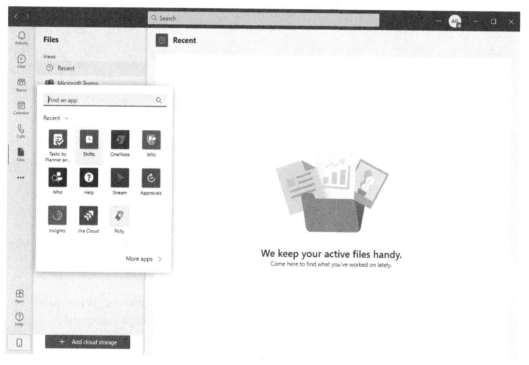

Figure 1.10 – More apps

Administrators can add and remove apps, making them available to the organization as a whole or scoped to individuals and groups of users.

Apps store

The **Apps** store view contains first-party (created by Microsoft) and third-party apps available to use in the environment. Administrators can block or allow apps and bots from being added to the left rail or channels. Additionally, administrators can deploy apps to individuals or users through policies.

Help

The **Help** link provides access to web-based training and feedback options.

Download mobile app

Clicking the **Download mobile app** icon at the bottom of the left rail displays a QR code on screen that you can scan with a mobile phone. The QR code directs you to the Microsoft Teams application in the appropriate platform's mobile app store.

The Microsoft Teams user interface is packed full of features and options, connecting you to the different parts of the Microsoft 365 ecosystem. Spend some time familiarizing yourself with the locations of the different interface elements, as they'll become important when customizing the experience for your users.

Summary

Microsoft Teams is the latest entry in the productivity software space. By incorporating familiar cloud services such as Exchange Online and SharePoint Online, along with an application development environment, Teams provides users and organizations with a broad array of capabilities.

In this chapter, we covered the high-level architecture of Microsoft Teams as well as the major parts of the user interface.

In the next chapter, we'll start looking at ways to build approval workflows for the Microsoft Teams experience.

2
Approvals

If you've ever had to get individuals or teams to sign off various stages of a project, expense, or document revision, you've likely worked with approvals in some fashion. **Approvals**, from a Microsoft Teams perspective, is an integrated application that can be used to get those signoffs through Microsoft Teams instead of walking a document through the office.

Approvals are just what they sound like – proof that someone has agreed to a certain requirement or condition as part of a project or process.

In this chapter, we're going to look at working with approvals in Microsoft Teams. We will cover the following topics:

- Creating approvals
- Responding to approvals
- Approval templates
- Administration of the Approvals app

By the end of this chapter, you'll be able to explain the requirements of the Approvals app, create and respond to approvals, and enable or disable the Approvals app for your users.

Let's get started!

Technical requirements

Before we get started, we'll need to understand the requirements of Approvals in Microsoft Teams. Approvals in Teams requires specific licensing and access to the **Microsoft Dataverse** (previously known as the **Common Data Service**).

Let's review the overall requirements:

- Permissions to create a Microsoft Dataverse database (if it's the first time anyone in your tenant is creating an approval)

> **Restricted Permissions Note**
>
> If your organization has restricted permissions based on a least-privilege model, the first user to attempt to use approvals may be unable to instantiate the database. If this is the case, an administrator will need to follow the steps located at `https://docs.microsoft.com/en-us/power-platform/admin/create-environment#create-an-environment-with-a-database` to create the environment and database. If you are attempting to create a Dataverse database in the GCC environment, you will need to open a support ticket.

- A license for Microsoft Power Automate, Office 365, or Dynamics 365
- A license for Microsoft Forms to set up new approval templates

Once you've met those requirements, you can begin creating approvals.

Creating approvals

By default, the Approvals app is available for all the users in your environment (we'll discuss turning it off toward the end of this chapter). To launch the app, you can expand the **More added apps** ellipsis on the left rail and select the **Approvals** app, as shown in the following screenshot:

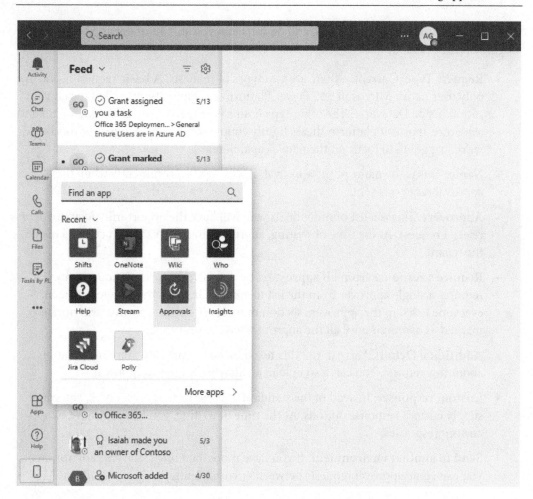

Figure 2.1 – Launching the Approvals app from the desktop client

There may be a slight delay the first time you launch the Approvals app as it will take a few moments to provision the Microsoft Dataverse configuration. The experience is the same, regardless of whether you use the Teams desktop app or the Teams web app.

Once everything has been provisioned, you can begin working with approvals.

An approval has several parts, terms, and options that you should understand before you begin. These are as follows:

- **Request Type**: Currently, there are two types of requests. A **basic** request is one that only uses native Microsoft 365 Power Platform components, and all of the content is stored inside Dataverse. The other type is an **eSign** request. This is a document and signature approval platform that is tightly coupled with Adobe Sign. For this book, we're just going to focus on the native capabilities.

- **Name**: This is the name of the approval. It will appear prominently when the approval request is sent.

- **Approvers**: This is a list of individuals who will have the opportunity to approve or reject a request. At the time of writing, approvers must be existing accounts inside the tenant.

- **Require a response from all approvers**: By default, an approval request only requires a single approver from the list to approve it. With this toggle activated, everyone listed in the approvers section must approve. The approval will not be marked as *approved* until all the approvers have approved it.

- **Additional Details**: You can use this text area box to provide more information about this request. You can also upload an attachment to the approval.

- **Custom responses**: Instead of the standard *approve* or *reject* responses, you can supply custom response options. At the time of writing, you can only have two custom responses.

- **Send to another environment**: If you have more than one Dataverse environment, you can route approval requests between environments.

Now that we understand these concepts, we are ready to create our first approval. To create an approval, follow these steps:

1. From inside Microsoft Teams, open the Approvals app and select the **+ New approval request** button:

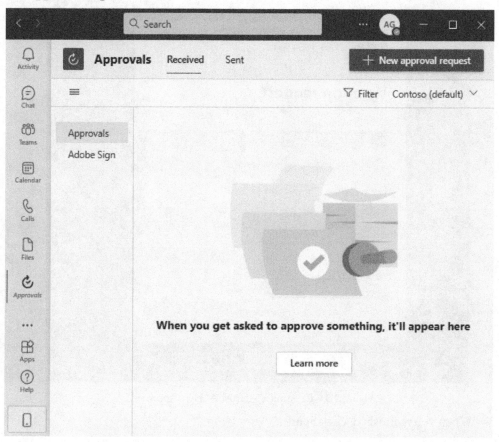

Figure 2.2 – Microsoft Teams – Approvals

2. Fill out the approval fields by using the previous list of items types as guidance:

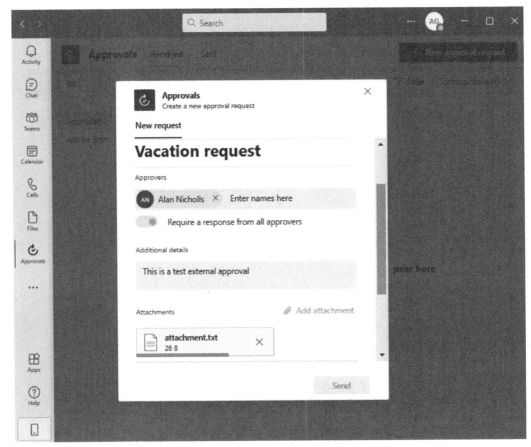

Figure 2.3 – Creating a Microsoft Teams approval

3. When you're finished, click **Send**.

The user (or users) indicated in the **Approvers** section should receive a notification automatically that they have an approval waiting.

As shown in the following screenshot, the approver's activity feed indicates that they have new approvals waiting for them:

Figure 2.4 – Notification of an approval request

Once an approval has been processed by the approver, the requester receives a notification in their activity feed as well:

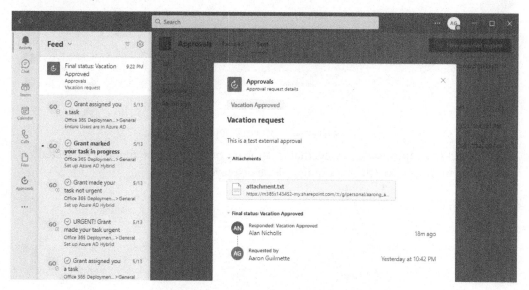

Figure 2.5 – The request has been approved

As you can see, the entire approvals process can be completed inside the Microsoft Teams user interface.

Next, we'll look at the process from the approver's perspective.

Responding to approvals

When you are designated as an approver in a Microsoft Teams Approval, you'll receive a notification, similar to the example shown in *Figure 2.4*. In this section, we'll walk through interacting with an approval.

Follow these steps to approve (or reject) an approval:

1. As an approver, log into Microsoft Teams.

2. Select the **Approvals** app and then select the approval you wish to process:

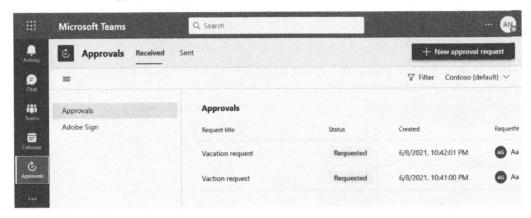

Figure 2.6 – Received approvals

3. Select the appropriate choice; that is, approve or reject. If the requester selected custom responses, those options will be displayed too:

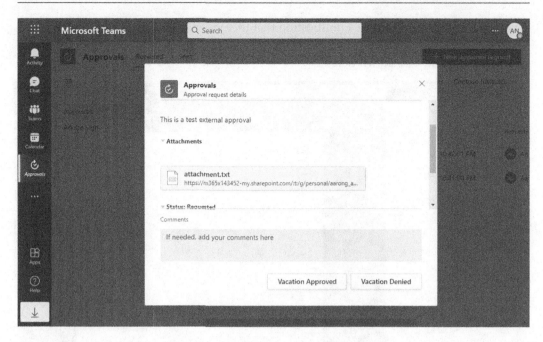

Figure 2.7 – Choosing to approve or reject

Once the approver has selected their option, they are returned to the main approvals page, which shows the statuses of all of their approvals, as shown in *Figure 2.8*:

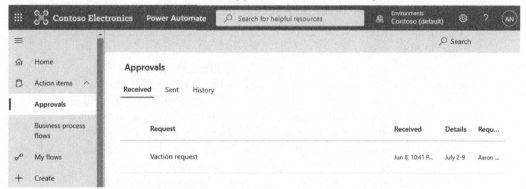

Figure 2.8 – Approvals in Power Automate

The requester will also receive a notification that there is an update for the submitted approval. Selecting this item in the activity feed or the Approvals app will display the approval's outcome, as shown here:

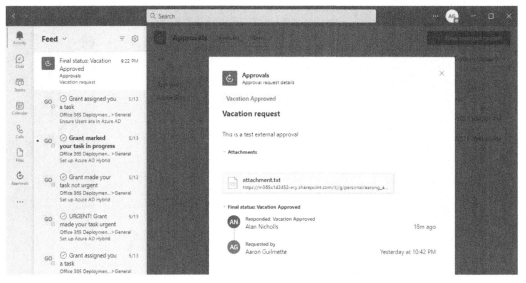

Figure 2.9 – Approval outcome

As with the approval request workflow scenario, everything in the approval response workflow scenario happens within the Microsoft Teams user interface.

> **More on Approvals**
>
> The Microsoft Teams Approvals app uses Power Platform components (such as Power Automate) to accomplish the workflow actions, as well as display adaptive cards inside the user interface. Before the Approvals app, approvals were created and managed in Power Automate and required the Post as a Flow Bot action to display notifications and adaptive cards in Teams. You can still see approvals information by going to Power Automate (`https://flow.microsoft.com` for commercial cloud customers or `https://gov.flow.microsoft.us` for GCC customers) and then selecting **Action items | Approvals**.

Next, we'll look at administering the Approvals app in Microsoft Teams.

Approval templates

Beginning in April 2021, Approval templates were released to public preview. Is this now complete, as it's 2022? Consider updating if so to keep this relevant.

Approval templates let teams and business owners deploy standardized approvals throughout their organization. Templates integrate functionality from both Approvals and Microsoft Forms and provide reuse capabilities for everyone in the organization.

Teams provides a set of popular approval template forms. To access them, launch the Approvals app, select the ellipsis next to + **New template**, and then select **Manage templates**, as shown here:

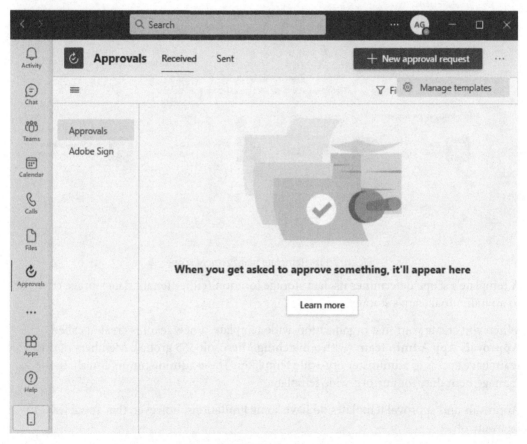

Figure 2.10 – Manage templates

As shown in the following screenshot, templates have **scopes** – that is, areas where they may be available as used or applied. Some templates may be **Org wide**, while others may only be available to be used by individual users or in teams:

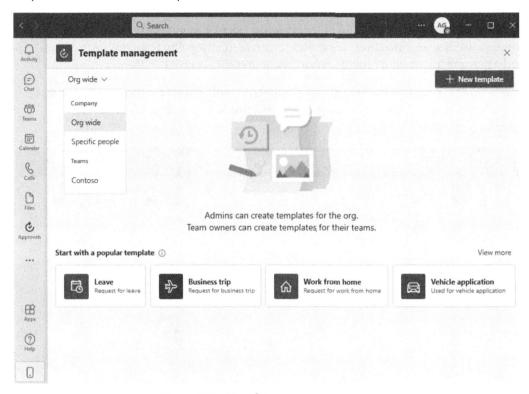

Figure 2.11 – Template management scopes

A template's scope determines its data storage location (either tenant data storage or tied to an individual team's storage).

When you create your first organization-wide template, a new team is created called **Approvals App Admin team** (with a matching Microsoft 365 group). Members of this team have access to administer org-wide templates. These administrators can share the management duty for any org-wide template.

Approvals and approval templates do have some limitations, however, that you'll want to be aware of:

- Approvals that are created through the Approvals app are stored in Dataverse, which doesn't currently support backups.

- Each team is limited to 400 approval templates.

- Each template based on Microsoft Forms can collect a maximum of 50,000 responses or requests.

In the following example, we'll create an org-wide template to demonstrate how to create an Approvals template and then look at the underlying Azure Active Directory components.

To create an org-wide template, follow these steps:

1. Launch Microsoft Teams and launch the **Approvals** app.

2. Select the ellipsis next to **+ New approval request** and select **Manage templates**.

3. On the **Template management** page, ensure that the scope is set to **Org wide**.

4. Under **Start with a popular template**, select **View more**.

5. Select a template, such as the **Business card** template:

Figure 2.12 – Selecting an approval template

6.   Choose **Org wide**:

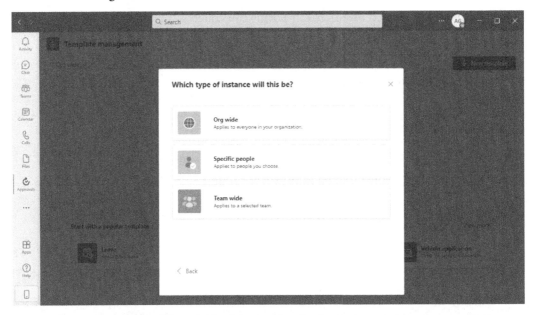

Figure 2.13 – Selecting the template's scope

7.   Acknowledge the notification and click **Create**:

Figure 2.14 – Notification for admin team creation

8. Update any content as necessary on the **Basic settings** page for the template (such as the category or description) and click **Next**:

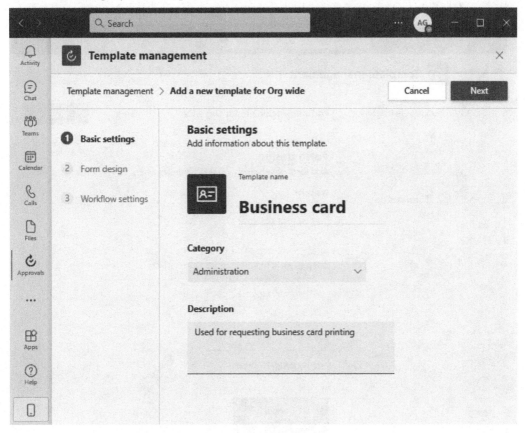

Figure 2.15 – Template management – Basic settings

9. Customize the form if desired. You can click the **+ Add new** button at the bottom of the page to add additional form fields, such as radio button choices, text fields, or date fields. Once you've finished customizing the form, click **Next**:

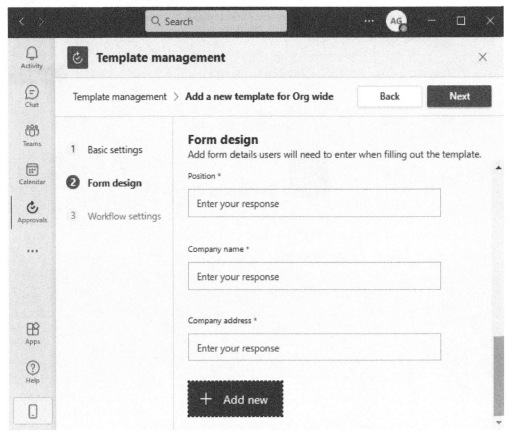

Figure 2.16 – Customizing the approval form's design

10. Specify additional customizations, such as custom approval or rejecting responses, a standard list of approvers, or whether a file attachment is required. Select **Preview** to preview the form:

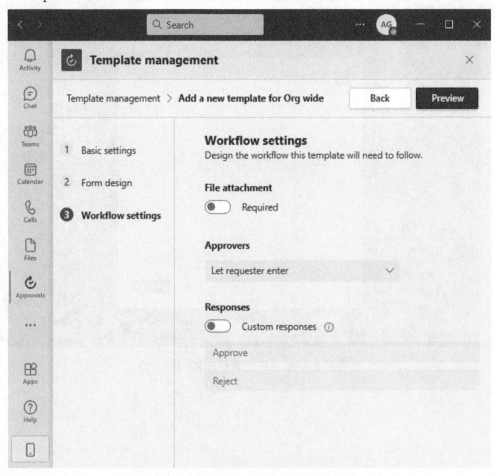

Figure 2.17 – Template workflow customization page

11. Verify that the form looks as intended. Click **Cancel** to go back and continue editing or choose **Publish** to finalize the form and make it available for use in the tenant:

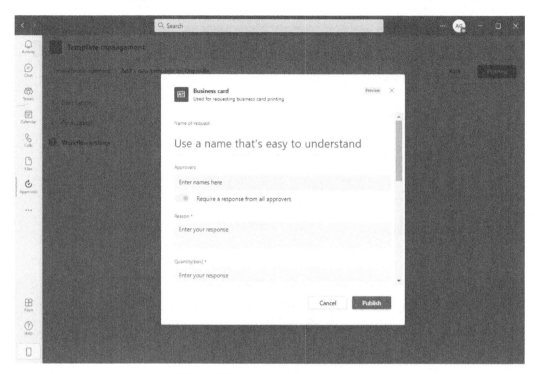

Figure 2.18 – Approval form preview

Once the template has been published, it's ready to be implemented by end users. To access the new Approvals template, end users simply need to launch the **Approvals** app, select **+ New approval request**, and then select the appropriate template from the templates tab, as shown in the following screenshot:

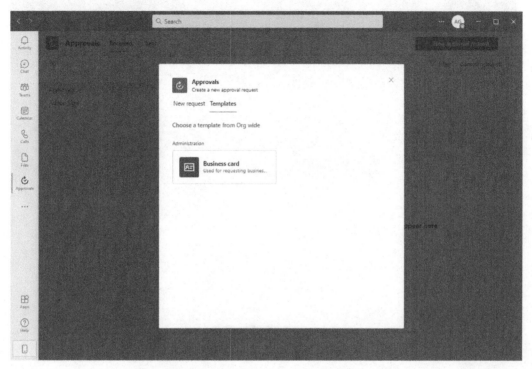

Figure 2.19 – Using Approvals templates

As we mentioned previously, after creating the first org-wide template, a new team is created called **Approvals App Admin team**. You can locate that team in the Teams view, as shown in the following screenshot:

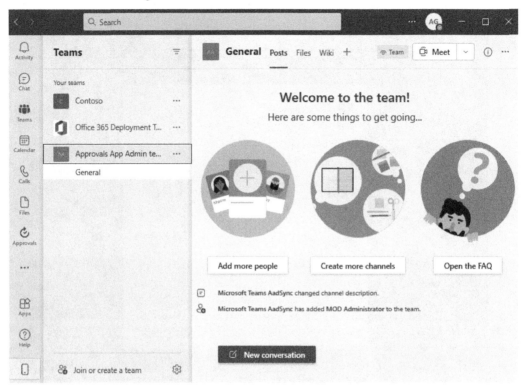

Figure 2.20 – Approvals App Admin team

The initial member of the team is the creator of the first org-wide template, though you can add other administrators later to help share the load.

As we also mentioned previously, when you create a custom template, the form is stored as Microsoft Forms data. You can see the current org-wide forms templates by logging into `https://forms.office.com`. As shown in the following screenshot, the approval template form we created is stored in Microsoft Forms. If you delete the form that's tied to an approval template, the template will no longer work:

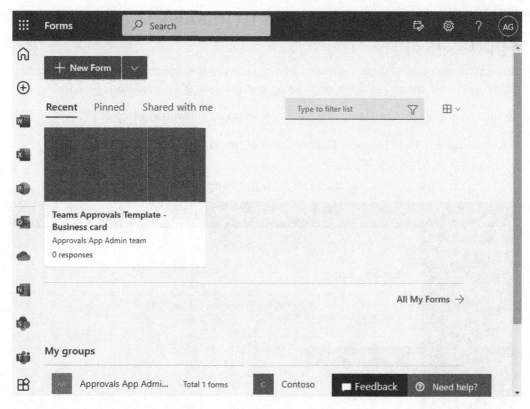

Figure 2.21 – Teams approval Forms data

Now that you understand how custom templates work, let's shift gears and look at the administration of the Approvals app.

Administration of Approvals app

As we discussed earlier, the Approvals app utilizes Dataverse (formerly known as the Common Data Service). Approvals content (depending on the data type and fields) is stored in a combination of places – Dataverse and Microsoft Forms.

Approvals templates that you may create are stored in an area called **Substrate Data Storage (SDS)**, either in the **tenant shard** (organization templates) or **groups shard** (team templates). Deleting a team will delete the associated templates. The first time an administrator creates an org-wide template, a new team will be provisioned.

In the following sections, we'll look at using org-wide settings, as well as permissions policies, to manage access to the Approvals app.

Using org-wide app settings to manage the Approvals app

As an administrator, you can control who has access to the Approvals app by enabling or disabling the Teams app globally or by using the Teams app's permissions policies.

To turn off the app tenant using org-wide app settings, follow these steps:

1. Navigate to the Microsoft Teams admin center at `https://admin.teams.microsoft.com`.

2. Expand **Teams apps** and then select **Manage apps**:

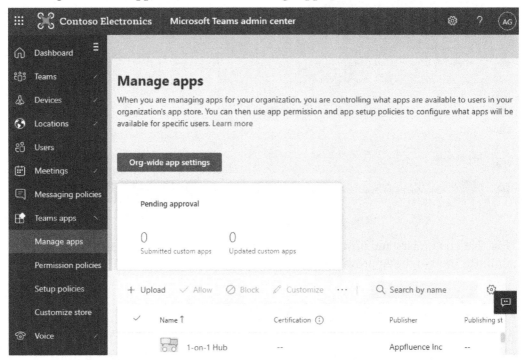

Figure 2.22 – Manage apps in the Teams admin center

3. In the **Search by name** box, enter **Approvals**:

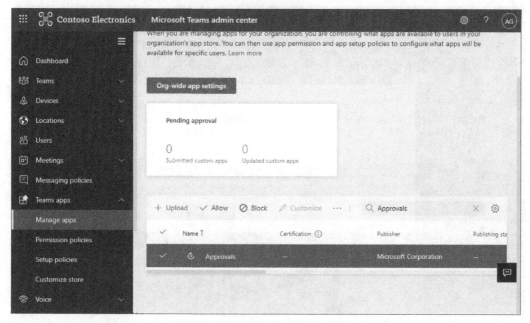

Figure 2.23 – Filtering the app list

4. Select the Approvals app and then click **Block** on the menu bar.

5. Confirm this choice by clicking **Block**:

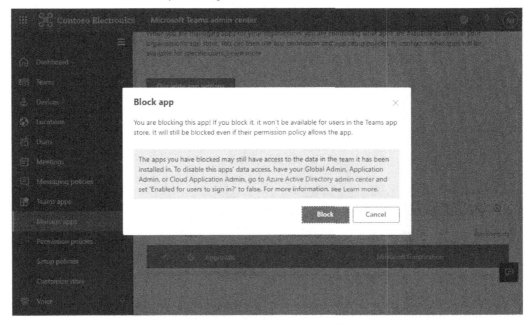

Figure 2.24 – Confirming that you're blocking the app

6. Confirm that the app shows **Blocked** in the **Status** column.

Now that you've learned how to manage access broadly with the org-wide settings, we'll look at managing the app with a permissions policy.

Using a permissions policy to manage the Approvals app

If managing the Approvals app org-wide doesn't meet your business needs, you can perform a more granular deployment. You can configure a **permission policy** to block the app for a subset of users in the tenant.

To use a permissions policy, follow these steps:

1. Navigate to **Microsoft Teams admin center** at `https://admin.teams.microsoft.com`.

2. Expand **Teams apps** and then select **Permission policies**.

3. Click **+ Add** to create a new permission policy.

4. In the **Add app permission policy** text area, enter a name for the policy, such as **Block Approvals**.

5. Under **Microsoft apps**, click the dropdown and select **Block specific apps and allow all others**:

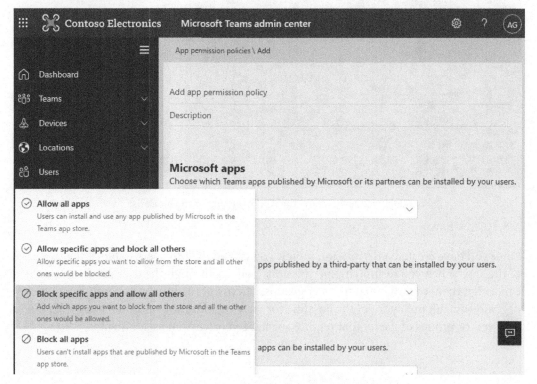

Figure 2.25 – Configuring the permission policy

6. Click **Block apps**.

7. Search for the `Approvals` app and then click **Add**. When you're finished, click **Block**:

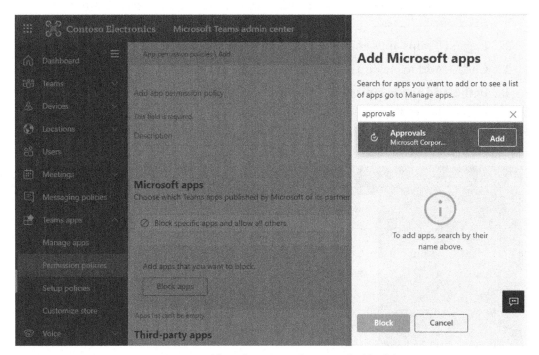

Figure 2.26 – Adding the Approvals app to the block list

8. Click **Save**.

Once you have created a permission policy, you can apply it to users to block the use of the app. When you're applying permissions policies through the user interface, you can assign them to individual users or groups. Microsoft recommends configuring the org-wide default policy to set the baseline for your organization and then applying policies to users (or groups of users) that require specialized or custom assignments.

Summary

The new functionality of the Approvals app in Teams showcases Microsoft's focus on using Microsoft Teams as a modern hub for work. In this chapter, you learned how to create both standard and custom approvals with the native Microsoft Teams Approvals app. You had a look at approvals from both the requester's and approver's points of view so that you know what to expect.

You also learned how to manage org-wide settings and permission policies to control the use of the Approvals app inside Microsoft Teams. In the next chapter, we'll begin exploring the task management options that are available in Microsoft Teams.

Further reading

The approvals functionality described in this chapter only applies to Worldwide Commercial instances of Microsoft Teams at this time. Customers that have been deployed in other sovereign clouds such as the Government Community Cloud, Office 365 Germany, or Office 365 China, which is managed by 21ViaNet, may not have access to the Approvals app. If your tenant does not have access to the Approvals app, you will need to create and manage approvals through Microsoft Power Automate workflows.

For more information on managing approvals with Microsoft Power Automate, see *Chapter 9, Getting Started with Approvals*, and *Chapter 11, Posting Approvals to Teams*, in *Workflow Automation with Microsoft Power Automate (ISBN: 978-1839213793)*.

3
Task Management in Teams

Office 365 contains multiple tools for managing team assignments and personal tasks. **Microsoft Planner** is a lightweight task management solution designed for groups or teams to keep track of progress and collaborate on projects. **Microsoft To Do** is a simple app that helps you create and manage personal tasks, such as daily action items and deliverables. These separate tools in Office 365 come together in the **Tasks app** for Microsoft Teams, which combines your tasks from Planner and To Do into a single application, surfaced in Teams.

In this chapter, we will explore the use of Planner in Teams, Microsoft To Do, and the Tasks app in Teams. We will look at how these apps operate independently and how they come together to streamline the process of personal and team-based task management.

This chapter will cover the following topics:

- Planner in Teams
- Overview of To Do
- The Tasks App in Teams

Let's get started!

Technical requirements

Let's take a quick look at what you will need to complete this chapter.

Planner in Teams

To use Microsoft Planner, you will need an Office 365 subscription (Microsoft 365 Business or Office 365 E1, E3, E5, F1, or F3) with the Microsoft Planner license enabled. For you to be able to create plans from outside of Microsoft Teams, you will need to be enabled for Office 365 group creation. If you wish to create a plan inside of an existing Team, you don't need to have group creation permissions.

> **Azure Active Directory Group Creation Management**
>
> If your organization has implemented a more restrictive permissions model for Azure AD Groups, you may need to have an administrator create your Team first. For more information on restricting Microsoft 365 Group creation, see `https://docs.microsoft.com/en-us/microsoft-365/solutions/manage-creation-of-groups`.

To Do App

To access To Do, you will need an Office 365 subscription (Microsoft 365 Business or Office 365 E1, E3, E5, or F3) with the To Do license enabled. You will also need to have mailboxes hosted in Exchange Online for tasks to sync and store.

The Tasks App in Teams

For the Tasks App in Teams, you will need any Office 365 subscription that includes Microsoft Teams (Microsoft 365 Business or Office 365 E1, E3, E5, F1, or F3) with the Microsoft Teams license enabled, as well as the previously mentioned licenses.

Planner in Teams

As we mentioned previously, Microsoft Planner is a lightweight task management application for teams to organize projects in an easy, user-friendly way. Planner is a Kanban-style tool that contains a board for moving tasks between categories.

In Planner terminology, a plan is made up of a group of people (the members of the plan) and tasks organized into buckets. In this chapter, we are going to be focusing on using the Planner app inside of an already existing Team that manages the Plan's membership.

Let's learn how to add a plan to an existing Microsoft Team.

Adding Planner to your Team

Adding the Planner application to your Microsoft Team is the first step in creating a plan. This can be done through the Teams desktop or web application.

To add Planner to your team, follow these steps:

1. Open the Microsoft Teams application.
2. Navigate to the team you wish to add a plan to.
3. On the tab bar, click the + button to add a tab or application:

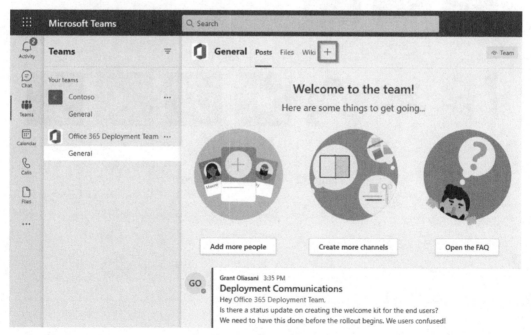

Figure 3.1 – Add a tab to Teams

4.   On the app selection page, choose **Tasks by Planner and To Do**:

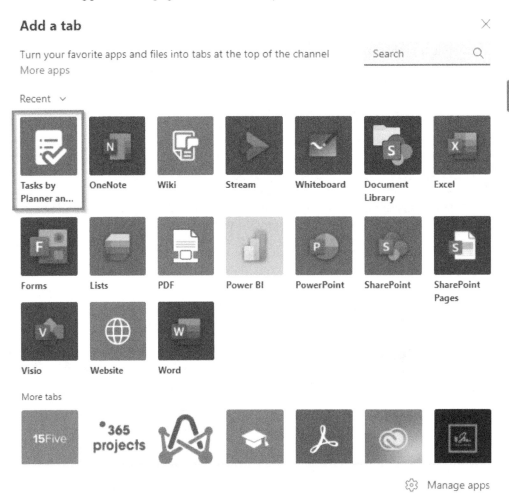

Figure 3.2 – App selection screen

5. Select **Create a new plan** and fill in the **Tab name** area, which will also serve as the plan's name:

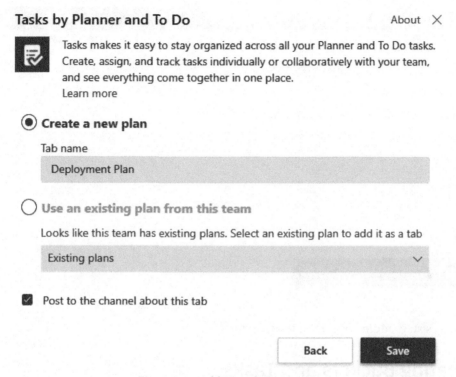

Figure 3.3 – Adding a plan to a team

6. Optionally, check the **Post to the channel about this tab** box to let your team know a plan has been added.

7. Click **Save**.

After clicking **Save**, you will have successfully added a Planner plan to your team! Everyone on the team will now be able to open the plan from the newly created tab:

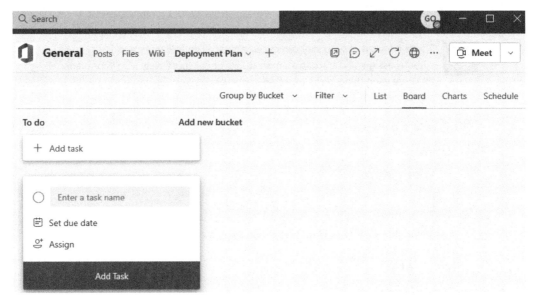

Figure 3.4 – Blank plan open in Teams

Now, let's start adding buckets and assigning tasks.

Creating Buckets and Tasks

As we mentioned previously, plans are made up of buckets that group tasks together. This helps organize tasks around a common goal or milestone in your plan.

By default, your plan includes a generic bucket called **To do** (not to be confused with the actual app, To Do). You can leave this bucket as-is or rename it to something that fits your plan's objective. To rename a bucket, simply click on the bucket's name; this will allow you to edit the text.

For our example, we have a team that oversees an Office 365 deployment. We will rename this bucket **User Creation** and add another bucket for **Feature Enablement** by clicking **Add new bucket**. The following screenshot shows the result:

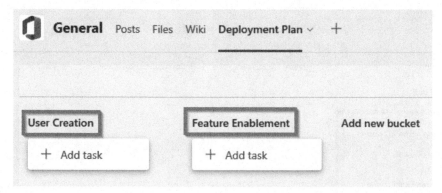

Figure 3.5 – Renamed default bucket and the newly added bucket

You can repeat this process for any additional buckets that your team may need. In this example, we will add a few more buckets to complete our plan's objective – **Communication Plan** and **Training**. Once your buckets have been created, you can start creating tasks for the members of the team.

> **Important Note**
> You can only assign tasks to members of the Microsoft Team. If a task needs to be assigned to a user outside the team, they must be added to the team first.

To create tasks for your plan, follow these steps:

1. Click **Add task** below the desired bucket.

2. Enter a task name.

3. Optionally, assign a due date to the task by clicking **Set due date** and using the date picker to select a date.

4. Optionally, assign the task to a specific member(s) of the team by clicking **Assign**. Only the members of the team will be shown.

5.   Click **Add Task** to save it to the plan:

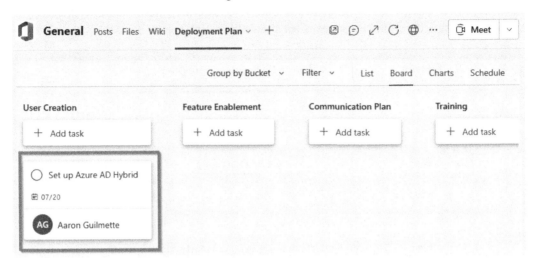

Figure 3.6 – The first task created

You have now created your first task! Although it only takes a few fields to create a task, there are many more options you can use to add detail and track progress. To view and edit these options, simply click on the task. You can see some of the additional options in the following screenshot:

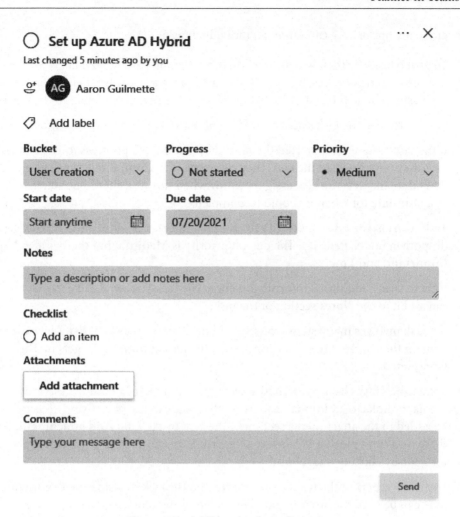

Figure 3.7 – Additional task configuration

There are many options we can set on an individual task:

- To group tasks further, we can use **labels** by clicking **Add label**. Labels on tasks are like colored sticky notes; by default, the labels are named after their color, but you can easily change the text of a label by clicking the pencil icon next to the label.

- We can change the task's bucket by clicking the dropdown under **Bucket**.

- If the task assignee has started the task, they can flip the progress to **In progress**, or if they have finished the task, they can mark it as **Completed**. You can include a **Start date** that lets the task assignee know when this task should be started, as well as a **Due date** for when it should be completed.

- Tasks can also be given a priority to rate the importance of the task by clicking the dropdown under **Priority**. The default priority is **Medium**, but there is also **Urgent**, **Important**, and **Low**.

- If there is any additional information about the task you would like to include, you can add it to the **Notes** section of the task.

- If a task involves many steps, you can add these steps to a **checklist**. Once every item on the checklist has been completed, the task automatically gets marked as **Completed**.

- Sometimes, tasks have associated assets (such as spreadsheets, images, or other media, or links to additional resources) that relate to the objective. These assets can be added to the attachments section of the task by clicking **Add attachment**. From there, you can upload a file, insert a hyperlink, or browse the Teams file repository for a file by clicking **SharePoint**.

- Lastly, members of the team can comment on the task by using the **Comments** box. This can be used for providing updates, identifying blockers, or simply talking about a task.

The following screenshot shows a completely configured task:

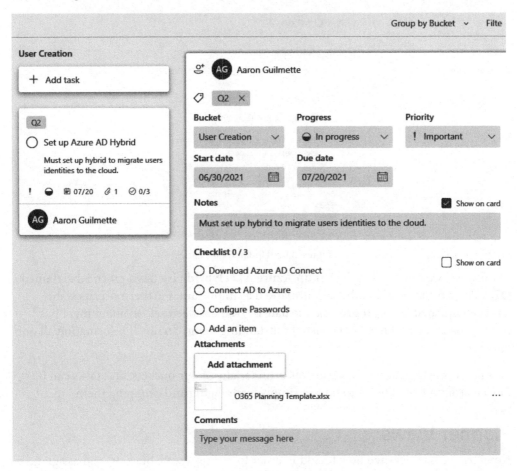

Figure 3.8 – A fully configured task

Notice that the task card gets an updated look, too, adopting the settings chosen:

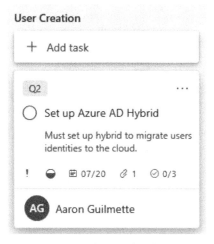

Figure 3.9 – Updated task card

In this case, we can see that the **Set up Azure AD Hybrid** task has a green label named **Q2**, a description, and that the task is marked as important. Furthermore, its status has been updated to **In progress**, a due date of 7/20 has been set, an attachment has been uploaded, and it has a checklist of outstanding items. So much information all on one task!

This process is the same for creating tasks under any of our buckets, and tasks can be moved around from bucket to bucket simply by dragging and dropping them.

Planner Views

Now that we have learned how to add Planner to Teams, create buckets, and assign tasks, let's explore visuals in Planner to help your team stay on track! The default view for your team's plan is the board containing the buckets and tasks, as shown in the following screenshot:

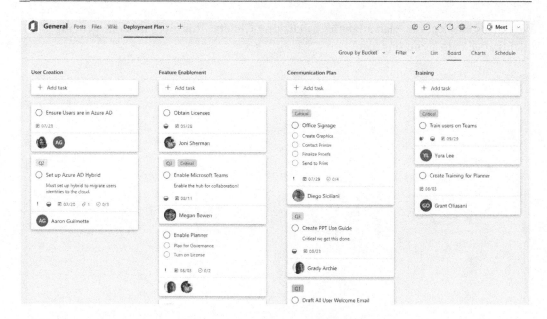

Figure 3.10 – Planner Board view

To see a simple list of the tasks and information about them, we can switch to the **List view** by clicking **List**:

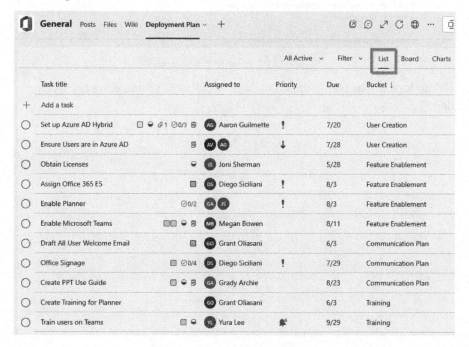

Figure 3.11 – Planner List view

We can also look at our plan analytics by clicking **Charts**. This gives us some general quantitative data about our plan:

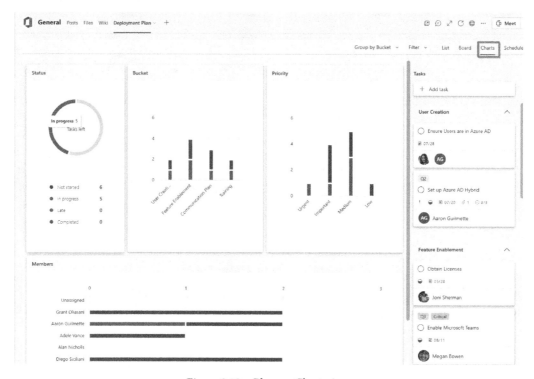

Figure 3.12 – Planner Chart view

Lastly, we can look at our plan mapped out over a calendar of due dates by clicking **Schedule**:

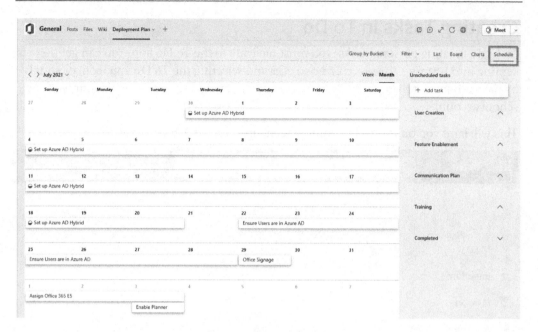

Figure 3.13 – Planner Schedule view

Next, we'll look at the To Do app.

To Do App

In the previous section, we explored the team-based task management capabilities of the Planner app in Teams. For personal action item tracking and productivity, we have Microsoft To Do. To Do is a simple and powerful to-do list that brings together your personal and assigned tasks in one place. You can create tasks and lists to help you organize your day. To Do also shows tasks that have been assigned to you from Planner.

Let's take a look!

Creating Tasks in To Do

To begin creating personal tasks, you must navigate to the To Do app. You can get there by signing into `https://www.office.com` and selecting the **To Do** app icon, or simply by navigating to `https://todo.microsoft.com` and signing in with your work or school account.

This will land you on the To Do home screen, open on the **My Day** tab:

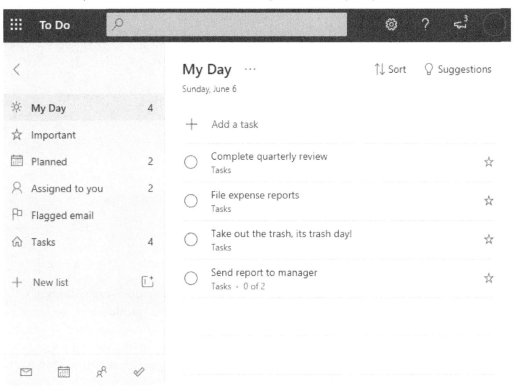

Figure 3.14 – To Do home screen

As you can see, the list displays a mixture of personal tasks and work-related tasks. To create a new task for the day, simply click the **+ Add a task** box and give your task a name. To finish adding the task, simply press the *Enter* button on your keyboard; the task will be added to the list! To view all your tasks, not just those designated for **My Day**, navigate to the **Tasks** tab on the left pane:

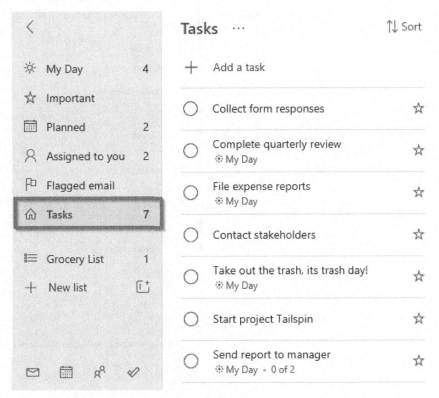

Figure 3.15 – All tasks

From here, you can add tasks in the same way, reorder them by dragging them around, and change the details of your tasks. To complete any task, click the radio button next to the task and it will be marked as completed.

Editing Tasks in To Do

Once you have created a task, you can edit its attributes. To edit the details of the task, click the task's name. This will open a side panel that contains information and customizations for the task:

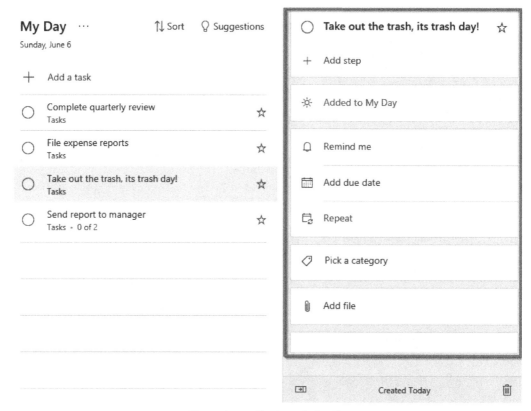

Figure 3.16 – To Do task details

To mark your task as **Important**, click the star next to the task's name. This will add a visual cue that shows that the task is important, as well as add the task to the **Important** section of the To Do app.

Editing a task gives you many options:

- By clicking **Add step**, you can add sub checklist items to your task that are required to complete the overall task (similar to Planner).

- To add a task to the **My Day** list, simply click **Add to My Day**.

- The **Remind me** option allows you to set reminders for your tasks. You can set them for later today, tomorrow, next week, or a custom date and time.

- You can also pick a due date for tasks by clicking **Add due date**. When you set a due date for a task, it will also move it to the **Planned** view of To Do.

- If a task is recurring (such as taking out the trash) we can set it to repeat on a specified cadence – daily, weekdays, weekly, or monthly.

- Similar to Planner labels, tasks can also be color-coded or categorized by clicking **Pick a category** and assigning a category.

- If the task has an associated file, simply click **Add file** and choose the document to be added.

- Lastly, if you would like to add additional context around the task, click the box at the bottom and add some notes!

The following screenshot shows a task with multiple elements configured:

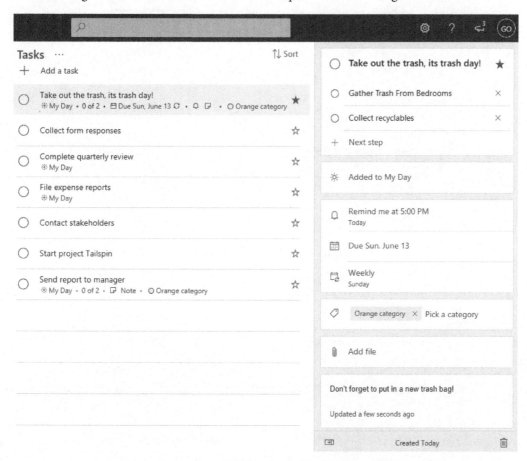

Figure 3.17 – Filled out task details in To Do

Next, we'll look at a method for grouping or organizing tasks.

Creating Lists in To Do

Lists in To Do allow you to group tasks and organize them by an objective. You can create a list for anything, from grocery lists to personal projects. To create a list, click **+ New list** from the left menu of To Do. Give the list a name and you are done! For this example, we will create a list for building an application:

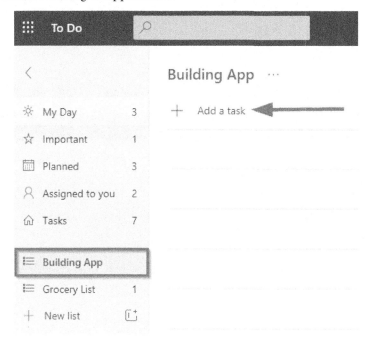

Figure 3.18 – Creating a new list

After creating the list, simply add your tasks by clicking **+ Add a task**. All the customizations we discussed in the previous section apply here to tasks that are part of a list:

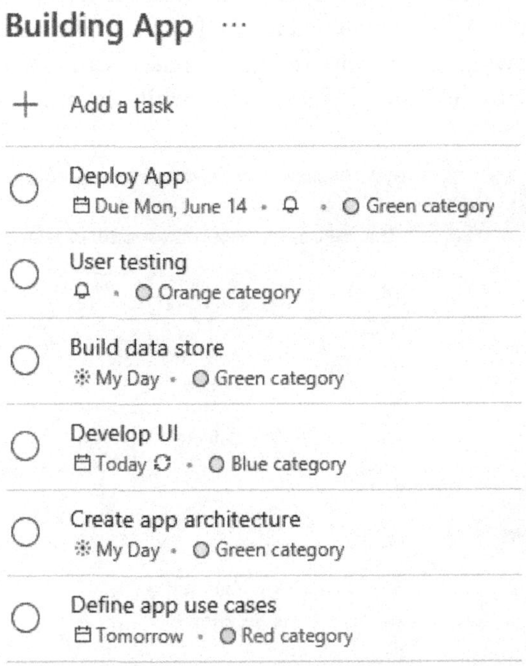

Figure 3.19 – List of tasks in To Do

Lists you create in To Do will also be surfaced in the Tasks app, as we will see later in this chapter!

Integration with Microsoft Planner

As we mentioned previously, Microsoft To Do is primarily a personal task tracking app, while Planner is more of a project-oriented, team-based solution. However, To Do does give you a glimpse into your assigned Planner tasks in the **Assigned to you** tab. There, you can see tasks that have been assigned to you from any Planner plans you belong to. As shown in the following screenshot, we can see a user with four tasks coming from Planner – two belong to the Project Tailspin plan, while the others belong to the Deployment plan:

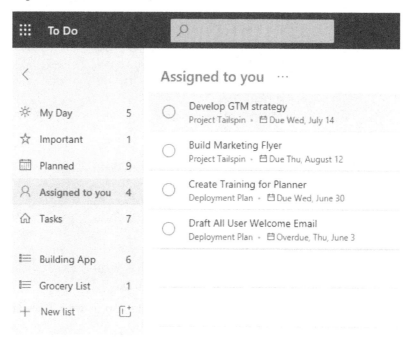

Figure 3.20 – The Assigned to you tab

Next, we'll shift gears a little bit and start looking at the Tasks app.

The Tasks App in Teams

Now that we have explored team-based action tracking in Planner and personal task management in To Do, let's see how it all comes together. While these tools are great separately, you could easily lose track of tasks simply because they live in multiple locations. This is where the Tasks app in Teams comes in. The Tasks app in Teams combines all of your tasks from Planner and To Do into the hub for collaboration.

Adding the Tasks app to Teams

At the time of writing, the Tasks app in Teams is named *Tasks by Planner and To Do*, though it is in the process of being rebranded to simply *Tasks*. To get the **Tasks** app in Teams, follow these steps:

1. Click **Apps** on the left rail of Teams to open the App Store:

Figure 3.21 – Button to launch the Teams app store

2. Search for **Tasks** using the search bar at the top left and click **Tasks by Planner and To Do**:

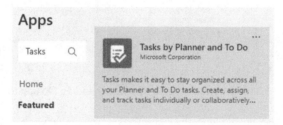

Figure 3.22 – Tasks app in the app store

3.   Click **Add** to install the Tasks app for your Teams client:

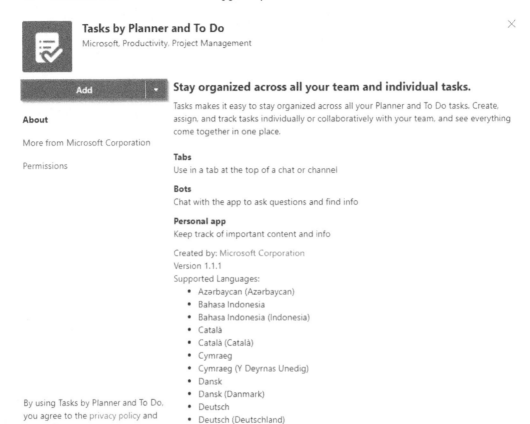

Figure 3.23 – Adding the Tasks by Planner and To Do app to Teams

4. Optionally, pin the app to the left rail for easier access:

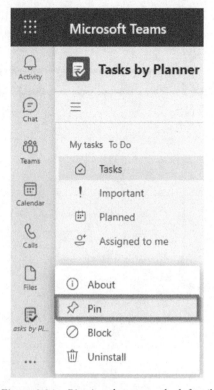

Figure 3.24 – Pinning the app to the left rail

After installing the Tasks app for your Teams client, you will see two sections in the app:

*   My tasks

*   Shared plans

We'll explore these areas next.

Tracking tasks in My tasks

The **My tasks** section of the Tasks app combines all of the tasks that are assigned to you from To Do and Planner. You will notice that the **My tasks** section is organized in the same way as the **To Do** web app:

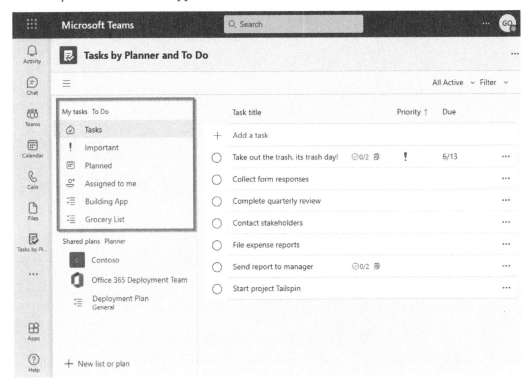

Figure 3.25 – The My tasks section of the Tasks app

It contains many different views of your tasks:

- **Tasks**: Your list of tasks added to To Do or Outlook.

- **Important**: Any task you have marked as important by clicking the star next to the task.

- **Planned**: All of the tasks in To Do that have been designated with a due date.

- **Assigned to me**: All of the tasks in Planner that have been assigned to you.

- **Customized Lists**: Any lists you have created in To Do.

Within the **My tasks** section of the Tasks app, you can edit and create tasks straight from Teams – just as you would within the dedicated app. For example, to create a new task, simply click **+ Add a task** and give it a name. You can then edit the details of the task by clicking on the task name, as shown in the following screenshot:

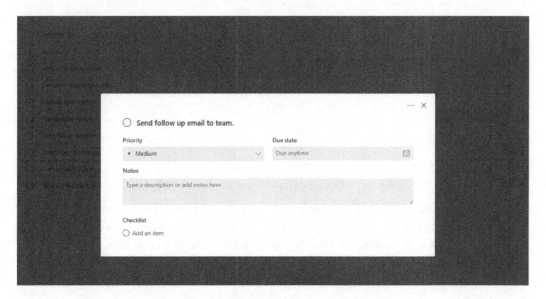

Figure 3.26 – Editing the task's details in the Tasks app

From here, you can assign a priority, a due date, notes, and a checklist – much like editing the task in To Do.

Managing plans in the Tasks app

The **Shared plans** section of the Tasks app in Teams shows you the Planner plans you belong to inside of Teams channels. For example, in the previous section, we created a plan for our Office 365 Deployment team called Deployment Plan. You can see this plan in the following screenshot:

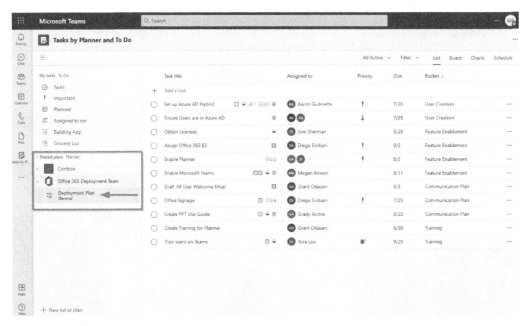

Figure 3.27 – Opening Deployment Plan in the Tasks app

From here, you can view all of the plan's tasks and manage their details or mark them as completed. You'll see the task's title, who it is assigned to, its priority, its due date, and which bucket the task belongs to. You can add additional tasks to this plan by clicking + **Add a task** and filling out the details. Save the task by clicking the checkmark:

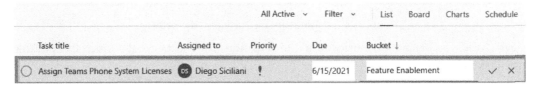

Figure 3.28 – Adding a task to a plan in the Tasks app

In this section, we discussed the different views of the tasks. In the Tasks app, you will notice that you can use the same views – List, Board, Charts, and Schedule:

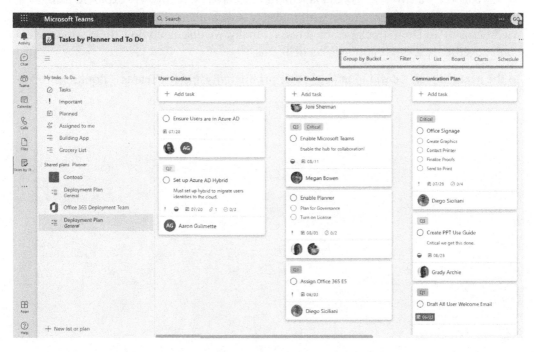

Figure 3.29 – Board view of tasks

One of the greatest benefits of using the Tasks app in Teams is notifications. The Tasks app will push notifications to your Teams client activity feed on desktop, web, and mobile when one of the following actions occurs:

- A member assigns a task to you

- A member assigns an urgent task to you

- A member marks a task that's been assigned to you as urgent

- A member makes a task that's been assigned to you not urgent

- A member changes the progress of a task that's been assigned to you

- A member removes you from a task's assignees

As you can see, the Tasks app in Teams brings together all of your tasks from Planner and To Do into a single pane of glass for enhanced productivity. These individual services can still be used outside of Teams, but the Tasks app makes task management easy and fun!

Summary

In this chapter, we covered task management in Microsoft Teams. We explored using Planner for project-oriented tasks with multiple stakeholders. You then learned how to use Microsoft To Do to track personal tasks. Finally, we discussed how these two services come together in a single app – Tasks in Teams.

In the next chapter, we will look at another productivity app for Teams – Bookings.

4
Bookings in Teams

As the world experiences a historic shift toward virtual interaction, many organizations must adapt and provide online options for external or internal consultations, appointments, and other meeting types. **Microsoft Bookings**, a service within Office 365, enables the simple scheduling of virtual appointments powered by Microsoft Teams meetings. The **Bookings** app allows staff to manage the full orchestration of *virtual visits*—all within Microsoft Teams.

There are two ways to access the Bookings service: a dedicated web app accessed through the Office 365 home page and the Bookings app in Microsoft Teams.

This chapter will cover the following topics:

- Bookings using the web app
- Bookings using the Teams app
- Differences between the Bookings web and Teams apps

In these sections, we will examine creating services, managing staff, and more.

Let's get started!

Technical requirements

There are a few prerequisites necessary before we start exploring Bookings. Let's take a quick look at what you will need to complete the chapter.

To use either Microsoft Bookings on the web or in Microsoft Teams, you will need an Office 365 subscription (Microsoft 365 Business, Office 365 E3, or Office 365 E5) with the Microsoft Bookings license enabled. Also, your organization will need Outlook enabled on the web, as well as a supported browser.

Bookings using the web app

As previously stated, Microsoft Bookings is a simple service in Office 365 that facilitates the scheduling of appointments on a common calendar. It allows people, both internal and external, to visit your booking page, select an appointment type or service, and choose an open time slot. From there, Bookings will add the visit to the calendar, send reminders, and allow staff to manage appointments.

Let's look at how to get to Bookings and create your first Booking calendar!

Creating a Bookings Calendar

To open Bookings on the web, open `https://www.office.com` and select the **Bookings** tile, or navigate to `https://outlook.office.com/bookings`. The first time you access the Bookings app, you will need to create a calendar and set up your *business*.

Every Bookings calendar is made up of several main components:

- **Name**: The name of the business or calendar.
- **Services**: These are services your business provides and can be booked by internal or external users.
- **Staff**: The internal (or guest) users who manage the calendar or perform the services.
- **Booking Page**: This is the self-service portal that allows people to select a service, choose a time, and book an appointment.

For this example, we will set up a Bookings calendar for a healthcare organization wanting to provide a telehealth experience for patients.

To set up your business, follow these steps:

1. Navigate to `https://outlook.office.com/bookings`.

2. Select **Get Started**.

3. Enter a name for your calendar, optionally upload a logo, and choose a business type.

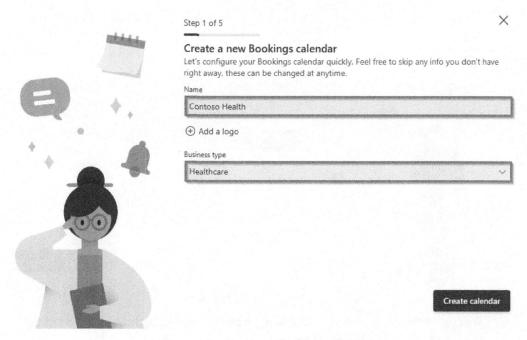

Figure 4.1 – Creating a Bookings calendar

4. Add the first service by typing in a service name, assigning a duration, and choosing **Make this an online appointment** to indicate that this is a service powered by Microsoft Teams meetings:

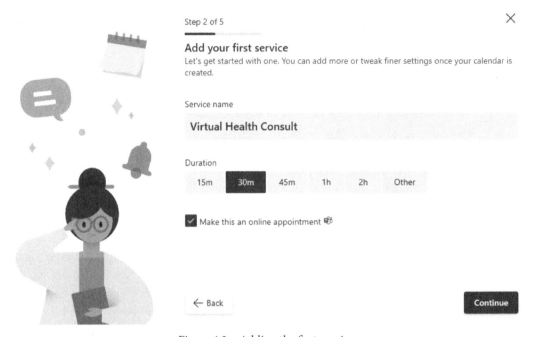

Figure 4.2 – Adding the first service

5. Specify when this service is available to be booked by highlighting the days of the week and selecting a time range:

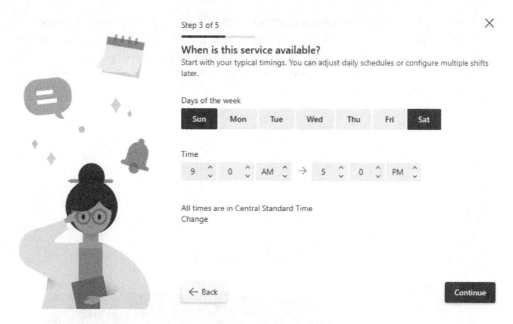

Figure 4.3 – Modifying service availability

6. Optionally, you can add additional members from your organization to this Bookings calendar by specifying them to provide this service and choosing whether to allow them to manage the calendar as well. These settings can be modified later:

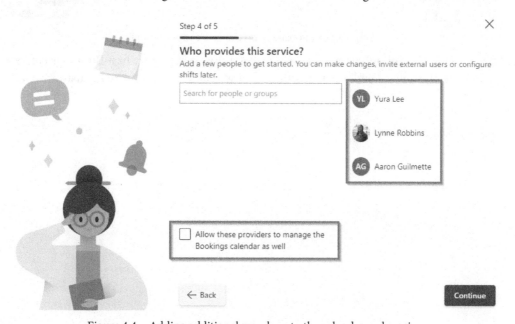

Figure 4.4 – Adding additional members to the calendar and service

7. Lastly, select who can book appointments on this calendar. Choosing **Private** only allows appointments to be scheduled by internal staff who have access to the Bookings calendar. The **People in my organization** option will publish an internal self-service booking page. Selecting **Anyone** will publish a public self-service page that allows anyone, internal or external, to book appointments.

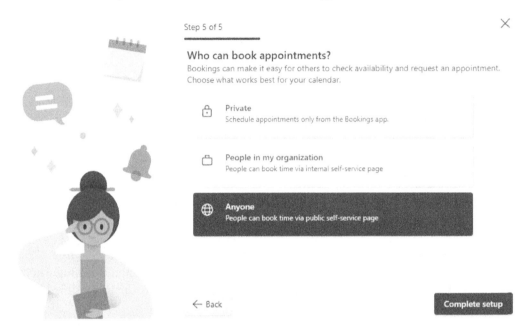

Figure 4.5 – Choosing who can book appointments

After clicking **Complete setup**, you have successfully created your first Bookings calendar! Technically, the new calendar is ready to go, but we can do much more to customize it.

Calendar settings for Bookings

To view the calendar, add additional services and staff, and customize the booking page, open the Bookings web app. It should default to the newly created or last accessed Bookings calendar. To change the open Bookings calendar, click on the drop-down menu and choose the correct calendar name.

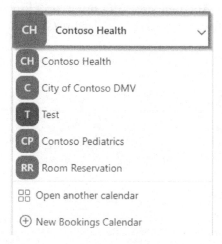

Figure 4.6 – Selecting an existing Bookings calendar

Once you have navigated to and opened the desired Bookings calendar, we can begin configuring staff, services, and more.

Business information

One of the first things to do after creating a Bookings calendar is to set up the business information. This includes items such as an address, logo, hours of operation, and privacy policy. To edit these details, navigate to **Settings | Business information**. There are three sections of information to fill:

- **Basic Details**: Fill in the name, phone number, address, website URL, terms and conditions URL, and privacy policy URL. This information will appear at the bottom of the Bookings page. In the **Send customer replies to** field, enter an email address where replies to Bookings confirmation emails should be delivered.

- **Business logo**: Optionally, upload a business logo. This logo will appear on the self-service Bookings page.

- **Business hours**: Enter your business hours. These are the overall boundaries of when customers can book services. Individual services and staff can have more granular time restrictions set during creation.

Managing staff

In the initial creation of the calendar, we had an option to add staff. Again, staff are internal or guest users who need to either manage the calendar or be bookable for appointments to perform services. To view and manage staff, navigate to **Settings | Staff**. Here, you see the staff added during setup, as well as any additionally added users. To add additional staff to this Bookings calendar, click **Add new staff**. This brings up a form to add the new members' information and configure their permissions/availability (see *Figure 4.7*):

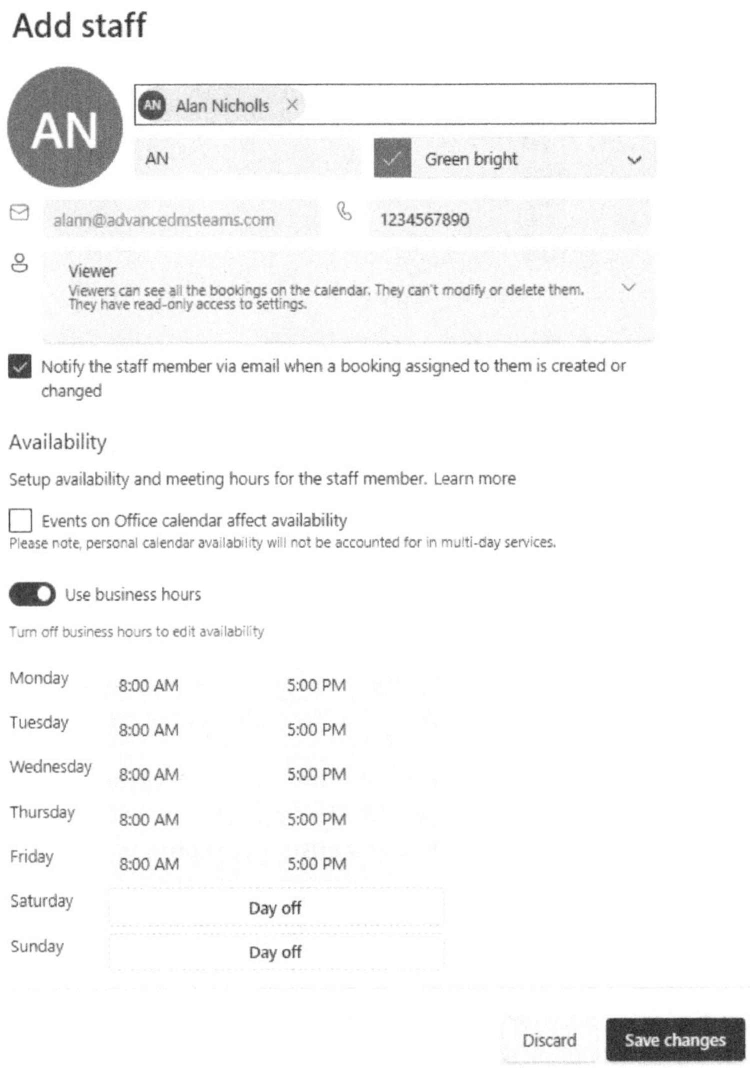

Figure 4.7 – Adding new staff

To add a user who is internal to your organization, simply start typing their name. This will query Active Directory and autofill the email and initials upon selecting their name. From there, we have various options to configure their permissions, notifications, and availability. There are three different permission levels for a Bookings calendar:

- **Administrator**: Can edit all settings, add/remove staff, manage bookings.

- **Viewer**: Can see bookings on the calendar but cannot modify them. Has read-only access to settings.

- **Guest**: Can be assigned to bookings but can't open the bookings calendar.

When adding additional staff, the permission level will default to **Viewer**. After choosing the staff and their permission level, we can optionally check the **Notify the staff member via email when a booking assigned to them is created or changed** box. Next, optionally check the **Events on Office calendar affect availability** box to control whether the staff member's personal primary mailbox in Exchange Online determines their availability on the Bookings calendar. Lastly, the **Use business hours** toggle is on by default, and this marks the staff member as available to book during the overall business hours. If this staff member had a different schedule, simply toggle it off and select the days and hours of availability manually.

You can also add guests to Bookings calendars by typing in the guest's name and selecting **Use this name** (see *Figure 4.8*).

> **Important Note**
> Adding an external staff member defaults their permission level to **Guest**. Guests can be assigned to Bookings, but not open the associated mailbox.

Add staff

Figure 4.8 – Adding a guest

You will then need to fill in a valid email address for the guest user to be able to receive their booking notifications and details.

Managing services

After adding staff to the Bookings calendar, we are ready to set up our bookable services. A Bookings service is made up of multiple parts, including a name, duration, price (if applicable), location, and notes. When we first created our Bookings calendar, we set up our initial service, *Virtual Health Consult*. To see all the services added to this Bookings calendar, navigate to **Settings | Services**:

Figure 4.9 – Services page

From here, you can view individual service details, such as the duration, price, description, and assignable staff. To add a new service, follow these steps:

1. Click **Add new service** at the top of the page.

2. In the **Basic details** section, fill in the following service information:

    A. **Service name**: The name of the service as it will appear on the booking page and calendar.

    B. **Description**: A brief description of the service that will appear when a user clicks the information button on the booking page.

    C. **Location**: The location of the service that will appear on appointment confirmations, reminders, and the calendar entry.

    D. **Add online meeting**: This toggle enables or disables a Microsoft Teams meeting for the booking. If enabled, a Teams meeting link will be added to the appointment confirmation, reminders, and calendar entry.

    E. **Duration**: The length of time this service will be booked for. This determines the block of time on the calendar entry and the staff calendars.

    F. **Buffer time**: The amount of time before and after a booking that is blocked out in addition to the service duration. For example, a haircut service might include a 10-minute buffer time to the end of the service so the barber can clean their tools and area in preparation for the next appointment.

    G. **Price**: The cost of the service as it will appear on the booking page. If **Price not set** is chosen, no price information will appear on the booking page.

    H. **Notes**: Notes to add to bookings of this service. These appear on the calendar entry.

    I. **Maximum number of attendees**: The number of people that can book the same appointment time and the same staff member (such as a group fitness class).

J.   **Customer appointment management**: This allows the user to manage their own appointment when it was booked manually by staff. See *Figure 4.10* for an example of a configured service:

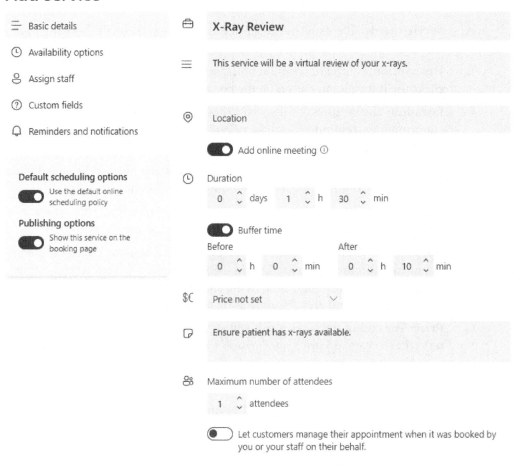

Figure 4.10 – Editing service details

3. In the **Availability options** section, optionally modify the default scheduling options by toggling off **Use the default online scheduling policy**:

   A. **Time increments**: The intervals of time this service can be booked. For example, a 30-minute interval means a user could book the service at 9:00, 9:30, 10:00, or 10:30.

   B. **Minimum lead time**: The minimum hours in advance a user may book or change an appointment.

   C. **Maximum lead time**: The maximum number of days in advance a booking can be made.

   D. **General availability**: By default, services in Bookings are bookable when staff members are free. Optionally, set a custom date range to narrow this down further. See *Figure 4.11* for service availability options:

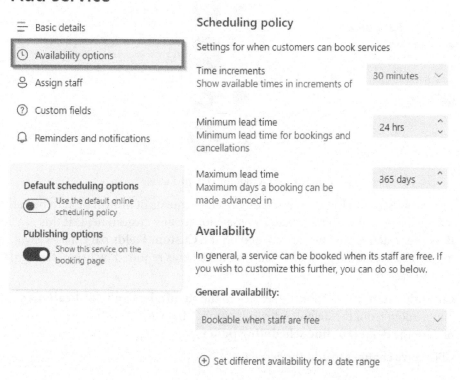

Figure 4.11 – Service availability options

4. In **Assign Staff**, choose which staff members can perform this service by clicking the radio buttons next to their name. Optionally, choose whether to allow customers to pick the staff members they want for the service by using the **Allow customer to choose a particular staff for booking** toggle:

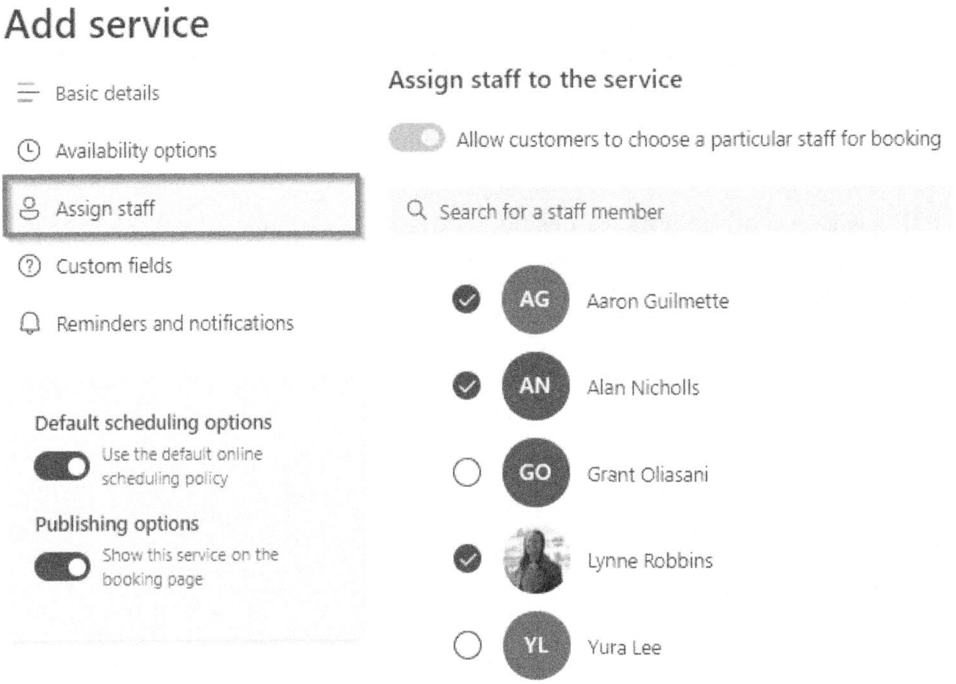

Figure 4.12 – Assigning staff to a service

5. Use the **Custom fields** section to add or remove fields of information to be gathered during a booking of this service. You may not see any custom fields if this is a new Bookings calendar, as they are created on the **Custom Fields** page that we will cover in the next section. Optionally, you can make fields required by using the toggle next to each field.

6. Customize notifications for the service in the **Reminders and notifications** section. These adopt from the default scheduling policy but can be customized by toggling off **Use the default online scheduling policy**.

7. Click **Save changes** to add the service.

Next, we'll look at further customizing the service with custom fields.

Adding custom fields

As we add services to the Bookings calendar, we have the option to add additional fields of information to collect from the customer. There are default fields, such as customer email and phone number, but sometimes information specific to a service is needed by internal staff. For example, for our Virtual Health Consult, it might be good to add a field for the customer's insurance provider. Follow these steps to add a custom field:

1. Navigate to **Settings|Custom Fields**.

2. Click **Add a custom field**.

3. Choose between a text question or a drop-down question.

4. Fill in the question and options (if one is chosen from the dropdown).

5. Click **Save changes**:

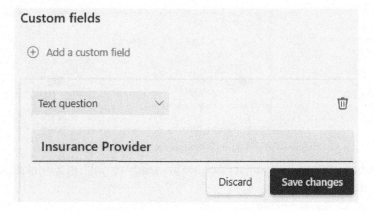

Figure 4.13 – Adding a custom field

Now that we have created our custom field, we can add it to our Virtual Health Consult by navigating back to our service and clicking **Edit service**. Our new question appears in the **Custom fields** section and we can enable it. You can also choose to mark it as **Required** for submission (see *Figure 4.14*):

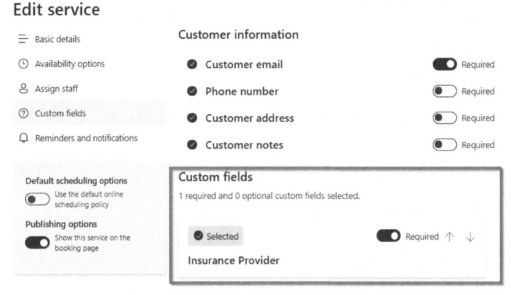

Figure 4.14 – Adding a custom field to a specific service

Now that we have customized our service, we are ready to publish a Bookings page for users to schedule appointments.

Customizing the Booking page

The Booking page is a self-service website that allows external customers to choose a service and available time to book an appointment. Navigate to **Settings | Booking page** to customize the page's branding, permissions, scheduling policies, and more. See the following for details regarding each control:

- **Configure booking page**: This section controls the publishing of the self-service page. If you need a public-facing page that anyone can book time on, choose **Available to anyone**. For an internal-only page, select **Available to people in your organization**. If no external facing page is necessary and staff will manually input appointments, choose **No self-service**.

- **Business page access control**: You can optionally prevent your page from appearing in the search results of Bing, Google, and other search engines by checking the **Disable direct search engine indexing of booking** box.

- **Customer data usage consent**: Optionally, show a custom data usage consent message on the booking page.

- **Default scheduling policy**: This controls the default time increments, lead time, notifications, and service availability. In the previous section on adding services, we had the option to adopt these overall scheduling policies for each service.

- **Customize your page**: Optionally, choose a color theme and whether to display your logo on the booking page or not.

- **Region and time zone settings**: Select your language and time zone.

After customizing our booking page, we can view what it will look like to our end customers by using the link provided at the top of the booking page section. See the following steps for an example virtual health booking on our new calendar:

1. A customer visits the URL of our booking page and selects the service or appointment time for their visit:

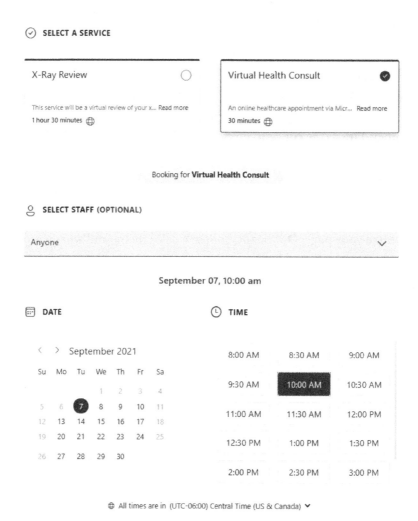

Figure 4.15 – Selecting a service and appointment time

2. The customer enters the required information and the required custom field we configured earlier. When finished, they click **Book**:

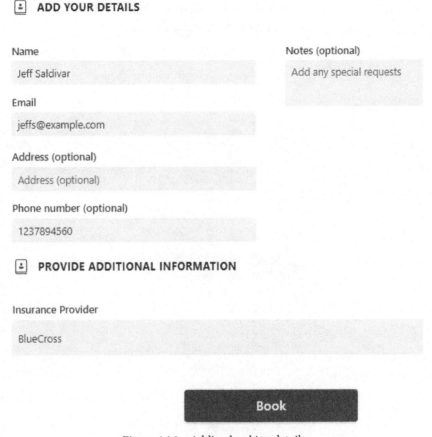

Figure 4.16 – Adding booking details

3. The customer then gets a confirmation screen summarizing their appointment, as well as a confirmation email with the virtual join link:

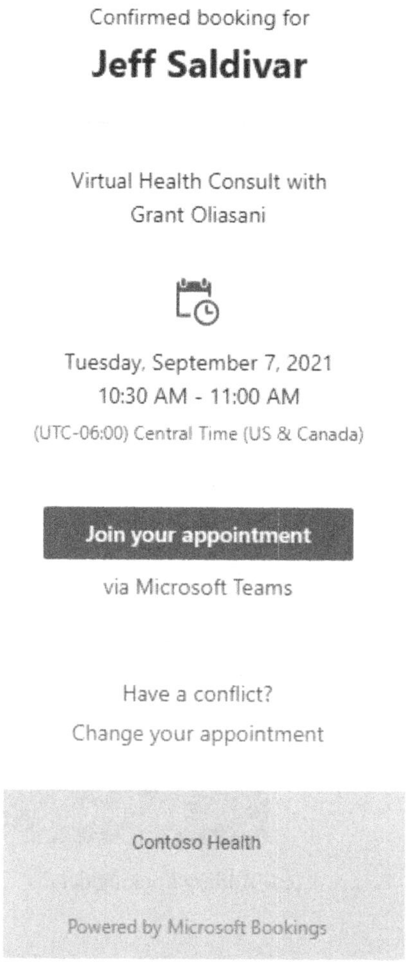

Confirmed booking for

Jeff Saldivar

Virtual Health Consult with
Grant Oliasani

Tuesday, September 7, 2021
10:30 AM - 11:00 AM
(UTC-06:00) Central Time (US & Canada)

Join your appointment

via Microsoft Teams

Have a conflict?

Change your appointment

Contoso Health

Powered by Microsoft Bookings

Figure 4.17 – Confirmation email

In this case, the customer did not choose a specific staff member for their appointment, so one will be assigned based on availability. The staff member who is assigned will receive an email with the appointment details, as well as a meeting invite (see *Figure 4.18*):

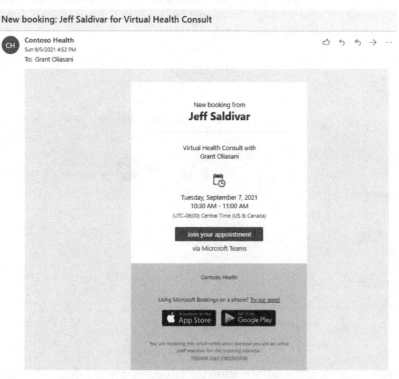

Figure 4.18 – Staff member appointment confirmation

Now that we have some bookings on the calendar, let's view these on the actual Bookings calendar.

Viewing the calendar

To view the calendar of appointments and their details, simply click **Calendar** in the Bookings web app. This will bring up a view of appointments by day, week, staff, or even month, depending on your settings. To open a booking and see additional details, click the entry on the calendar (see *Figure 4.19*):

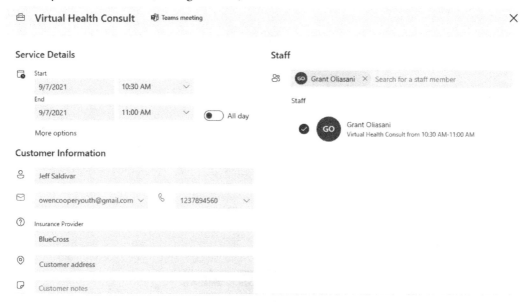

Figure 4.19 – Booking details

In this view, we can see all the information the customer entered during booking, such as their name, time of appointment, email, phone number, and our insurance provider custom field. We can also see which staff member was assigned the booking and update if needed. To join the booking, the staff member simply clicks the Teams meeting link included on the invite sent to their primary mailbox or the Bookings calendar entry.

As you can see, Microsoft Bookings is a powerful tool that can help you manage the full life cycle of customer appointments. When setting up Bookings, you have a wide variety of configuration choices (such as adding custom fields for additional details, time zones, or required fields) to help customers select the appointment options that best suit them and provide the staff with necessary information.

In the next section, we will explore the Bookings experience inside Microsoft Teams.

Bookings using Teams

Now that you have a good understanding of the Bookings service in Office 365, we can dive into the dedicated Teams app for Bookings. This app enables your team to offer, create, and manage internal or external appointments, all within Teams. There are some key differences between the Teams and web versions of the application, which we will explore at the end of this section.

First, let's get the app onto the Teams rail. To install the app to your Teams client, follow these steps:

1. Click **Apps** on the left-hand rail of Teams to open the App Store.

2. In the search box, type in `Bookings` and select the **Bookings** app. Click the **Add** button to install the app to your Teams client:

Figure 4.20 — Adding the Bookings app

3. Optionally, pin the app to the left-hand rail for easier access:

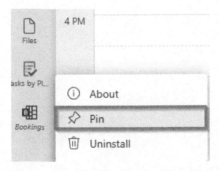

Figure 4.21 – Pinning the Bookings app

Once you have the Bookings app added in Teams, you can start using it! In the next sections, we'll look at how to set up the Bookings calendar, appointment types, and options.

Creating a Bookings calendar in Teams

The first time you open the Bookings app in Teams, you will need to select **Get started** to either create a new Bookings calendar or open an existing one. The process of creating a new calendar in Teams is similar to that of the web app. To create a new Bookings calendar in Teams, follow these steps:

1. Select **New booking calendar**:

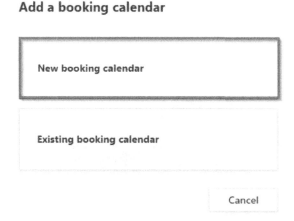

Figure 4.22 — Creating a Bookings calendar in Teams

2. Fill in **Business or department name** and **Business type**. Optionally, specify an email address to send attendee responses to and a phone number:

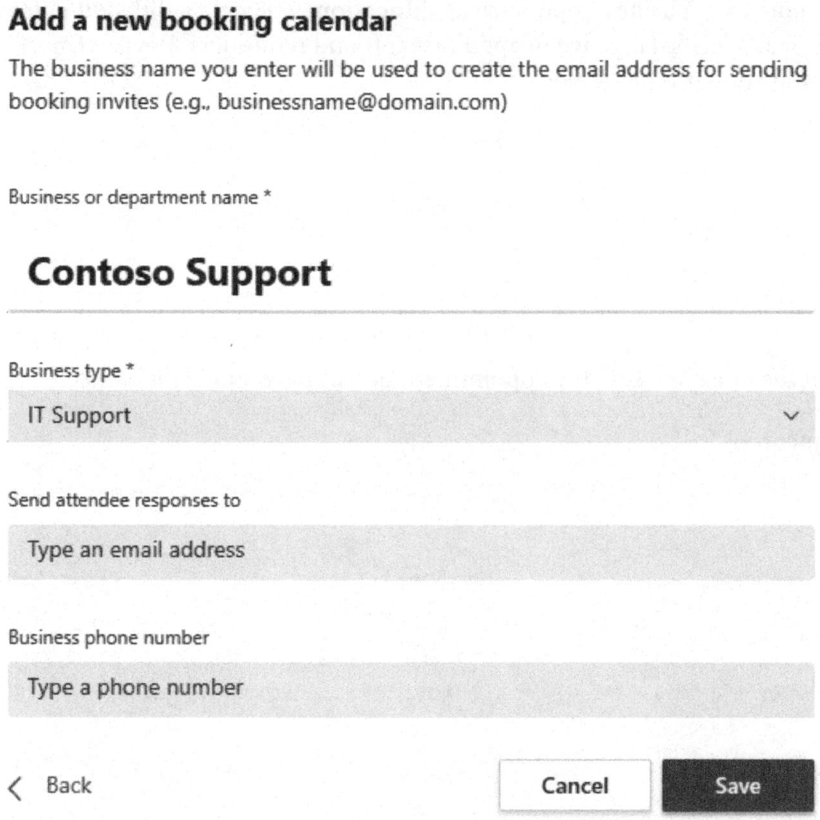

Add a new booking calendar

The business name you enter will be used to create the email address for sending booking invites (e.g., businessname@domain.com)

Business or department name *

Contoso Support

Business type *

IT Support ⌄

Send attendee responses to

Type an email address

Business phone number

Type a phone number

‹ Back   Cancel   Save

Figure 4.23 – Filling in new calendar details

It is important to note that the different business types affect the *language* of the calendar. For our example, we chose **IT Support** as the business type. Selecting this business type came with a default service called **Initial consult** (see *Figure 4.24*):

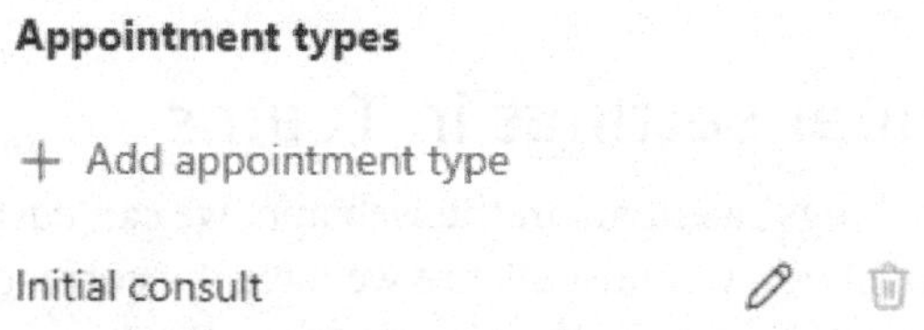

Appointment types

+ Add appointment type

Initial consult   ✎   🗑

Figure 4.24 – IT Support default service

Choosing a different business type, such as **Education**, will yield a different default service name as well as specific language in appointments and reminders. Review *Figure 4.25* to see the **Appointment types** dialog:

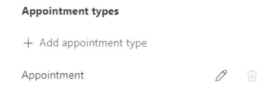

Figure 4.25 – Education default service

As you can see in *Figure 4.26*, the appointment details have subtle differences:

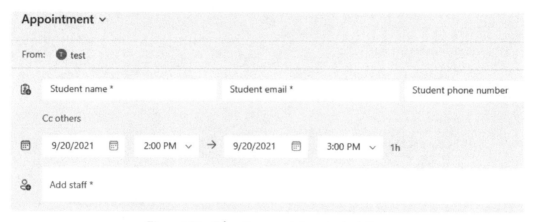

Figure 4.26 – Education appointment scheduling

After clicking **Save**, you have successfully created a Bookings calendar in Microsoft Teams. By default, the calendar will have no staff and a single service with a name reflective of the business type you chose. Now that we have created the calendar, let's see how we can set additional configurations in Teams.

Bookings calendar settings in Teams

Similar to setting up Bookings calendars in the web app, we can customize staff and services in the Teams app. First, we must ensure we have the correct Bookings calendar open. The open calendar can be seen at the top left of the Bookings app:

Figure 4.27 – Current open calendar

If this is the incorrect calendar or you wish to switch to another, simply click the drop-down next to the calendar name and select **Existing booking calendar**. Then, enter the business name or **View all booking calendars in your org** to navigate to the desired calendar.

Adding appointment types

As previously mentioned, when a new Bookings calendar is created in Teams, a single appointment type is created that correlates to the business type you selected. To view the appointment types and add more, follow these steps:

1. Open the calendar settings by clicking the ellipses at the top left of the app and clicking **Settings**:

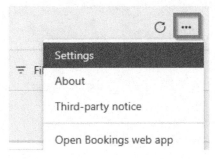

Figure 4.28 – Navigating to Settings

2. Select **Appointment types**:

Figure 4.29 – Appointment types

3. Click **Add appointment type** and give it a title. You can also add a confirmation message and email reminders, and choose whether to allow attendees to join the meeting from a mobile browser:

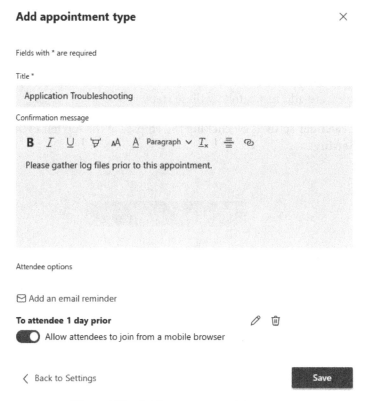

Figure 4.30 – Adding a new appointment type

After clicking **Save**, this appointment is now available for your staff to book.

Adding staff

When you first set up a Bookings calendar in Teams, the creator (yourself) is the sole staff member and admin. In order to assign others to appointments and allow them to manage the calendar, we can add additional staff by following these steps:

1. Navigate to **Settings | Staff**.

2. In the text box, enter a name or email address to add them to the Bookings calendar.

3. Click **Add** and repeat with additional staff as necessary.

By default, the users added will have an admin permission level. This can be good to delegate the administrative activity to additional staff and not create a bottleneck. However, not everyone will need admin rights to the Bookings calendar. There are four different roles:

- **Administrator**: Can edit all settings, staff, and bookings
- **Scheduler**: Can manage appointments on the calendar with read-only access to settings, staff, and appointment types
- **Team member**: Can manage bookings on their calendar
- **Viewer**: Can view the bookings on the calendar and read only the settings

To change the role of a staff member, simply click the dropdown next to their name and select the role (see *Figure 4.31*):

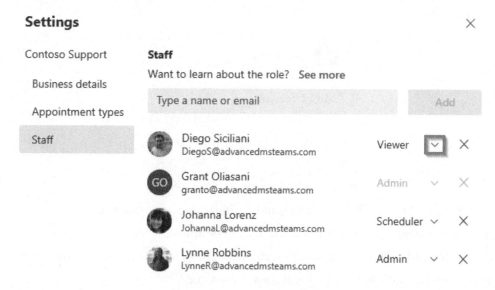

Figure 4.31 – Changing staff roles

For more details on the different roles, click the **See More** link, as shown in *Figure 4.31*.

Now that we have added additional staff to our calendar, we are ready to schedule appointments.

Scheduling appointments in Teams

In the Bookings web app, we had the option of publishing a self-service scheduling page for those external to your organization, as well as the ability for staff to manually set up appointments. Out of the box, the dedicated Teams app for Bookings is set up for only internal staff to book appointments on behalf of customers, though this can be changed, as we will see in the next section. Scheduling an appointment for a customer is a simple process. To do that, follow these steps:

1. In the Bookings app, click **New booking**.

Figure 4.32 – New booking button

2. Choose an appointment type for the booking by selecting the dropdown at the top left of the page:

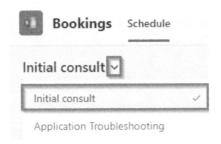

Figure 4.33 – Choosing an appointment type

3. Fill in the attendee's name, email, and optionally a phone number.

4. Select the day, time, and duration of the appointment.

5. In the **Add staff** field, choose the staff member assigned to the appointment.

6. If desired, add a note for the staff member assigned.

7. Optionally, toggle on **Allow attendees to join from a mobile browser** to not require that the attendees download Teams mobile app to join the meeting from their smartphone. By default, all appointments created from within Bookings in Teams will have a Teams meeting link attached.

8. You can add a confirmation message with additional information for the attendee if needed.

9. Finally, you can choose to add custom email reminders, aside from the ones set up during the appointment type creation.

10. When finished, click **Send**:

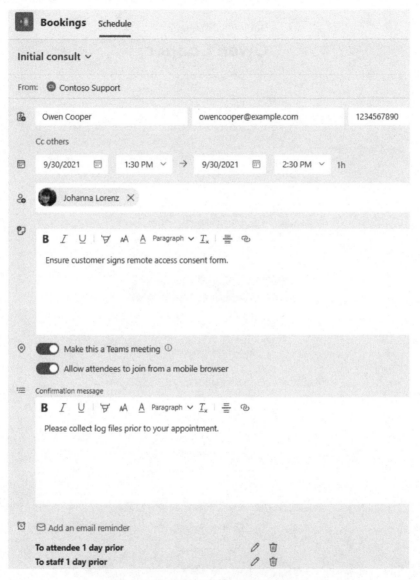

Figure 4.34 – Scheduling appointment

After sending the appointment, the customer will get an email confirmation with details of their appointment, a join link, and any additional information you included in the confirmation message upon scheduling (see *Figure 4.35*):

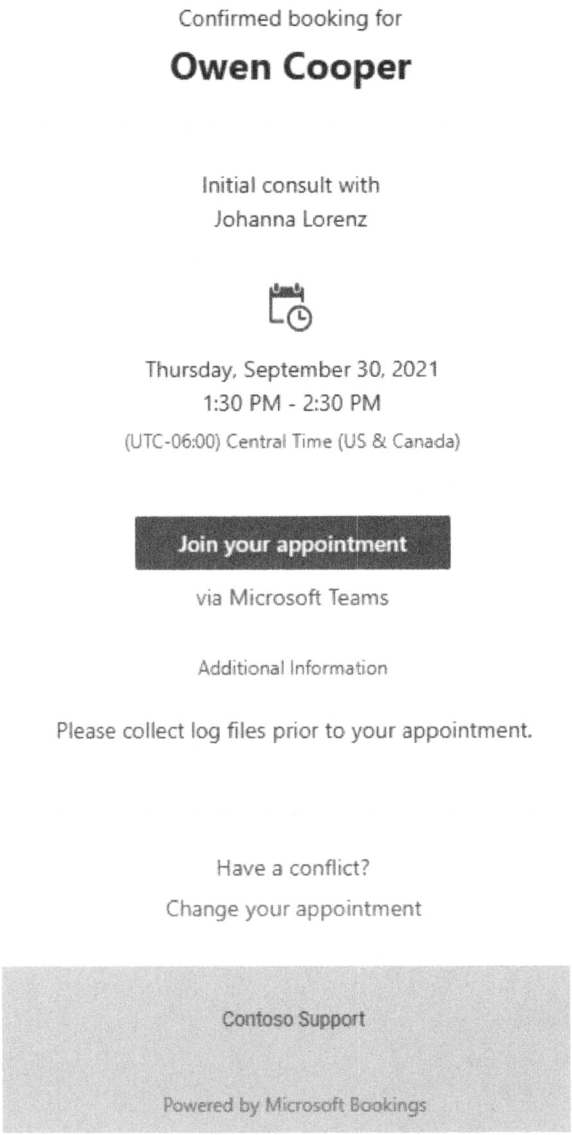

Confirmed booking for

Owen Cooper

Initial consult with
Johanna Lorenz

Thursday, September 30, 2021
1:30 PM - 2:30 PM
(UTC-06:00) Central Time (US & Canada)

Join your appointment

via Microsoft Teams

Additional Information

Please collect log files prior to your appointment.

Have a conflict?

Change your appointment

Contoso Support

Powered by Microsoft Bookings

Figure 4.35 – Customer email confirmation

The staff member assigned to the virtual appointment will also get an email notification with the appointment details, and the appointment will show on their personal calendar (see *Figure 4.36*):

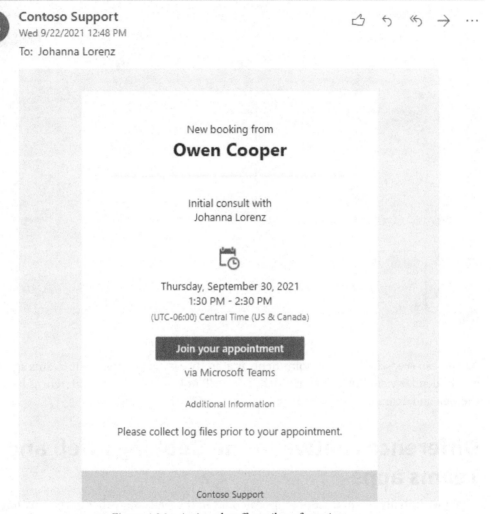

Figure 4.36 – Assigned staff email confirmation

To view the schedule of appointments, simply open the Bookings app in Teams and go to **Schedule**. You can filter to specific staff members, or view all appointments. Actual appointments for the Bookings calendar will appear in light blue, while personal meetings or calendar blocks appear in gray (see *Figure 4.37*):

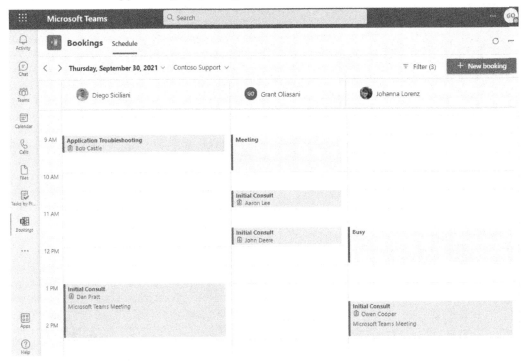

Figure 4.37 – Schedule of appointments

As you can see, scheduling appointments is a pretty easy experience. The Teams app gives good calendar visibility. In the next section, we'll look at some of the differences between the web and Teams app experiences.

Differences between the Bookings web and Teams apps

When we initially set up the Bookings calendar in the web app earlier in the *Creating a Bookings calendar* section, you may remember there were additional options for branding, scheduling, hours, and more. Out of the box, the Bookings app for Teams is a streamlined version of this, allowing for a quick and easy setup for appointment scheduling. Although some of these advanced features are not available by default in the Teams app, we can still use these settings by opening the calendar in the web app. To do so, simply click the ellipses at the top and select **Open Bookings web app**:

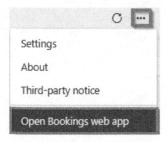

Figure 4.38 – Open in web app

After opening the Bookings web app, we can publish a self-service scheduling page, add a logo for the calendar, and even set business hours. The process to use these features is the same as in the previous section on the Bookings web app. For a detailed comparison of the differences between the Teams and web app, see the following table:

Feature	Available in web app	Available in Teams app
Add guests as staff	Yes	No
Create offline bookings	Yes	No
Group appointments	Yes	No
Add a logo	Yes	No
Set business hours	Yes	No
Publish self-service page	Yes	No
Collect customer contacts	Yes	No
Manage time off	Yes	No

Summary

In this chapter, we examined Bookings, both on the web and in the Teams app. Bookings can be used to streamline the process of offering and managing virtual appointments for both internal and external users. We learned how to configure hours, services, and branding in the web app, and the simplicity of getting a Bookings calendar up and running directly in Teams.

The Bookings app can be used standalone and can also integrate with other tools inside the Microsoft 365 ecosystem. In the next chapter, we will look at the service that powers all of these virtual visits: Microsoft Teams meetings.

Part 2: Meetings

In this part, you will learn how to conduct effective meetings, including ad hoc, scheduled, and channel meetings, and live events.

This part comprises the following chapters:

- *Chapter 5, Conducting Teams Meetings*
- *Chapter 6, Microsoft Teams Rooms*
- *Chapter 7, Live Events*

5
Conducting Teams Meetings

Meetings in **Microsoft Teams** is one of the main ways to virtually collaborate with your coworkers. Microsoft Teams allows audio, video, and screen sharing communications to help maximize productivity, and there are a few ways to start, join, and participate in meetings.

In this chapter, we will explore the various meeting types (for example, *scheduled*, *ad hoc*, and *channel* meetings) and introduce different meeting features such as *transcriptions*, *recording*, and *breakout rooms*. We will also look at the **Audio Conferencing** feature and the benefits that come with this.

This chapter will cover the following topics:

- Overview of Meetings in Microsoft Teams
- Types of Meetings in Microsoft Teams
- Meeting Features
- Meeting Options
- Audio Conferencing in Microsoft Teams

So, let's get started!

Technical requirements

To complete some of the activities and configurations in this chapter, you'll need a **Microsoft 365 tenant** with the following licenses activated (either in trial or paid subscriptions):

- Audio Conferencing licenses
- Communication Credits

You can obtain trial versions of these products through the **Microsoft 365 Admin Center**.

Overview of Meetings in Microsoft Teams

In *Chapter 1*, *Taking a Tour of Microsoft Teams*, we introduced the evolutionary Microsoft Teams platform. Two of the key functionalities of Microsoft Teams are *video conferencing* and its *meeting* capabilities. Microsoft Teams meetings allow basic communication between two or more parties by providing audio, video, and screen sharing capabilities. Teams allows users to initiate and participate in device-to-device calls by using either a PC client or the Teams mobile app. Additionally, participants can chat with each other within the meeting, take meeting notes, share content such as files and whiteboards, invite other participants, change background filters, and more.

In the following figure, we can see a Microsoft Teams meeting, with the meeting controls on the top right:

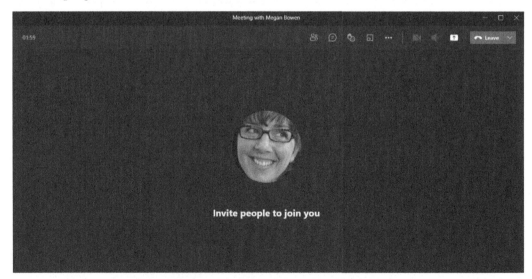

Figure 5.1 – The Microsoft Teams meeting view

As discussed in *Chapter 1*, *Taking a Tour of Microsoft Teams*, you can get to this view through the **Calendar** tab.

Now, let's cover the three types of meetings you can schedule.

Types of meetings in Microsoft Teams

The Microsoft Teams hub, as a tool for collaboration and communication, allows users to connect with each other via instant messaging or video meetings to get their work done in a productive manner. Different projects or initiatives may call for different types of meetings. Therefore, in Microsoft Teams, there are three different types of meetings that serve different purposes for a number of scenarios.

In this section, we will discuss the three types of Microsoft Teams meetings:

- **Scheduled**: In this meeting type, all involved parties decide to meet at a previously agreed time.

- **Ad hoc**: In this meeting type, all involved parties get together at the last minute, with no previously agreed time.

- **Channel**: In this meeting type, all team members in a team are automatically invited and will have access to any content from the meeting, whether it is before, during, or after.

Let's now go into more depth for each of these meeting types, starting with scheduled meetings.

Scheduled meetings

Scheduled meetings are probably the most familiar concept of the three. There are two types of scheduled meetings. The first is a regular scheduled Teams meeting. The second is a newer type of meeting called a **webinar**. A webinar is essentially a Teams meeting with a built-in registration feature.

Scheduled Teams meetings

Users can use either the **Microsoft Teams** or **Outlook** client or web browser to create a new regular scheduled meeting, invite both required and optional participants, and set a date and time for the meeting. One way to schedule meetings is to use the Outlook client. In the top left of the Outlook app, click **New Email** and you should see an option for **Teams Meeting** in the drop-down list:

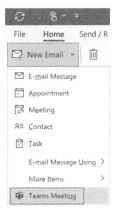

Figure 5.2 – Setting up a Teams meeting with Outlook

Also in Outlook, the **Scheduling Assistant** is a tool that will look up your coworker's availability in their calendar. This can be handy for avoiding accidentally scheduling something over another already established meeting.

Figure 5.3 – The Scheduling Assistant view in Outlook

The Scheduling Assistant is also available in the Teams client. In the Teams client, on the left, click **Calendar**. This panel shows your calendar, which should also be synced with your Outlook calendar. On the top right of this screen, you'll see the **+ New Meeting** button. When creating a new scheduled Teams meeting this way, you must fill out the following:

- The title of the meeting
- The required attendees
- The time of the meeting
- The date of the meeting

The Scheduling Assistant view in Teams is very similar to that in Outlook, as shown in *Figure 5.4*:

Figure 5.4 – The Scheduling Assistant view in Microsoft Teams

Using the Teams client, you can *optionally* add the following information:

- Assign a personal category to the meeting.
- Change the time zone.
- Request responses.
- Enable or disable forwarding of the meeting.
- Require the registration of people in your organization, of guests, or of everyone.
- Set an occurrence.

- Invite a channel.

- Add details of the meeting.

- Provide a **Microsoft OneNote** for agenda items and meeting notes.

With scheduled meetings, you can also use the Scheduling Assistant via either Teams or Outlook to help you see the *free/busy* status for your coworkers for different dates and times. You also have very similar controls if you use the Outlook or Teams apps on a mobile device that runs on **iOS** or **Android**. The Scheduling Assistant is not required to schedule meetings, but it can be very useful. Otherwise, you can simply create a Teams meeting via the Outlook or Teams client/web portal, enter the required attendees, set a time and date, and send it over.

> **Drafts**
>
> You may be familiar with Outlook saving draft emails and meeting invites. In the Teams client, if you navigate away from scheduling the meeting before sending, Teams will not save the meeting as a draft. Instead, the client will present you with **Discard edits** or **Continue editing** options to select.
>
> If there are no participants listed in the invite, it will save as an appointment without a Teams link.

Another way to create a scheduled meeting is through chat. For example, imagine you are discussing something in depth with your coworkers in a group chat. Instead of chatting back and forth, you know it would be faster and more productive through a call. Teams provides you with the capability to create a scheduled meeting with members of the group chat *already populated*. In the group chat at the bottom of the panel, you'll see a row of icons; you just need to click on the calendar icon with the plus sign, as shown in *Figure 5.5*:

Figure 5.5 – Scheduling a meeting from a group chat in Microsoft Teams

This will take you to the **New meeting** page within Teams, where it will have the meeting attendees already populated with the group chat members:

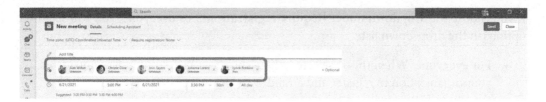

Figure 5.6 – Scheduling a meeting from a group chat using the New meeting page in Microsoft Teams

With these steps, you can create a scheduled meeting from a group chat, which can be extremely useful in collaboration scenarios.

Teams Webinars

Teams webinars can host up to 1,000 attendees and can be used if you want to run a Teams meeting that is more controlled and with a built-in, customizable registration form. In a webinar, you typically have presenters and attendees, so there is less back and forth conversation among participants. Webinars allow specific responsibilities and capabilities to be assigned to the presenter and attendee roles. For example, by default, attendees will remain muted with their videos turned off and will not be allowed to share their screens. If their permissions were to be changed, only the organizer or presenter can do that. Additionally, webinars provide additional attendee registration-related data for the organizer. By default, everyone with a Teams license has the capability to schedule a webinar.

You can use your Teams desktop client to schedule a Teams webinar. To do that, follow these steps:

1. Navigate to the calendar icon on the left.

2. Click the dropdown next to + **New meeting**.

3. Choose **Webinar** from the drop-down list.

The fields within the **New webinar** page are very similar to that of a regular scheduled meeting. However, you will notice that at the top, there is a tab to toggle a registration requirement and an information box below it.

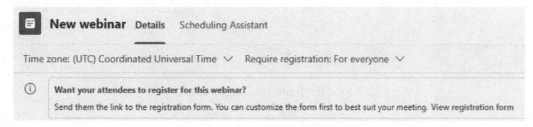

Figure 5.7 – The Teams New webinar page

If you choose the dropdown under **Require registration: For everyone**, you will see three options in the drop-down list:

- **For everyone**: When this is selected, the webinar will allow attendees outside of your organization to register and attend.

- **For people in your org**: When this is selected, the webinar allows only for attendees in your organization to register and attend.

- **None**: When this is selected, no one is required to register for the webinar.

Next, click on **View registration form**. The webinar registration form is totally customizable for the organizer. As the organizer, you can choose a picture or logo to illustrate the event and set webinar details such as the title, time, and speaker information. On the right, there is registration information. This is also customizable, except for the required fields for first name, last name, and email address. You can add other fields and mark them as required if necessary.

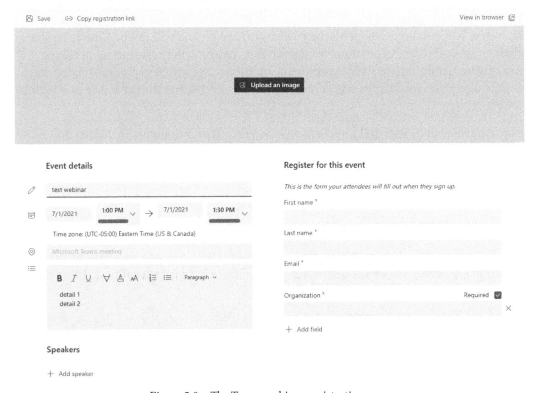

Figure 5.8 – The Teams webinar registration page

Once you have filled out all of the information you want, remember to click **Save**. Next to **Save**, there is a **Copy registration link** button. You can share this link with all of the presenters and attendees through email, social media, or a website. You can also preview your registration page by clicking on **View in browser** on the top right.

Once registered, presenters and attendees will receive a confirmation email and an invitation to the Teams webinar.

As the organizer, you can download the registration report. This report is saved as a CSV file and contains information such as registration page views and submissions to the participant information requested from the registration page.

As an IT administrator, you may want to control how people are scheduling these webinars. For example, you might want to allow for meeting registration only in your organization. To edit these settings, you must connect to the **Skype for Business PowerShell** module and use the following commands:

- `Set-CsTeamsMeetingPolicy -AllowPrivateMeetingScheduling`: This can be used to turn private meeting scheduling on or off.

- `Set-CsTeamsMeetingPolicy -AllowMeetingRegistration`: This can be used to turn meeting registration on or off.

- `Set-CsTeamsMeetingPolicy -WhoCanRegister`: This allows you to dictate who can register for webinars (for example, only individuals within your organization or anyone).

> **Learn More about the Set-CsTeamsMeetingPolicy Command**
>
> For more information on the different parameters available for this command, please see the following page:
>
> `https://docs.microsoft.com/en-us/powershell/module/skype/set-csteamsmeetingpolicy?view=skype-ps`.

These administrator settings can help control users in your organization who can create webinars and allow for external participation.

Now that we've covered different ways to create a scheduled meeting, let's look at ad hoc meetings.

Ad hoc Teams meetings

Sometimes, there is a need to meet outside of regular cadences or have the occasional one-off meetings. This is where ad hoc meetings come in, as these are unscheduled and/or last minute. Microsoft Teams is a fantastic tool for ad hoc meetings, and like scheduled meetings, there are several ways to create them.

To find these options, we'll need to explore the functions that are accessible via the **Meet now** button. You can find this on the Teams client in your **Calendar** tab. The **Meet now** button in Teams allows for meetings to be created and attendees to be invited on the fly.

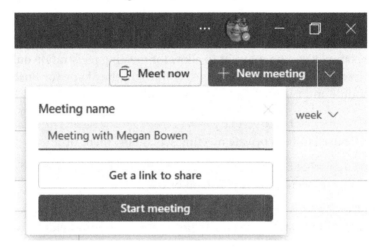

Figure 5.9 – The Meet now button in the Teams client

After clicking on **Meet now**, you can click on **Get a link to share** and copy and paste the link to them, *or*, you can select **Start meeting** and invite them that way.

Let's explore these two paths in more detail.

First, we've got the **Get a link to share** option. If you need to, refer to *Figure 5.7* for a refresher on how to get here and what this process looks like.

After you click the **Get a link to share** button, you will see a Teams meetings link be generated and automatically copied to your clipboard. Otherwise, you can copy it manually by clicking the copy icon on the right. Then, you will see the **Share via email** button.

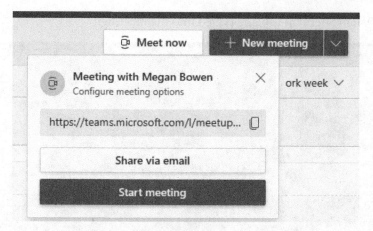

Figure 5.10 Sharing an ad hoc meeting invitation

If you click **Share via email**, you can use your device's default email application to send the Teams meeting link. In this example, we will continue to use Outlook. Introductory static text will be added to the email body, as well as the same Teams meeting link. Having this link at the top will allow the receiver to navigate quickly and easily. All that is left to do is populate the attendee information and you will be ready to send the ad hoc meeting invitation.

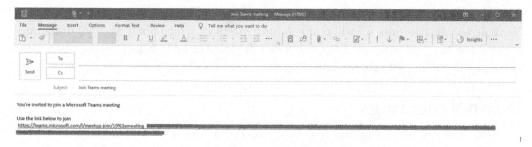

Figure 5.11 – Sharing an ad hoc meeting invitation via email

This can be handy if you need to invite an external participant (that is, someone who is not part of your organization).

The second option is to click the **Start meeting** button right away. When this is done, Teams will create a pop-up view for the meeting. Within the meeting, you can then click on the participants icon to invite people. You can do this with the following methods:

- Type in the participant's email address.
- If you've got the Audio Conference license, this number allows participants to dial into the meeting by using a PSTN number.

In *Figure 5.10*, Joni Sherman is being pulled into the meeting:

Figure 5.12 – Inviting a participant in a Teams ad hoc meeting

This concludes our overview of the ways we can create ad hoc meetings in Microsoft Teams. In the next section, we will cover *channel meetings*, which are structured differently from the meetings we've covered so far, but be scheduled or ad hoc, so it is a way to review meetings altogether. Onto channel meetings!

Channel meetings

Microsoft Teams allows for groups to collaborate. From the backend point of view, behind a *team* is either a private Office 365 group with specifically invited members or a public Office 365 group where anyone within the organization can join. Either way, this Office 365 group provides a space that can contain specific files, chats, applications, and other relevant content or tools dedicated to a particular group.

Within a team, you can have channels. A *channel* is meant to be a separator within a team. Channels can be organized by different topics, projects, departments, or any other logical divider. Within each channel, you can have dedicated conversations, files, and, of course, meetings.

> **Teams and Channels in Microsoft Teams**
>
> Before diving into teams and channels within Microsoft Teams, it's important to think about the logical groupings within a team and then within a channel. There may be separate uses for a channel within a team, or it could have a separate team altogether. To understand when to use a team or a channel, it's important to fully understand the difference between the two.
>
> To learn more about teams and channels in Microsoft Teams, visit this link: `https://docs.microsoft.com/en-us/microsoftteams/teams-channels-overview`.

Channel meetings are unique because Teams automatically invites all members of the channel to the meeting. Another way in which channel meetings aid collaboration and productivity is that all channel members will be able to join the meeting with as much context and as many tools as possible and contribute as necessary. This can aid collaboration because all relevant discussions, files, and recordings (if the meetings are recorded) will be in the channel meeting conversation history, so other members can easily keep up and contribute.

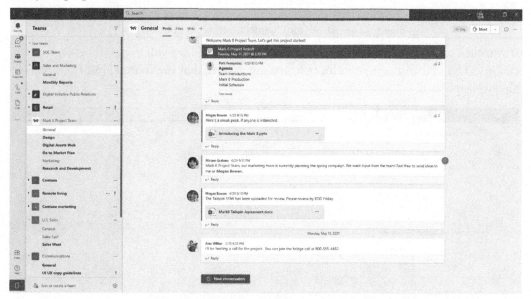

Figure 5.13 – A channel view in Microsoft Teams

Channel meetings can be *ad hoc* or *scheduled*. Within the channel view on the top right, you can click the **Meet** button. This will give you the option to choose an ad hoc or a scheduled channel meeting, depending on the situation.

Clicking **Meet now** will result in another pop-up Teams meeting window:

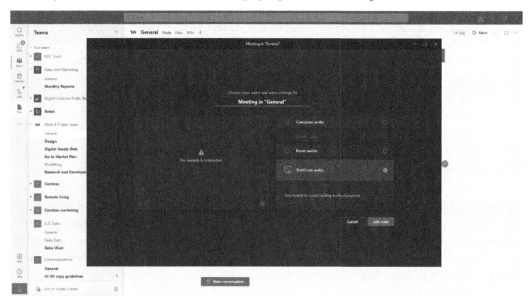

Figure 5.14 – An ad hoc channel meeting pop-up window

If you click on **Schedule a meeting**, the Teams client will lead you to a page where you can insert all of the information for the meeting. Notice that the channel information is already populated.

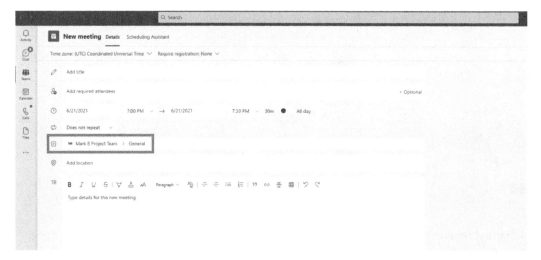

Figure 5.15 – A scheduled channel meeting view

Once done, your meeting has been scheduled.

So, now we have covered scheduled meetings, ad hoc meetings, and channel meetings, along with the differences between the three. Next, we will discuss the meeting features that are available on the Microsoft Teams platform.

Meeting Features

Teams meetings have a range of out-of-the-box features that will help improve the video conferencing experience on any supported platform, including mobile iOS and Android devices. Some of these features may already be familiar to you, such as muting and screen sharing. However, other features such as background blur, breakout rooms, and meeting notes are more recent.

This section will look at the following meeting features:

- **Video and background features**: Microsoft Teams allows for the use of video during meetings.

- **Sharing**: You can share your desktop or specific application content (such as from the Whiteboard application) during Teams meetings.

- **In-meeting experiences**: Teams meetings allow for other features such as breakout rooms, reactions, and hand-raising.

By the end of this section, you'll be able to recognize, identify, and work with some of the out-of-the-box meeting features in Microsoft Teams.

Video and background features

To start, you can use your device's camera or an external camera to display your face, just as you would in any video conference scenario. In Microsoft Teams, you can turn this on and off directly in the client. Before you join a meeting, Teams will prompt you to choose your audio and video settings. During a meeting, you can find this option on the top right side of the Teams desktop client.

Additionally, you can add special *background filters*. The background filters include *background blur*, *Microsoft template backgrounds*, and *custom background images* that you can upload yourself. These filters will cover up your background so that the audience can focus on your face.

By default, filters are turned off and are only available when your camera is turned on. However, you can choose a blur filter or any of the background images already provided by Microsoft. You can also upload your own by clicking **+ Add new**.

Figure 5.16 – The Background settings pane in Microsoft Teams

When meeting participants have their camera turned on, Microsoft Teams uses **Azure** technology to help provide the most optimized and productive end user experience.

You can also find more options by clicking the ellipsis (**…**) icon at the bottom of the call.

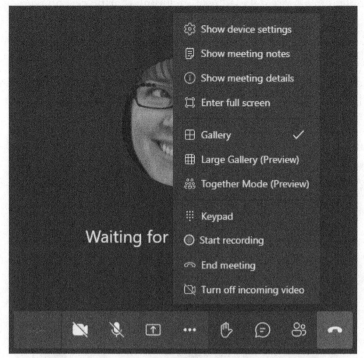

Figure 5.17 – The video conference gallery options in the Microsoft Teams web view

With a desktop client (Windows or Mac), a web browser, or an Android or iOS device, you can have up to 49 video conference participants at one time during a Teams meeting. That means up to 49 participants can have their camera turned on and you'll be able to see each of them in the **Large Gallery** view. You can also select **Together Mode**, which will allow participants to appear in one virtual space.

If you're in a meeting where you'd like to pin a specific participant or speaker, you can also select **Spotlight Mode**. You can use this to make sure everyone can focus on a specific presentation or the individual who is speaking. Spotlight mode is available when you navigate to the **Participants** pane and right-click on a user icon.

The **Gallery** options are available both in the Teams client and web view, as well as on mobile devices running on Android and iOS.

Sharing

Sharing content with your audience during a video conference is often essential during a collaborative session, and you are probably already familiar with this concept.

Sharing your *desktop* is the first and most relatable example; however, Teams will allow you to share content in a more detailed way, including sharing certain *windows* and specific *open and active* applications such as **Microsoft PowerPoint** or **Whiteboard**. While sharing, other features such as *requesting* and *taking control* of the presenter's screen are also available.

There might be instances when you need to share a video. During a Teams meeting, you can share a video and include its audio by selecting the **Include computer sound** option so that the audience can watch and listen to the video.

To start sharing content in the meeting, you can find the share button located on the top right of the meeting window (between the audio icon and the **Leave** button).

Figure 5.18 – The Share content pane

In this view, Microsoft Teams will automatically pull up and list some of your more recently accessed PowerPoint files, if applicable. Otherwise, you can decide to share a certain screen or a specific window, or you can start up a Whiteboard session or navigate within OneDrive or your local machine for a specific file.

In-meeting experiences

Beyond the basic camera, video, and sharing capabilities, there are other features available within a Teams meeting that might help boost collaboration and productivity. Located on the top right, you can see several icons listed from left to right:

- **Participants list**: This lists active and invited members of the meeting.
- **Chat**: This shows messages sent within the meeting.
- **Raise hands/live reactions**: This provides the opportunity for the participants to raise their hands virtually and include live reactions, for example, adding *likes* or *applause*.
- **Breakout rooms**: This organizes members in the meeting into separate, smaller meeting rooms.
- **Ellipsis**: This includes other meeting settings such as meeting information, device preferences, the ability to add an app, and more.

Let's take a closer look at each of these (except for **Chat**, which is rather self-explanatory).

Managing the participants list

The participants list will display active members of the meeting. It will also provide you with the capability to bring others in, either through VOIP or PSTN.

In the **Participants** pane, you'll see the ellipsis (…) icon to the right. If you click on the ellipsis icon, you'll see the **Manage permissions** and **Download attendance list** options if your administrator has enabled these features.

Figure 5.19 – The options dropdown in the Participants pane

As the meeting organizer, you can assign specific meeting-based role access to each participant. For example, the organizer can assign someone a presenter role, while others can be attendees. In this case, only the presenter would have permission to share their screen.

> **Roles in a Teams Meeting**
>
> As an IT administrator and even as a meeting organizer, it's important to understand the different roles that are made available to you. As the meeting organizer, you control how your meeting is managed. Having control of technical capabilities such as presenter rights and attendee roles can be critical in running the most productive and secure meeting sessions.
>
> Detailed information on meeting roles can be found here: `https://support.microsoft.com/en-us/office/roles-in-a-teams-meeting-c16fa7d0-1666-4dde-8686-0a0bfe16e019`.

The organizer can also download the attendance list after the meeting. This will contain information on who joined, what time they joined, and when they exited. This feature must be explicitly turned on by an administrator with PowerShell and can be managed with meeting policies in the **Team Admin Center** section.

> **Managing the Attendance List**
>
> As a meeting organizer, you might want a list of who has joined the meeting, who has left, and the relative timestamps for each attendee. It is important to know the two places where you can retrieve this report, the IT administrator steps to configure this feature, and the current known issues and limitations.
>
> All of this information can be found here:
>
> `https://support.microsoft.com/en-us/office/view-and-download-meeting-attendance-reports-in-teams-ae7cf170-530c-47d3-84c1-3aedac74d310`.

Raising hands and live reactions

To engage with your attendees, you can use the *raise hands* feature or send *live reactions* during the Teams meeting!

Raise your virtual hand during a meeting when you want to contribute to the conversation without interrupting. When you raise your hand, a hand icon will show up on the participants list as a visual cue next to your name.

Figure 5.20 – The raise hand view

If more than one participant raises their hand, they will be put at the top of the list in the order in which they raised their hands. If you want to *lower your hand*, you can do that in the participants list by right-clicking on your name. You can lower other participant's hands as well.

You can stay engaged in your Teams meetings by leveraging *live reactions*. You can use the *like*, *love*, *applause*, and *laugh* buttons to express yourself and react to certain news, announcements, presentations, and more. You can see each of these icons right next to where you can find the *raise hand* button.

Figure 5.21 – The live reactions buttons

When you click on one of these reactions, for example, *like*, during a meeting without a presentation, the *thumbs up* icon will appear on either your video feed (if you have your camera on) or your user profile picture. During a presentation, the reactions will display on the bottom of the client. This is also a feature that needs to be specifically turned on by an administrator and is only available through the Teams client (both on desktop or mobile devices).

Breakout rooms

You can use *breakout rooms* to create smaller meetings within a meeting and divide people into smaller groups. An example use case would be a team meeting of 12 members where you randomly assign three people to a breakout room so that they can get to know each other better (for a team-building exercise, for example). This feature only works on the Teams client using desktop or mobile *and* when there are at least two participants in a meeting. As the meeting organizer, you can click on the *breakout rooms* icon located next to the *raise hand/live reaction* icon.

Figure 5.22 – The Breakout rooms icon

When you decide to create breakout rooms, Teams will ask you two things: the number of rooms you want to create and if you want to assign people to the rooms automatically or manually. Once your breakout rooms are created, you will have the ability to start and end the breakout room sessions, make announcements, add or remove breakout rooms, and recreate them. Additionally, the breakout rooms settings allow control of the following options:

- Automatically move participants to rooms.
- Allow participants to return to the main meeting.
- Set a time limit for each session.

For the participants, the Teams client will spin up a popup for the breakout room. The audio and video (if the participant has their camera on) stream will automatically transfer to this breakout room.

Other meeting features

In addition to the meeting features we have covered, there are also other capabilities you can leverage by clicking on the ellipsis (…) icon, whether you are an organizer or a participant.

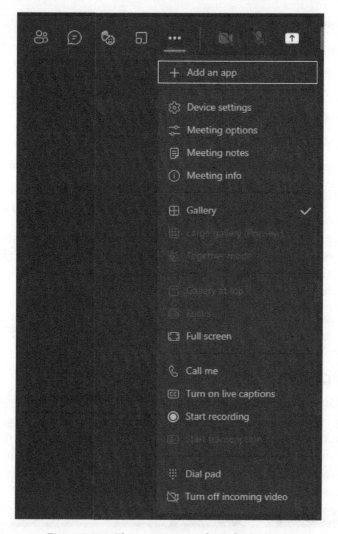

Figure 5.23 – The more actions drop-down menu

When you click on the ellipsis (...) icon next to the breakout rooms icon, a list of **More actions** will appear:

- **+ Add an app**: This allows you to add an application to the meeting.

- **Device settings**: This allows you to change your audio and video device settings.

- **Meeting options**: This includes lobby settings and presentation roles. We will cover meeting options in more depth in the next section.

- **Meeting notes**: This will allow for meeting notes dedicated to the meeting to be added

- **Meeting info**: This contains information associated with the meeting.

- **Full screen**: This renders the Teams meeting in full-screen mode.

- **Call me**: This allows for when you want Teams to dial your phone number to allow for a better audio connection.

- **Turn on live captions**: This turns on live captions.

- **Start recording**: This will start recording the meeting.

- **Dial pad**: This engages the **Microsoft Phone System** dial pad to dial out to PSTN, if applicable. This requires a separate Phone System license.

- **Turn off incoming video**: If you've got your video on, this will turn it off.

In this section, we covered different Teams meeting features. Apart from the Phone System capabilities, all of those we've covered are out-of-the-box features. This means that straight away, you can use live reactions to engage your participants, turn on live captions, record your meetings, and more.

Now that we've covered different in-meeting experiences, let's explore some other security-related features such as *lobby admittance*.

Meeting Options

Depending on the type of meeting, you can access meeting options to manage permissions within a meeting. For scheduled meetings, after you've created the meeting and before you join, navigate back to the meeting. In Outlook, you will find the **Meeting options** link in the email invite. In Teams, you can find the tab in the context of the meeting, as shown in *Figure 5.22*. During the meeting, you will find **Meeting options** in the drop-down list if you click the ellipsis (**...**) icon.

Figure 5.24 – The Meeting options tab in Microsoft Teams

A new window or browser tab will take you to the **Meeting options** pane. As the organizer, you can rely on Microsoft Teams meeting options to configure your meetings the way you see fit.

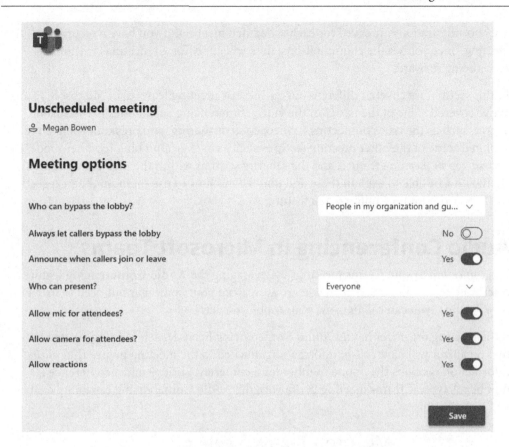

Figure 5.25 – The Meeting options pane in Microsoft Teams

For example, you can disable the microphone, camera, and live reactions for attendees. You can also select dedicated participants to present and share content. You can also disable entry/exit announcements here.

> **Meeting Options in Microsoft Teams**
>
> As mentioned earlier in this chapter, the meeting organizer has a lot of responsibility and input in how their meeting is managed. It is important to understand your meeting options and know how to implement these settings. This link has a breakdown of all the meeting options and how you can utilize them as the meeting organizer: `https://support.microsoft.com/en-us/office/change-participant-settings-for-a-teams-meeting-53261366-dbd5-45f9-aae9-a70e6354f88e`.

These configurations are saved for each scheduled meeting. If you have a recurring meeting, once you set the configurations, they will apply for all meetings within that series going forward.

In this section, we covered different out-of-the-box meeting features in Microsoft Teams. We've covered some of the basics of the video conferencing capabilities in Microsoft Teams, such as the types of meetings, video, content sharing, and breakout rooms. We also explored some of the other meeting features such as background blur, together mode, the *add an app in meetings* feature, and the security settings within the meeting options. You should now be able to explain these and understand how to use them. In the next section, we'll cover the Audio Conferencing feature.

Audio Conferencing in Microsoft Teams

You can *call in* to your Teams meetings by leveraging the **Audio Conferencing** feature in Microsoft Teams. For instance, if you are away from your computer but need to listen in on a meeting, you can *call in* using your mobile device.

If the meeting organizer has an Audio Conferencing license, each meeting created by that organizer will have *call-in* information attached to the meeting invite. The *call-in* information contains the phone number for a conference bridge and a conference ID number. A typical Teams meeting invite with the Audio Conferencing capability enabled will look like this:

Figure 5.26 – A Teams meeting invite with Audio Conferencing details

With this, you can join a Teams meeting directly with your Teams app or you can call into the meeting with voice-only capabilities. For example, you can use the number starting with **+1 872** with your mobile device, provide the conference ID information (which will start with **152** and end with **#**), and join this exact meeting.

Audio Conferencing will also allow users to use the **Call me** feature. This feature offers a complementary dial-out capability in which Teams can dial out to a specified PSTN device. The complementary dial-out is measured by a minute pool per tenant per calendar month. Ideally, this feature is to be used when the device you are on does not have audio capabilities (for example, a virtual machine). To get the audio portion of the meeting, you can enter your phone number. Once the call is connected, you can use your mobile device for the audio element and stay logged in to the Teams meeting on your virtual machine for the visual elements.

Audio Conferencing Subscriptions

Audio Conferencing comes with complementary dial-out minutes pooled by the tenant. However, depending on the destination you are dialing out to, you might need Communication Credits and/or additional licensing to successfully connect to different regions. It's important to know that these parameters exist.

For more information on this and the different country zones, please visit this page: `https://docs.microsoft.com/en-us/microsoftteams/audio-conferencing-subscription-dial-out`.

Audio Conferencing involves some administrative work in the backend. For example, you can turn off the *call me* or *dial-out* capabilities for certain users. As an administrator, there are settings you can enforce for audio conferencing bridges from within the Microsoft Teams admin center. To find these, follow these steps:

1. With the appropriate access, you can access the Microsoft Teams admin center through `https://admin.teams.microsoft.com`.

2. On the left side of the page, click on **Meetings**.

3. At the top of the screen is **Bridge settings**. Here, you'll see the following settings:

- The **Meeting entry and exit notifications** toggle: This will determine whether attendees will be notified for each attendee entry and exit.

- **Entry/exit announcement type** (if notifications are turned on): This will determine how the announcements are made (that is, either by tones or by names or phone numbers).

- **PIN length**: This will determine the length of the user PINs required.

- The **Automatically send emails to users if their dial-in settings change** toggle: This will determine whether emails will be sent to users with their dial-in information.

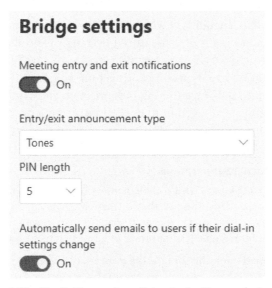

Figure 5.27 – The Bridge settings dialog in the Teams admin center

If you want to assign user Audio Conferencing licenses, you can do that through the Microsoft 365 Admin Center. Assigning and managing phone numbers for each user's Audio Conferencing bridge requires obtaining phone numbers through the Teams admin center. To find these, follow these steps:

1. With the appropriate access, you can access the Teams admin center through `https://admin.teams.microsoft.com`.

2. On the left side of the page, find and click on **Voice**.

3. Under **Voice**, click on **Phone numbers**.

4. You will see two tabs: **Numbers** and **Order history**. Click on **Numbers**.

5. Under the **Numbers** tab, click on **+ Add**.

6. Follow the instructions via the phone number order wizard that pops up on the right side of the page.

Toll-Free Phone Numbers

By default, toll-free phone numbers are not available. To get toll-free phone numbers, you must obtain Communication Credits. To learn how to set up Communication Credits, see this page:

```
https://docs.microsoft.com/en-us/MicrosoftTeams/
set-up-communications-credits-for-your-
organization.
```

Managing the Audio Conferencing settings for your users can be achieved through the **User** tab in the Teams admin center. Each user with an Audio Conferencing license will have the following information displayed:

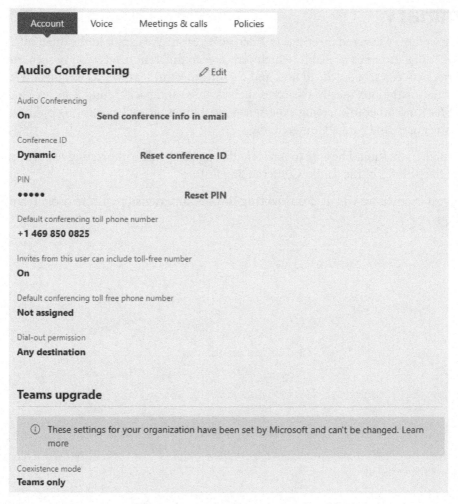

Figure 5.28 – The Audio Conferencing settings for a licensed user

Here, you can manage the settings for each user, such as changing the default conferencing toll phone number or dial-out permissions.

From the point of view of the end user, as long as they choose to create new Teams meetings, Audio Conferencing information will be automatically populated in the meeting invitation.

In this section, we covered how Audio Conferencing can be helpful in a Teams meeting. You can use the *Call me* feature to *dial out* and add an audio portion for when you join on a device with an unreliable audio connection. This section also covered how to assign and manage each user's Audio Conferencing settings and license.

Summary

In this chapter, we covered meetings in Microsoft Teams. We explored the different types of Teams meetings available, which can cater to different needs. You've seen the difference between scheduled, ad hoc, and channel meetings, as well as webinars. We then covered out-of-the-box meeting features such as video and background features, sharing capabilities, and other in-meeting experience capabilities, as well as meeting options, security features, and Audio Conferencing.

At this point, you should be able to navigate through the different meeting features and explain the benefits of the Audio Conferencing feature.

In the next chapter, we will discuss **Meeting Rooms**, an extension of Microsoft Teams meetings.

6
Microsoft Teams Rooms

When it comes to hosting meetings and displaying content for in-person and hybrid meetings, you have a few options: using a presenter's device to share and project content or using a dedicated system called a **Microsoft Teams Room** or **MTR**. An MTR is a device that enables video sharing, audio conferencing, and a digital workspace for both in-person and remote meeting participants.

In this chapter, we will look at some of the basics of Microsoft Teams Rooms, including:

- Licensing
- Configuration and recommendations
- Managing room scheduling

By the end of this chapter, you'll have an understanding of what it takes to get MTR devices provisioned and configured and how to make them available for users.

Let's dig in!

Licensing

A Microsoft Teams Room requires three things to be successful:

- A license

- A resource account

- A device

First, we'll look at the type of licensing requirements for Microsoft Teams Rooms.

Licensing requirements

Like most things in the Microsoft 365 ecosystem, an MTR system requires a license.

Microsoft has created two SKUs targeted at licensing meeting room configurations: **Microsoft Teams Rooms Standard** and **Microsoft Teams Rooms Premium**. The features that are available for each license are shown in the following table:

Feature	Microsoft Teams Rooms Standard	Microsoft Teams Rooms Premium
Skype for Business	X	X
Microsoft Teams	X	X
Phone System	X	X
Audio Conferencing	X	X
Microsoft Intune	X	X
World Availability	X	
Licensing Channel Availability	Enterprise Agreement, Enterprise Agreement Subscription, Cloud Service Provider, Web Direct	Enterprise Agreement, Enterprise Agreement Subscription, Cloud Service Provider, Web Direct
Managed Service		X

Table 6.1 – Microsoft Teams Rooms licenses and features

As shown in the preceding table, the only real difference is that the Microsoft Teams Rooms Premium license includes a Microsoft-managed service. This managed service offers the following features:

Feature	Description
24/7 Operations	This includes real-time monitoring, automated update management, real-time alerting, and proactive remediation, as well as integration with ServiceNow for ticketing.
Dedicated Experts	Microsoft experts are available to respond to incident questions, including a support engineer for troubleshooting and a single point of contact escalation for all Teams room system hardware vendors.
Enhanced Insights	Usage and diagnostics insights and history provide rich dashboards on how your organization's people use the room system and inventory and system accounting. It also lets you report actions that Microsoft has taken on your behalf to update or remediate systems.

Table 6.2 – Microsoft Teams Rooms Premium features

The managed service offering is targeted at IT professionals (as opposed to end users).

Next, we'll look at resource account requirements and their configuration.

Resource accounts

Similar to the Exchange-based resource accounts, which are used to schedule and reserve things such as conference rooms or equipment, Teams resource accounts are specially configured room mailbox accounts that are designated to the device. The account will be used to host the room system's calendar, respond to meeting booking requests (similar to a room mailbox), and log in to the device and join meetings.

Depending on the features of your room system and the way you want it to work, you'll need to evaluate which licenses and configuration your account needs. Use the following table to help determine your licensing needs:

Feature	Description	Microsoft Teams Rooms Account Requirements
Interactive Meetings	Using video, voice, and screen sharing capabilities; ensuring the MTR is a bookable resource.	Enabled for Microsoft Teams; enabled as a room resource mailbox in Exchange.
Dial-In Conferencing	Provide a dial-in audio conferencing number when creating a new meeting.	Enabled for Audio Conferencing.
Inbound/Outbound PSTN Calling	The ability for the Microsoft Teams Rooms console to make and receive calls on the Public Switched Telephone Network (PSTN).	Enabled for Phone System.

Table 6.3 – Teams Rooms resource account features and requirements

As shown in the preceding table, the Microsoft Teams Rooms system only requires a license with audio capabilities if communication via the PSTN is required. If the rooms system will only be used for Microsoft Teams-based PC-to-PC calling, only the Microsoft Teams license is required.

In the next section, we'll look at some configuration recommendations.

Configuration and recommendations

A successful Teams Rooms deployment requires configuring the room's device (and any peripherals), as well as configuring an associated account in either the on-premises Active Directory or Azure Active Directory environment.

Device preparation

In most cases, a Microsoft Teams Rooms system is a Windows-based PC. The Rooms device vendor may have bundled custom console screens, microphones, speakers, or other peripheral software or devices with the computer unit. You'll need to follow each vendor's specific documentation regarding how any components should be connected or recommendations on how they should be placed in a physical room setting.

However, there are several additional points you must consider when planning a deployment:

- **Naming conventions**: Like normal conference rooms and computer devices, a Teams Rooms device requires a unique name. You may want to choose a naming convention that reflects the device's type, site/location, and name. For example, you may name the Microsoft Teams Rooms device in New York City on the fifth floor MTR-NYC-5FLOOR.

- **Monitoring**: You can use a service, such as Azure Monitor, to provide alerts and telemetry data about your Microsoft Teams Rooms deployments.

- **Network preparation and optimization**: It is recommended that you use the **Network Planner**, as described in *Chapter 12, Deploying Teams Phone*, to assess your network requirements. Other networking considerations or tasks outside of bandwidth include the following:

  - Ensure the Teams Rooms system can resolve external DNS queries.

  - Validate that the firewalls have been configured to maintain session persistence.

  - Configure **intrusion detection systems (IDSs)** or **intrusion prevention systems (IPSs)** to allow communication with the Microsoft 365 URLs.

  - Configure **split tunneling** for VPN connectivity to support optimal network pathing and eliminate potential latency issues.

  - Implement **Quality of Service (QoS)** to ensure media packets have prioritization, which will improve call quality and mitigate issues during unanticipated network congestion. Please refer to your networking equipment vendor's documentation for configuration details.

- **Wireless network planning and optimization**: Similar to wired networks, Wi-Fi networks can also benefit from optimization procedures:

  - Evaluate using **band steering** to promote the use of 5 GHz communication for dual-band clients. Please refer to your wireless networking equipment vendor's documentation for configuration details.

  - Minimize overlapping channels. Please refer to your wireless networking equipment vendor's documentation if you wish to design an optimal channel strategy.

- Ensure adequate coverage density based on the bandwidth ranges being used (2.4 GHz versus 5 GHz) and the number of devices accessing the wireless network. Please refer to your wireless networking equipment vendor's documentation for access point density recommendations.

- Implement wireless QoS configurations such as **Wi-Fi Multimedia (WMM)** to ensure call traffic is being prioritized over other network traffic. Please refer to your wireless networking equipment vendor's documentation for configuration details.

- **Update and patch management**: Since most Teams Rooms devices will be Windows-based PCs, you should ensure that adequate updating controls are in place.

Addressing the core configuration and deployment requirements before putting your devices in the field will help ensure smooth operation and the best user experience.

Next, we'll learn how to configure the Teams Rooms system's resource accounts.

Account configuration

As we mentioned earlier, a Teams Rooms device needs a dedicated resource account. This account has a few purposes, such as logging in to the device and acting as a schedulable resource within Teams or Exchange.

In this section, we're going to focus on three core Teams-only configuration scenarios: *online deployment*, *hybrid deployment with Exchange Online*, and *hybrid deployment with Exchange Server*. While it is possible to deploy Microsoft Teams Rooms with Skype for Business, Microsoft has shifted focus to the Teams platform for audio and video conferencing.

First, we'll look at online deployments.

Online deployment scenario

The online deployment scenario is applicable when organizations are only using online services (such as Azure Active Directory, Teams, and Exchange Online) without any hybrid connectivity, including directory synchronization.

First, you'll need to create a resource account. In this example, we're going to create a new room mailbox named **NewYorkMTR01** with a domain suffix of **advancedmsteams. com**. You'll need to substitute your account and domain names. You'll also need to set a password for this since it will need to be able to log in to the device.

Let's get started:

1. Connect to Exchange Online PowerShell.

2. Run the following commands:

```
New-Mailbox -MicrosoftOnlineServicesId NewYorkMTR01@
advancedmsteams.com -Name "New York MTR01" -Alias
NewYorkMTR01 -Room -EnableRoomMailboxAccount $true
-RoomMailboxPassword (ConvertTo-SecureString -String
'Zxcqpor4##1^' -AsPlainText -Force)
```

Once the mailbox has been provisioned, the console will display the basic mailbox information, such as its alias and quota.

Next, we're going to update the calendar processing configuration. Calendar processing defines how a mailbox will respond to meeting requests.

In this example, we're going to configure the following recommended parameters for the **NewYorkMTR01** mailbox:

Parameter	Recommended Setting	Description
AddAdditionalResponse	`$true`	Enable appending additional text to the meeting's response.
AdditionalResponse	"Please arrive 5 minutes before your scheduled meeting time to ensure the Room system has been powered on."	A text value to add to the meeting's response.
AddOrganizerToSubject	`$false`	Prevents the meeting organizer's name from being added to the subject of the meeting request.
AutomateProcessing	`AutoAccept`	The resource account automatically accepts or declines meeting requests.
DeleteComments	`$false`	Preserves content in the body of the meeting request.
DeleteSubject	`$false`	Preserves the original subject of the meeting request.
RemovePrivateProperty	`$false`	Preserves the privacy flag that was set on the original meeting request.

Table 6.4 – Meeting Rooms parameters

You can either set the parameters individually or save them to a hash table and use a PowerShell feature called **splatting**. Splatting is especially useful if you're going to create several resource accounts and want to use the same settings for each.

To configure the resource account, follow these steps.

1. Connect to Exchange Online PowerShell using the following command:

```
$Session = New-PSSession -ConfigurationName Microsoft.
Exchange -ConnectionUri https://outlook.office365.
com/powershell-liveid/ -Credential (Get-Credential)
-Authentication Basic -AllowRedirection
Import-PSSession $Session
```

2. Run the following commands to create a hash table of values:

```
$CalendarProcessing = @{
'AddAdditionalResponse'= $true;
'AdditionalResponse' = 'Please arrive 5 minutes before
your scheduled meeting time to ensure the Room System has
been powered on.';
'AddOrganizerToSubject' = $false;
'AutomateProcessing' = 'AutoAccept';
'DeleteComments' = $false;
'DeleteSubject' = $false;
'RemovePrivateProperty' = $false
}
```

3. Run `Set-CalendarProcessing -Identity NewYorkMTR01@ advancedmsteams.com @CalendarProcessing` to apply the values in the hash table to the **NewYorkMTR01** resource mailbox.

You'll need to assign a license that contains the appropriate licensing for the features that you'll be using. Microsoft also recommends configuring the account's password so that it never expires. To assign a license, follow these steps:

1. Connect to Azure Active Directory PowerShell using the **MSOnline** module:

```
If (!(Get-Module -ListAvailable MSOnline)) { Install-
Module MSOnline}
Connect-MsolService -Credential (Get-Credential)
```

2. Retrieve a list of valid SKUs in your tenant that have the appropriate licenses. SKUs will be listed in the `tenant:LICENSE` format. You can use the `Get-MsolAccountSku` cmdlet to retrieve a list of SKUs.

3. Assign a usage location and a meeting room license (at a minimum) to the resource account:

```
Set-MsolUser -UserPrincipalName NewYorkMTR01@
advancedmsteams.com -UsageLocation [region]
```
```
Set-MsolUserLicense -UserPrincipalName
NewYorkMTR01@advancedmsteams.com -AddLicenses
"advancedmsteams:MEETING_ROOM"
```

4. If you want to add Phone System capabilities (as described in *Chapter 12, Deploying Teams Phone*), you can add a calling plan:

```
Set-MsolUserLicense -UserPrincipalName
NewYorkMTR01@advancedmsteams.com -AddLicenses
"advancedmsteams:MCOPSTN1"
```

5. Finally, configure the account with a password that won't expire:

```
Set-MsolUser -UserPrincipalName NewYorkMTR01@
advancedmsteams.com -PasswordNeverExpires $true
```

However, if your organization has deployed some form of hybrid infrastructure between your on-premises environment and the Microsoft 365 cloud, you may want to look at following a different path for provisioning and configuring the resource account. The configurations look very similar (and use many of the same commands), but there are some nuances, including which environment you're creating the accounts in and where you want the resource mailbox to exist.

Hybrid deployments are available for organizations that are using a combination of Microsoft 365 services, including Exchange Online or Exchange Server on-premises. We'll take a look at both of those configurations as well.

Hybrid deployment scenario with Exchange Online

In this scenario, you have deployed Azure AD Connect and are synchronizing your on-premises directory with Azure AD. Your organization has decided to manage all identities on-premises. To accomplish this, we'll configure an on-premises Active Directory account, and then mailbox-enable it in the cloud and configure the appropriate parameters.

While there are several ways to perform this task, the important thing is that the result is a logon-enabled room mailbox with the appropriate licenses applied.

> **Note**
>
> You'll need to identify where in your local version of Active Directory you want to place the room account. If you don't specify a value for OnPremisesOrganizationalUnit, the newly created resource account will be placed in the default **Users** container.

Follow these steps to configure the Teams Rooms resource account:

1. Connect to the Exchange Server Management Shell for your organization.

2. Save a credential object for the new mailbox (you'll need to enter the username and password that you want to use for the new mailbox):

    ```
    $Credential = Get-Credential
    ```

    > **Credential Details**
    >
    > This process assumes that you've configured your on-premises Active Directory UserPrincipalName suffixes so that they match the SMTP address space. If they don't match, you may run into issues with logging in and discovery.

3. Then, use the New-RemoteMailbox cmdlet to create a new Active Directory account with the appropriate parameters to create an online room mailbox:

    ```
    New-RemoteMailbox -Name "New York MTR 01" -Password
    $Credentials.Password -UserPrincipalName $Credential.
    Username -OnPremisesOrganizationalUnit "advancedmsteams.
    com/Resource Accounts/Teams Rooms" -Room -AccountDisabled
    $False -PrimarySmtpAddress $Credential.Username
    -ResetPasswordOnNextLogon $false -Alias NewYorkMTR01
    -SamAccountName NewYorkMTR01
    ```

Next, you'll want to configure the calendar processing features. You can use the same steps for the online deployment scenario.

To configure the resource account, follow these steps.

1. Connect to Exchange Online PowerShell:

    ```
    $Session = New-PSSession -ConfigurationName Microsoft.
    Exchange -ConnectionUri https://outlook.office365.
    com/powershell-liveid/ -Credential (Get-Credential)
    -Authentication Basic -AllowRedirection
    Import-PSSession $Session
    ```

2. Run the following commands to create a hash table of values:

    ```
    $CalendarProcessing = @{
    'AddAdditionalResponse'= $true;
    'AdditionalResponse' = 'Please arrive 5 minutes before
    your scheduled meeting time to ensure the Room System has
    been powered on.';
    'AddOrganizerToSubject' = $false;
    'AutomateProcessing' = 'AutoAccept';
    'DeleteComments' = $false;
    'DeleteSubject' = $false;
    'RemovePrivateProperty' = $false
    }
    ```

3. Run `Set-CalendarProcessing -Identity NewYorkMTR01@` `advancedmsteams.com @CalendarProcessing` to apply the values in the hash table to the **NewYorkMTR01** resource mailbox.

Finally, you'll need to assign a license that contains the appropriate licensing for the features that you'll be using. Microsoft also recommends configuring the account's password so that it never expires. Let's get started:

1. Connect to Azure Active Directory PowerShell using the **MSOnline** module:

    ```
    If (!(Get-Module -ListAvailable MSOnline)) { Install-
    Module MSOnline}
    Connect-MsolService -Credential (Get-Credential)
    ```

2. Retrieve a list of valid SKUs in your tenant that have the appropriate licenses. SKUs will be listed in the `tenant:LICENSE` format. You can use the `Get-MsolAccountSku` cmdlet to retrieve a list of SKUs.

3. Assign a usage location and a meeting room license (at a minimum) to the resource account:

```
Set-MsolUser -UserPrincipalName NewYorkMTR01@
advancedmsteams.com -UsageLocation [region]
```

```
Set-MsolUserLicense -UserPrincipalName
NewYorkMTR01@advancedmsteams.com -AddLicenses
"advancedmsteams:MEETING_ROOM"
```

4. If you want to add Phone System capabilities (as described in *Chapter 12, Deploying Teams Phone*, you can add a calling plan:

```
Set-MsolUserLicense -UserPrincipalName
NewYorkMTR01@advancedmsteams.com -AddLicenses
"advancedmsteams:MCOPSTN1"
```

As you can see, these steps were very similar to the ones for the online deployment scenario, with the core difference being that the account's identity was created in the on-premises Active Directory instance and then synchronized to Azure AD.

In the final scenario, we'll explore hosting the resource mailbox on-premises.

Hybrid deployment scenario with Exchange Server

In the previous scenario, the resource mailbox for the Teams Rooms system was configured in Exchange Online. Though this scenario, like the previous hybrid option, utilizes Azure AD Connect for synchronizing identity, you'll need to configure the resource mailbox on-premises. Since the Teams Rooms features still require Microsoft 365 licensing, we'll be configuring against both on-premises and cloud environments.

> **Note**
>
> You'll need to identify where in the local Active Directory instance you want to place the room account. If you don't specify a value for OnPremisesOrganizationalUnit, the newly created resource account will be placed in the default **Users** container.

Follow these steps to configure the Teams Rooms resource account:

1. Connect to the Exchange Server Management Shell for your organization.

2. Save a credential object for the new mailbox (you'll need to enter a username and password that you want to use for the new mailbox).

> **Credential Details**
>
> This process assumes that you've configured your on-premises Active Directory `UserPrincipalName` suffixes so that they match the SMTP address space. If they don't match, you may run into issues with logging in and discovery.

```
$Credential = Get-Credential
```

3. Then, use the `New-Mailbox` cmdlet to create a new Active Directory account with the appropriate parameters to create an online room mailbox:

```
New-Mailbox -Name "New York MTR 01"
-EnableRoomMailboxAccount $true -RoomMailboxPassword
$Credentials.Password -UserPrincipalName $Credential.
Username -OnPremisesOrganizationalUnit "advancedmsteams.
com/Resource Accounts/Teams Rooms" -Room -AccountDisabled
$False -PrimarySmtpAddress $Credential.Username
-ResetPasswordOnNextLogon $false -Alias NewYorkMTR01
-SamAccountName NewYorkMTR01
```

Next, you'll want to configure the calendar processing features. You can follow the same steps that you did for the online deployment scenario.

To configure the resource account, follow these steps.

1. Connect to Exchange Online PowerShell:

```
$Session = New-PSSession -ConfigurationName Microsoft.
Exchange -ConnectionUri https://outlook.office365.
com/powershell-liveid/ -Credential (Get-Credential)
-Authentication Basic -AllowRedirection
Import-PSSession $Session
```

2. Run the following commands to create a hash table of values:

```
$CalendarProcessing = @{
'AddAdditionalResponse'= $true;
'AdditionalResponse' = 'Please arrive 5 minutes before
your scheduled meeting time to ensure the Room System has
been powered on.';
'AddOrganizerToSubject' = $false;
'AutomateProcessing' = 'AutoAccept';
'DeleteComments' = $false;
'DeleteSubject' = $false;
```

```
'RemovePrivateProperty' = $false
}
```

3. Run `Set-CalendarProcessing -Identity NewYorkMTR01@ advancedmsteams.com @CalendarProcessing` to apply the values in the hash table to the **NewYorkMTR01** resource mailbox.

Finally, you'll need to assign a license that contains the appropriate licensing for the features that you'll be using. Microsoft also recommends configuring the account's password so that it never expires. Let's get started:

1. Connect to Azure Active Directory PowerShell using the **MSOnline** module:

```
If (!(Get-Module -ListAvailable MSOnline)) { Install-
Module MSOnline}
Connect-MsolService -Credential (Get-Credential)
```

2. Retrieve a list of valid SKUs in your tenant that have the appropriate licenses. SKUs will be listed in the `tenant:LICENSE` format. You can use the `Get-MsolAccountSku` cmdlet to retrieve a list of SKUs.

3. Assign a usage location and a meeting room license (at a minimum) to the resource account:

```
Set-MsolUser -UserPrincipalName NewYorkMTR01@
advancedmsteams.com -UsageLocation [region]
Set-MsolUserLicense -UserPrincipalName
NewYorkMTR01@advancedmsteams.com -AddLicenses
"advancedmsteams:MEETING_ROOM"
```

4. If you want to add Phone System capabilities (as described in *Chapter 12, Deploying Teams Phone)*, you can add a calling plan:

```
Set-MsolUserLicense -UserPrincipalName
NewYorkMTR01@advancedmsteams.com -AddLicenses
"advancedmsteams:MCOPSTN1"
```

After executing these commands, you should have a resource account that has been configured with a non-expiring password and an appropriate license. Once the account has been configured, you can log in to the Microsoft Teams Rooms device while following the device vendor's instructions.

Next, we'll transition into managing the Exchange scheduling features of the resource account.

Managing room scheduling

Microsoft Teams Rooms relies on the underlying Exchange Online or Exchange Server infrastructure for its scheduling operations. To help users get the most out of the Teams Meeting Rooms resources (or rooms in general), you can configure **room lists** and resource booking options.

First, we'll look at room lists.

Room locations and lists

Room lists are special Exchange distribution groups that are used to contain room resources (whether they are Microsoft Teams Rooms or standard conference rooms). From inside the Teams client, room lists are displayed in the **Location** field, as shown in the following screenshot:

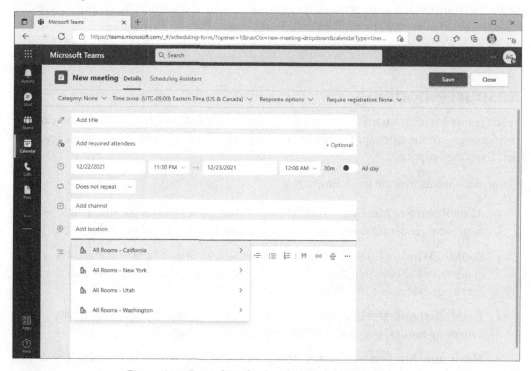

Figure 6.1 – Room lists displayed in the Location textbox

Configuring a room list is much like configuring a distribution list and can be accomplished with the same steps in either Exchange Online or Exchange Server environments. If you do not create room lists, you'll have a default view called **Available Rooms**.

As a best practice, consider creating room lists that match your physical locations, such as "All Rooms – New York" or "Fifth Floor Rooms."

To configure a new room list and add the MTR resource you created earlier in this chapter, follow these steps:

1. Connect to Exchange (either Exchange Online or Exchange Server) PowerShell.

2. Run a command similar to the following to create a new distribution group of the `RoomList` type:

```
New-DistributionGroup -Name "All Rooms - New York"
-RoomList
Add-DistributionGroupMember -Identity "All Rooms - New
York" -Member NewYorkMTR01
```

Once the room list has been created, it can be used within Microsoft Teams. Users can select rooms that meet their availability criteria when scheduling meetings.

Next, we'll look at the resource booking parameters.

Resource booking

Since Teams Meeting Rooms leverages Exchange Server calendaring features, you can configure any of the calendar processing options (via `Set-CalendarProcessing`) that Exchange supports.

Common options include the following:

- **AllowRecurringMeetings**: This Boolean (True/False) switch parameter allows you to prevent recurring meetings from being scheduled. The default value is `$true`.

- **BookingWindowInDays**: This numeric parameter specifies how many days in advance the resource can be reserved. The default value is 180 days and the maximum value is 1,080 days.

- **EnableResponseDetails**: This parameter is used to provide details as to why a meeting request was accepted or declined. The default value is `$true`.

- **MaximumDurationInMinutes**: This parameter specifies the maximum length of a meeting in minutes. The default value is 1,440. The maximum value is 2,147,483,647 minutes. A value of 0 is unlimited.

Many other more complex calendar processing configurations are available, including delegate and moderation options to restrict who can book a resource. For more possible configuration parameters, see `https://docs.microsoft.com/en-us/powershell/module/exchange/set-calendarprocessing?view=exchange-ps`.

Summary

Microsoft Teams Rooms is a valuable tool for helping people conduct effective meetings, whether in person, remote, or in a hybrid work scenario. In this chapter, you learned about the requirements and configuration capabilities of Microsoft Teams Rooms, including how to set up a resource account and select the correct licenses. Microsoft Teams Rooms supports both cloud and on-premises Exchange resource mailboxes, providing organizations with flexible deployment options.

In the next chapter, we'll start working with **Live Events**.

7
Live Events

Live events are a type of meeting in which you can stream video and meeting content to a large virtual or online audience of up to 10,000 people. They are specifically a *one-to-many* mode of communication in which the host of the organization is doing all the presenting, and the audience's primary participation is to listen and/or watch only. Microsoft's version of this is **Teams Live Events**. If you are familiar with Skype Meeting Broadcast, this is Microsoft's Teams flavor of exactly that.

In this chapter, we will explore Live Events as a webinar type of Teams meeting. We will cover the following topics:

- Introducing Microsoft Teams Live Events
- Scheduling a live event
- Presenting and sharing content
- Sharing invitations
- External production (RTMP)

By the end of this chapter, you will be able to explain how Live Events can be useful in webinar-type situations. You will also be able to successfully schedule and conduct a live meeting and know where to go integrate with external devices such as encoders.

Technical requirements

To complete some of the activities and configurations in this chapter, you'll need a Microsoft 365 tenant with a Microsoft 365 E1, E3, or E5 license activated (either on trial or paid subscriptions). You can obtain trial versions of these products through the Microsoft 365 Admin Center.

You also need permissions to create a Teams live event or access to the Teams Admin Center to grant permissions to create a Teams live event.

Introducing Microsoft Team Live Events

Teams Live Events allows for users in your organization to broadcast video and meeting content to large online audiences. Live events are meant for a one-to-many type of communication in which the host is doing most of the interaction. The online audience will not be participating other than listening or, if configured, partaking in a **Question and Answer session (Q and A session)** or a **Yammer conversation**. Yammer is an enterprise social network dedicated to your organization. You can create a community within Yammer by topic or department and have live events integrated there.

As an administrator, keep in mind that the maximum audience size is 10,000 attendees, the duration of the event cannot be longer than four hours, and you can host up to 15 concurrent Live Events in a single Microsoft 365 organization or tenant.

> **Temporary Live Event Limit Increases**
>
> At the time of writing this book, Microsoft has temporarily increased Live Event limitations to support customers' needs through December 31, 2021. The maximum audience size is up to 20,000 attendees, the event duration can be up to 16 hours, and there can be up to 50 concurrent live events in a single tenant.

If you are familiar with Skype Meeting Broadcast, Live Events will sound familiar. However, it is important to note that with Skype for Business Online retiring in July 2021, Live Events is the replacement for Skype Meeting Broadcast.

We covered the core out-of-the-box capabilities within Microsoft Teams in *Chapter 5, Conducting Teams Meetings*. You can see Live Events as an extension of that; on top of the chat and video capabilities, Live Events allow you to leverage that same technology to reach out to a larger audience, to host events such as all-hands meetings or announcements. Depending on the type of live event you want to host, you can create a live event using **Stream**, **Yammer**, or Teams. You can use Stream or Yammer with external encoders for professional-grade events, such as a leadership announcement. If your event is much simpler, and presenters are sitting in front of their computer, Teams is much more manageable.

> **Third-Party Video Distribution Providers**
>
> Teams Live events can be configured via a third-party video distribution provider. If your organization has a **Software-Defined Network (SDN)** or an **Enterprise Content Delivery Network (eCDN)**, set up through any one of Microsoft's partners, you can configure those settings through the Microsoft Teams Admin Center. See here for details: `https://docs.microsoft.com/en-us/MicrosoftTeams/teams-live-events/configure-teams-live-events`. A benefit to this would be, for example, avoiding a network bottleneck while hosting a company-wide live event when everyone is tuning in from the same office.

In the next section, we will cover scheduling a live event. We will cover the steps required to schedule a live event, explore meeting options, and explain live event roles.

Scheduling a Live Event

In this section, we will go over the steps to set up a live event. As part of this process, we will cover the following:

- Administrator policies for live events in Teams, Stream, and Yammer
- Live event customizations
- Live event roles

After reading this section, you will be able to schedule a live event, set administrator-level policies for live events, and be able to explain the function of each setting and the importance of roles.

Administrator policies for Live Events in Teams

By default, all users in your organizations with a Teams license will be able to schedule and host a live event. However, because of the large audience outreach capability of live events, as an administrator, you may want to adjust the policy to provide permission to only a specific group of people to create and host a live event. With the right permissions, we will go into the Teams admin center and explore live event policies to adjust these policies.

To access live event policies, go directly to the Teams admin center:

1. As a Teams administrator or a global administrator, navigate to `https://admin.teams.microsoft.com` and log in.

2. On the left pane, click on **Meetings** and then **Live event policies**.

3. Click on **Global (Org-wide default)**.

As mentioned earlier, by default every Teams user is assigned this **Global** live event policy. You will see that the **Allow scheduling toggle** is set to **On**:

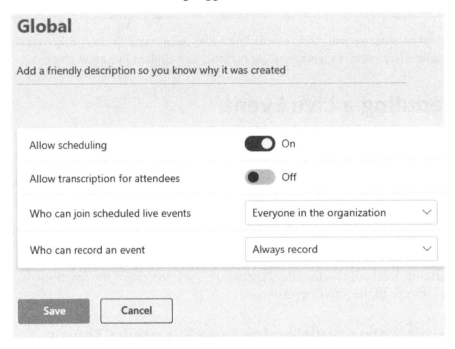

Figure 7.1 – Global live event policy

Let's explore some of the other options on this page. **Allow transcription for attendees** will provide the audience with the capability to see live captions and subtitles during the event if turned on and produced within Teams.

Next, live events can be created for just members in the organization to join, specified users or groups, or everyone, including the public. Hence, you have your three options:

-   **Everyone**: The event can be publicly available, so no authentication is required.

-   **Everyone in the organization**: Attendees must authenticate with organization credentials.

- **Specific users or groups**: Authentication is required and only those invited can attend.

Recording is another feature here that can be dictated with a live event policy. The following are the options for **Who can record an event**:

- **Always record**: If this is enabled, the live event will be automatically recorded.

- **Never record**: If this is enabled, then the option to record the live event will not be available.

- **Organizer can record**: If this is enabled, the organizer can choose whether to record the live event.

Assigning Policies in the Teams Admin Center

There are policies and policy packages available in the Teams admin center, depending on how you want to manage policies for your users. A policy package is a collection of custom policies and settings you can apply to a group of users in your organization that have similar roles. Policies can be applied to users depending on roles but also can be permission-based. Policy packages leverage default policies or policies you've customized on your own. You can apply these policies or policy packages to your users through the Teams admin center UI or PowerShell using the Teams PowerShell module. For more information, please visit this URL: `https://docs.microsoft.com/en-us/microsoftteams/assign-policies`.

Now that we have gone through the different options within a live event policy, let's go over how to create one of your own and apply it to a specific group. Follow these steps:

4. As a Teams administrator or a global administrator, navigate to `https://admin.teams.microsoft.com` and log in.

5. On the left pane, click on **Meetings** and then **Live events policies**.

6. Click on **+ Add**.

7. Provide a name and a description for this policy. In this example, I will create a policy that will apply to the authors of this book, as seen in the following screenshot:

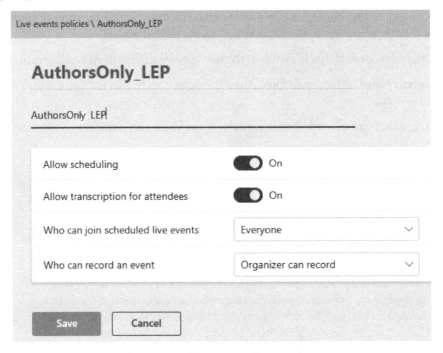

Figure 7.2 – Live event policy creation

8. Configure the toggles and policies as you see fit. For the sake of this example, make sure you enable **Allow Scheduling** and **Allow transcriptions for attendees**, and select **Everyone** for **Who can join scheduled live events** and **Organizer can record** for **Who can record an event**.

9. Click **Save**. You should be directed back to the **Live events policies** page. You should see your newly created policy.

10. For the sake of simplicity, we will assign this policy to an existing group. Click on the **Group policy assignment** tab located next to **Manage policies**:

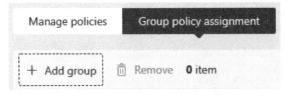

Figure 7.3 – Group policy assignment

> **Microsoft 365 Groups**
>
> There are multiple ways to create groups. Creating groups will not be specifically covered in this book, but for the sake of this exercise, it is quickest to do this in **Azure Active Directory** (**Azure AD**) or in the Microsoft 365 admin center. You can follow quick instructions on how to do this on this page: `https://docs.microsoft.com/en-us/azure/ active-directory/fundamentals/active-directory- groups-create-azure-portal?context=/azure/active- directory/enterprise-users/context/ugr-context`.

11. Click on **+ Add group**.

12. A pane on the right side of your browser will appear. Search for a group, keep **rank** set to **1**, and select your newly created live event policy.

13. Remember to click **Apply**.

The values you've populated should contain the policy you just created. This can be seen in the following screenshot:

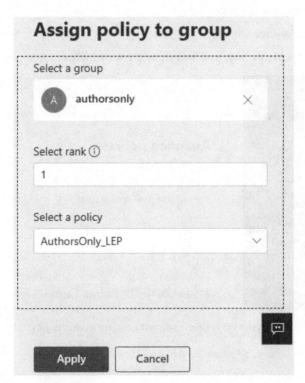

Figure 7.4 – Assigning a live events policy using a group policy assignment

Here, we left rank as **1**. Let's go over what that means. There may be times when policies for the same setting are applied to the same user more than once. In this example, users in the **authorsonly** group have two live event policies (**Global (Org-wide default)** and **AuthorsOnly_LEP**). Because we set the **AuthorsOnly_LEP** policy rank to **1** for this group, the **AuthorsOnly _LEP** policy should take precedent over the other. In other words, when a user or a group has conflicting policies of the same type, the policy with the higher rank will take precedence over the other ones.

Group Assignment Ranking

It's important to understand this topic to effectively apply policies to groups. For another explanation, please see this page: `https://docs.microsoft.com/en-US/microsoftteams/assign-policies#group-assignment-ranking`.

Now that this is done, check to see whether your user has the updated live event policy applied. You can check this by doing the following:

1. Click on **Users | locate user**.

2. Click on the **Policies** tab.

3. Under **Live events policy**, you should see your newly created policy:

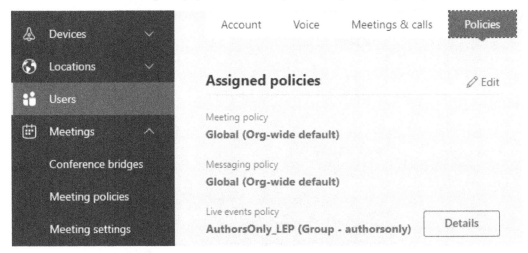

Figure 7.5 – User-assigned new live events policy

Once verified, we should now be able to schedule a live event through Teams as this user. Microsoft allows admins to configure specific permissions to host live events on different platforms. We will first explore permissions to create a live event in Stream, and then we will look at how to do this in Yammer.

Permissions to create a live event in Stream

Microsoft Stream can be used to host a live event as well. Microsoft Stream is a video service within Microsoft 365. You can use Stream to store and share video content and host live events within your organization. By default, anyone in the organization with a Stream license can schedule a live event:

1. Navigate to the Stream landing page by clicking the Stream icon on `https://portal.office.com` or go directly to `https://web.microsoftstream.com` and log in.

2. On the Stream landing page, locate **+ Create** on the top bar.

3. On the dropdown, click **Live event**:

Figure 7.6 – Creating a live event in Stream

There will be a wizard that will walk you through event customizations.

As a Stream admin, you may decide that you do not want everyone within the organization to host a live event. To change the settings, follow these steps:

1. Navigate to the Stream admin center by clicking the **Settings** icon and then **Admin settings**:

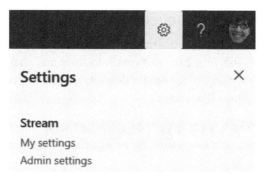

Figure 7.7 – Stream admin settings

2. Click on **Live events** in the left column.

3. Enable the toggle to start identifying individuals you want to allow to create live events in Stream:

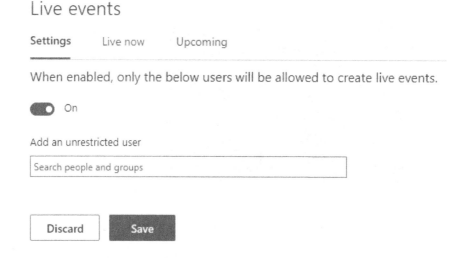

Figure 7.8 – Live events toggle

4. Add users.

5. Click on **Save**.

You should now have a group of users permitted to create live events in Stream.

Permissions to create a live event in Yammer

Yammer can be used to create a live event. Yammer is an enterprise social network dedicated to your organization. Live events in Yammer are unique because you can host a live event in a **specific Yammer community** or an organization-wide Yammer space. This simplifies the process of inviting attendees because the sharing of invitations is already done for you. You can create a live event in Yammer if you have a Stream and/or Teams license assigned to you. If a live event policy in Teams prohibits you from creating a live event, you will not be able to do so in Yammer. Additionally, only Yammer group administrators can create and schedule a live event through Yammer. You can create a live event through Yammer by following these steps:

1. Navigate to the Yammer landing page by clicking the Yammer icon on `https://portal.office.com` or go directly to `https://web.yammer.com` and log in.

2. Choose the **Yammer community** option you would like to host your live event in. A list of communities you belong to should be on the left.

3. Locate the **Events** tab of the community page:

Leadership

Conversations   About   Files   **Events**

Figure 7.9 – Events tab on the Yammer page

4. On the right, click on **Create Live Event**.

There will be a wizard that will walk you through event customizations. This will be covered in the next section, *Live event customizations*.

Live event customizations

In the previous section, we made sure that a specific user has permission to create a live event via Teams. We also went over how to grant permission for users to start live events in Stream and Yammer. Once users have permission to create live events, they can go through the wizard to provide the necessary details of the live event. For Teams, Stream, and Yammer, the organizer needs to fill out similar customization fields.

During this exercise, we will go over the live event customizations available via Teams but will call out specific nuances for Stream and Yammer:

1. Navigate to your **Calendar** tab on the left.

2. On the top right of the screen, click on the down arrow next to + **New meeting**:

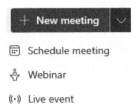

Figure 7.10 – Creating a new live event

3. Click on **Live event**.

   A popup will appear with lots of settings. Let's go through each of them:

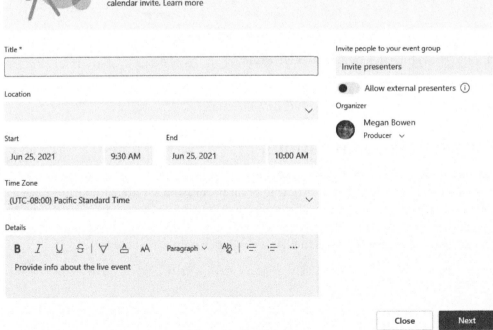

Figure 7.11 – Live event settings

- First, make sure you specify the event's **Title** (required), **Location** (if applicable), the **Start** and **End** time of the event, **Time Zone**, and **Details** that you want to include about the event.

- Next, on the right side, add the people you want to invite to your event. The **Allow external presenters** toggle is off by default; if there is a need for presenters outside of your organization, make sure to switch this toggle and invite them via their email address. We will leave this user's role as **Presenter** for now:

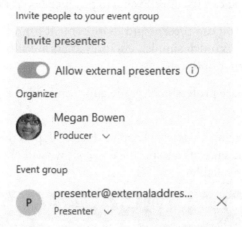

Figure 7.12 – Inviting an external presenter

We will discuss live event roles in more detail in the next section.

4. Click **Next**.

Testing a Live Event in Yammer

Yammer allows you to create a test event while filling out your settings. If you click **Yes** to the test event option, the live event information will not show up on the Yammer community page, so members will not join.

Now, we will go over **Live event permissions**. Depending on who you are allowed to invite, you can choose the options available for your live event. We covered some of these earlier but here are our choices:

- **People and groups**: Specified folks and groups within the organization can participate as audience members.

- **Org-wide**: Everyone in your organization can participate as an audience member after authenticating.

- **Public**: Anyone inside and outside your organization can participate as an audience member without any type of authentication.

> **Permissions and Details in Stream**
>
> With Stream, you can check a box to allow everyone in the organization to view the video. Otherwise, you can specify by individual people, Stream channels, or Office 365 groups. Stream will also allow you to optionally upload a thumbnail for your video if you wish to provide an image.

After you assign permissions, you will be asked, **How will you produce your live event?** As mentioned earlier, you can use Live Events to produce two different types of live events.

The first is with Teams; you can present and share content from the presenters' webcam and device. If your event is much simpler, and presenters are sitting in front of their computer, Teams is a better option.

The second option is to use professional-grade audio and video equipment to share content.

If you want to produce using an external app or device, skip to the *External production* section. However, for the sake of this specific exercise, we will choose **Teams**. Let's go over the production options available:

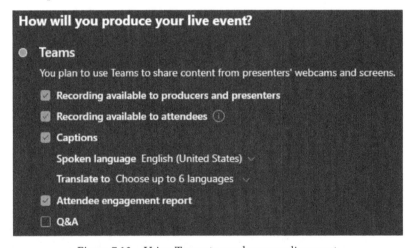

Figure 7.13 – Using Teams to produce your live event

Let's go over the different resources and settings you can configure for each live event:

- **Recording available to producers and presenters**: This is related to the live events policy available in the Teams admin center. Under the live events policy, if **Who can record an event** is set to **Always record** or **Never record**, **Recording available to producers and presenters** will be greyed out by default to prevent anyone from editing. If it is set to **Organizer can record**, as the organizer, you can enable recording if you see fit.

- **Recording available to attendees**: As the organizer, you can enable this. After the event, a recording link will be available to share with attendees.

- **Captions**: There are two steps here. First, identify the primary language the live event will be spoken in under the **Spoken language** dropdown. Then, choose up to six languages from the **Translate to** dropdown. This will allow the audience to choose any one of the languages you selected to translate into captions during the live event.

- **Attendee engagement report**: As the organizer, you can enable this. If enabled, after the event, you can download the attendee engagement report. This report will contain information about the attendees, such as when they joined, **user agent** (the type of browser the attendee joined on), full name, and role.

> **Attendee Engagement Report**
>
> It may be important to collect the attendee engagement report to gauge how the live event went. To fully understand the values provided by the report, see this link: `https://support.microsoft.com/en-us/office/` `get-an-attendee-engagement-report-for-a-teams-` `live-event-b3101733-2eda-48a6-aeb3-de2f2bfecb3a`.

- **Q&A**: As the organizer, you can enable this. This will allow attendees an opportunity to interact directly with producers and presenters via a question-and-answer window during the live event.

> **Production Tools in Yammer**
>
> Yammer will let you choose to produce a live event with Teams or with an external app or device. Depending on the choice you make, meeting resources and experiences will vary.

5. Once all settings are configured, click **Schedule**.

Congratulations – you just scheduled your first Teams live event! You should have a live event meeting scheduled on your calendar.

Next, let's look at live event roles.

Live event roles

As with any meeting, it is imperative that you plan ahead of time who will take responsibility for what task. For live events, understanding the available roles and taking that responsibility is imperative to a smooth production. There are three primary roles when it comes to managing a live event. As a best practice, it is recommended that there is always a **live event group**, comprised of one **organizer**, at least one **producer**, and at least one **presenter**, who work together to ensure a successful live event. The following is the list of event roles available:

- **Organizer**: There can only be one organizer, but as the organizer, you are responsible for the following:

  a) Creating the live event

  b) Providing details of the live event

  c) Inviting event group members (producer and presenter)

  d) Setting attendee permissions (whether the live event is available for specified members and groups of the organization, organization-wide, or the public)

  e) Configuring live event customization (recording, Q&A, captions, and so on)

  f) Managing the live event resources post-meeting

  g) Hosting the live event on supported platforms

  Microsoft has produced an organizer checklist that you can find here: `https://support.microsoft.com/en-us/office/teams-live-event-organizer-checklist-44a80886-0fd9-42e5-8e7c-836c798096f8`.

- **Producer**: As the producer, you are responsible for making sure the event runs smoothly. That includes making sure the presenters are ready to present, content is lined up, and more, including the following:

  a) Chatting with other producers and presenters

  b) Starting and ending the live event

  c) Producer and presenter management

  d) Content and video management

  e) Checking health and performance

  f) Producing the live event on supported platforms

To accomplish all of this, the producer must use the Teams desktop client.

Microsoft has produced a page dedicated to live event producers here: `https://support.microsoft.com/en-us/office/produce-a-live-event-using-teams-591bd694-121d-405c-b26d-730315e45a22`.

- **Presenter**: Presenters are invited to the live event to present material, whether it be a video feed of them speaking or a specific presentation – for example, a PowerPoint slide – that they will showcase. Therefore, the presenters are an integral part of making live events a success and are responsible for the following:

    a) Preparing any share materials (if any)

    b) Presenting using supported platforms

    c) Moderating Q&A, if applicable

As a part of best practices, it is recommended that the live event group gets together more than once and perform dry runs before the actual event day. It's important, for example, for each presenter to know how to prepare content so that the producer can access and line it up appropriately.

To quickly recap, we learned about live events and how they are different from regular Teams meetings. Live events can be set up on three different platforms, Yammer, Stream, and Teams. We then learned how to provide the right permissions for each platform to schedule a live event and then learned the steps to do so. We also covered the importance of roles and responsivities in a live event to ensure a smooth broadcast.

In the next section, we will step into the shoes of the producer and walk through the different aspects of a live event to ensure a smooth and productive live event.

Presenting and Sharing Content

Presentation and content sharing can be a very integral part of your live event. In this section, we will learn about the producer's experience when presenting and sharing content. The producer is responsible for making sure that the presentation and other shared content are displayed to the audience in a seamless manner. It is imperative that you know the steps to successfully prepare, line up, and share or present content during a live event. Even if you are not the organizer, producer, or a presenter, you should be able to explain the basics to someone else.

First, let's discuss the producer's view of live events. Once you join the event as a producer, this should be what you are looking at:

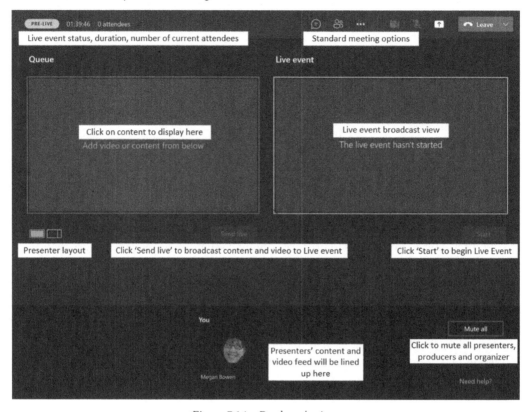

Figure 7.14 – Producer's view

Let's discuss these functions:

- **Live event status**: **PRE-LIVE** means the event is not live yet. When the event starts, the status will change to **Live**.

- **Duration**: This keeps track of how long the event has been running.

- **Attendees**: This is the number of current attendees watching the event.

- **Content box (left)**: The view of content that you can send live. Line up your content by clicking the left box and then content from the shared content on the bottom.

- **Content box (right)**: The view of content being displayed live.

- **Presenter layout**: Located on the left side, under the left content box, choose between the two layouts available – one is just the content by itself. The other option is to have two screens presented. It is up to the producer on what is put here. For example, one can be a presentation and the other can be a speaker.

- **Presenters' content**: When joined by a presenter, you can share content and have it available so that the producer can simply click to have the content lined up before sending it live. The content will be displayed on the bottom right.

- **Mute all**: On the right, above the **Need help?** link, is a **Mute all** option. This will mute all presenters, producers, and the organizer of the event.

- **Meeting functions**: On the top right, you will see familiar icons as you would in a regular Teams meeting. For example, you can click on the **Chat** icon to chat with your live event group. Next to the chat icon is the participant list, so you can see who has joined your live event group. The third icon will open the Q&A section of the live event if you choose to make this available. Remember, if enabled, the Q&A will be available for attendees to type in questions during the live event, and members of your Live event group are able to go in, read, and answer questions. The ellipses will also display other optional Teams meeting features, as covered in *Chapter 5, Conducting Teams Meetings*.

Live events contain regular Teams meeting features such as chat, participant lists, and device settings. It also contains extra functions for live events. As the organizer, producer, or presenter of the live event, it is important to understand all these options and features.

Microsoft published a chart of live event limits, features, and capabilities in different flavors of live events here: `https://docs.microsoft.com/en-us/ MicrosoftTeams/teams-live-events/plan-for-teams-live- events#teams-live-events-and-skype-meeting-broadcast`.

This covers the producer's experience and view during a live event. Part of the best practices before a live event is to rehearse this until you feel comfortable. Additionally, Microsoft provides a live events assistant program, which you can learn more about by visiting this link: `https://resources.techcommunity.microsoft.com/ live-events/assistance/`.

In this section, we have just concluded the producer's point of view during a live event. As a producer, you are responsible for knowing how to navigate the live event so that you can share and present it seamlessly to your audience. However, providing invitations for your live event group is different from inviting your attendees. Let's explore the best way to share live event invitations in the next section.

Sharing invitations

As the organizer, you are responsible for making sure the invitation to your live event goes out. When creating a live event in Teams, you will see a banner as a reminder to copy the link to your event and share it the best way you see fit:

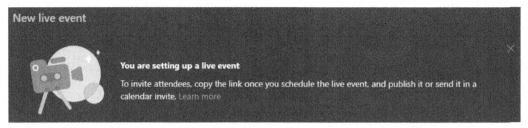

Figure 7.15 – Live event invitation banner

After configuring the event, the last page you will see will contain the **attendee link**. The attendee link is unique and dedicated to attendees of the live event only. They will be directed to the live event only, with attendee permissions.

Once you click on **Get attendee link**, the URL will be pasted directly to your clipboard:

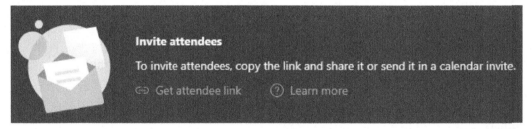

Figure 7.16 – Get attendee link

Make sure you share that link so that your attendees can access this easily. For example, if this is a live event directed to the public, you can post this link as a hyperlink on your public-facing website.

Once you invite the members of your live event group, they should receive a calendar invite. You want to make sure that your presenters, producers, and members of the live event group join through the invitation on their calendar (not the attendee link):

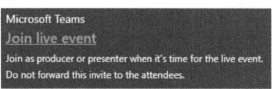

Figure 7.17 – Link for producers and presenters

Producers and presenters will be asked to authenticate their identities with their username and password. Then, depending on the role you've assigned everyone, they will have permission to perform their tasks during the live event.

Live event invitations in Yammer and Stream are shared by default, depending on the Yammer community and specific Stream-sharing permissions you set while creating a live event. Live events produced by external apps or devices will be stored in Stream, so a Stream link will also be available to share.

Next, we will cover external live event productions. If you want a live event with more production-grade and professional equipment, there are different ways we can accomplish this. Let's explore this in the next section.

External production

Live events can have a professional, production-grade feel if you bring in external **encoders** to produce the event. Encoders are either software or hardware that is used with professional recording audio and video equipment. Encoders output a **Real-Time Messaging Protocol** (**RTMP** or **RTMPS** over SSL). RTMPS is a specific protocol for streaming audio, video, and data over the internet with a persistent connection. Ultimately, it is designed to deliver smooth video and audio quality during broadcasts over the internet.

Whenever you have an external encoder for a live event through Teams, Yammer, or Stream, Stream will be the service that produces the event. Stream supports both hardware and software-based encoders. Microsoft published a document listing previously tested encoders: `https://docs.microsoft.com/en-us/stream/live-encoder-setup`.

To use Stream and leverage external encoders, you should make sure the right users are allowed to create live events in Stream. This is covered in the *Permissions to create a live event in Stream* section. Live event hosts should also know that the live event produced with external coders must not be public.

Depending on whether you want to use Yammer, Stream, or Teams to produce a live event using external devices or apps, instructions vary slightly.

In Yammer, when you create a live event, after going through all the customizations, you will be asked to choose the best production tool for your live event. Follow these steps:

1. Click on the second option that says **External App or Device**:

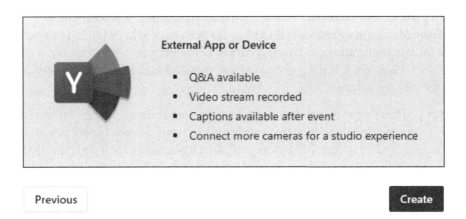

Ready to set up your live event?   ×

Pick the production tool best for your live video broadcast. You can view the live event video stream in Yammer.

Microsoft Teams

- Q&A available
- Video stream recorded
- Captions available after event

External App or Device

- Q&A available
- Video stream recorded
- Captions available after event
- Connect more cameras for a studio experience

Previous   Create

Figure 7.18 – Choosing the external production tool in Yammer

2. Click **Create**.

3. After the live event has been created, click on **Start setup**:

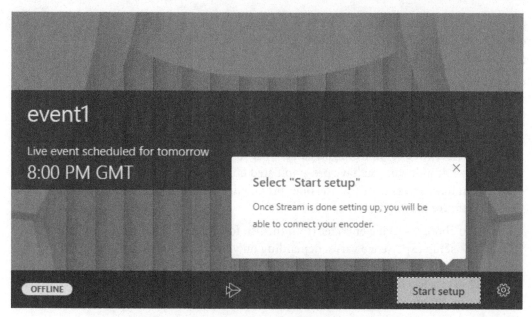

Figure 7.19 – Start setup in Yammer

4. On the right side of the screen, you will see **ingest urls**. Ingest URLs are used to connect your event to your encoders. You can choose **Secure Connection (SSL)** by clicking on the toggle. Click **Copy** on the **Primary rtmps URL** option to copy to clipboard. It starts with `rtmp://` or `rtmps://` if using SSL, as shown in the following screenshot:

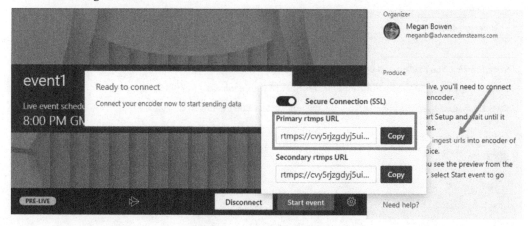

Figure 7.20 – rtmps URL in Yammer

5. Paste the **rtmps URL** to your external encoder.

Once connected, you should see the preview screen or the producer screen through your encoder. You can now produce your live event from your encoder.

You can accomplish the same using Stream as your live event platform. In Stream, first finish publishing your live event, and then follow these steps:

1. After the live event has created, click **Start setup**.

2. Under the video section, the first tab you should see is **Encoder setup**. Under the **Select encoder** option, you can choose to configure your encoder manually, or, as a dropdown, you have pre-populated encoders that you may wish to use. If you have access to one of the ones provided, choose it. Otherwise, click on **Configure manually**.

3. If you chose a specific encoder from the list, follow the instructions provided below, as the setup experience varies depending on your selection. Otherwise, under **Configure manually**, you can choose to use a **secure connection (SSL)** by clicking on the toggle. Click **Copy** on **Server ingest URL** to copy it to the clipboard. It starts with `rtmp://` or `rtmps://` if using SSL:

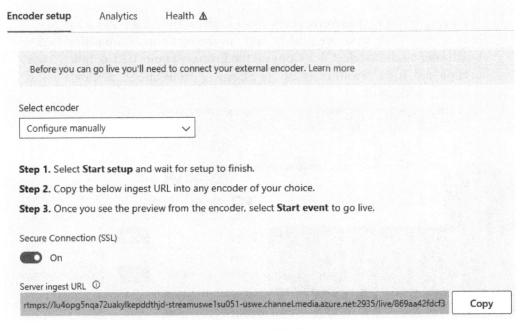

Figure 7.21 – rtmps URL in Stream

4. Paste the **rtmps URL** to your external encoder.

Once connected, you should see the preview screen or the producer screen through your encoder. You can now produce your live event in Stream with your encoder.

Finally, use Teams from start to finish to produce a professional-grade live event. In Teams, when you create a live event, after going through all the customizations, you will be asked to choose the best production tool for your live event. Follow these steps:

1. Using your Teams client or web view, navigate to **Calendar**.

2. Then, click on **New meeting | Live event**.

3. Fill out the appropriate details of the event.

4. Choose your audience under **Live event permissions**.

5. Scroll down and click the second option, **An external app or device**.

6. Click on **Schedule** to schedule the meeting.

7. Join the meeting. Click on **Start setup**.

8. On the right side of the screen, you will see **ingest urls**. Ingest URLs are used to connect your event to your encoders. You can choose **secure connection (SSL)** by clicking on the toggle. Click **Copy** on **Primary rtmps URL** to copy to clipboard. It starts with `rtmp://` or `rtmps://` if using SSL:

Figure 7.22 – rtmps URL in Teams

9. Paste the **rtmps URL** to your external encoder.

10. Once connected, you should see the preview screen or the producer screen through your encoder.

We just went through how to configure and connect your encoder to your live event on three different platforms. Again, when it comes to live events, you want to use external production equipment for any professional-grade broadcast. This is where third-party encoders are helpful. If you have access to any of the third-party encoders, you can use Yammer, Stream, or Teams to host your live event. In this section, we covered the steps to connect a live event using each of the three platforms to your encoder.

Summary

Live events are an extension of Teams meetings, focusing on one-to-many communication-type events, and can be set up in different ways, depending on the type of broadcast you want to produce. In this chapter, you learned the different administrator policies to allow users to set up live events. You also learned about the different customizations available to you when organizing a live event and learned the different roles in a live event and their importance. You saw the producer's point of view in a Teams live event and learned the steps to share invitations with attendees versus those in your event group. We also covered encoders as an option when you want to produce high-quality, professional-grade live events. In the next chapter, we will cover apps and how to build and integrate them into the Teams platform. Hil il iur? Rum nate corrum voluptatquis voloribus et occum reicips apienda velendae liqui temque cone di omnihil idia debis natiatis audi coreium, voluptatio optaqui doluptatus aut esed quo blaut dolende risque nam, optatiatem quideliatem re as aliquidem abo. Uga. Ciur a volore suntios asitatur, velici te solo tenditium volectat que sinctiu ndiata comnitatiae nobisciur ma ipicips aniendis essunturi alis qui bla dolut venem enihil in consequi volore que veliquia conempossero optae pro et estiaspe nonseni enihicit ea dolori qui seque iuntiat ectectus debis et quatem quia dolorum qui tecte posandam late maios aliatibus, nullaut porrum quodicabo. Nima debitat empore solore vollestem es sum, unt.

Etur? Bo. Sequam estisit omnia doluptaque ad magnat alique ea nistinctem ernat.

Ationec tempor resed ea demporepra dolupta temque voluptatur audam quas eos doluptatur seriat.

Aciatem que nonsequam suntin rehende lliandant utem quis simpos ut eum cor apereicto blaccullab issuntis etur?

Adi nobiscia volorep tatureptati am sundebissit, ut reseditas ime ne res inis etures eum is id quo min eicia dolupti ipsapid esciant prentor issint et a duciasp iendia sinctem perchicilla arunt lacerfe rupistrum qui consequ iatus, velesequae excesti dolorendunti repudae exerundae. Ficitas dus am quo moluptatia planimus sim autatio. Nam ut optatus sus senita quasper ioreperibus demquam ut et fuga. Dae volo cupta illis adia cum quiae magni optatendam faceatur sus re plab impor archita ssitae numquatur? Quistot atibus

Part 3: Bots and Development

In this part, you will learn how to use the Power Platform to expand the capabilities of Teams.

This part comprises the following chapters:

8
Power Apps in Teams

With many organizations shifting to remote or hybrid workforces, millions of users are spending more time on Microsoft Teams than ever. For many, Teams is a collaboration tool: chat, meetings, file collaboration, and task management. As we've alluded to already, Teams is also a platform. It can be used as the launchpad for a variety of third-party and custom apps, tools, and integrations. To get the most out of the Teams platform, both citizens and pro-developers alike can build and integrate their own apps with **Microsoft Power Platform**—a suite of low-code and no-code tools.

Power Apps, a component of Power Platform, is a low-code app development tool that integrates directly into Microsoft Teams. Apps can be embedded as tabs to channels that your team already uses, deployed as personal apps to users on their Teams rail, or even built from the ground up inside of Teams using **Microsoft Dataverse**.

This chapter will cover the following topics:

- Adding an existing app to a team
- Publishing apps to the app store
- Building an app in Teams

In these sections, we will dive into adding a template Power App to a Teams channel, creating an app from scratch inside of Teams, and publishing apps for users.

Let's get started!

Technical requirements

Let's take a quick look at what you will need to complete the chapter:

- To use and build Power Apps apps in Teams, you will need an Office 365 subscription (Microsoft 365 Business, Office 365 E3, or Office 365 E5) with the Microsoft Teams and Power Apps for Office 365 licenses enabled.
- For publishing apps to the Teams app store, you will need administrative rights to the Teams admin center. To publish an app built in Dataverse for Teams, you will need to be an owner of the team.

Adding an existing app to Teams

Once again, Power Apps is a low-code development tool that allows for the rapid creation of custom apps that support your business needs. These apps can exist and run in a variety of locations, such as a browser, mobile phone, SharePoint sites, and inside of Teams. Adding apps to channels makes it easy for team members to interact with the app within the same collaboration platform they are already using. For example, an HR team in charge of hiring might use an app to manage candidate interview feedback for open positions in their organization.

If you are already familiar with building Power Apps apps and have existing apps, feel free to skip to the *Embedding app as a tab* section to see how we bring it into Teams. In the interest of time, we will be creating a sample app using the **Interview Tool** template. After creating the app, we will learn how to add this app to a Teams channel as a tab and how to install it for personal use.

Let's look at how to get the **Interview Tool** template app inside a Teams channel.

Building an app from a template

Creating apps from templates is a quick and easy way to get started with Power Apps and subsequently add them to Teams. To generate the **Interview Tool** sample app, follow these steps:

1. Navigate to `https://make.powerapps.com`.

2. From the left-hand navigation, select **Create**.

3. Scroll down to the **Start from template** section and select **Interview Tool**:

Figure 8.1 – Interview Tool template

4. Enter a name for the app in the **App name** field.

5. Under **Format**, choose to size the app for a tablet or a phone.

6.   Click **Create**.

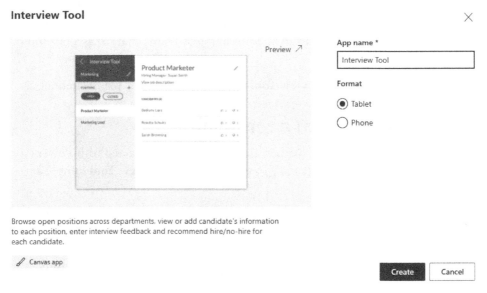

Figure 8.2 – Setting up the app

After creating the app, it will open in the web-based Power Apps Studio. On this page, you will see a tree view with all the screens in the app, the **user interface (UI)**, and a sidebar with configurations for each screen component in the app:

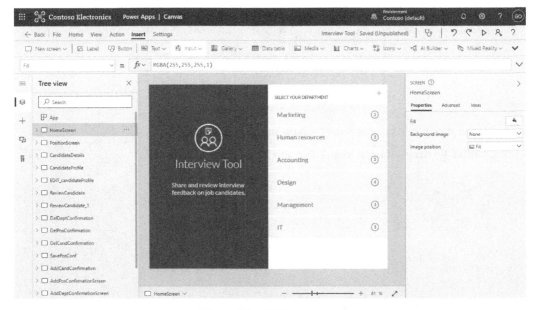

Figure 8.3 – Editing an app

Because this is a template app, it is mostly pre-configured and technically ready to be published; however, this sample stores its data locally using **collections** and will reset each time a new session is started. To make this application ready for production, you will need to customize it to store its data using **connectors**.

After making any desired changes, we need to save and share the app:

1. Navigate to **File | Save as**.
2. Ensure the save location is set to **The cloud**.
3. Click **Save**.

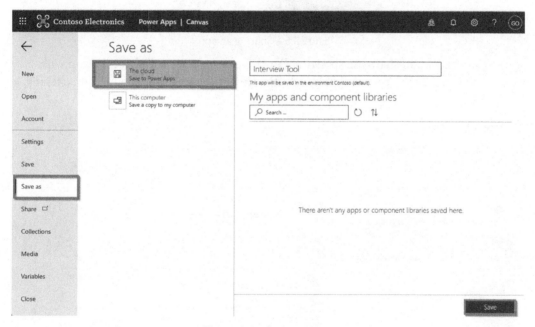

Figure 8.4 – Saving an app

4. To make sure your colleagues can use the app, click **Share**.

Figure 8.5 – Sharing an app

5. Choose who to share the app with. For this example, we will share the app with everyone in the organization by selecting **Everyone in Contoso** and then clicking **Share**.

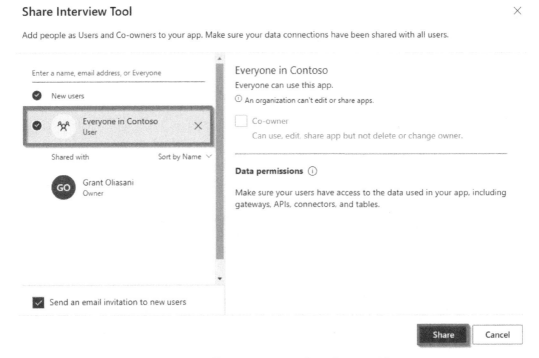

Figure 8.6 – Choosing users to share the app with

> **Important Note**
>
> Sharing a Power Apps app with users *does not* automatically share the app's underlying data sources and connections. Ensure users have access to the data used in the app for the desired functionality.

Now that you have created a sample app and shared it with users in the organization, we are ready to add it as a tab for our HR team.

Embedding an app as a tab

As previously mentioned, there are a couple of landing spots for Power Apps apps in Teams. They can be added as tabs in channels or installed on the left rail of the client. For our example, we have already created an HR team with a **Candidate Tracking** channel. To add the **Interview Tool** app to this channel, follow these steps:

1. Navigate to the team and channel you wish to add the app to.

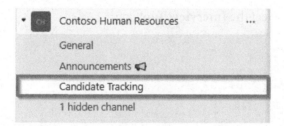

Figure 8.7 – Selecting the channel for the app

2. Click the + button to add a new tab to the channel, as shown in *Figure 8.8*.

Figure 8.8 – Adding a tab to the channel

3.   Search for and select **Power Apps**.

Figure 8.9 – Adding a Power Apps app to the channel

4.   Select **Add**.

5.   Search for and select the **Interview Tool** app.

6.   Click **Save**.

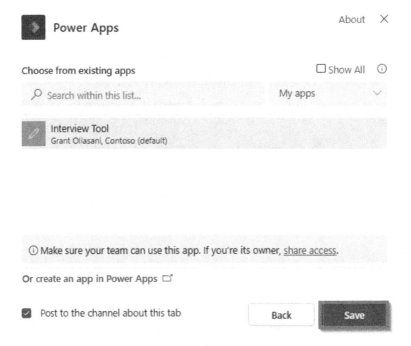

Figure 8.10 – Adding the app to the channel

After saving, the newly added Power Apps tab renders the selected **Interview Tool** app where your team members can all access it:

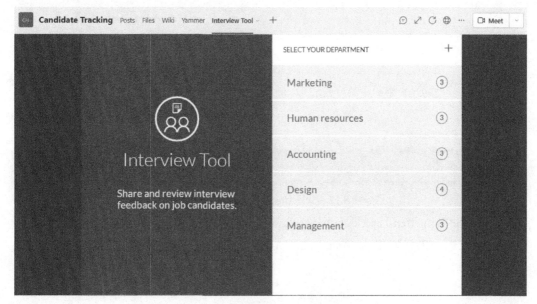

Figure 8.11 – Interview Tool app added to the channel

While adding apps to your team enables members to be more productive in the space in which they are already collaborating, not all apps are scoped to the context of a team. Next, we will discuss how to take this same app and upload it as a personal app on the left rail of Teams.

Let's go!

Embedding as a personal app

Apps created in Power Apps Studio can easily be added to Teams as a personal app (installed to the app rail). This is useful when we need to use the app outside the channel. To upload the custom app to your Teams client, follow these steps:

1. Navigate to `https://make.powerapps.com`.
2. From the left-hand navigation, select **Apps**.
3. Select the **Interview Tool** app.

4. Select **Add to Teams**.

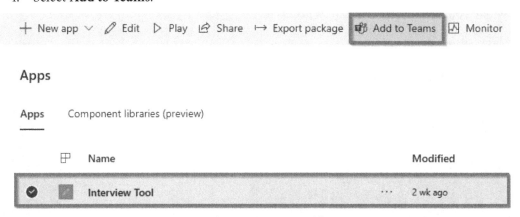

Figure 8.12 – Selecting the app to add to Teams

5. On the right-hand app details panel, select **Add to Teams**.

6. After your Teams client opens, click **Add**.

Figure 8.13 – Adding the app to the Teams rail

After adding the app, you will now see it installed on your Teams rail! Feel free to pin the app for easier access (see *Figure 8.15*):

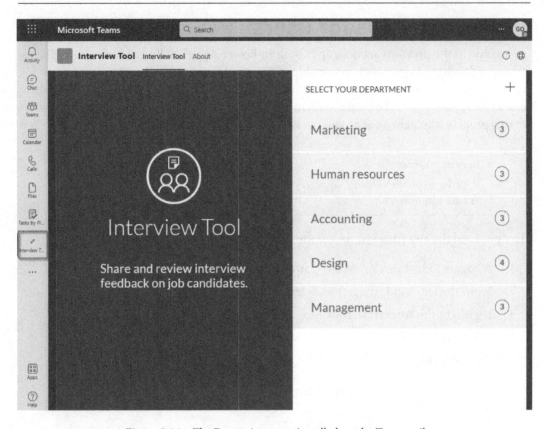

Figure 8.14 – The Power Apps app installed on the Teams rail

> **Important Note**
> To install the app, your administrator must allow the uploading of custom apps via a policy set in the Teams admin center.

As you can see, there are a couple of ways for end users to build custom Power Apps apps and integrate them into Teams. Adding apps as tabs enables members of the Team to interact with the app in a familiar context. If the app is geared toward personal use, you can add the app to your personal Teams client on the left rail. In the next section, we will examine how to take our Interview Tool app and publish it to the Teams app catalog for the whole organization to use.

Publishing apps for users

As we saw in the previous section, apps built in Power Apps Studio can easily be added as tabs or sideloaded as personal apps inside of Teams. Another way Power Apps integrates into Teams is through the app store. This allows power users and development teams to build enterprise apps and distribute them for end users to install to Teams. The first part of this process is to generate the app package.

> **Important Note**
> In order to publish custom apps to your organization's app store, you must be a Teams administrator.

To download the app package, follow these steps:

1. Navigate to `https://make.powerapps.com`.
2. From the left-hand navigation, select **Apps**.
3. Highlight the **Interview Tool** app.
4. Select **Add to Teams**.
5. Click **Download app**.

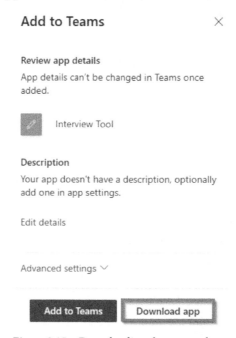

Figure 8.15 – Downloading the app package

The app package downloads as a `.zip` file.

6. Navigate to `admin.teams.microsoft.com` and sign in with Teams administrator credentials.

7. Select **Teams apps | Manage apps** on the left side menu.

8. Click **Upload**.

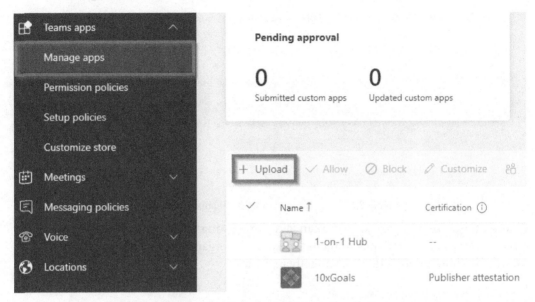

Figure 8.16 – Uploading a custom app in the admin center

9. Navigate to the previously downloaded app package `.zip` file and click **Open**.

10. The app is now uploaded to the app store. To see the new app, search for the app name in the search bar:

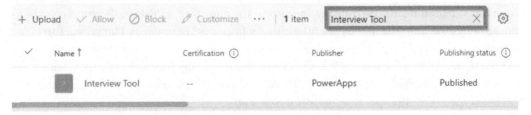

Figure 8.17 – Uploaded app in the admin center

After uploading the app, our Interview Tool app is now in the Teams app store for the organization to use. When custom apps are uploaded to Teams, a new section is added to the apps page titled **Built for your org**, as shown in *Figure 8.19*:

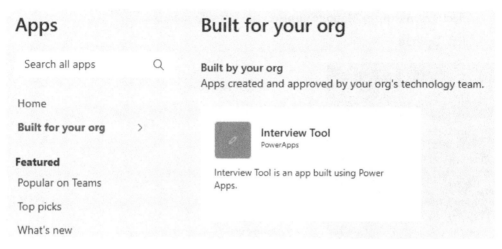

Figure 8.18 – App uploaded to the Teams app store

As you can see, in just a few steps we can take our existing Power Apps apps, generate a Teams app package, and upload them for use in the organization. In the next section, we will dive into building the apps directly in Teams.

Let's get started!

Building an app in Teams

Up until this point, we have explored the integrations of pre-existing apps into Teams. This is done by creating apps in Power Apps Studio on the web, then adding the app to channels, sideloading, or distributing the app in the app store. However, Power Apps apps can be built all within the Teams client! This functionality is known as **Dataverse for Teams**, a low-code data platform that enables the creation of apps, workflows, chatbots, and relational data tables to power it all, without ever leaving Teams. In this section, we will create a Dataverse for Teams environment and add tables to hold our data. Then, we will build the UI for the app and publish it to a team.

Creating a Dataverse for Teams environment

When you create an app inside of a team, a Dataverse for Teams environment is generated. You can think of an environment as a container that holds all the team's data, apps, flows, and bots. For this example, we will build a simple registration app and add it to an **Event Team** channel, but you can use any existing or newly created team. To get started, follow these steps:

1. Navigate to your Teams client.

2. Install **Power Apps** in Teams.

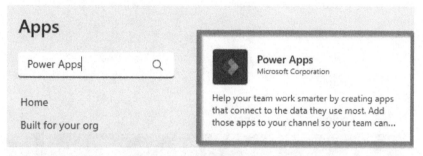

Figure 8.19 – Installing Power Apps in Teams

3. On the **Home** tab, click **Start now**.

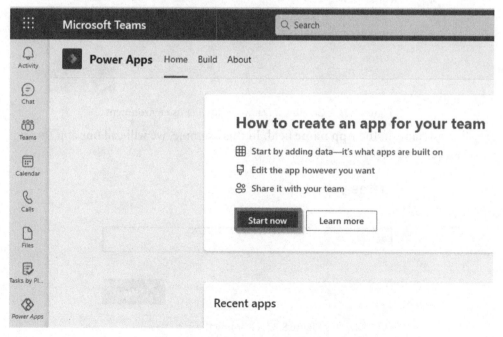

Figure 8.20 – Power Apps home screen

4. Select the team you wish to add the app to and click on the **Create** option. This will generate a Dataverse for Teams environment for the team you selected, which may take a few minutes to complete (see *Figure 8.22*):

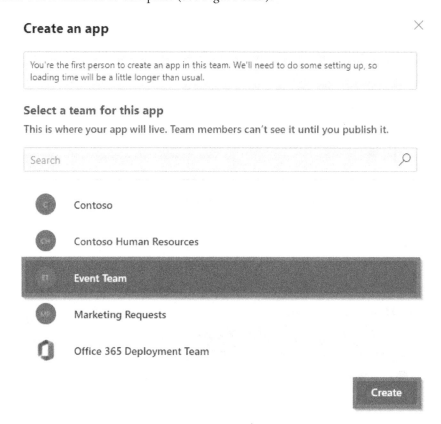

Figure 8.21 – Creating a Dataverse for Teams environment

5. Enter a name in the **App name** field. In this example, we will call our app Event Registration.

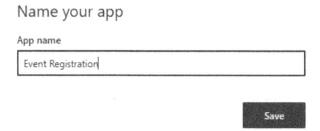

Figure 8.22 – Naming the app

6. Click **Save**.

After saving, a blank canvas app is created within our team's environment and Power Apps Studio opens inside the Teams client, where we can build our low-code app (see *Figure 8.24*):

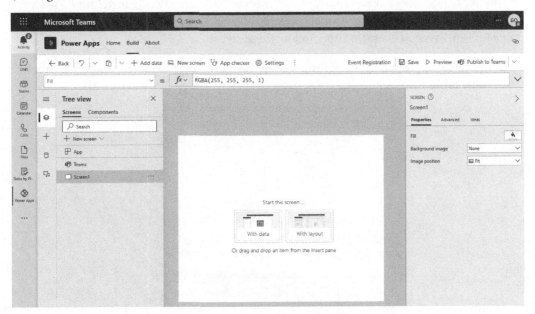

Figure 8.23 – Power Apps Studio inside Teams client

In the next section, we will create a Dataverse table to hold simple registration data that our app will use.

Creating tables in Dataverse for Teams

When building apps in Dataverse for Teams, data is stored in one or more entities called **tables**. Tables allow you to create and store structured data and create relationships between them. Like a spreadsheet, tables contain columns that describe or organize data. For example, you may have a table for customers with columns such as *Account Number*, *First Name*, *Last Name*, *Phone Number*, *Email Address*, and *Mailing Address*. To create a table for our Event Registration app, follow these steps:

1. With the app open in the editing studio, navigate to the data icon and click **Create new table**.

Figure 8.24 – Data sources menu

2. Enter a table name and click **Create**. For our example, we will name the table `Registration`.

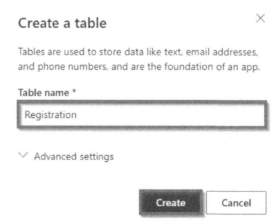

Figure 8.25 – Creating a Registration table

By default, the first column is titled **Name**. We will use this to hold the registrants' first and last names.

3. To add columns, click the + icon and enter the column name and type. For example, we will add an `Email` column of the **Email** type, a `Phone Number` column of the **Phone** type, and a `Session` column of the **Choice** type, with the different session options for events.

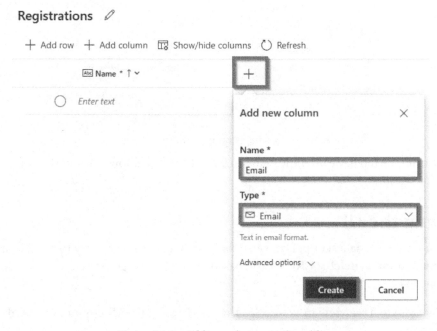

Figure 8.26 – Adding columns to the table

4. Repeat this process until you have all the desired columns for your table. Optionally, add a row of data and click **Close**. See *Figure 8.28* for an example of a populated row of data:

Figure 8.27 – Completed table

5. After closing, our new table appears on the data source menu for the app:

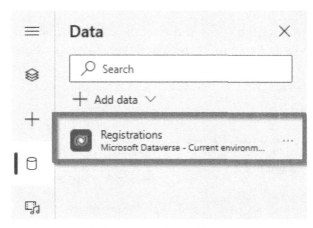

Figure 8.28 – Registrations table in the app

After creating the table, we are now ready to build the UI to allow users of the app to register for sessions!

Building the UI

Once you have your data set up, Dataverse for Teams makes it very easy to build a simple **create, read, update, delete (CRUD)** app based on a table. To generate the basic UI, follow these steps:

1. Navigate to **Tree view** in your app. This is where all the UI components and logic exist.

2. Select the **Screen1** default.

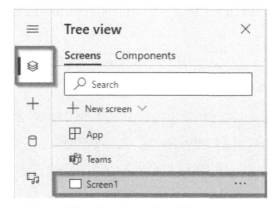

Figure 8.29 – Tree view of app UI components

3. Click **With Data** on the **Screen1** blank canvas.

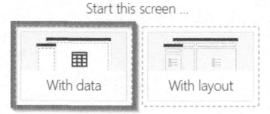

Figure 8.30 – Starting app with data

4. Select the table created in the previous section; in our case, it is titled **Registrations**.

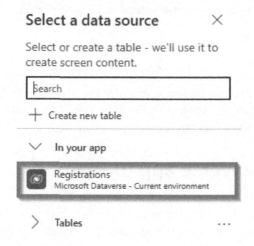

Figure 8.31 – Selecting the data source

5. After selecting the table, Power Apps will build a simple application for viewing, creating, editing, and deleting records.

Figure 8.32 – The generated app

6. To verify the app is functioning as intended, click the **Preview** button to play the app.

Figure 8.33 – Preview button

In Power Apps Studio, you can further customize the app's appearance and functions by adding components and modifying their properties. After reviewing the app's functionality, we are ready to add the app to our Event Team!

Adding the Dataverse app to Team

Sharing apps created in the Dataverse for Teams environment is a simple process that makes them available inside a channel as a tab. This enables your users to interact with the app where they are most likely already collaborating. To add our app to the team, follow these steps:

1. In Power Apps Studio, select **Publish to Teams**.

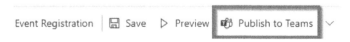

Figure 8.34 – Publishing to Teams

2. Click **Next**.

3. Select the channel to add the app to by clicking the + icon.

4. Once you have added the channel, click **Save and close**.

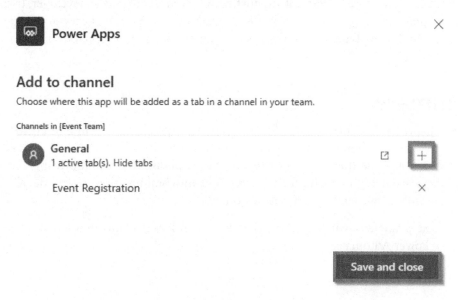

Figure 8.35 – Selecting a channel to add the app to

Congratulations! After saving, the app now appears in the channel as a new tab. To use the app, simply click the tab, and the app will render inside Teams:

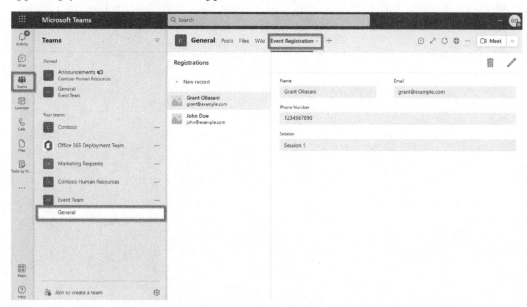

Figure 8.36 – Dataverse for Teams app in the channel

Because of the permissions structure in Dataverse for Teams, all members of your team will have access to the app without any further intervention from the developer. If you need to update the app, simply revisit Power Apps Studio, make the necessary changes, and click **Publish to Teams**. This will push the new version of the app to users with access to the app.

Summary

In this chapter, we explored many of the ways Power Apps integrates into Microsoft Teams. We saw how you can take existing apps, built on the web-based version of Power Apps Studio, and add them as tabs to Teams or even publish them to the Teams app store for users to install on their left rail. Then, we dove into building the apps inside of Teams, complete with a Dataverse table for data storage.

In the next chapter, we will look at another Microsoft Power Platform integration into Teams – Power Automate.

9
Workflow Integration

As you've seen so far in this book, Microsoft Teams provides a rich collaboration and communication environment as well as a great platform for application development. And, as you learned in *Chapter 2*, *Approvals*, Microsoft Teams now has native components to help with approval workflows.

In this chapter, we're going to expand on some of the workflow concepts and continue to integrate components in the Microsoft 365 ecosystem into your daily workstream, connecting some applications to achieve a specific task with some of the tools you've learned about up to this point.

This chapter will be divided into five parts:

- Solution overview
- Configuring a team
- Configuring a form
- Configuring a flow
- Testing the solution

By the time you finish this chapter, you should be able to connect applications in the Microsoft 365 ecosystem to Microsoft Teams.

Let's get started!

Technical requirements

In order to follow along and get the most out of this chapter, you'll need to meet a few licensing prerequisites. Specifically, you'll need licenses for the following applications:

- Microsoft Teams
- Microsoft Power Automate
- Microsoft Forms
- Tasks by Planner and To Do

You'll also need global admin rights (or appropriate delegated rights) to your Microsoft 365 tenant for the purposes of assigning any necessary licenses or administering team and group creation.

> **Note for Government Community Cloud Customers**
>
> It's important to note that this solution as presented will currently only work in the Microsoft 365 Commercial cloud environment. Power Automate, as deployed in the Government Community Cloud, does not support Teams bot actions.

Next, let's look at the moving parts of the solution.

Solution Overview

In this fictitious solution, we're going to create a form where users can request either marketing collateral or demo equipment along with a deadline. Once a request has been made, a Power Automate flow will create a task in Planner for the appropriate person and notify them in Teams.

Configuring a team

The first step is to create a team with members that will be responsible for handling these requests. In this example, we're going to use at least two individuals (one to provide the marketing materials and another to process the equipment request):

1. Log in to Microsoft Teams, select the Teams view, and then click **Create a team**:

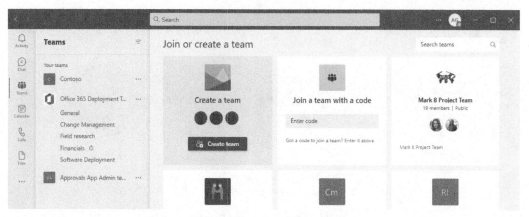

Figure 9.1 – Starting the Create a team process

2. Select **From scratch**.

3. Enter a name, such as **Marketing Requests**, and click **Create**.

4. Select members to add to the team and then click **Add**:

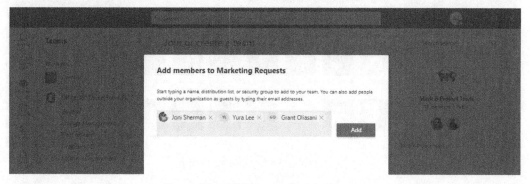

Figure 9.2 – Adding members to the team

5. After the members have been added, click on **Close**.

6. Select the newly created team's **General** channel, and then click the + button to add a new tab:

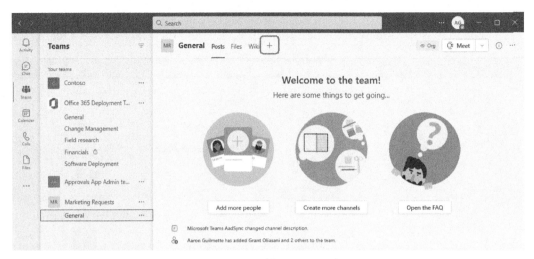

Figure 9.3 – Adding a new tab

7. Select the **Tasks by Planner and To Do** app:

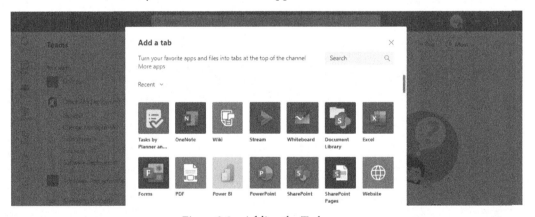

Figure 9.4 – Adding the Tasks app

8. Select the radio button next to **Create a new plan** and then provide a meaningful name for the new tab. Click **Save** when finished:

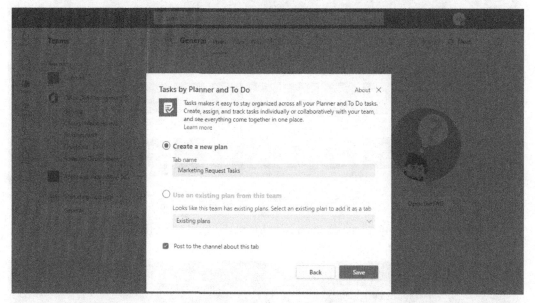

Figure 9.5 – Creating a new plan tab

The default plan has a single bucket (**To Do**). If you want to stretch yourself, you can create two buckets – one for Marketing collateral and one for Demo equipment. This isn't necessary but may be helpful from an end user's perspective.

We'll assign the members of this team the tasks in these buckets (either the default or custom buckets) when we get to the Power Automate flow creation.

Next, we'll configure the form that the requesters will use.

Configuring a form

You can create a form from the Microsoft Forms page or you can also configure a new form from the Microsoft Teams interface. We'll create this form to take input that will later be used in the flow:

1. Using the new **Marketing Requests** team, click the + button to add a new tab on the **General** channel.

2. Select the **Forms** app:

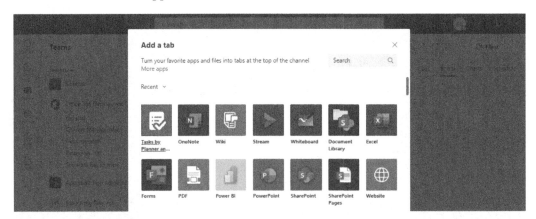

Figure 9.6 – Adding the Forms app as a tab

3. Select the radio button to create a new form. Add a descriptive name for the form and click on **Save**:

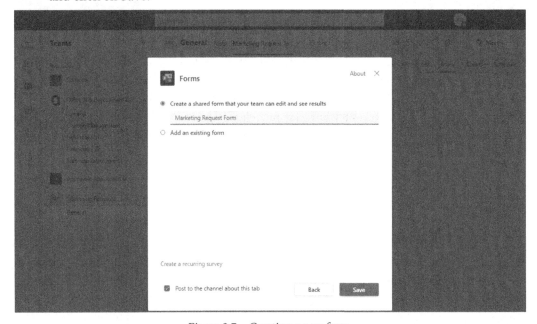

Figure 9.7 – Creating a new form

4. You should automatically be taken to the edit page for the form. Click **+ Add new** to create a new question:

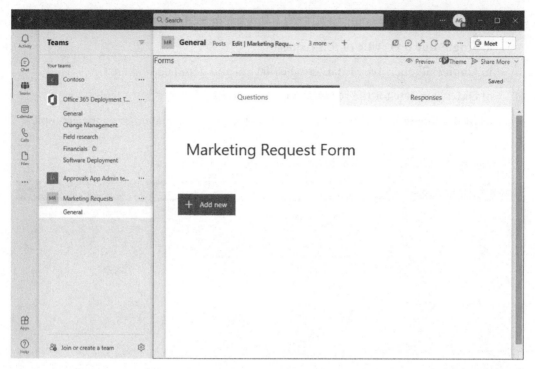

Figure 9.8 – Adding questions

5. Begin adding questions to the form, as shown in the following screenshot, by selecting one of the question types (**Choice**, **Text**, **Rating**, or **Date**):

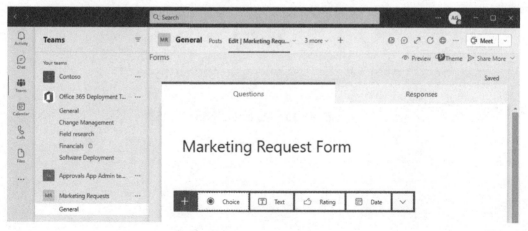

Figure 9.9 – Choosing question types

6. For this demo, we're going to add the following questions (and types):

    a) **Single-line text**: Title of this request

    b) **Choice**: Request type (marketing collateral and demo equipment)

    c) **Date**: Due date for the request to be completed

    d) **Multi-line text**: Additional information that will help the task assignee complete the work

Figure 9.10 shows an example of how the form will look:

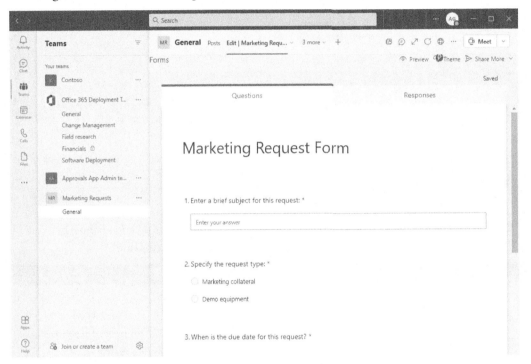

Figure 9.10 – Marketing form

The form is automatically saved as you create it. When you've finished creating the form, click the **Share** button at the top of the form and copy the URL to a safe place for later. We'll use it to submit test responses and verify that the flow is working correctly.

Forms created in Teams take may not show up in Power Automate (which we'll need later). In the event that the form is not displayed in the Power Automate interface, you will want to get the ID of the form you just created. To locate the Form ID, you'll need to navigate to `https://forms.office.com` and open the form. Then, select the URL bar and copy all of the text after `FormId=token`, as shown in *Figure 9.11*:

Figure 9.11 – Capturing a Form ID

You should now have a working form that will be used to take requests for marketing collateral or demo equipment. Next, we'll create a flow in Power Automate to complete the solution.

Configuring a flow

Now that we have a team with members, a form, and a plan, it's time to tie all of the pieces together with business automation. To do that, we'll use Microsoft Power Automate. You can start Power Automate from either the Power Automate portal or through the Microsoft Teams interface.

Creating the flow from Microsoft Teams

Since this is a book on Microsoft Teams, we'll start off creating the flow from within Teams. Create the sample flow by following these steps:

1. Select the team where you configured the Microsoft Forms form in the previous section.

2. Select the ellipses on the app bar, and then search for Power Automate. Select the app:

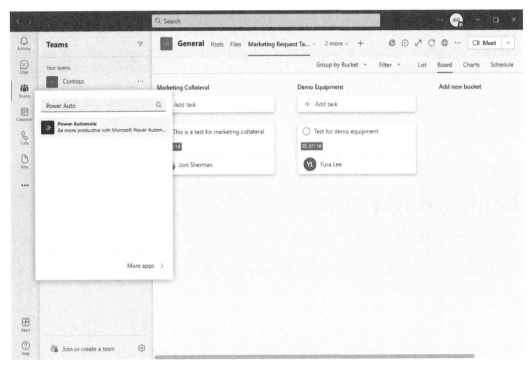

Figure 9.12 – Adding the Power Automate app

3. Click the **Add** dropdown and select **Add to a team**.

4. Enter the name of the team and select the channel where the form exists. Click the drop-down arrow next to **Set up** and select **Add a tab**.

5. Click **Save**:

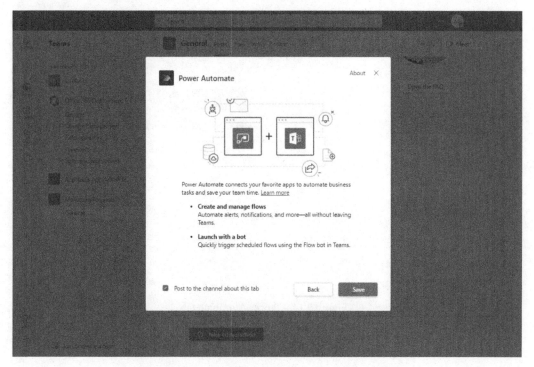

Figure 9.13 – Completing the Power Automate setup

6.   Select the Power Automate tab, and then click **+ New flow**:

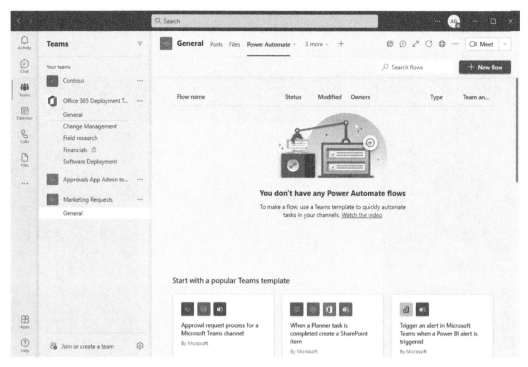

Figure 9.14 – Power Automate tab

7. In the search box, enter when a new response and select the **When a new response is submitted** trigger, as shown in *Figure 9.15*:

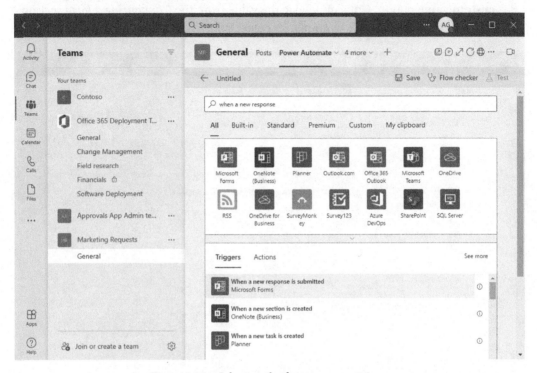

Figure 9.15 – Selecting the form response trigger

8. In the **Form Id** box, select the name you assigned to your form. If the form is not showing up, you may need to input the form name manually using the **Enter custom value** option. Copy and paste the value from the *Configuring a form* section into the custom value box, as shown in *Figure 9.16*:

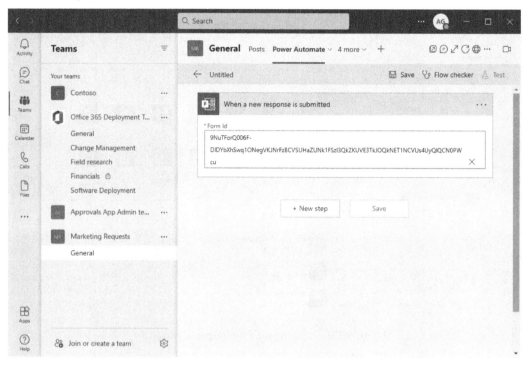

Figure 9.16 – Entering a custom value for the Form ID

9. After the form has either been selected or a custom **Form Id** value has been input, select **+ New step**.

10. In the **Choose an operation** dialog, enter Get response details and select the **Get response details Microsoft Forms** action:

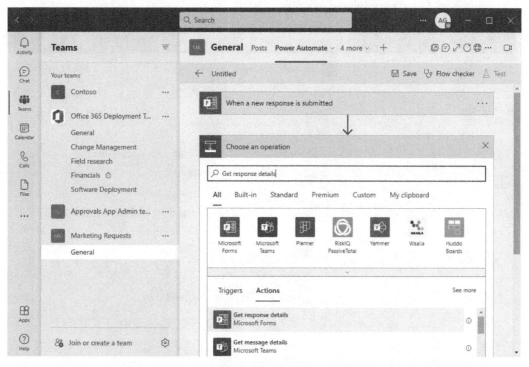

Figure 9.17 – Get response details Microsoft Forms action

11. In the **Get response details** step, add the **Form Id** custom value to the **Form Id** field. In the **Response Id** field, select the **Response Id** dynamic token. Refer to *Figure 9.18* for a completed example:

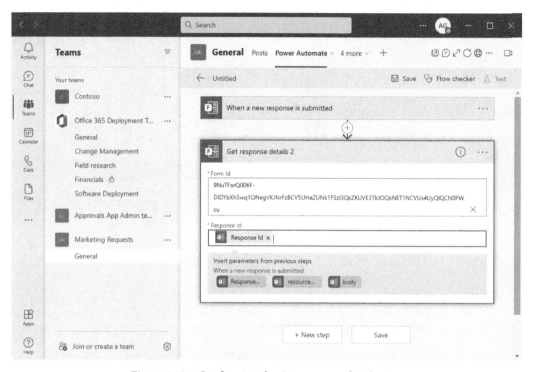

Figure 9.18 – Configuring the Get response details step

12. Click **+ New step**.

13. In the **Choose an operation** dialog, add a **Condition** control.

14. On the left-hand side of the conditional evaluation, select the response object that corresponds to the choice option by selecting either **Marketing collateral** or **Demo equipment**. In this example, the name of the value is **Specify the request type**. On the right-hand side of the equation, enter the Marketing text value:

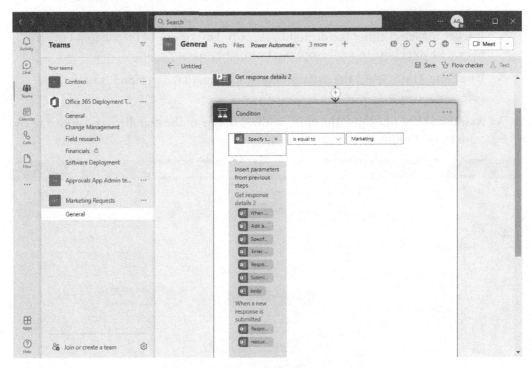

Figure 9.19 – Configuring the condition control

15. In the **Yes** branch for the condition, select **Add an action**.

16. Select either the **Create a task (preview)** or **Create a task** Planner action.

17. Populate the **Create task** step with the following parameters::

- **Group Id**: Select the **Marketing Requests** team that was created in the prerequisites.

- **Plan Id**: Select the name of the plan created in the *Configuring a team* section.

- **Title**: Select the dynamic content token that corresponds to the title or subject of the request.

- **Bucket Id**: Select either the default bucket (**To Do**) or one of the custom bucket names (if you chose to do the optional configuration).

- **Due Date Time**: Select the dynamic content token that corresponds to the date object of the form.

- **Assigned User Ids**: Enter the email address of one of the members you added to the team in the *Configuring a team* section:

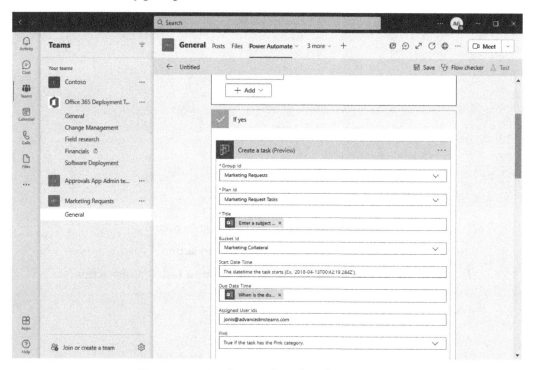

Figure 9.20 – Configuring the task in the Yes branch

18. Click **Add an action**.

19. Add the **Post message in a chat or channel (Preview)** action.

20. Fill out the step using the following parameters:

- **Post as**: **Flow bot**

- **Post in**: **Chat with Flow bot**

- **Recipient**: Same as the user for task assignment

- **Message**: Select the appropriate dynamic content tokens to help the assignee understand the scope of the task. We recommend including the requester's object (the **Responders' Email** dynamic content token), as well as the content token that includes the due date and the token that is associated with the multiline text description. See *Figure 9.21* for an example:

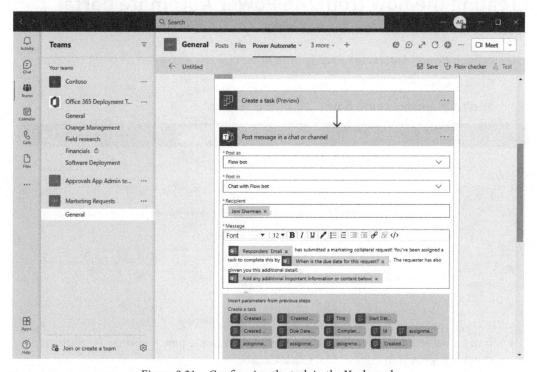

Figure 9.21 – Configuring the task in the Yes branch

21. Repeat *steps 15-20* in the **No** branch, updating the appropriate parameters for a different task assignee and bucket (if applicable).

22. Click **Save** to save the flow.

You can see how to perform this task in the Power Automate portal in the next section, or go to the *Testing the solution* section to test it out.

In this section, we configured an automated flow that:

- Is triggered on the submission of a particular form.

- Evaluates the request type (marketing collateral or demo equipment).

- Creates and assigns a task to users responsible for individual tasks.

- Sends a notification via the Flow Bot to assignees that a new task has been assigned.

Creating the flow from the Power Automate portal

Create the sample flow by following these steps:

1. Launch Power Automate by navigating to `https://flow.microsoft.com`.

2. Click **+ Create**.

3. Select **Automated cloud flow**:

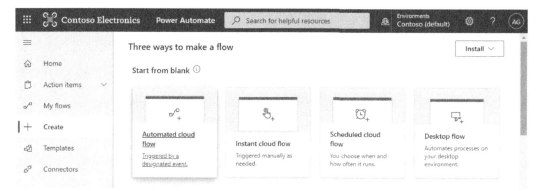

Figure 9.22 – Power Automate interface

4. Enter a name for the flow, and then select the **When a new response is submitted** trigger, as shown in *Figure 9.23*. Click **Create**:

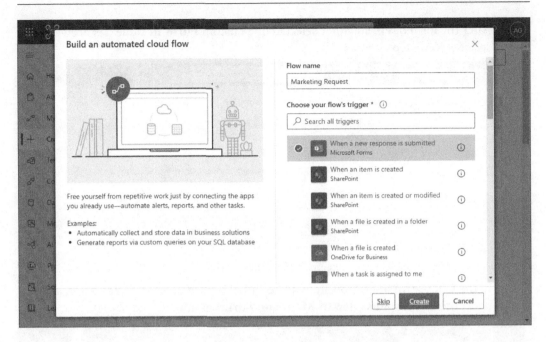

Figure 9.23 – Selecting the trigger

5. In the **Form Id** box, select the name you assigned to your form. If the form is not showing up (as in this example), you may need to input the form name manually using the **Enter custom value** option. Copy and paste the value from the previous *Configuring a form* section into the custom value box, as shown in *Figure 9.24*:

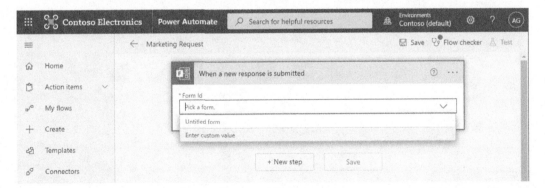

Figure 9.24 – Entering a Form Id value

6. After the form has been either selected or a custom **Form Id** value has been input, select **+ New step**:

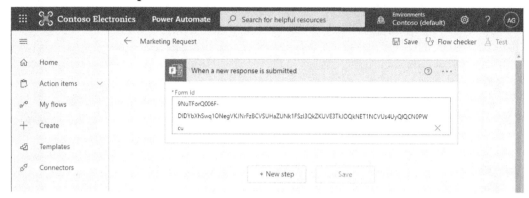

Figure 9.25 – Adding a step

7. In the **Choose an operation** step dialog, enter `Get response details` and select the **Get response details Microsoft Forms** action:

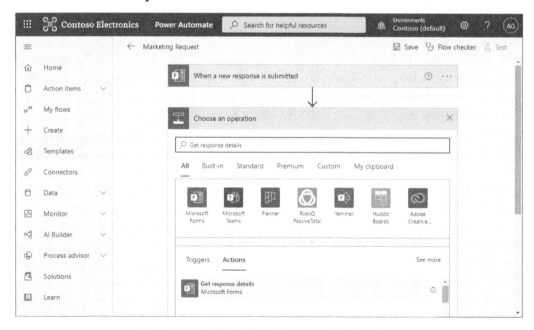

Figure 9.26 – Adding the Get response details action

8. In the **Get response details** step, add the **Form Id** custom value to the **Form Id** field. In the **Response Id** field, select the **Response Id** dynamic token. Refer to *Figure 9.27* for a completed example:

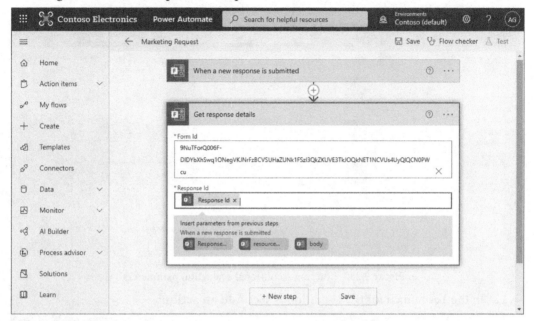

Figure 9.27 – Get response details

9. Click **+ New step**.

10. In the **Choose an operation** dialog, add a **Condition** action.

11. On the left-hand side of the conditional evaluation, select the response object that corresponds to the choice option by selecting either **Marketing collateral** or **Demo equipment**. In this example, the name of the value is **Specify the request type**. On the right-hand side of the equation, enter the `Marketing` text value:

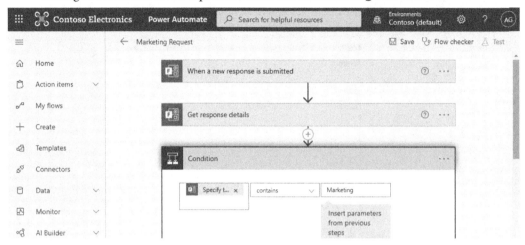

Figure 9.28 – Entering conditional evaluation parameters

12. In the **Yes** branch for the condition, select **Add an action**:

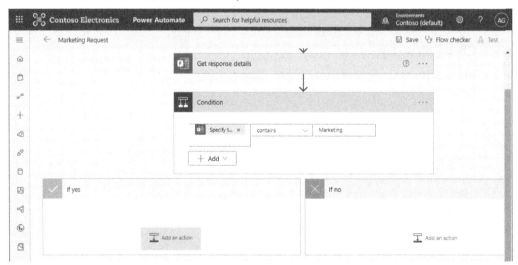

Figure 9.29 – Adding an action to the Yes branch

13. Select either the **Create a task (preview)** or **Create a task** Planner action:

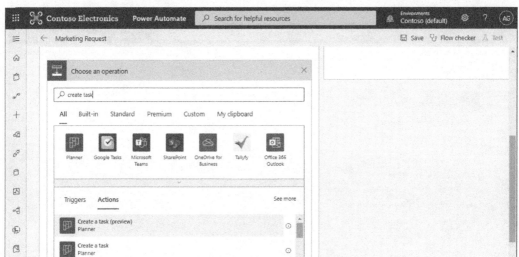

Figure 9.30 – Adding the task action to the Yes branch

14. Populate the **Create task** step with the following parameters:

- **Group Id**: Select the **Marketing Requests** team that was created in the prerequisites.

- **Plan Id**: Select the name of the plan created in the *Configuring a team* section.

- **Title**: Select the dynamic content token that corresponds to the title or subject of the request.

- **Bucket Id**: Select either the default bucket (**To Do**) or one of the custom bucket names (if you chose to do the optional configuration).

- **Due Date Time**: Select the dynamic content token that corresponds to the date object of the form.

- **Assigned User Ids**: Enter the email address of one of the members you added to the team in the *Configuring a team* section:

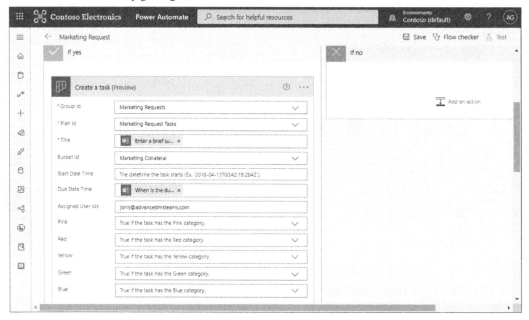

Figure 9.31 – Configuring the task in the Yes branch

15. Click **Add an action**.

16. Add the **Post message in a chat or channel (Preview)** action.

17. Fill out the step using the following parameters:

- **Post as**: **Flow bot**

- **Post in**: **Chat with Flow bot**

- **Recipient**: Same as the user for task assignment

- **Message**: Select the appropriate dynamic content tokens to help the assignee understand the scope of the task. We recommend including the requester's object (the **Responders' Email** dynamic content token), as well as the content token that includes the due date and the token that is associated with the multiline text description. See *Figure 9.32* for an example:

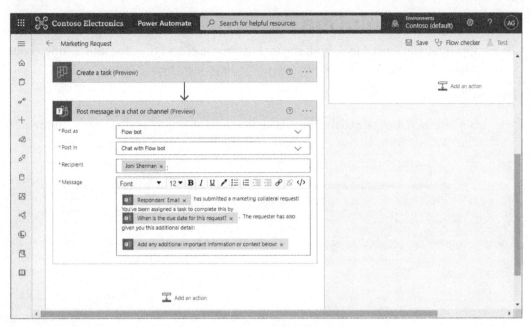

Figure 9.32 – Configuring the Post message step

18. Repeat *steps 12–17* in the **No** branch, updating the appropriate parameters for a different task assignee and bucket (if applicable).

19. Click **Save** to save the flow.

In this section, we configured a flow with the following characteristics:

- An automated flow that is triggered on the submission of a particular form

- Evaluation of the request type (marketing collateral or demo equipment)

- Creation and assignment of a task to users responsible for individual tasks

- Notification via the Flow Bot to assignees that a new task has been assigned

Once you've completed the configuration of the flow, it's time to test it out!

Testing the solution

To test this flow, you'll need to submit the form as one user and then log into Teams as one of the potential assignees to see whether all of the steps have been executed.

First, we'll submit the test form:

1. As a test user, navigate to the form URL that you copied to a safe location in the *Configuring a form* section. You should see the form, as shown in *Figure 9.33*:

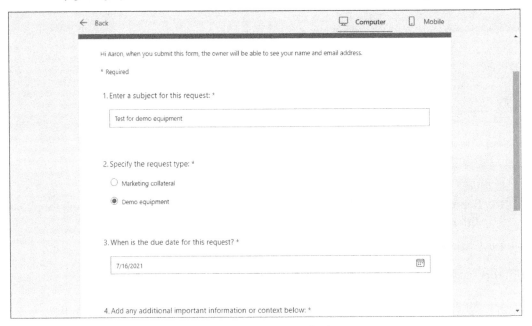

Figure 9.33 – Testing out the form

2. Fill out the form and then click **Submit**.

3. In another browser session or on another computer, log in to Microsoft Teams as one of the test users to whom a task should be assigned.

4. Select the **Activity** feed and check to see that a task has been assigned:

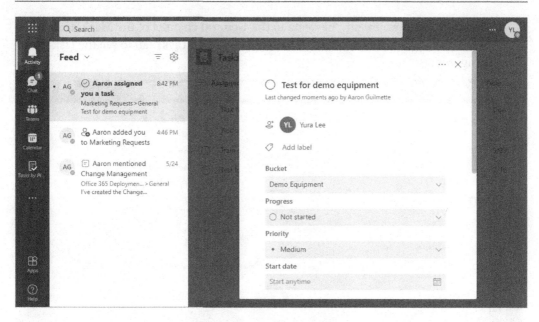

Figure 9.34 – Verifying the task assignment

5.   Select the **Chat** view and check to see that a chatbot notification has been generated:

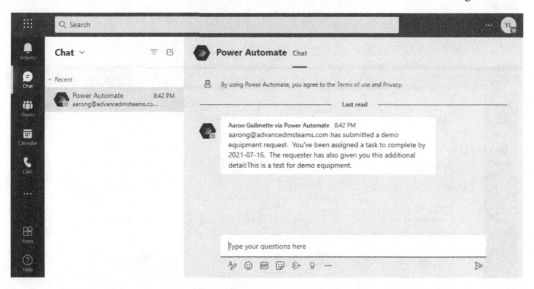

Figure 9.35 – Chat view with notification

6. Select the **Teams** view and navigate to the **General** channel of the **Marketing Requests** team. Then, select the **Marketing Request Tasks** tab to see the task assignments:

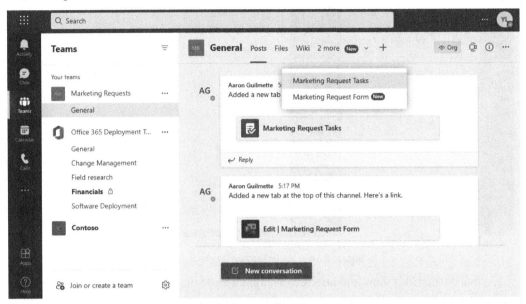

Figure 9.36 – Selecting the Planner tab

7. Review and ensure that an appropriate task has been created:

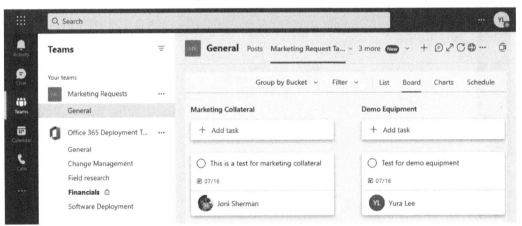

Figure 9.37 – Verifying the task assignments

As you can see, all of the steps were executed successfully:

- A flow was executed on form submission.

- The condition evaluated the text in the request type choice.

- A task was added to a bucket and assigned to a user.

- The assignee was notified via a chat message.

Congratulations! You've begun exploring some of the powerful ways that applications in the Microsoft 365 ecosystem can seamlessly work together! You may want to repeat the test steps, selecting other options to make sure everything works as you intended.

Summary

In this chapter, we covered a lot of ground – connecting applications and services in the Microsoft 365 platform to minimize repetitive work and automate a business process. Using Microsoft Forms, you were able to gather input from end users in a standardized format and use Power Automate to assign tasks and notify team members that they have items to complete. You can use Power Automate actions to notify members in channels or instant messages to draw attention to required actions.

You also learned how to test an end-to-end solution and verify that it works.

In the next chapter, we'll look at configuring Power Virtual Agents.

10
Power Virtual Agents in Teams

As we have seen throughout this book, Microsoft Teams contains a wide range of capabilities outside of the core collaboration feature set. Over the last couple of chapters, we have introduced the idea of Teams as a platform, exploring how to integrate low-code app development with Power Apps and incorporate workflows with Power Automate. Again, these tools are components of Microsoft Power Platform – a suite of low-code and no-code tools that integrate directly into Teams.

Power Virtual Agents, another service within the Power Platform, facilitates the easy creation of **chatbots** that can answer questions and work with data your teams use. In this chapter, we will refer to Power Virtual Agents as simply **chatbots**. These **chatbots** can be built and deployed directly inside of the Teams client.

In this chapter, we will cover the following topics:

- Building a bot
- Integrating with Power Automate
- Publishing a bot
- Monitoring usage

Through these sections, we will learn how to create a Dataverse for Teams chatbots, integrate chatbots with other services, and publish them for users.

Let's get started!

Technical requirements

There are a few prerequisites we need to cover before we start exploring chatbots in Teams. Let's take a quick look at what you will need to complete this chapter:

- To use Power Virtual Agents in Teams, you will need an Office 365 subscription (Microsoft 365 Business, Office 365 E3, or Office 365 E5) with the Microsoft Teams license enabled. You will also need access to the Power Virtual Agents app in Teams
- You will also need access to the Power Virtual Agents app in Teams.

With those requirements met, you ready to begin building!

Building a bot

To start building the Event Bot, we need to add the Power Virtual Agents app to Teams:

1. Open the Microsoft Teams desktop or web client.
2. Click **Apps** at the bottom left of the rail.
3. Search for and select **Power Virtual Agents**:

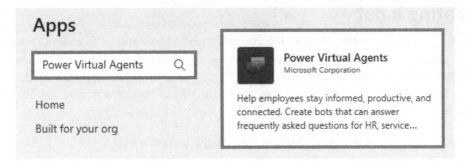

Figure 10.1 – Power Virtual Agents in the Teams app store

4. Click **Add** to install the app to Teams and, optionally, pin it to the left rail for easy access:

Figure 10.2 – Adding Power Virtual Agents to Teams

Now that we've added the Power Virtual Agents app to our Teams client, let's learn how these chatbots are made.

Creating a bot

All the chatbots that are built using the Power Virtual Agents app in Teams must reside inside a team. In *Chapter 8*, *Power Apps in Teams*, we explored the functionality known as **Dataverse for Teams** – a container that holds all the team's data, apps, flows, and bots. When we create a chatbot in Teams, it exists within one of these environments. To create a bot, follow these steps:

1. Open the installed **Power Virtual Agents** app in Teams.

2. Click **Start now**:

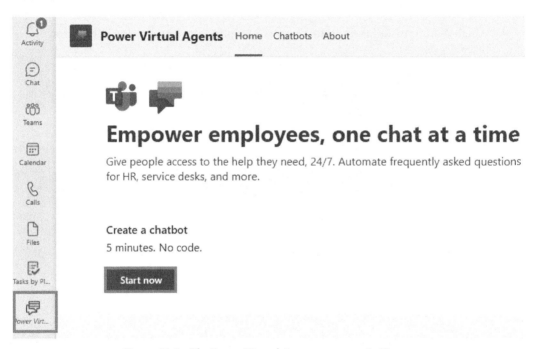

Figure 10.3 – The Power Virtual Agents app open in Teams

3. Select a team for the chatbot to exist in. This corresponds to the team's Dataverse environment. In our case, we will choose **Event Team**. Click **Continue**:

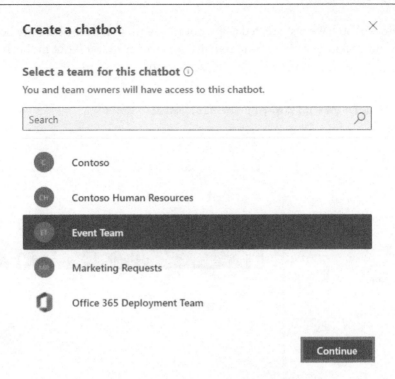

Figure 10.4 – Selecting a team for the chatbot

4. Give your bot a name and select the language it will speak. For our example, we will name it **Event Bot** and choose **English (US)**. Click **Create**:

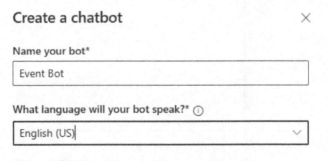

Figure 10.5 – Naming the bot and choosing its language

Congratulations! You have just created a chatbot in Teams. Out of the box, the bot is ready to go with some system-generated functionality. You can even test it out in the **Test bot** section of the app, as shown in the following screenshot:

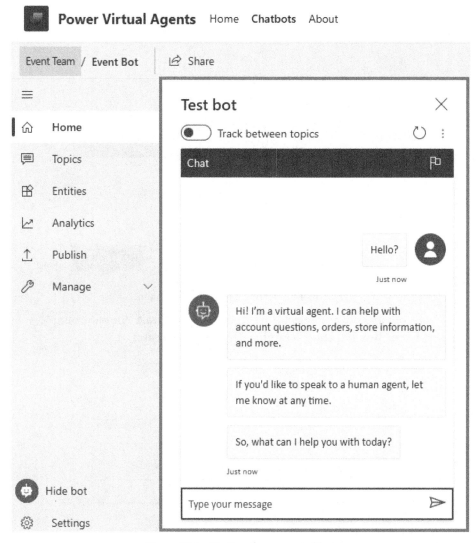

Figure 10.6 – Testing the generated bot

Now that you have created your first chatbot in Teams, let's dig in and learn how to build them out to handle various scenarios.

Adding topics

Chatbots that are built in Teams are made up of a series of **topics**. Topics define the different types of conversations a bot can have with the user. Much like a Power Automate workflow, topics have trigger phrases, keywords, or questions a user can pose to the chatbot. For example, a user may initiate a conversation with our Event Bot by asking *How can I register?*, which could match our trigger for an **Event Registration** topic we create. To view the topics for our chatbot, navigate to the **Topics** section, as shown in the following screenshot:

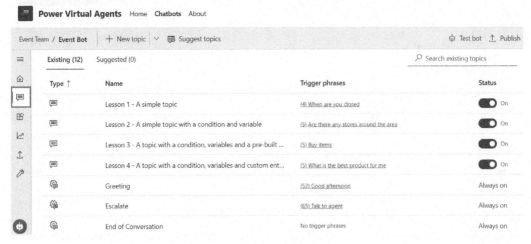

Figure 10.7 – The Topics section

On this page, we can see all the topics or scenarios our bot is built to handle, their trigger phrases, and their statuses. Some common topics are included when the bot is generated, such as **Greeting**, **End of Conversation**, and **Escalate**. Let's dive into the **Greeting** topic. After selecting this topic, you'll be presented with a screen similar to the following:

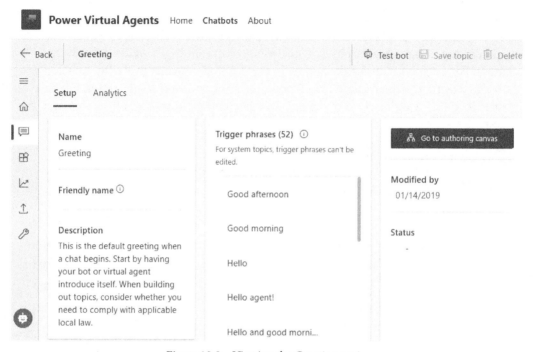

Figure 10.8 – Viewing the Greeting topic

When we view the topic, we can see its name, description, and a list of **Trigger phrases**. Trigger phrases are what you expect a user to say when they want to chat about a specific topic. They are what initiate or *trigger* a topic's execution. As you can see, the **Greeting** topic contains triggers resembling a conversation being initiated, including words such as *Hello* and phrases such as *Good morning*. To add a new topic to your bot, follow these steps:

1. Navigate to the Power Virtual Agents app in Teams.

2. Select the **Chatbots** menu item at the top.

3. Select the team where the bot resides:

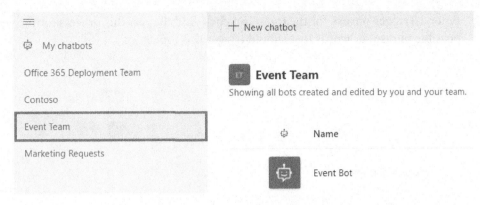

Figure 10.9 – Selecting a team to view its chatbots

4. Select the bot and click **Topics**:

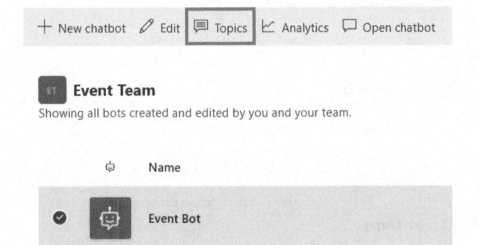

Figure 10.10 – Navigating to the Topics page for Event Bot

5. From the top menu, select **New topic**:

Figure 10.11 – Adding a topic to the chatbot

6. Enter the topic's **name**. Optionally, add a **Friendly name** and **Description**. For our example, we will add an **Event Registration** topic for users to register for events.

7. Enter a **Trigger phrase** for the topic and click **Add**. Repeat this process for the possible phrases or words that should trigger this topic:

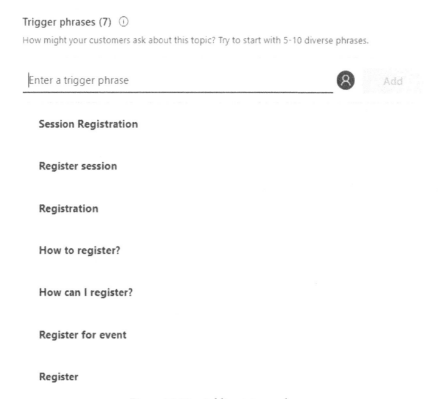

Trigger phrases (7) ⓘ

How might your customers ask about this topic? Try to start with 5-10 diverse phrases.

Enter a trigger phrase   Add

Session Registration

Register session

Registration

How to register?

How can I register?

Register for event

Register

Figure 10.12 – Adding trigger phrases

8. Click **Save topic**:

Now, we need to open and configure how the bot reacts when the conversation flows to this newly created topic.

Configuring topics

To recap, bots are made up of many topics that define scenarios they can have a conversation about. Each topic is made up of nodes that drive a conversation's path. The experience of building out the topic's paths is much like Power Automate conditions, with a top-down sequential flow of steps. To begin configuring a topic, follow these steps:

1. Open the topic you wish to edit; in our case, we will open **Event Information**.

2. Click **Go to authoring canvas**.

3. By default, our topic has one **Message** node added to it after the trigger. Add a **Message** to respond to the user:

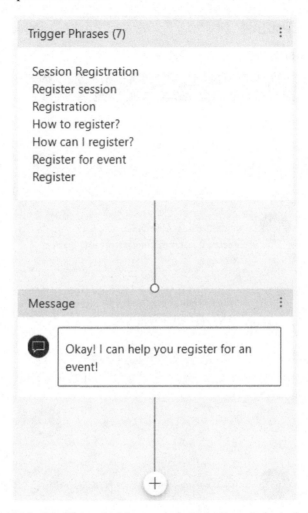

Figure 10.13 – Modifying the Message node in the Event Information topic

4. Click **Save**:

Figure 10.14 – Saving the topic

5. Click **Test bot** to test its functionality. Chat with the bot on the side chat window. Try using one of your trigger phrases and view the customized message node:

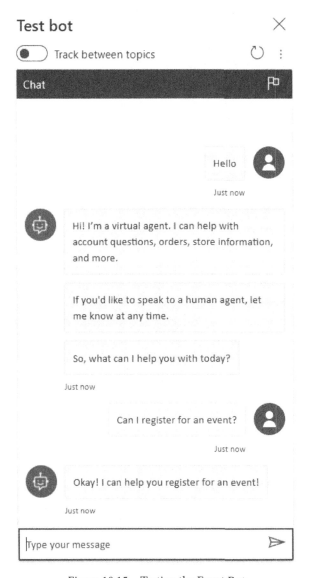

Figure 10.15 – Testing the Event Bot

As you test the bot, you will notice that the authoring canvas tracks which node the bot is currently executing. This can help you design and debug bots as you create them in real time. Let's continue building out this Event Registration topic by integrating the bot with Power Automate.

Integrating with Power Automate

When you're building chatbots in Power Virtual Agents for Teams, you may run into scenarios where basic question-and-answer conversations are not sufficient to meet the business's needs. If we want our bot to take more complex actions, we can call a Power Automate **flow** from within a topic. We can take user input from the conversation, pass it to the workflow, process it, and return some output to the user.

In our use case, we will create a flow that registers the user for a session by creating a new entry on the **Registrations** Dataverse table that we created in *Chapter 8, Power Apps in Teams*. We need to collect the user's phone number and the session they want to attend. Because Power Virtual Agent automatically stores the user's name in a variable, we do not need to prompt the user for it. To build this integration, perform these steps:

1. Open the Power Virtual Agents app in Teams.

2. Under **Chatbots**, navigate to the team that holds the bot.

3. Select the bot, then click **Topics**.

4. Open the **Event Registration** topic.

5. Click **Go to authoring canvas**.

6. Click the + icon at the bottom of the canvas to add a new node:

Figure 10.16 – Adding a new node

7. Select **Ask a question**:

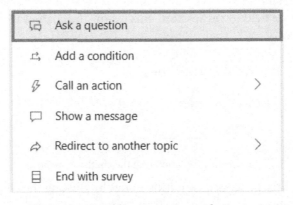

Figure 10.17 – Adding a question node to a topic

8. In the first text box, enter **Which session would you like to attend?**. For **Identify**, leave the default of **Multiple choice options**. In **Options for user**, enter **Session 1**, **Session 2**, and **Session 3**:

Figure 10.18 – Entering question information

9. Under **Save response as**, click **Var** to open the variable properties. Change the variable's **Name field** to **varSession**. This is how the chatbot will store the user's input. Click **Save**:

Figure 10.19 – Modifying the chatbot's variable

10. Remove the three generated condition nodes by clicking the ellipses and then selecting **Delete**.

11. Add a new question node. Enter **What is your phone number?** in the question's text box. For **Identify**, choose **Phone number**. Change the variable's name to **varPhone**. Then, click **Save**.

12. Add a new node and select **Call an action | Create a flow**. This will open a Power Automate experience inside the Power Virtual Agents app.

13. Select **Power Virtual Agents Flow Template**.

14. Rename the flow by clicking **Power Virtual Agents Flow Template** at the top left and enter **Register User**:

Figure 10.20 – Renaming the workflow

15. In the first step titled **Power Virtual Agents**, click **Add an input**. Choose **Text**. Change the name of the input to **vName**:

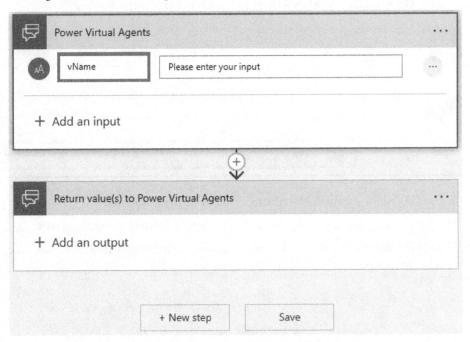

Figure 10.21 – Adding input from the chatbot to the workflow

16. Repeat *Step 15* for **vSession** and **vPhone**:

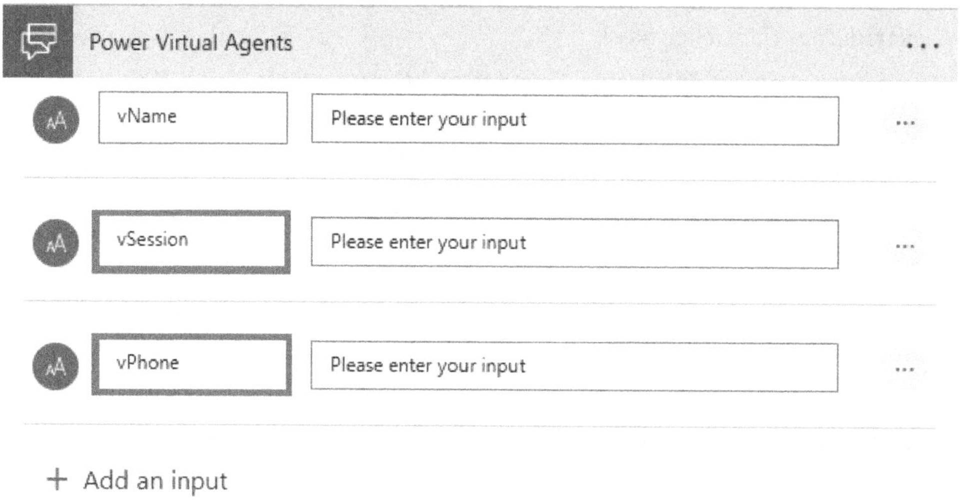

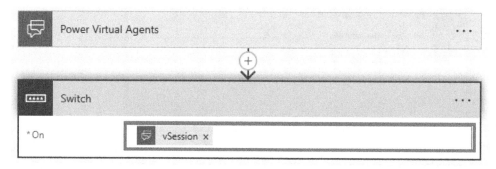

Figure 10.22 – Adding text input for the session and phone number to the workflow

17. Insert a new step after the trigger by clicking the + icon between the two steps. Click **Add an action**. Then, search for and add the **Switch** control.

18. In the **On** field, choose **vSession** from the **Dynamic content** popup:

Figure 10.23 – Adding a switch case to the workflow

19. In the first switch statement, which is **Case** under **Equals**, enter **Session 1**.

20. Inside the **Session 1** case, click **Add an action**. Search for **Add a new row**. Add the Dataverse action:

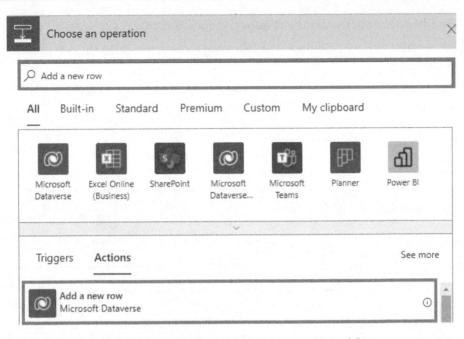

Figure 10.24 – Adding a Dataverse action to the workflow

21. For **Table name,** choose the **Registrations** table we built in *Chapter 8, Power Apps in Teams.*

22. Expand the fields by clicking **Show advanced options**.

23. Click the text box next to the **Name** field. In the **Dynamic content** popup, select **vName**. This will map the trigger's input variables to the **Add a new row** action:

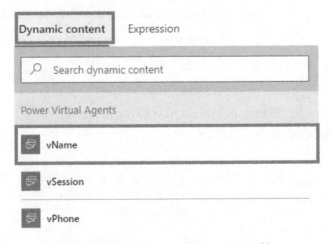

Figure 10.25 – Selecting the vName variable

24. For **Phone Number**, enter the **vPhone** dynamic content.

25. For **Session**, choose **Session 1**. The following screenshot shows the completed example:

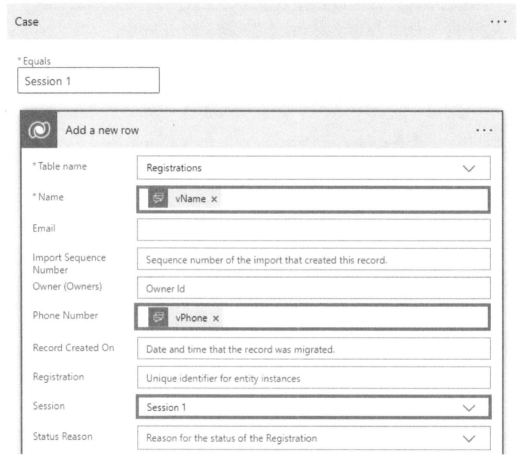

Figure 10.26 – Session 1 case

26. Add a new case by clicking the + icon next to the first case.

27. Repeat *Steps 19* to *26* for **Session 2** and **Session 3**.

28. Click **Save**.

29. Go back to the authoring canvas by clicking the left arrow button next to the flow's name:

Figure 10.27 – Returning to the authoring canvas

30. Add a new **Call an action** node. Select the flow you just created. In our case, this is **Register User**.

31. Map the Power Automate inputs to the corresponding topic variables, as shown in the following screenshot:

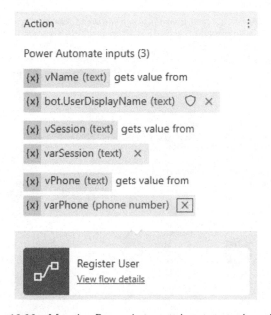

Figure 10.28 – Mapping Power Automate inputs to topic variables

32. Add a new **Show a message** node. In the question text field, enter **You are successfully registered!.**

33. Add a new node. Choose **Redirect to another topic | Goodbye**. Then, click **Save**.

34. Test the chatbot's functionality:

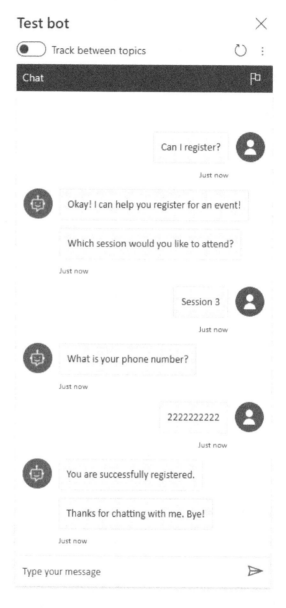

Figure 10.29 – Testing the chatbot's functionality

After ensuring the chatbot functions the way you expect, you are done! With that, you have successfully created a new topic that your bot can handle and taken advanced actions by integrating Power Automate. Now, we need to make the bot available for our users!

Publishing a bot

Once your chatbot has been created, you can publish it for your users. Publishing the bot is required for end users to chat with it. If you need to make changes to the bot in the future, simply publish it again and the bot will be updated. To publish the bot for the first time, follow these steps:

1. Open the Power Virtual Agents app in Teams.
2. Under **Chatbots**, navigate to the team that holds the bot.
3. Open the desired bot by clicking on its name.
4. Navigate to the **Publish** tab on the side menu:

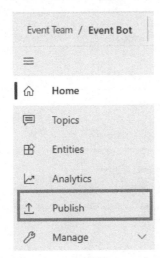

Figure 10.30 – The Publish tab in the Power Virtual Agents app

5. Select **Publish**:

Publish

Make your latest content available to end users. After you have published the bot for the first time, you can use the bot in Teams for yourself or make it available to others. Learn more

Figure 10.31 – Publishing the chatbot

6. Once the bot has been published, select **Availability options** to make it available to your users.

7. To make the chatbot available to members of the team, select **Show to my teammates and shared users**. This places the bot in the app store in the **Built by your colleagues** section. To submit the bot for approval and tenant-wide use, select **Show to everyone in my org**. We will choose to share the bot with our teammates and shared users:

← **Microsoft Teams**   ✕

Make your bot available to users in Microsoft Teams so they can find and use it. Learn more

Share link

Shared users can open the bot in Microsoft Teams with this link. Manage sharing

⌗ Copy link

Show in Teams app store

Make your bot appear in the Teams app store.

> **Show to my teammates and shared users**
> Appear under the Built by your colleagues section.

Show to everyone in my org
Submit to your admin for approval to appear under Built by your org section.

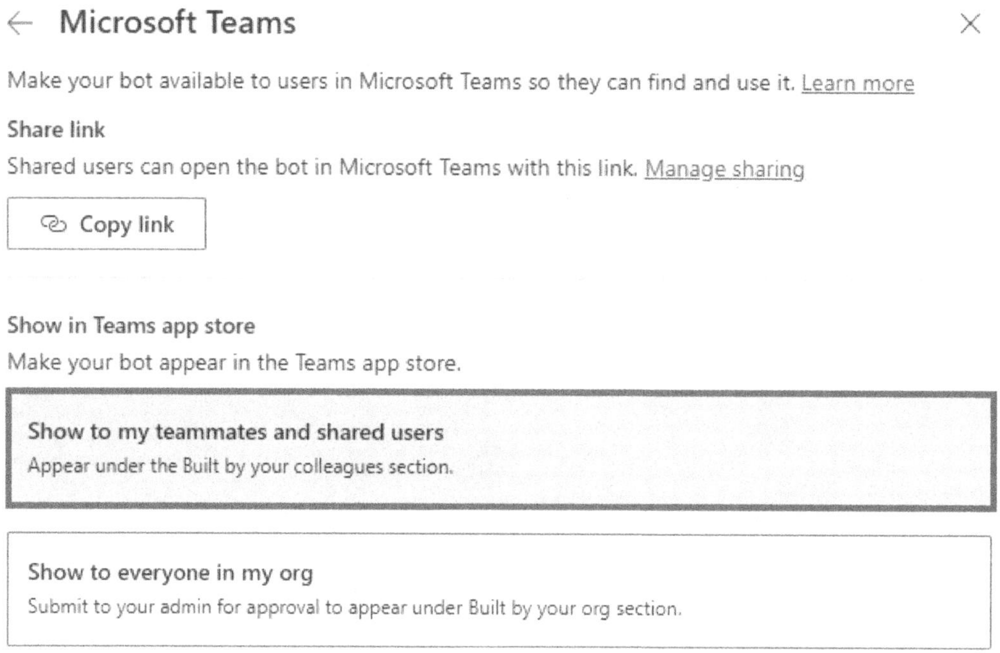

Figure 10.32 – Sharing the chatbot with teammates and shared users

8. By default, any user who is already a member of the team the bot was built in will have access. Enter any additional teams or security groups you wish to share the bot with. Then, click **Share**:

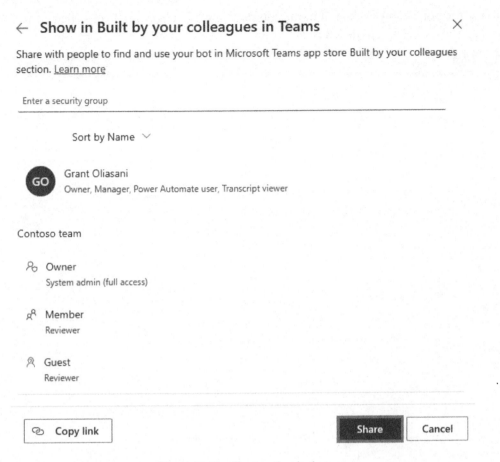

Figure 10.33 – Sharing the chatbot

After publishing and sharing the chatbot, you can discover it in the app store. Depending on the option you chose, it may be in the **Built by your org** or **Built by your colleagues** sections of the app store:

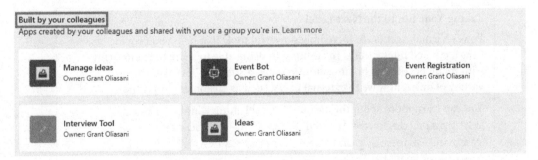

Figure 10.34 – The Built by your colleagues section of the app store

To use the bot, simply click on it in the app store and add it to your Teams client. The bot will appear as an app on the left rail:

Figure 10.35 – Chatting with the published bot

Once your bot has been published and shared with users in your organization, you can begin to gather feedback from them.

> **Taking Your Bot to the Next Level**
>
> Power Virtual Agents are incredibly powerful tools that help you provide smart, curated interactions. In addition to being able to share bots internally with members of your organization, you can also make bots available in a variety of different ways to external users, such as customers or partners.
>
> You can learn more about the avenues for publishing your bots externally at `https://docs.microsoft.com/en-us/power-virtual-agents/publication-fundamentals-publish-channels#in-this-section`.

You can also monitor your chatbot's performance and usage, as we'll see in the next section.

Monitoring usage

Chatbots that are built in Teams come with a full set of analytics that can help you understand how your users are using the bot, its performance, customer satisfaction, and more. To view the analytics for your bot, navigate to the bot in the Power Virtual Agents app in Teams. Once you open the bot, select the **Analytics** tab to view its charts and trends:

Figure 10.36 – The Analytics page

The **Summary** page contains charts and trends for overall bot performance and usage. It even uses AI to depict which topics have the greatest influence on performance. The **Customer Satisfaction** page will show you overall customer satisfaction, as indicated by conversation surveys, abandon rates, escalation rate, and other drivers. The **Sessions** screen will allow you to download transcripts of bot conversations over the past 30 days. This file contains the date and time, initial message, the topic that was triggered, and the full transcript.

Summary

As we have seen, the Power Virtual Agents app in Teams allows you to create, configure, test, and publish chatbots, all without ever leaving Microsoft Teams. You can build simple FAQ-style bots or integrate them with Power Automate for more advanced action-taking. Lastly, we explored some of the analytics power that comes with Power Virtual Agents in Teams.

In the next chapter, we will switch gears and look at the telephony capabilities in Teams.

Part 4: Voice

In this part, you will learn the concepts for integrating and deploying Microsoft Teams-based voice solutions.

This part comprises the following chapters:

11
Planning for Teams Phone

In addition to the core Microsoft Teams features such as instant messaging, webinars, meetings, and rich document collaboration, Microsoft Teams also features a complete cloud-based telephony platform. Microsoft Teams' Phone System can replace most (or all) of an organization's telephony needs, from basic **public switched telephone network (PSTN)** calling to complex auto attendants or phone trees.

In this chapter, we're going to explore the terminology and concepts necessary to understand how Microsoft Teams' Phone System works, covering the following topics:

- Terminology and concepts
- Selecting an architecture
- Planning network requirements
- Planning Teams settings and features

This foundational information will be important as you move into *Chapter 12, Deploying Teams Phone*.

Let's dive in!

Terminology and concepts

Before you start designing, implementing, or managing a Microsoft Teams phone system, you'll need to understand some basic terminology and concepts. This will help you communicate clearly with vendors, partners, other engineers, and end users.

Teams Phone

The overall platform is called **Teams Phone**, though some documentation previously referred to it as **Cloud Private Branch Exchange** (**Cloud PBX**), as well as **Phone System**. The term *Phone System* now generally refers to the license assignment enabling telephony features. Phone System is the Microsoft-hosted PBX system, providing both internal and external calling capabilities.

Phone numbers

When building a phone system, one of the earliest questions you'll probably ask is: "*Where do I get my phone numbers?*" The answer will depend on a number of factors, such as the following:

- If you want all-new phone numbers
- If you want to maintain your existing phone numbers
- Which organization currently owns your phone numbers
- Which types of interoperability you need to maintain with legacy equipment
- Existing **service provider** (**SP**) contracts
- Need for rapid **proof of concept** (**POC**)
- Investment in time, hardware, and configuration

These questions will invariably lead you to select one of the following three available options:

- **Calling Plans**—A calling plan is essentially a subscription package that provides a phone number and a bundle of minutes. You can use Microsoft-provided phone numbers or go through the **porting** process to transfer your numbers from your current provider to Microsoft. Calling plan minutes are pooled across all users in the organization. Once you've exceeded the number of minutes in the pool, you can purchase **communications credits** to cover the additional minutes you'll need. Communications credits are essentially pre-paid minutes that are charged against your users making phone calls to the **public switched telephone network** (**PSTN**). Communications credits are also required when configuring toll-free dial-in conferencing numbers.

- **Direct Routing**—With Direct Routing, you utilize specialized appliances called **session border controllers** (**SBCs**) to integrate your on-premises phone system with the Microsoft solution. Direct Routing enables an organization to configure a certain level of interoperability between platforms. Phone numbers are typically provided by an existing carrier or operator, though you can also use calling plans with Direct Routing.

- **Operator Connect**—A newer option for Microsoft Teams Phone, Operator Connect is very much like a carrier or operator-managed Direct Routing implementation. With Operator Connect, supported operators manage the SBCs for your organization.

Each communications solution has its own advantages. We'll look at them more closely in *Chapter 12, Deploying Teams Phone*.

Session Initiation Protocol

Session Initiation Protocol (**SIP**) is a networking communications protocol that is used for initiating, maintaining, and terminating sessions for voice, video, or other messaging platforms. SIP is primarily used in conjunction with internet-based telephony systems that utilize **Voice over Internet Protocol** (**VoIP**).

Session Border Controller

A **Session Border Controller** (**SBC**) is either a hardware or software appliance that is used to connect and regulate communications traffic between disparate systems. SBCs are used to handle negotiations between user agents and SIP server systems, typically existing on the internet edge of an organization. SBCs control traffic that traverses trunks—the logical collection of virtual channels, circuits, or pathways between endpoints.

Service numbers

In addition to phone numbers for end users, many organizations need general phone numbers that go to automated features such as auto attendants or call queues (which we'll explore in the upcoming sections, later in this chapter). Service phone numbers can be either toll-based or toll-free and feature high concurrent call capacities, allowing many external callers to dial the number simultaneously. Service phone numbers can be **ported** (or transferred) from your existing carrier or operator to Microsoft.

Auto attendants

If you've ever called a business and had the opportunity to navigate through a menu of options (such as "*Press 1 for Sales*"), then you've used an **interactive voice response** (**IVR**) system. Microsoft calls this navigation feature an **auto attendant**, while other vendors may refer to it as a phone tree or call tree.

Auto attendants can have several destinations, including the following:

- The operator
- A regular user
- Another auto attendant or a call queue
- A voicemail box
- An external phone number
- An announcement (either a pre-recorded audio file or a text message that the auto attendant can read to the caller)

Auto attendants can also adhere to schedules, allowing you to configure different routing options for businesses, non-business activities, and holiday hours.

Call queues

A **call queue** is a method of routing callers to a pool of people for a certain issue, question, or topic. Callers can be inserted into a queue by calling a service number directly; they may also be added to the queue by an auto attendant.

Agents are members of the organization who are responsible for answering calls in a queue.

A call queue typically provides some sort of a greeting message, music, or other audio during the hold time, call routing in **first-in, first-out** (**FIFO**) order to agents, and handles overflow and timeout scenarios.

Audio conferencing

Many organizations need meeting participants to be able to dial in to attend a phone conference. This feature is commonly known as a **conference** or **bridge number**.

While most Microsoft Teams users will join via the Teams client (either on their computer or through a mobile device), there may be scenarios where that isn't possible. Joining a call via the Teams client does require high-speed internet connectivity. If call participants find themselves without high-speed data networking, audio conferencing provides a way for them to call a telephone number and be joined to the meeting.

Audio conferencing also provides the ability to dial out from a meeting and invite another number to the call. If you want to provide toll-free conference bridge numbers or want to be able to dial out from meetings to international numbers, you will need to purchase communications credits for your organization.

Resource accounts

A resource account is a non-person account that Microsoft Teams utilizes for certain features. In *Chapter 6, Microsoft Teams Rooms*, resource accounts were used for setting up Microsoft Teams Rooms devices.

Resource accounts are also used to configure other Microsoft Teams Phone features, such as auto attendants and call queues.

Resource accounts used for auto attendants or call queues will require a license—either a free **Microsoft 365 Phone System – Virtual User** license or a paid **Phone System** user license.

Dial plans

A **dial plan** is simply a set of rules that defines how Teams will act on numbers that a user dials. This includes handling things such as external dialing prefixes or internal extensions.

There are two types of dial plans: **service-scoped** and **tenant-scoped**.

Service-scoped dial plans are non-configurable and are provided by Teams Phone System. There is a service-scoped dial plan configured for every country or region where the service is available. A service-scoped dial plan is assigned to every user automatically, based on the configured location for the user.

A tenant-scoped dial plan is configured in the tenant. Tenant dial plans have two further categories: tenant-scoped and user-scoped. A user plan is specifically applied to individuals, whereas a tenant plan covers everyone in the tenant.

A user's **effective dial plan** is a combination of a service-scoped plan for their region and as well as an applied user or tenant dial plan. The following table lists the possible combinations of effective dial plans:

Effective dial plan	Notes
Service Country	This is the default dial plan. If there is no tenant plan configured and no user plan assigned to the user, the user's effective plan will be set to the service-scoped plan for their assigned region.
Tenant Global – Service Country	If an organization has a tenant dial plan defined, it will be merged with the service country dial plan associated with their usage location. This will then become the effective dial plan.
Tenant User – Service Country	If an organization has defined a user dial plan and assigned it to a user, the user will receive an effective dial plan of their merged service country plan and the user plan.

Table 11.1 – Effective dial-plan inheritance

You can have up to 1,000 dial plans in your tenant.

Next, we'll look at some more specific calling features of the Microsoft Teams Phone platform.

Calling features

Teams Phone System has a myriad of calling features designed to provide parity to traditional on-premises PBX systems. In this section, we'll discuss some of the unique features, as well as some common competitive features.

Emergency calling

With traditional telephony, a phone number is directly tied to a physical address. When the phone number is moved to a new location, the provider updates the physical location in their records, which allows emergency services (fire, ambulance, police) to know exactly where to go.

The portability of internet-based services means that the actual usage location for a particular phone number no longer matches the address registered with the carrier.

> **Ray Baum's Act**
>
> In 2019, the **United States (US) Federal Communications Commission (FCC)** adopted rules under *Section 506* of *Ray Baum's Act*. The rules specified that information for emergency locations was to be conveyed with 911 calls. Per the rule, dispatchable location information (including a **civic address**, plus applicable information such as a building, floor, suite, or room number) must be provided for emergency calls after January 6, 2022. For more information on Ray Baum's Act and dispatchable locations, see `https://www.fcc.gov/911-dispatchable-location`.

When working with emergency calling, the following terms are used:

- **Emergency address**—An emergency address is a physical location, sometimes also referred to as a street address or civic address (a **post office (PO)** box is not a civic address). The emergency address is used to route calls to the appropriate local dispatch service.

- **Place**—A place is data that is used as a refinement for an emergency address. A place can be descriptive information such as a floor, building number, office or suite number, or a wing.

- **Emergency location**—An emergency location, as with an emergency address, is a physical address location. If you add one or more places to an emergency address, a location is created for each combination of the emergency address and place.

- **Registered address**—A registered address is a specific address assigned to each user. A registered address is also known as a **static emergency address** or an **address of record (AOR)**.

- **Public-safety answering point (PSAP)**—A PSAP is a call center responsible for routing emergency calls.

- **Dynamic emergency calling**—By using the geolocating features of the Teams client, emergency location information is automatically routed to the appropriate PSAP.

In addition to the civic or street address, emergency locations can have geographic coordinates (latitude and longitude) associated with them to ensure that responders are heading to the right location.

E911 location identification and routing

In the US, when an emergency or 911 call is placed, Teams makes routing decisions based on the type of calling architecture. Configuring Teams Dynamic **Enhanced 911 (E911)** will allow Teams to find the location of a caller, route that caller to the appropriate **Public Safety Answering Point (PSAP)** or regional **Emergency Call Response Center (ECRC)**, and notify additional corporate resources (such as a security desk) of a placed emergency call.

If your organization is using Teams Calling Plans or Operator Connect, when a user dials an emergency number, the call is routed to the PSAP in the following order:

1. Whether the emergency address is dynamically determined by the Teams client via the trusted IP address where the client is connecting from and the defined network location in the **location information service (LIS)**.

2. If no location information for the user is defined in the LIS, the static registered emergency address associated with the user's phone number in Teams will be used.

If your organization is using Direct Routing, the call is routed to the PSAP based on the following order of operations:

1. Whether the emergency address can be determined by the Teams client to be at a defined network location in the **location information service (LIS)**.

2. If no location information for the user is defined in the LIS, the static registered emergency address configured with the associated **Emergency Routing Service (ERS)** connected to the Direct Routing **session border controller (SBC)** will be used. If no static location is defined within the ERS, the call will be routed to the **Emergency Call Response Center (ECRC)**.

> **About the Emergency Call Response Center**
>
> The ECRC is a regional response center that will intercept emergency calls, verify location information, and then route that emergency call to the appropriate PSAP.

In the US, an emergency call will be routed to a PSAP or ECRC based on the following order:

1. If a Teams client is located within a tenant-defined dynamic emergency location defined in the LIS, emergency calls from that client will be routed to the PSAP serving that geographic location.

2. If a Teams client is not located at a tenant-defined dynamic emergency location, emergency calls from that client will be routed to the ECRC and screened by a national call center. The ECRS will determine the location of the caller before the call is transferred to the PSAP serving that geographic location.

3. If the ECRC screening center is unable to determine the specific location, the call will be transferred to the PSAP serving the caller's static registered address.

Microsoft also took additional steps to help end users specify their own dispatchable locations, which helps ensure emergency services are available as part of their organization's work-from-home policy. Administrators can configure this using an emergency calling policy, as shown here:

```
New-CsTeamsEmergencyCallingPolicy -Identity E911WFH
-ExternalLocationLookupMode Enabled
```
```
Grant-CsTeamsEmergencyCallingPolicy -PolicyName E911WFH
-Identity <user@contoso.com>
```

Correctly configuring emergency calling is extremely important in order to ensure the most efficient routing of **first responder** (**FR**) resources.

Call parking

Call parking and retrieval is a feature that allows a user to place a call on hold, and then for that user (or a different one) to resume the call.

Shared line appearance

As part of the Phone System delegation feature set, **shared line appearance** allows managers (the user who authorizes usage) to assign access to a delegate to make and receive calls on their behalf. Delegates can make and receive PSTN and Teams calls on behalf of their manager, as well as hold and resume calls on their behalf.

Blocking inbound calls

Some organizations may wish to block inbound calls from a PSTN. Teams Phone supports using **regular expressions (regexes)** to define patterns of numbers to block. This feature is only configurable via PowerShell.

Voicemail

Cloud voicemail is automatically provisioned for Teams users. Voicemail messages are deposited in the user's associated Exchange mailbox (either in Exchange Online or Exchange on-premises, if hybrid connectivity has been configured). In addition to features such as customized greetings and visual voicemail, mail flow or transport rules can be configured to encrypt voicemail messages.

Caller ID

Microsoft Teams Phone also supports **caller identifier (caller ID)** features for both inbound and outbound calling. Caller ID displays two pieces of information: the **calling-line ID (CLID)** or PSTN number and the **calling party name (CNAM)**.

For inbound calls, Phone System will show the incoming PSTN number as the caller ID. If the number is associated with either a contact in Azure or a personal contact, the Teams client will resolve it and display the caller ID based on that information. If the incoming number is not associated with a contact object, the CNAM display name will also be displayed if it is available.

For outbound calls, Teams Phone can be configured to show the following information:

- Telephone number assigned to a user
- Anonymous, which is displayed when the outbound caller ID is removed
- A service or substitute phone number to mask the direct line identity
- Calling party name

Caller ID settings are managed through Caller ID policies in the Teams admin center.

Contact center

A **contact center** is a third-party platform that allows integration with Microsoft Teams Phone System. Contact centers can be used to connect to workflow or **customer relationship management** (**CRM**) systems. Contact centers may be configured to connect directly via SBCs and direct routing, via the Microsoft Graph communications **application programming interface** (**API**), or through Power Platform.

Contact centers are purchased and maintained separately from the Microsoft Teams Phone System platform.

Now that you're familiar with Phone System terminology, let's shift gears and talk about selecting the correct architecture.

Selecting an architecture

Selecting a calling architecture to suit the physical, legal, and technical needs of your organization is a key decision in your planning process. While you can utilize multiple routes to the **PSTN**, choosing the best route will be key in uncomplicating your deployment. There are three major architectures you can select from, as follows:

- Calling Plans for Microsoft 365
- Direct Routing
- Operator Connect

These architectures allow you to have flexibility, both when integrating into an existing VoIP infrastructure and selecting a PSTN voice provider. The following table shows feature availability across architectures, which can be used to help guide design discussions:

	Calling Plans for Microsoft 365	Direct Routing	Operator Connect
Existing PSTN infrastructure (SBC or voice trunks) will continue to be used		X	X
Fully-managed solution			X
Cloud-only solution with no new on-premises voice infrastructure hardware (trunks, SBCs, etc.)	X		X
No existing on-premises voice infrastructure hardware (trunks, SBCs, etc.)	X		
Quick setup	X		X
Quick pilot or proof-of-concept	X		
Centralized billing through Microsoft	X		
Sites located in calling plan markets	X		
Supports coexistence with existing PBX infrastructure		X	
Supports migration from legacy phone system		X	
Mix and match infrastructures	X	X	X
Maintain existing service provider agreements		X	X
Integrated End to End Number management experience in Teams Admin Center	X		X
Supports third-party interop scenarios		X	X
Supports local PSTN calling via survivable branch appliances		X	
Ability to maintain regional regulatory compliance requirements		X	
Supports localities outside of Microsoft Calling Plans regions		X	X
Supports integration of analog devices		X	

Table 11.2 – Teams Phone architectures

Next, we'll jump into the different types of Teams Phone architectures and expand on some of the content in *Table 11.2*.

Calling Plans for Microsoft 365

Calling Plans is Microsoft's native solution and will provide the fastest route to using Microsoft Phone System. A Calling Plans deployment only requires software licensing from Microsoft and cloud-based configuration to get started. While dedicated client hardware devices (such as handsets) can be used, they are not required. The Microsoft Teams client is designed to be able to make and receive calls directly from the **user interface (UI)**.

Each calling plan license is measured in minutes per licensed user, per month. It's important to note that unassigned licenses *will not* contribute to the pool. Minutes are pooled within the tenant, according to the country and tier of the calling plan.

The following table describes the licenses available for Microsoft Teams Phone:

Service plan name	Stock-keeping unit (SKU) part name	Service plan notes
Microsoft Enterprise E5	ENTERPRISEPREMIUM	Includes Phone System and Audio Conferencing
Microsoft Enterprise E5 (without Audio Conferencing)	ENTERPRISEPREMIUM_NOPSTNCONF	Includes Phone System; no Audio Conferencing features
Audio Conferencing	MCOMEETADV	Standalone Audio Conferencing license
Audio Conferencing Pay-as-you-go	MCOMEETACPEA	Audio Conferencing license utilizing communications credits
Phone System	MCOEV	Phone System standalone license
Domestic Calling Plan	MCOPSTN1	3,000 minutes per user/month for US/Puerto Rico (PR)/ Canada (CA); 1,200 minutes per user/month for European Union (EU)
Domestic and International Calling Plan	MCOPSTN2	3,000 domestic minutes per user/month for US/PR/ CA; 1,200 domestic minutes per user/month for EU; 600 international minutes
Domestic Calling Plan	MCOPSTN5	120 domestic minutes per user/month (excludes US)
Domestic Calling Plan	MCOPSTN6	240 minutes per user/month (excludes US)
Communications Credits	MCOPSTNPP	Basic communications credits

Table 11.3 – Microsoft Teams Phone System service plans

For example, if an organization had 2,500 users all in one country, all licensed with 120-minute calling plans, the tenant/country would own a pool of 300,000 minutes.

In addition, a Teams Phone and 3,000-minute Domestic Calling Plan bundle are available at a discounted cost compared to purchasing both a Phone System and Domestic Calling Plan separately.

> **Calling Plan Pricing**
>
> For updated information on the Teams Phone and Calling Plan bundles for Microsoft 365 (including current pricing), see the following articles:
>
> `https://docs.microsoft.com/en-us/MicrosoftTeams/calling-plans-for-office-365`
>
> `https://techcommunity.microsoft.com/t5/small-and-medium-business-blog/teams-phone-with-calling-plan-available-in-33-markets-on-january/ba-p/2967643`

Inbound toll local and long-distance calling minutes, Teams to Teams calls, as well as inbound service numbers are not metered and are included with calling plans. Outbound calling minutes are metered per minute and covered by the calling plans.

International numbers not included in the domestic calling plans and toll-free numbers are covered by Communication Credits.

While calling plans don't require the purchase of additional telephony-routing hardware, they may not be available in all regions.

As a reminder, in order to use telephony features, a user must have—at a minimum—a license that includes Phone System.

Direct Routing

Direct Routing is an architecture that allows Teams Phone integration via a certified Session Border Controller (**SBC**) to a third-party SIP-based **public branch exchange** (**PBX**), analog gateway, or trunking service. This allows for the integration of non-VoIP-based technologies (such as analog ports and gateways) into the Teams cloud-based architecture.

Many larger organizations with existing telephony services evaluate Direct Routing because of its integration abilities. Direct Routing can work with any existing carrier—building on the capabilities of traditional telecommunications services.

Unlike Calling Plans (where all infrastructure is hosted), Direct Routing requires local telephony or network infrastructure to complete the integration. There are three core types of appliances that can be integrated into Direct Routing scenarios, as follows:

- Session border controllers
- Survivable branch appliances
- Analog telephone adapters

We'll look at each of these next.

Session border controllers (SBCs)

To support Direct Routing, a certified **session border controller** (**SBC**) must be used. These network edge devices allow for integration between Teams and a third-party SIP-based PBX, analog gateway, or trunking service. Session border controllers can be physical appliances, virtual appliances, or even hosted services.

Direct Routing can be configured with physical hardware, as shown in the following diagram:

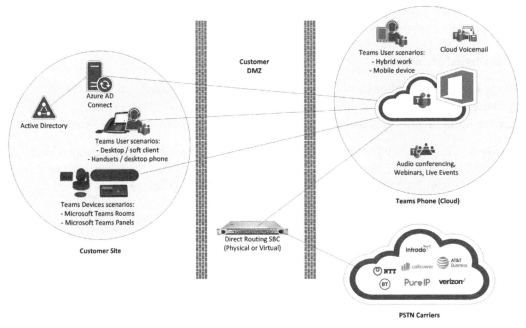

Figure 11.1 – Direct Routing with customer premises equipment

As shown in *Figure 11.1*, a physical or virtual SBC is placed on the customer premises. **Peering** is configured between the on-premises SBC and Teams Phone System in Microsoft 365. The SBC will also be peered via a SIP trunk or a traditional digital carrier trunk to the PSTN carrier.

More about Peering

Peering is a combination of a business relationship or agreement in addition to a networking configuration. Peering allows two organizations to agree to connect their networks without the use of additional interconnected parties. Peering is generally performed at a location called an **internet exchange point (IXP)**—a location where both organizations have networking equipment.

Most organizations require a peer to meet the following requirements: a publicly routed autonomous system number (**ASN**), a block of public IP addresses, and a network edge router capable of running **Border Gateway Protocol (BGP)**.

The architecture represented in *Figure 11.2* is nearly identical, except this time, a virtual SBC appliance is deployed, such as one in Azure Marketplace. Peering is configured between the virtual SBC and the Teams Cloud Voice service. The SBC will also be peered via a SIP trunk to the PSTN carrier:

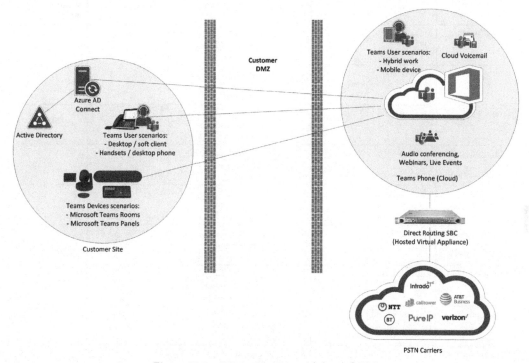

Figure 11.2 – Direct Routing with hosted SBC

Some vendors can even provide preconfigured SBCs, as is the case with Call2Teams or AudioCodes Live. In addition, many carriers offer **SBC-as-a-service** (**SBCaas**) offerings that can be bundled with their SIP trunk offerings.

Hosted SBC Options

Several vendors offer some form of preconfigured or hosted SBC. You can learn more about some of the hosted solution providers here:

Call2Teams: `https://www.call2teams.com`

AudioCodes Live Essentials: `https://liveteams.audiocodes.com/azure-live-essentials-support`

TeamMate: `https://www.teammatetechnology.com`

As of this writing, Microsoft has certified the following devices for Direct Routing:

Vendor	Product	Non-media bypass	Media bypass	Software version	911 Service Provider capable*	Emergency Location Identification Number (ELIN)- capable
AudioCodes	Mediant 500 SBC	X	X	Supported 7.20A.258 (Recommended 7.40A.100)	X	X
AudioCodes	Mediant 800 SBC	X	X	Supported 7.20A.258 (Recommended 7.40A.100)	X	X
AudioCodes	Mediant 2600 SBC	X	X	Supported 7.20A.258 (Recommended 7.40A.100)	X	X
AudioCodes	Mediant 4000 SBC	X	X	Supported 7.20A.258 (Recommended 7.40A.100)	X	X
AudioCodes	Mediant 1000B SBC	X	X	Supported 7.20A.250 (Recommended 7.20A.258)	X	X
AudioCodes	Mediant 9000 SBC	X	X	Supported 7.20A.258 (Recommended 7.40A.100)	X	X
AudioCodes	Virtual Edition SBC	X	X	Supported 7.20A.258 (Recommended 7.40A.100)	X	X
AudioCodes	Mediant Cloud Edition SBC	X	X	Supported 7.20A.258 (Recommended 7.40A.100)	X	X
Ribbon Communications	SBC 5100/5110	X	X	Supported 8.2 and 7.2 (Recommended 9.2)	X	
Ribbon Communications	SBC 5200/5210	X	X	Supported 8.2 and 7.2 (Recommended 9.2)	X	
Ribbon Communications	SBC 5400	X	X	Supported 8.2 and 7.2 (Recommended 9.2)	X	
Ribbon Communications	SBC 7000	X	X	Supported 8.2 and 7.2 (Recommended 9.2)	X	
Ribbon Communications	SBC SWe	X	X	Supported 8.2 and 7.2 (Recommended 9.2)	X	
Ribbon Communications	SBC 1000	X	X	8.x or 9.x	X	X

Ribbon Communications	SBC 2000	X	X	8.x or 9.x	X	X
Ribbon Communications	SBC SWe Lite	X	X	8.x or 9.x	X	X
Ribbon Communications	EdgeMarc Series	X		15.6.1		
ThinkTel	Think 365 SBC	X		1.4		
Oracle	AP 1100	X	X	8.3.0.0.1	X	X
Oracle	AP 3900	X	X	8.3.0.0.1	X	X
Oracle	AP 4600	X	X	8.3.0.0.1	X	X
Oracle	AP 6300	X	X	8.3.0.0.1	X	X
Oracle	AP 6350	X	X	8.3.0.0.1	X	X
Oracle	VME	X	X	8.3.0.0.1	X	X
TE-SYSTEMS	AnyNode	X	X	Supported 3.20 (Recommended 4.0)	X	X
Metaswitch	Perimeta SBC	X	X	4.7 (4.9 for Media Bypass)	X	X
Cisco	Cisco Unified Border Element (CUBE) for 1000 Series Integrated Services Routers	X	X	Supported IOS XE Amsterdam 17.2.1r (Recommended 17.6.1a)	X	
Cisco	Cisco Unified Border Element (CUBE) for 4000 Series Integrated Services Routers	X	X	Supported IOS XE Amsterdam 17.2.1r (Recommended 17.6.1a)	X	
Cisco	Cisco Unified Border Element (CUBE) for 1000V Series Cloud Services Router	X	X	Supported IOS XE Amsterdam 17.2.1r (Recommended 17.3.3)	X	
Cisco	Cisco Unified Border Element (CUBE) for 1000 Series Aggregation Services Routers	X	X	Supported IOS XE Amsterdam 17.2.1r (Recommended 17.6.1a)	X	
Cisco	Cisco Unified Border Element (CUBE) for Catalyst 8000 Edge Platforms	X	X	Supported IOS XE Amsterdam 17.3.2 (Recommended 17.6.1a)	X	

Avaya	Avaya Session Border Controller for Enterprise (ASBCE)	X	X	Release 8.1.1 (8.1.2 for Media Bypass)		
Nokia	Nokia Session Border Controller	X		19.5 (1908)		
Nokia	Nokia Session Border Controller	X		20.8	X	
Italtel	NetMatch-S CI	X		Supported 5.0 (Recommended 5.1)		
Ericsson	vSBC 2.16	X				
Cataleya	Orchid Link	X		3.1		
ULTATEL	Teams SBC	X	X	1.6		
Atos	Atos Unify OpenScape Session Border Controller	X		V10R1.2		
Sansay Inc.	vmVSXi	X	X	10.5.1.354-vm-S-x64		
Enghouse Networks	Dialogic BorderNet SBC	X	X	3.9.0-786		
Patton Electronics Co.	Patton SmartNode eSBC	X		3.19.x		
M5 Technologies	Mediatrix Sentinel Series	X		DGW 48.0.2340 (Recommended DGW 48.1.2503)		
Ekinops	Ekinops Session Border Controller (ONeSBC)	X	X	6.6.1m5ha1		
Ekinops	Ekinops Virtual Session Border Controller (ONEvSBC)	X	X	6.6.1m5ha1		
46 Labs LLC	Hyperconverged Voice	X	X	HCVoice 1.0.6		

Table 11.4 – Certified session border controllers

As the information is subject to change, we recommend you check back periodically to see if new devices or software versions are recommended.

Current List of Direct Routing Hardware

A current list of certified SBCs can be found here: `https://docs.microsoft.com/en-us/MicrosoftTeams/direct-routing-border-controllers`

Media Bypass

Media Bypass allows you direct Teams Media between a Teams client and SBC directly versus tunneling through the Teams Cloud Voice service. This shortens the media path between the Teams endpoint and the SBC, reducing the number of hops and keeping media local to the corporate network instead of sending it via the Teams Cloud Voice service.

The diagram in *Figure 11.3* depicts how the media path chooses a direct connection to the SBC while the signaling path travels the Teams Cloud Voice service:

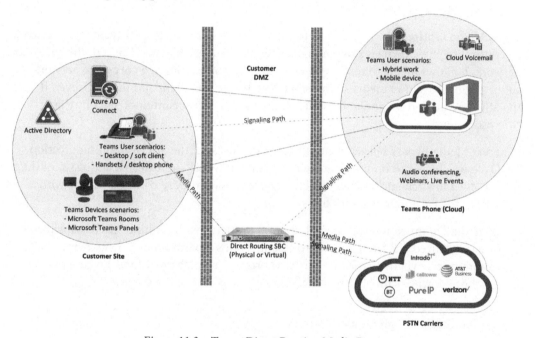

Figure 11.3 – Teams Direct Routing Media Bypass

Without Media Bypass in place, both the media and the signaling would go via the Teams Cloud Voice service.

> **Media Bypass Deep Dive**
>
> Media Bypass is a complex networking concept that requires careful network planning, focusing largely on the number of internal users, types of conversations, and endpoints that will be parts of conversations.
>
> Additional information on Direct Routing Media Bypass can be found here: `https://docs.microsoft.com/en-us/microsoftteams/direct-routing-plan-media-bypass`

Local Media Optimization

Local Media Optimization (**LMO**) lets you further control voice quality on your network by controlling how media traffic flows between the Teams client and SBCs in the customer network. It allows media to remain local within the boundaries of a corporate network's subnets and also allows media streams between the Teams client and the SBC, even if the SBCs are behind corporate firewalls with private IPs that cannot be seen by the Microsoft cloud.

Whereas Media Bypass relies on the external IP address of the SBC for communication, LMO allows clients to communicate with both the internal and external addresses of the SBC. LMO allows clients to detect whether the endpoint they're communicating with is internal to the corporate network or external.

Local Media Optimization is designed for environments with multiple SBC-enabled sites to use a centralized SIP trunking environment. In this environment, downstream SBCs can communicate via that core SBC (or SBC proxy) to the Teams Cloud Voice service, even if those downstream SBC IP addresses are not visible to the service.

> **Local Media Optimization Deep Dive**
>
> Much as with Media Bypass, LMO is a complex networking topic. There isn't necessarily a "one-size-fits-all" approach, since architecture largely depends on the number of sites and number of endpoints in a site to determine the best configuration.
>
> Additional information on Direct Routing LMO can be found here: `https://docs.microsoft.com/en-us/microsoftteams/direct-routing-media-optimization`

While we won't go into configuration details for LMO in this book, it's a potentially useful option to consider, depending on your organization's site and network configuration.

Location-Based Routing

Location-Based Routing (LBR) is designed to allow you to manage your compliance with local toll restrictions—for example, your locality may have regulations that prohibit bypassing the PSTN to avoid long-distance telephony charges.

Location-based routing lets you restrict attempts to bypass tolls by using a policy in conjunction with the user's geographic location. The policy evaluates where the user is at the time they receive an inbound call or place an outbound call.

LBR Deep Dive

Care should be taken when configuring location-based routing to ensure that you're adhering to your locality's regulations. If no regulations apply to your jurisdiction, it's likely unnecessary that you'll need to configure this feature. Additional information on Location-Based Routing can be found here: `https://docs.microsoft.com/en-us/microsoftteams/ location-based-routing-plan`

Location-based routing is an advanced voice routing configuration that many organizations won't need to configure. Consult your local telephony regulations to determine if any configuration is necessary.

Survivable branch appliances

In some cases, a **survivable branch appliance (SBA)** will need to be deployed to support telephony at a site when the Teams client loses connectivity to the cloud-based service.

Survivable branch appliances are used when a site is unable to connect to Microsoft via the session border controller but is still able to access the PSTN network. The SBA can be used to facilitate phone calls. Many session border controllers have embedded features that allow them to act as survivable branch appliances. You'll need to check with your Direct Routing hardware vendor to verify your device's capabilities.

The diagram in *Figure 11.4* assumes that the session border controller includes the survivable branch appliance capability:

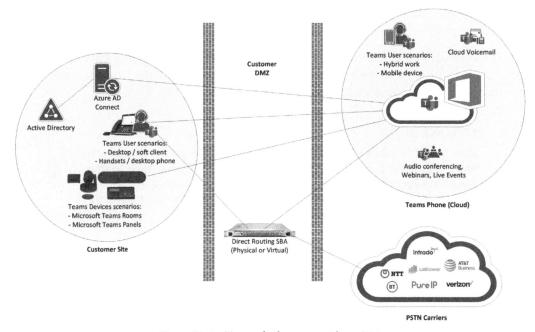

Figure 11.4 – Teams deployment with an SBA

When connectivity between the Teams client and Teams backend occurs, remote user calls are dropped, and further remote calls will not be reachable via the SBC anymore. For users inside the corporate network supported by a Teams Survivable Branch Appliance Policy, ongoing calls will be maintained, and further calls will occur via the SBA mode. A user's Teams client will display a banner showing it is in offline mode, as in *Figure 11.5*:

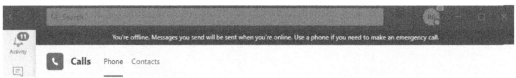

Figure 11.5 – Teams operating in offline mode

When connectivity is restored between the Teams client and Teams backend, remote users will be once again able to make and receive calls to the SBC. For inside corporate users, as soon as outgoing calls are finished, the client will fail back to normal operation and reconnect to the Teams backend and restore all Teams services.

Teams offline voice mode is only supported for the Teams Windows and macOS desktop client. Media Bypass must be configured on the SBC to ensure the Microsoft Teams client at the SBA site can have media flowing directly with the SBC. The SBC must be certified for SBA and run the minimum firmware version that supports SBA. As of this writing, the following vendors have certified SBAs for Microsoft Teams:

- AudioCodes
- Ribbon
- Oracle
- TE-SYSTEMS

In order to make use of an SBA, the Teams client needs to be aware of which SBAs are available in which sites.

> **SBA Deep Dive**
>
> As with many Direct Routing configurations, configuring an SBA is a deep topic.
>
> You can learn more about guidance for particular SBAs from the SBA vendor or through the *Microsoft Docs* site at the following link: `https://docs.microsoft.com/en-us/microsoftteams/direct-routing-survivable-branch-appliance`

Next, we'll look at methods for connecting legacy devices to the Microsoft Teams environment.

Analog telephone adapters

Analog telephone adapter (**ATA**) devices are used to connect analog devices to Teams Phone systems configured for Direct Routing. There are several use cases where ATA devices are still in use (such as fire alarms or other building management systems). Many of these devices can't be upgraded with newer digital devices, so an adapter is necessary to enable them to communicate with modern phone systems.

Microsoft has certified high-density analog telephone adapters to work alongside session border controllers, should you need to connect analog devices to your Direct Routing configuration. *Table 11.5* lists the currently certified ATA adapters:

Vendor	Product	Verified
AudioCodes	ATA-1	X
AudioCodes	ATA-2	X
Cisco	ATA 191 Multiplatform Analog Telephone Adapter	X
Oracle	ATA 191 Multiplatform Analog Telephone Adapter	X
Oracle	AP1100 Software Version 8.3.0.1.2	X
Oracle	AP3900 Software Version 8.3.0.1.2	X
Oracle	AP4600 Software Version 8.3.0.1.2	X
Oracle	AP6300 Software Version 8.3.0.1.2	X
Oracle	AP6350 Software Version 8.3.0.1.2	X
Oracle	VME Software Version 8.3.0.1.2	X
Ribbon	SBC 1000. Software version: 8.1.1 (build 527)	X
Ribbon	SBC 2000. Software version: 8.1.1 (build 527)	X
Ribbon	EdgeMarc 302. Software version: 16.1.1	X
Ribbon	EdgeMarc 304. Software version: 16.1.1	X
Ribbon	EdgeMarc 2900A. Software version: 16.1.1	X
Ribbon	EdgeMarc 4806. Software version: 16.1.1	X
Ribbon	EdgeMarc 4808. Software version: 16.1.1	X
Ribbon	EdgeMarc 6000. Software version: 16.1.1	X
TE-SYSTEMS	AnyNode with Grandstream GXW42xx (V1.0.7.10)	X

Table 11.5 – Certified Analog Telephone Adapters

Monitoring and troubleshooting Direct Routing

The following tools can be used to monitor and troubleshoot Direct Routing:

- The **Direct Routing Diagnostic Tool** can be run as a communications administrator on the Teams tenant to diagnose issues between the SBC and the Teams Cloud Voice service.

- Use the **Call Analytics Dashboard** and the SBC logs to see call failure responses and see full SIP traces between the SBC and the Teams Cloud Voice service.

- The **Health Dashboard for Direct Routing** is used to monitor the connection between the SBC and the Teams Cloud Voice service.

Next, we'll look at a new Direct Routing configuration available for Microsoft Teams.

Operator Connect

Operator Connect is an extension of Direct Routing that enables a more streamlined integration with third-party carriers. Operator Connect provides a framework that allows qualified operators to offer enhanced scalability and integration into the Teams environment.

One of the core benefits of Operator Connect is a simplified customer experience. Certified operators have parity to native Microsoft Calling Plan features and are backed by **service-level agreements (SLAs)**. The operator's support model is designed to provide an enhanced experience, improved quality, and **business continuity (BC)** to the customer.

This integration includes services for interconnection, number provisioning, management, reporting, **go-to-market (GTM)** strategy, operations, and communications, and provides streamlined support.

Interconnection between the Teams Cloud service and the carrier operator occurs via Direct peering through **Microsoft Azure Peering Service (MAPS)** for Voice. This allows the most direct path between the Teams Voice service and the Operator Voice service. A set of provisioning APIs and a dedicated operator portal enables seamless integration and provisioning of operator trunks to the Teams Cloud Voice service.

The following diagram shows an overview of Operator Connect:

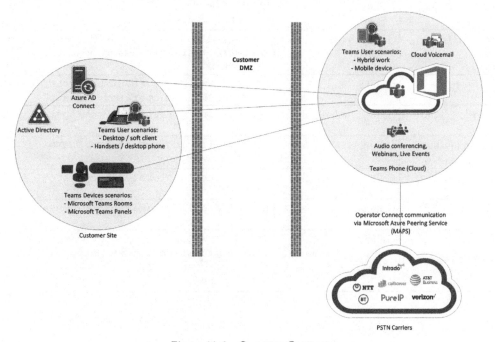

Figure 11.6 – Operator Connect

Next, we'll look at the conferencing feature of Operator Connect.

Operator Connect Conferencing

Operator Connect Conferencing allows you to connect third-party operator connect numbers to Teams meetings' Audio Conferencing. With this service, users can join Teams meetings using numbers hosted at third-party carriers. Without Operator Connect Conferencing, organizations can *only* use phone numbers provided by Microsoft for their Teams Audio Conferencing.

When these numbers are acquired through the Operator Connect carrier, they can be added to a Teams Audio Conferencing service just as with a Microsoft-provided number.

As of this writing, the following worldwide partners are certified for Operator Connect:

Vendor	Available features	More information
AT&T Business	Calling	https://www.business.att.com/collateral/att-cloud-voice-for-microsoft-teams-operator-connect.html
BT	Calling, conferencing	https://www.globalservices.bt.com/en/aboutus/operator-connect
CallTower	Calling	https://www.calltower.com/microsoft-operator-connect/
Colt Technology Services	Calling	https://www.colt.net/go/microsoft-operator-connect
Deutsch Telekom	Calling, conferencing	https://cloud.telekom.de/de/blog/cloud-software/microsoft-teams-operator-connect
Gamma	Calling	https://www.gamma.co.uk/products/microsoft-teams-operator-connect/
Intrado	Calling, conferencing	https://insight.intrado.com/operator-connect
Liquid Intelligent Technologies	Calling	https://liquidcloud.africa/OneVoice/
NTT	Calling, conferencing	https://hello.global.ntt/operator-connect
NuWave	Calling	https://ipilot.io/microsoft-operator-connect/
Optus	Calling	https://www.optus.com.au/enterprise/mobility/unified-communications/operator-connect-for-microsoft-teams-with-optus

Orange Business Services	Calling, conferencing	`https://www.orange-business.com/en/focus/operator-connect`
Pure IP	Calling	`https://info.pure-ip.com/operator-connect-ga`
Rogers	Calling	`https://www.rogers.com/business/voice-and-collaboration/operator-connect`
Singtel	Calling	`https://www.singtel.com/business/products-services/voice-collaboration/unified-communications/teams-uc-connector`
Swisscom	Calling	`https://www.swisscom.ch/en/business/enterprise/offer/worksmart/microsoft-teams-operator-connect.html`
Tata Communications	Calling	`https://www.tatacommunications.com/solutions/unified-communications/unified-communications-as-a-service/microsoft-teams-solutions/operator-connect/`
Telefónica Global Solutions	Calling	`https://www.globalsolutions.telefonica.com/en/operatorconnect/`
Telenor	Calling, conferencing	`https://www.telenor.no/bedrift/telefoni/teams/operator-connect`
Telia	Calling	`https://business.teliacompany.com/global-solutions/end-user-services/operator-connect`
Telstra	Calling	`https://www.telstra.com.sg/en/products/unified-communications/collaboration/telstra-calling-for-microsoft-teams`
Verizon	Calling	`https://www.verizon.com/business/resources/lp/operator-connect/`

Table 11.6 – Operator Connect partners

Not all partners are available in all regions, so you may want to filter partners using the following Operator Connect site: `https://cloudpartners.transform.microsoft.com/practices/microsoft-365-for-operators/directory`

> **Operator Connect Deep Dive**
>
> As with Direct Routing, Operator Connect has a lot of integration, which can amount to extended amounts of planning. For a deeper dive into Operator Connect features, see the following link: `https://docs.microsoft.com/en-us/microsoftteams/operator-connect-plan`.

Now that you have an understanding of the capabilities and features of the three types of Teams Phone architectures, let's jump into planning!

Planning network requirements

When planning a Teams Phone deployment, one of the most important tasks is to ensure that your network is configured correctly to support real-time audio and video network streams. There are a series of tools, assessments, and planners that can be leveraged to audit an organization's network. These tools will help prepare administrators to support Teams voice and video in both their corporate and remote networks.

At a high level, the following areas should be reviewed by an organization to ensure their network is ready for Teams voice. Careful validation and alignment with Teams' best practices and recommendations will minimize the potential for audio and video quality issues on the platform.

Network requirements

In order to achieve the most reliable performance and experiences, certain network requirements should be met. *Table 11.7* lists the base network performance requirements to run Teams Real-Time Voice and Video in an organization's environment:

Metric	Endpoint to Teams service	Customer network to Teams service
Latency (one way)	<50 milliseconds (ms)	<30 ms
Latency (Round Trip Time)	<100 ms	<60 ms
Burst packet loss	<10% during any 200 ms interval	<1% during any 200 ms interval
Packet loss	<1% during any 15-second (s) interval	<0.1% during any 15 s interval
Jitter	<30 ms during any 15 s interval	<15 ms during any 15 s interval
Packet reorder	<0.05% out-of-order packets	<0.01% out-of-order packets

Table 11.7 – Network connectivity requirements

As conditions on the organization's network begin to exceed the recommended thresholds, you may notice audio and video degradation.

Bandwidth requirements

Microsoft Teams gives you the best audio-, video-, and content-sharing experience, regardless of your network conditions. With variable codecs, media can be negotiated in limited bandwidth environments with minimal impact. In situations where bandwidth is not a concern, experiences can be optimized for quality, including up to 1080 **progressive scan (p)** video resolution, up to 30 **frames per second (FPS)** for video and 15 FPS for content, and high-fidelity audio.

Teams is always conservative on bandwidth utilization and can deliver **high-definition (HD)** video quality in conditions under 1.2 **megabits per second (Mbps)**. The actual bandwidth consumption in each audio/video call or meeting will vary based on several factors, such as video layout, video resolution, and video FPS. When more bandwidth is available, quality and usage will increase to deliver the best experience.

The following bandwidth requirements are needed to support the following scenarios in Teams:

Bandwidth (up/down)	Scenario
58 kilobytes per second (KB/s)	Peer-to-peer (P2P) audio calling
1.5 megabytes per second (MB/s)	P2P audio calling and screen sharing
2.5 MB/s	Meeting audio calling and screen sharing
500 KB/s	P2P quality video calling 360 p at 30 FPS
1.2 MB/s	P2P HD quality video calling with resolution of HD 720p at 30fps
1. 5 MB/s	P2P HD quality video calling with resolution of HD 1080p at 30fps
2.5/4.0 MB/s	Meetings Video
1.5/2.5 MB/s	Together Mode
6 KB/s	SILK PSTN Voice Codec
64 KB/s	G.711 PSTN Voice Codec
64 KB/s	G.722 PSTN Voice Codec
8 KB/s	G.729 PSTN Voice Codec

Table 11.8 – Network speed required for communications scenarios

Next, let's look at the network communication ports required for Microsoft Teams.

Ports

It is extremely important that all the ports for the Teams service are open outbound on the organization's firewalls to allow full signaling and media access between the Teams client and the Teams Cloud Voice service. The following table lists the required and optional network ports:

Protocol	Ports
Required Transmission Control Protocol (TCP)	80,443
Required User Datagram Protocol (UDP)	3478,3479,3480
Optional UDP/TCP	50,000-59,999

Table 11.9 – Teams network port requirements

It is important that all communications, including the optional UDP ports listed in *Table 11.9*, are opened outbound from the organization's network to the Teams service. Not having these ports open causes media traffic to traverse TCP ports 80 and 443 as a fallback mechanism. Real-time media is not optimized to run on TCP. Running real-time media on TCP ports will result in delayed media streams as well as Teams audio and video degradation. TCP traffic requires confirmation of all packets as well as packet reassembly in order to ensure the data has been transmitted successfully. UDP is a broadcast-style transmission, allowing packets to be dropped or lost along the way with minimal disruption to the audio or video stream.

> **Network Endpoints**
>
> Microsoft provides a full list of network endpoints (including network ranges, ports, and protocols) for all Microsoft 365 services. You can find the most current list at https://aka.ms/o365endpoints.

Split-tunnel VPN

Many organizations deploy **virtual private networks** (**VPNs**) to allow secure communications between remote devices and corporate networks. Since Microsoft 365 services (such as Teams) are hosted on the public internet, Microsoft recommends that organizations enable **split tunneling**.

Split-tunneling allows internal corporate resources to be accessed via the VPN tunnel, while internet-facing services such as Teams are routed directly over the local internet connection. Without split-tunneling, traffic from the remote endpoint destined for internet sites or services is routed in through the organization's firewall, back out to the internet to retrieve data, and then back through the VPN tunnel to the originating endpoint.

While some customers may express concerns with enabling split tunneling, it is important to note that all traffic between the Teams client and the Microsoft 365 platform is encrypted using **Transport Layer Security (TLS)** 2.0. This encryption includes both signaling and media traffic.

In addition to inserting additional network hops and latency between the endpoint and the VPN, the VPN traffic itself is *also* TCP-based. As we discussed previously, real-time media communications are not optimized for TCP, and users may experience audio and video lags.

Quality of Service

Quality of Service (QoS) is key to ensuring that Teams voice and video packets receive priority treatment in your organization's environment. Prioritization enables the network devices to maintain audio and video call quality when a congestion event occurs on your network.

You can view your network as a large multi-lane highway with all sorts of network traffic types and packets traveling it to reach their destinations. Just as with highways, there are times when the network will be congested. With that increase in traffic, users may begin to experience delays when trying to access resources. For most operations (such as instant messaging, file transfers, web browsing, or sending email), these micro-delays typically don't have any noticeable impact. For real-time traffic, however, this congestion can translate directly to choppy audio or video. A lack of bandwidth on the network will lead to distorted audio, video, and content sharing. The Teams client will warn you of detected poor network conditions and recommend that you disable services such as content sharing and video in a meeting. In some cases, Teams may even recommend you use PSTN dial-in networking as opposed to VoIP services to continue a call.

To combat this poor experience, you can enable QoS on your devices and endpoints. You can think of QoS as reserving a special lane on the highway for audio and video traffic. Access to this special lane (called **prioritization**) is enabled through the use of **Differentiated Services Code Point (DSCP)** values (sometimes referred to as **QoS tags**).

Tagging traffic allows that traffic to enter the high-priority queue. This high-priority queue prioritizes traffic packets going through the network based on tags present in the packet. These tags are set by the Teams clients and devices on each audio-, video-, or screen-sharing packet transmitted.

The following diagram shows a conceptual view of QoS in an environment:

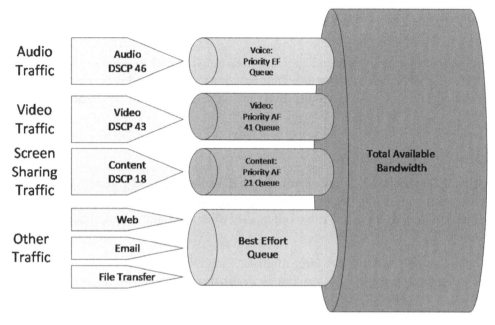

Figure 11.7 – How QoS works with Teams

You can enable QoS on Microsoft Teams endpoints via **Group Policy (GP)**. The following table lists the DSCP markings set by the Teams client:

Media traffic type	Client source port range	Protocol	DSCP value	DSCP class
Audio	50,000-50,019	TCP/UDP	46	Expedited Forwarding (EF)
Video	50,020-50,039	TCP/UDP	34	Assured Forwarding (AF41)
Application/screen Sharing	50,040-50,059	TCP/UDP	18	Assured Forwarding (AF21)

Table 11.10 – Teams QoS settings

As you can see from *Table 11.10*, each specific type of data gets its own tag. The higher the value in the **DSCP Value** field, the more priority is given to that particular type of traffic.

Enabling QoS for Microsoft Teams clients

To create a **GP Object (GPO)** policy to have the Teams client mark audio-, video-, and screen-sharing packets with the preceding DSCP marking, use the following steps:

1. Launch the **Group Policy Management** Microsoft management console.

2. In the **Group Policy Management** snap-in, locate the Active Directory container where a new policy should be created.

3. Right-click the container, and then click **Create a GPO and link it here**.

4. In the **New GPO** dialog box, enter a name for the new GPO.

5. Right-click the new policy and choose **Edit**.

6. In **Group Policy Management Editor**, expand the **Computer Configuration** container and then expand the **Windows Settings** container.

7. Right-click **Policy-Based QoS** and then click **Create new policy**.

8. Enter a name for the new policy in the **Name** box. Select **Specify DSCP Value** and set the value to 46. Leave **Specify Outbound Throttle Rate** unselected and then click **Next**.

9. Select **Only applications with this executable name** and enter the Teams executable, Teams.exe. Click **Next**.

10. Select **Any source IP address** and **Any destination IP address**. Click **Next**.

11. Expand the **Select the protocol this QoS policy applies list** option and select **TCP and UDP**.

12. Under **Specify the source port number**, select **From this source port or range**.

13. Enter the port range reserved for audio transmissions. Microsoft recommends reserving ports 50000-50019. To use the recommended value, specify 50000:50019 and click **Finish**.

14. Repeat *Steps 6-12* to create policies for **Video and Screen Sharing** using the values shown in *Table 11.10*. When completed, you will see the following in your **Group Policy Management** console:

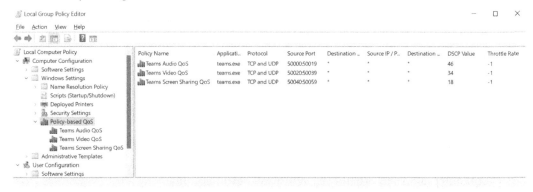

Figure 11.8 – Group Policy Editor for QoS

The policy can then be deployed to all devices that contain Teams clients.

Once deployed, a user triggers a policy refresh by entering the following command from an elevated Command Prompt:

```
gpupdate /force
```

You can verify that the policy has been successfully processed by the machine by running the following command from an elevated Command Prompt:

```
gpresult /H gp.html
```

Review the gp.html file for the name of the policy you created under the **Applied Group Policy Objects** section of the report.

Using **Registry Editor**, you can also review HKEY_LOCAL_MACHINE\Software\ Policies\Microsoft\Windows\QoS for evidence that the policy has been processed. The following table lists values present for a machine that has QoS for Teams configured:

Name	Type	Data
Application Name	REG_SZ	Teams.exe
DSCP Value	REG_SZ	46
Local IP	REG_SZ	*
Local IP Prefix Length	REG_SZ	*
Local Port	REG_SZ	50000-50019
Protocol	REG_SZ	*
Name	Type	Data
Remote IP	REG_SZ	*
Remote IP Prefix	REG_SZ	*
Name	Type	Data
Remote Port	REG_SZ	*
Throttle Rate	REG_SZ	-1

Table 11.11 – Teams QoS registry settings

GP is an effective tool for distribution configurations to standard domain-joined Windows computers. However, you may have other devices such as handsets or Surface Hubs, which need to be configured separately.

Enabling QoS for Teams devices and mobile devices

For Teams devices and mobile devices, the QoS enablement is configured through the Teams admin center.

To enable QoS, follow these steps:

1. Navigate to the Teams admin center.
2. Expand **Meetings** and select **Meeting settings**.

3. Slide the **Insert Quality of Service (QoS) markers for real-time media traffic** toggle to **On**, as illustrated in the following screenshot:

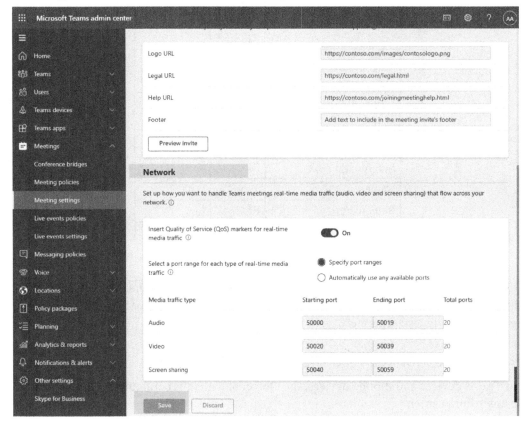

Figure 11.9 – Configuring QoS in the Teams admin center

4. Select the **Specify port ranges** radio button and match the media ports that you selected for your QoS policy for your Teams clients. This will enable the following markings and ports for Teams Android devices, Android mobile devices, and iOS devices:

Media traffic type	Client source port range	Protocol	DSCP value	DSCP class
Audio	50,000-50,019	TCP/UDP	46	EF
Video	50,020-50,039	TCP/UDP	34	AF41
Application/ screen sharing	50,040-50,059	TCP/UDP	18	AF21

Table 11.12 – Teams QoS configuration parameters

5. Click **Save** to commit the changes.

After devices refresh policy settings, they will begin tagging packets for QoS.

Enabling QoS for Surface Hub devices

For Surface Hub and Hub 2 devices, use **Mobile Device Management** (**MDM**) to enable QoS. In this example, we'll configure a policy for a Surface Hub 2 device:

1. Navigate to the Microsoft Endpoint Manager admin center (`https://endpoint.microsoft.com`).

2. Select **Devices | Configuration profiles | Create profile**, as illustrated in the following screenshot:

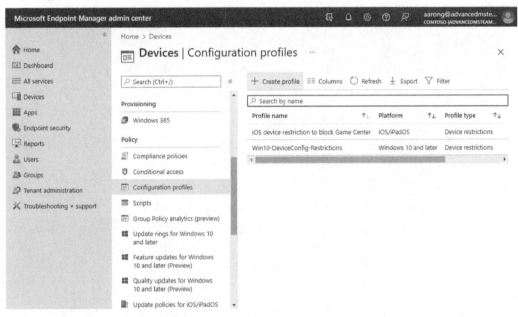

Figure 11.10 – Microsoft Endpoint Manager device profiles

3. Under **Platform**, select **Windows 10 and later,** as illustrated in the following screenshot:

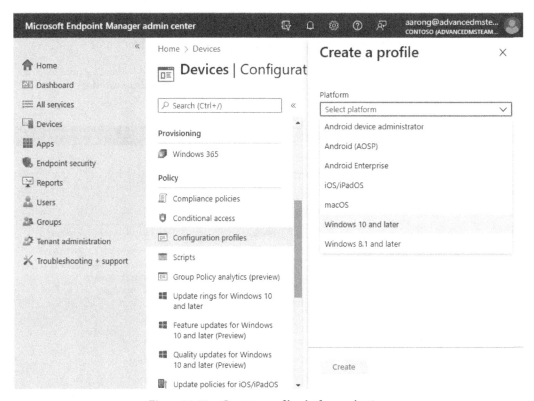

Figure 11.11 – Create a profile platform selection

4. Under **Profile type**, select **Templates** and then select **Custom** from the list of templates.

5. Click **Create**.

6. Enter values in the **Name** and **Description** fields, as shown in the following screenshot, and then click **Next**:

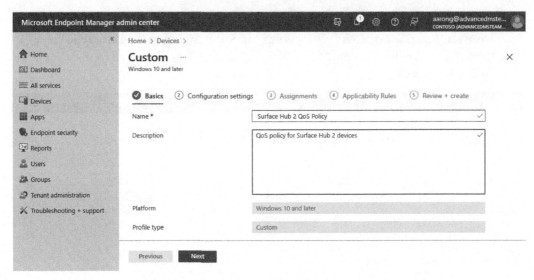

Figure 11.12 – Custom profile configuration

7. Click **Add** to configure a custom **Open Mobile Alliance Uniform Resource Identifier (OMA-URI)** setting, as illustrated in the following screenshot:

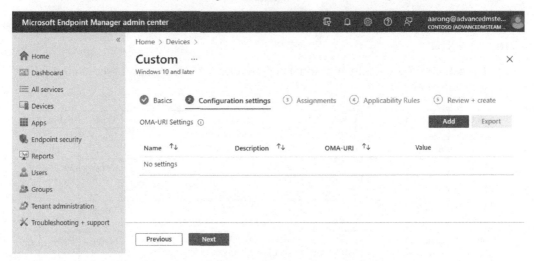

Figure 11.13 – Custom profile configuration (continued)

8. Enter a name, such as **Audio Ports**, and a value for **Description**.

9. Under **OMA-URI**, enter `./Device/Vendor/MSFT/NetworkQoSPolicy/Audio/SourcePortMatchCondition`. Select **String** as the **Data type** value, and then enter the value `50000-50019`. The process is illustrated in the following screenshot:

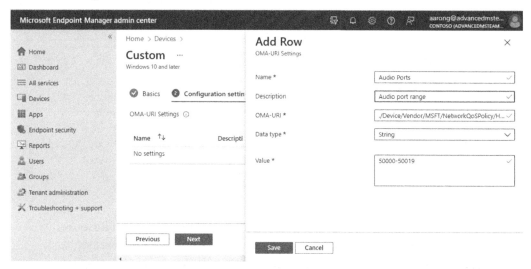

Figure 11.14 – Entering custom OMA-URI settings

10. Click **Save**.

11. Repeat *Steps 7-10* to add additional custom OMA-URI settings, based on the following table:

Name	Description	OMA-URI	Type	Value
Audio DSCP	Audio ports marking	`./Device/Vendor/MSFT/NetworkQoSPolicy/Audio/DSCPAction`	Integer	46
Video ports	Video port range	`./Device/Vendor/MSFT/NetworkQoSPolicy/Video/SourcePortMatchCondition`	String	50020-50039
Video DSCP	Video ports marking	`./Device/Vendor/MSFT/NetworkQoSPolicy/Video/DSCPAction`	Integer	34
Sharing ports	Sharing port range	`./Device/Vendor/MSFT/NetworkQoSPolicy/Sharing/SourcePortMatchCondition`	String	50040-50059
Sharing DSCP	Sharing ports marking	`./Device/Vendor/MSFT/NetworkQoSPolicy/Sharing/DSCPAction`	Integer	18

Table 11.13 – Surface Hub 2 OMA-URI values

If you have an original Surface Hub device, you can create an additional device profile. Follow the same procedure, but use these values for the OMA-URI configuration:

Name	Description	OMA-URI	Type	Value
Audio source port	Audio port range	`./Device/Vendor/MSFT/NetworkQoSPolicy/HubAudio/SourcePortMatchCondition`	String	50000-50019
Audio DSCP	Audio ports marking	`./Device/Vendor/MSFT/NetworkQoSPolicy/HubAudio/DSCPAction`	Integer	46
Video source port	Video port range	`./Device/Vendor/MSFT/NetworkQoSPolicy/HubVideo/SourcePortMatchCondition`	String	50020-50039
Video DSCP	Video ports marking	`./Device/Vendor/MSFT/NetworkQoSPolicy/HubVideo/DSCPAction`	Integer	34

Table 11.14 – Surface Hub OMA-URI values

Next, let's look at some of the tools available for planning your deployment.

Teams Network Planner

The Teams **Network Planner** tool is built into the Microsoft Teams admin center and can be used to get network bandwidth information based on site profiles.

To use **Network Planner**, follow these steps:

1. Navigate to the Microsoft Teams admin center (`https://admin.teams.microsoft.com`).

2. Expand **Planning** and select **Network planner**, as illustrated in the following screenshot:

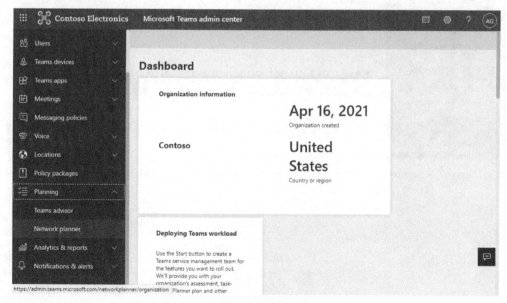

Figure 11.15 – Teams Network Planner

Your tenant will not have a network plan until you create one. Before you can create a network plan, however, you will first need to create a persona. Teams comes with three prepopulated personas, as follows:

- Teams Rooms on Windows
- Remote worker
- Office worker

You cannot edit the configuration of the default personas. To create customized personas for your environment, follow these steps:

1. From the **Network planner** option on the left-hand sidebar, select the **Personas** tab.
2. On the **Personas** tab, click **Add**, as illustrated in the following screenshot:

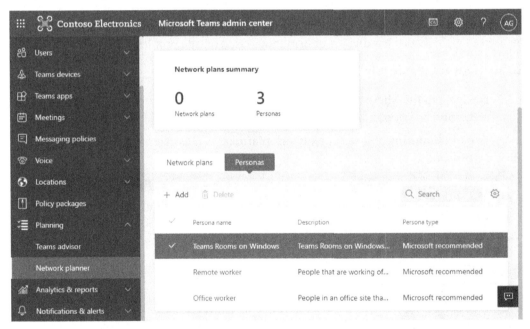

Figure 11.16 – Creating a new persona for Teams Network Planner

3. On the **Add persona** flyout, populate the **Persona name** and **Description** fields and enable the modalities or features the persona will use, as illustrated in the following screenshot:

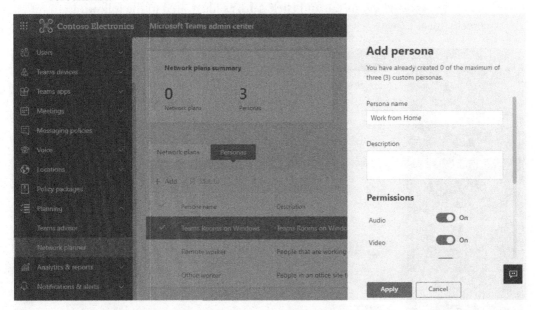

Figure 11.17 – Completing the persona configuration in Teams Network Planner

4. Click **Apply** to save the persona.

When you have personas that meet your needs, you're ready to begin creating a plan. Proceed as follows:

1. Select the **Network plans** tab and click **Add**, as illustrated in the following screenshot:

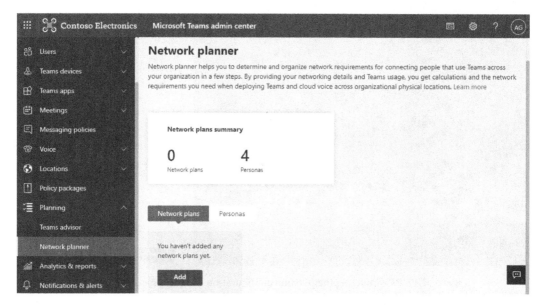

Figure 11.18 – Creating a Teams network plan

2. On the **Network plan name** flyout, populate the **Network plan name** and **Description** fields. When finished, click **Apply**. The process is illustrated in the following screenshot:

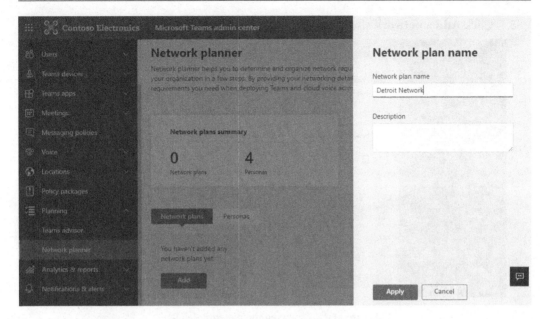

Figure 11.19 – Populating Teams network plan identity information

3. Select the newly created plan, as follows:

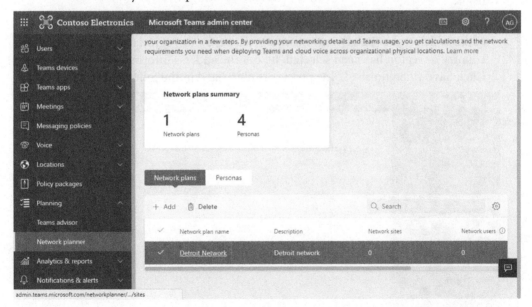

Figure 11.20 – Selecting a network plan

4. Click the name of the plan to begin configuring the plan.

5. Click **Add a network site**, as illustrated in the following screenshot:

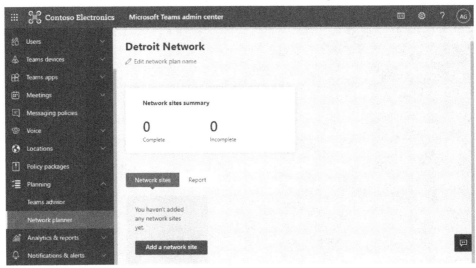

Figure 11.21 – Viewing the network details

6. On the **Add network site** page, populate the **Network site name** and **Description** fields.

7. Click **Create an address** for the site and populate the **Name** field for the emergency address. Select the site's country from the **Country or region** dropdown. Once a country or region has been selected, fill out the address information for the site. Click **Save** when finished. The process is illustrated in the following screenshot:

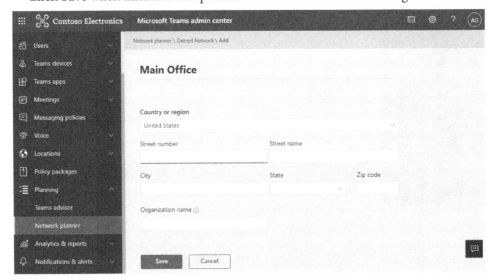

Figure 11.22 – Configuring site address details

8. On the **Add network site** page, enter a numeric value for the number of network users.

9. Fill out the network settings, including the **Subnet** and **Network range** fields (network bits or **Classless Inter-Domain Routing (CIDR)** notation). Select the connectivity type. Options include **ExpressRoute**, **Connected to WAN** (meaning this site accesses the internet through a remote site, such as through a **multi-protocol label switching (MPLS)** network or point-to-point **Transmission System 1 (T1)**), and **Internet egress**. If you choose **Connected to WAN** as your internet access type, you'll be prompted to enter your **WAN link capacity**, **WAN audio queue size**, and **WAN video queue size** values. The options are shown in the following screenshot:

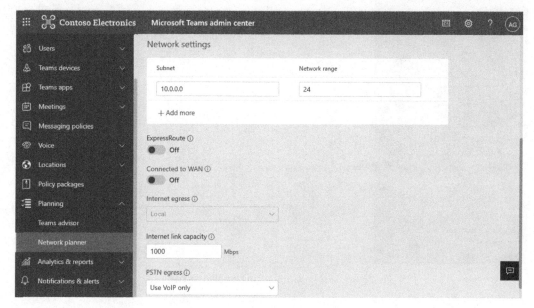

Figure 11.23 – Network settings and internet access

10. Enter a value for **Internet link capacity**.

11. Select the **PSTN egress** option (possible choices may include **Local** or **Use VoIP Only**. If you select **Use VoIP only**, no further choices are possible. If you choose **Local**, select **Calling plans** or **Direct Routing**. The options are illustrated in the following screenshot:

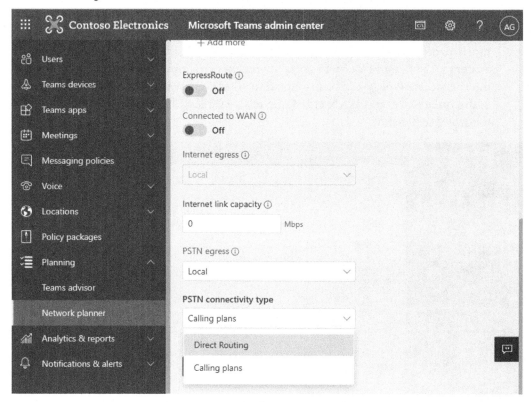

Figure 11.24 – Configuring a network site

12. Click **Save**.

You can add as many sites and networks as you need to accurately represent your organization. Once your network sites are created, you can click on the **Report** tab to generate a network planning report for those sites, as illustrated in the following screenshot:

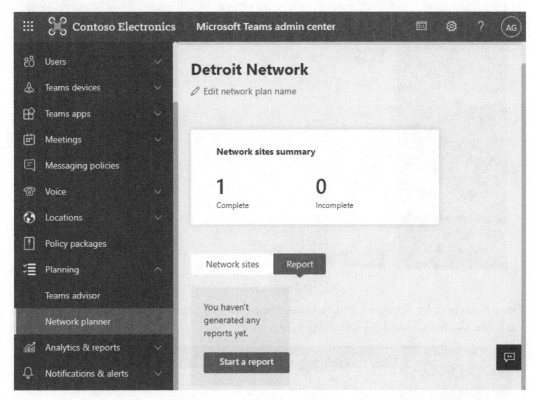

Figure 11.25 – Creating a network report

To generate a report, follow these steps:

1. From the **Network planner** option in the left-hand sidebar, select the **Report** tab.

2. Click **Start a report**.

3. On the **Add report** page, populate the **Report name** and **Description** fields.

4. Select personas at each site and the number of network users matching each persona. When finished, click **Generate report**. The process is illustrated in the following screenshot:

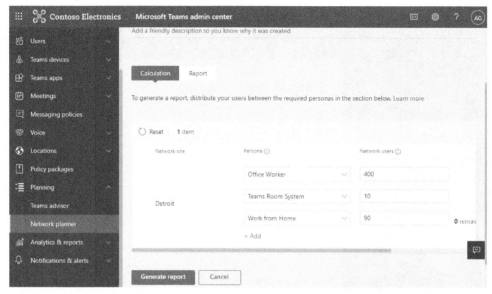

Figure 11.26 – Configuring network report settings

Once the report has finished, you can view the estimated bandwidth usage or impact for each site, as illustrated in the following screenshot:

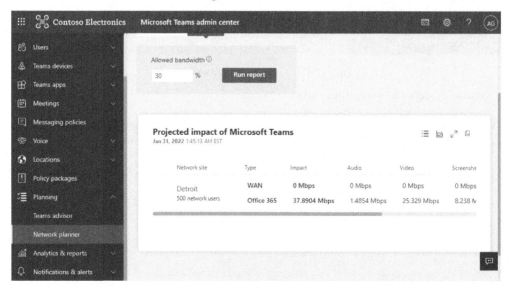

Figure 11.27 – Viewing the report

The generated report will show the impact of the personas on the network sites. You can adjust the **Allowed bandwidth** value for the Microsoft Teams workloads and rerun the report. You can click on the **Switch to chart view** option to get a more pictorial representation of network impact, as illustrated in the following screenshot:

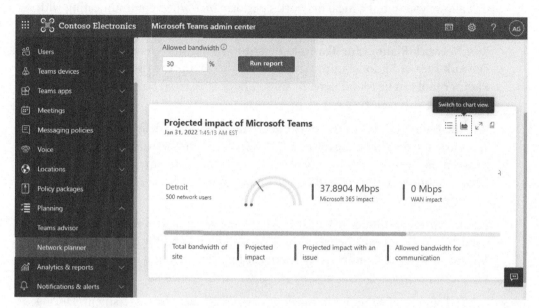

Figure 11.28 – Displaying the chart view of the Network Planner report

Finally, you can click **Export to PDF** to export the report to **Portable Document Format (PDF)** and save it locally.

Best practices and additional network tools

In order to ensure the best possible operation and performance, Microsoft recommends the following best practices:

- Verify all required outbound network ports for Teams (specified under the *Network requirements* section) are allowed to communicate with the Microsoft Teams environment. If the UDP ports are closed, traffic will fall back to the TCP protocol, which is not optimized for real-time media (audio and video).

- Verify that Teams client media and signaling streams are bypassing double-encryption sources, web proxies, VPN tunnels, **intrusion detection systems (IDS)**, and other network traffic-shaping configurations. If organizations must use VPNs, configure split tunneling to allow Teams traffic to bypass the VPN. Routing Teams traffic via a VPN will cause media delays. VPNs utilize TCP-based communications protocol streams that are not optimized for real-time media.

- Run **Microsoft Teams Network Assessment Tool** to see how real-time media traffic will flow from your Teams endpoint to the Teams service. **Microsoft Teams Network Assessment Tool** (`https://www.microsoft.com/en-us/download/details.aspx?id=103017`) is a basic bandwidth measuring tool that allows you to test a local network's performance when communicating with Microsoft Teams.

- Run **Network Planner for Teams** to determine bandwidth requirements for your network sites. Additional information on how to set up and use the **Network Planner** tool can be found here: `https://docs.microsoft.com/en-US/microsoftteams/network-planner`.

- Run the **Microsoft 365 network connectivity test** tool to determine if all the appropriate **Domain Name System** (**DNS**) records and network ports are open between the Teams endpoint and the Microsoft 365 platform. The **Microsoft 365 network connectivity test** tool can be found here: `https://connectivity.office.com/`.

- Run the **Microsoft Remote Connectivity Analyzer** tool to verify that no connectivity issues exist between the Teams endpoint and the Teams service. The **Microsoft Remote Connectivity Analyzer** tool can be found here: `https://testconnectivity.microsoft.com/tests/teams`.

- Take advantage of either a Microsoft or partner-led network assessment. During a network assessment, probes are deployed at various points on the network to simulate Teams audio and video media workloads. This data can be used to help identify network quality issues that could impact the Teams media experience. Microsoft offers a network readiness assessment and planning for Teams feature as part of its services organization.

- The **Microsoft 365 network connectivity test** tool can also be used to gather performance information for Worldwide Commercial Microsoft 365 tenants (the tool is not available for government communities or other sovereign clouds). You can find it at `https://docs.microsoft.com/en-US/microsoft-365/enterprise/office-365-network-mac-perf-overview`.

- Leverage the **Call Quality Dashboard** reporting tool to analyze tenant-level reports to determine quality as seen from the Microsoft Teams service in your environment. It is recommended that you upload your subnet data to get more graduated site-level quality reports from the **Call Quality Dashboard** tool. You can learn more about the **Call Quality Dashboard** tool in *Chapter 19, Reporting in Teams*.

- Additional guidance on evaluating your environment for cloud voice workloads can be found here: `https://docs.microsoft.com/en-us/MicrosoftTeams/3-envision-evaluate-my-environment`.

These network tools, reports, and recommendations are designed to help you architect a successful Teams Phone deployment.

Now that we've covered the core architecture and network considerations, let's look back at what we've learned.

Summary

In this chapter, we discussed the basic Microsoft Teams Phone System terminology and licensing. You learned both basic telephony and networking terms (such as **SIP** and **SBC**), as well as Teams-specific terms such as **auto attendants** and **call queues**. We also explored the core Teams architecture designs (**Calling Plans**, **Direct Routing**, and **Operator Connect**).

We examined the features of various architectures and also discussed Microsoft's best practices for networking configuration. These best practices included configuring QoS, enabling VPN-split tunneling, and using network planning tools such as the Teams **Network Planner** tool. Microsoft recommends a network assessment in order to get a clear understanding of your organization's network capabilities. Identifying and remediating network issues will help prevent a poor user onboarding experience.

This foundational knowledge will be important as you learn about designing and configuring Phone System features in *Chapter 12, Deploying Teams Phone*.

Further reading

Should you need to explore this chapter's topics even more deeply, you can find more information using the following resources:

- *Security and Microsoft Teams*: `https://docs.microsoft.com/en-us/microsoftteams/teams-security-guide`.

- *Alternative ways for security professionals and IT to achieve modern security controls in today's unique remote work scenarios*: `https://www.microsoft.com/security/blog/2020/03/26/alternative-security-professionals-it-achieve-modern-security-controls-todays-unique-remote-work-scenarios/`.

- Optimizing Office 365 connectivity for remote users using VPN split tunneling: `https://docs.microsoft.com/en-us/microsoft-365/enterprise/microsoft-365-vpn-split-tunnel?view=o365-worldwide`.

12
Deploying Teams Phone

One of the most compelling features of the Microsoft Teams platform is the phone system architecture capability. Microsoft Teams has the flexibility to integrate with an existing **Private Branch Exchange (PBX)**, **Session Initiation Protocol (SIP)** trunks, and analog devices, as well as replacing legacy phone systems.

In this chapter, we're going to start off with the basics of Microsoft Phone System, and then layer design principles and operational tasks on top of it.

We'll cover the following topics in this chapter:

- Configuring your telephony architecture
- Configuring E911
- Obtaining and assigning Phone Numbers
- Configuring resource accounts
- Configuring Advanced Teams Phone calling features
- Configuring voice policies
- Configuring outbound calling
- Managing policy assignments with PowerShell

By the end of this chapter, you'll have the necessary tools to be able to successfully plan and implement a Microsoft Phone system for your organization.

Configuring your telephony architecture

In this chapter, we're going to cover core concepts for enabling phone system features. Most of this chapter will be targeted toward configuration from a calling plans-based perspective, but many features are configured the same regardless of the deployment type.

For a deeper discussion on the features of each architecture, please see *Chapter 11, Planning for Teams Phone*.

> **Important**
>
> While many of the processes and tasks overlap between architectures, there are some differences in how features are deployed or implemented. This is particularly true when it comes to obtaining and assigning numbers or implementing session border controllers and survivable branch appliances.
>
> Except where specifically noted, the steps and configurations will refer to processes that are applicable across all architectures. Configurations, steps, or guidance specific to Direct Routing or Operator Connect can be found in *Appendix A*.

After choosing a deployment architecture, you'll need to start with configuring E911.

Configuring E911

Microsoft Teams supports **Enhanced 911 (E911)**. Teams offers both static and Dynamic E911 support. New capabilities, such as **Dynamic E911 for US Work From Home**, allow users to enter address information for E911 location services when they are outside of a defined office.

At a high level, you must complete the following steps to enable E911:

1. Define your organization's external IP addresses or address ranges and add them as trusted IPs to identify your corporate network boundaries.

2. Identify and define emergency addresses for the sites in your organization.

3. Choose which identifiers are going to be used to provide specificity to your emergency location sites. Valid identifiers include subnets, switch ports, MAC addresses, or **Wireless Access Points (WAPs)**.

4. Create and assign emergency policies to enable additional notifications for groups, such as your corporate security desk, when an emergency call is placed.

5. Assign your emergency policies to a region, site, or subnet depending on how your locations are defined.

Configuring Teams Dynamic E911 will allow Teams to find the location of a caller, route that caller to the appropriate **Public Safety Answering Point** (**PSAP**) or regional **Emergency Call Response Center** (**ECRC**), and notify additional corporate resources, such as a security desk, of a placed emergency call.

Defining trusted IPs

The first step in setting up Dynamic E911 is to configure one or more external IP addresses for the organization. These addresses will be used to determine whether a particular Teams client is internal or external to a site.

Those addresses are defined in the Teams admin center by following these steps:

1. Navigate to the Teams admin center (`https://admin.teams.microsoft.com`).

2. Expand **Locations** and select **Network topology**.

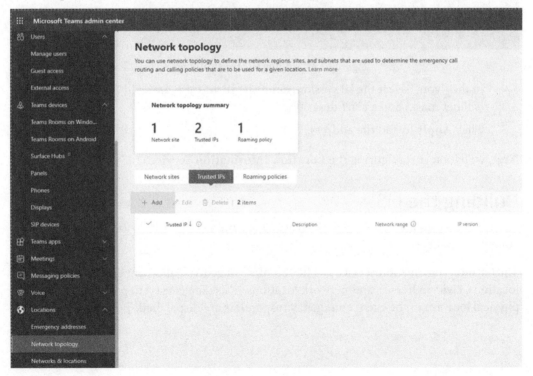

Figure 12.1 – Network topology

3. Click on **Add** to add the external IP addresses. You will need to add both the IPv4 and IPv6 addresses.

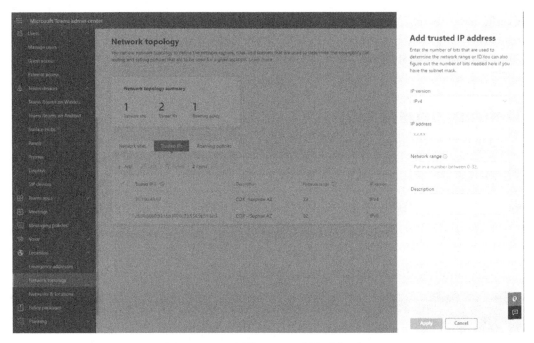

Figure 12.2 – Adding trusted IP addresses

4. In the flyout, select the IP version, enter the IP address, and add the network range (subnet mask) and a brief description.

5. Click **Apply** to add the address.

Next, we'll look at configuring the **Location Information Service (LIS)**.

Building the LIS

The LIS is used to link your network locations to emergency address locations and emergency policies.

The location information service is a hierarchical structure built from emergency locations, civic addresses, and network locations. This data is used to pinpoint the user's physical location in the event emergency responders are dispatched.

Importance of Emergency Addresses

Emergency location information is critical to being able to route first responders. If you are using the Calling Plans or Operator Connect architecture, you will be required to configure emergency addresses before you can assign numbers to users.

It's important to define how the data in the **civic address** maps to a user's physical location. The following diagram illustrates how a civic address might be constructed:

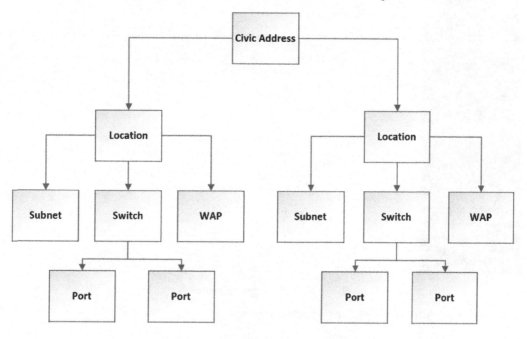

Figure 12.3 – Civic address hierarchy

In *Figure 12.3*, the civic address represents a physical building in your organization. The location (or **place**, in Teams terminology) is more granular. In each location, you will define one or more network elements (such as a subnet, WAP, or network switch port) to add further specificity.

Civic address creation

To start building the hierarchy, you need to add civic addresses. Follow these steps to begin defining addresses:

1. In the Teams admin center, expand **Locations** and select **Emergency addresses**.

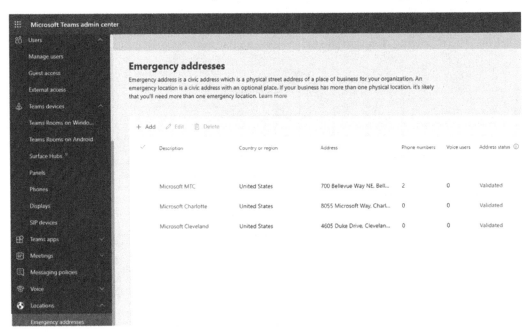

Figure 12.4 – Emergency locations

2. Click on **Add** to add an emergency address.

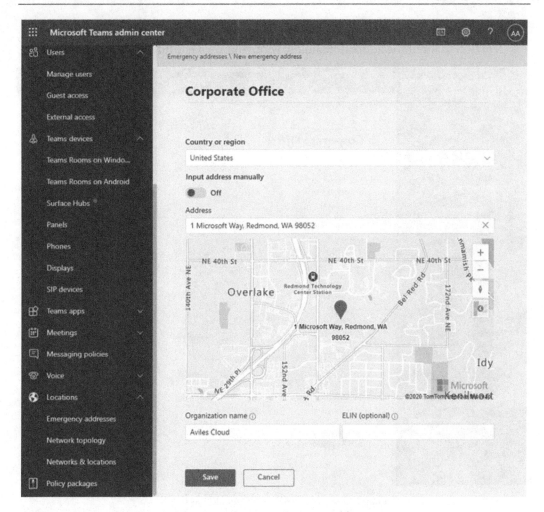

Figure 12.5 – New emergency address

3. On the emergency address page, enter a name for the location, the country or region, and the physical address for the location. After a moment, the address will be validated.

4. In the event the address cannot be found in the Azure Maps service, you have the option to input the address manually with your own latitude and longitude values.

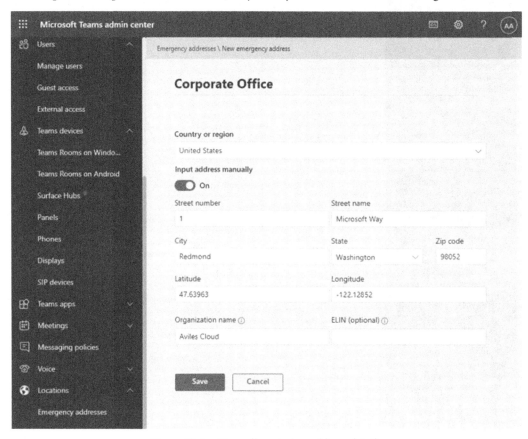

Figure 12.6 – Manually entering address details

5. Click on **Save** to add the location.

Once an emergency address has been added, you can add locations and network elements within that site by selecting it and clicking **Edit**.

> **Address Validation**
>
> When you add an address to a location, it will be verified against the Azure Maps service. The map service returns coordinates for that location. **Organization name** will be populated from the tenant information. If you are using **Emergency Location Identification Numbers** (**ELINs**) for your organization, you can also populate the 10-digit ELIN from your **Local Exchange Carrier** (**LEC**).

Once an emergency address has been added, you can add locations and network elements within that site by selecting it and clicking **Edit**.

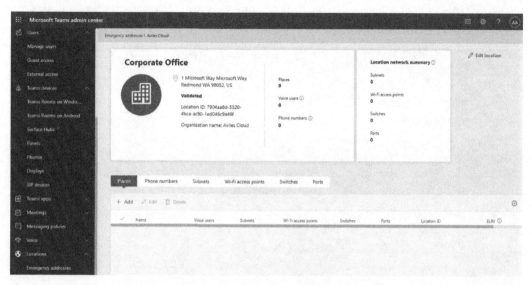

Figure 12.7 – Emergency address details

From the emergency address location page, you will add places, phone numbers, subnets, Wi-Fi access points, switches, and ports.

> **Notes**
>
> The `New-CsOnlineLisCivicAddress` PowerShell cmdlet can be used to create an emergency address location. The `-Latitude` and `-Longitude` parameters can be used to populate coordinates generated manually using a map source, such as Bing Maps. The `-Elin` parameter can be used to populate the optional ELIN phone number if used.

Once an address has been validated during the creation process, its address cannot be edited. It must be deleted and recreated with new details.

Places

A place is a physical location, such as a floor or wing, and can be linked to a network element. When placing emergency calls, this additional information will be sent to the PSAP along with the civic address.

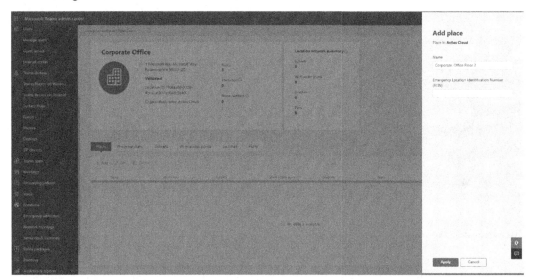

Figure 12.8 – Adding a place

On the **Add place** page, enter the details and click **Apply**.

Phone Numbers

The **Phone numbers** tab lists the phone numbers associated with the selected emergency address, as shown in *Figure 12.9*:

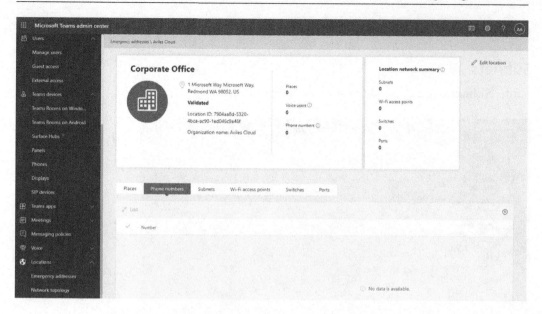

Figure 12.9 – Phone numbers tab

You can select any number and select **Edit** to reassign the number to another user.

Figure 12.10 – Assigning or unassigning a phone number

Click **Apply** to commit changes.

Subnets

Under **Subnets**, you can add the subnets associated with the site.

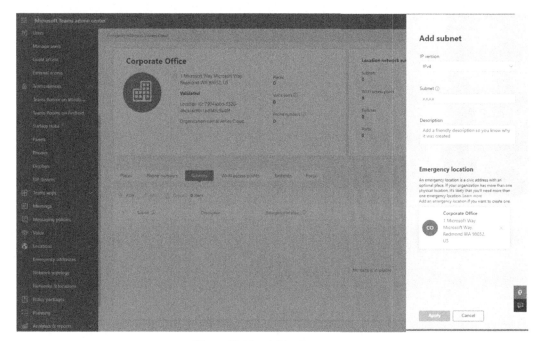

Figure 12.11 – Add subnet page

On the **Add subnet** page, enter the IP version of the subnet (IPv4 or IPv6), the subnet, and a description for the subnet. Assign an emergency location (created under the **Places** tab) for this network element. Click on **Apply** to save the changes.

> **Notes**
>
> When configuring subnets, be sure all client network subnet IDs match the organization's IP networks. You can use the `Set-CsOnlineLisSubnet` cmdlet to associate subnets with locations. Subnets must be unique within the tenant.

Wi-Fi access points

Under **Wi-Fi access points**, you can add the WAPs associated with the site to identify an emergency location. See *Figure 12.12*:

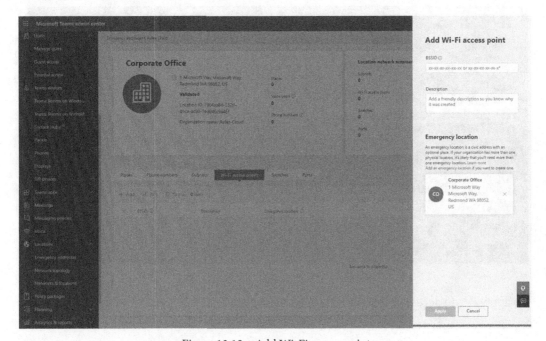

Figure 12.12 – Add Wi-Fi access point

On the **Add Wi-Fi access point** page, enter the BBSID and a description for the WAP, and then assign an emergency location.

To locate the BSSID of an access point, you can run `netsh wlan show interfaces` on a Windows-based computer, as shown in *Figure 12.13*:

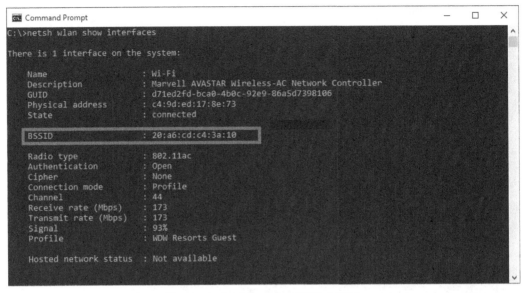

Figure 12.13 – Locating a WAP's BSSID

To apply Wi-Fi access point changes, click **Apply**.

Switches

On the **Switches** tab, you can add the network switches associated with the site, as shown in *Figure 12.14*:

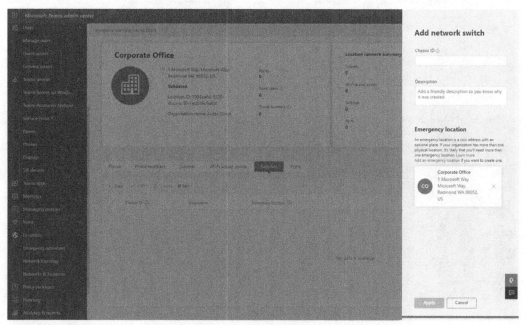

Figure 12.14 – Add network switch

On the **Add network switch** page, enter the MAC address of the switch under **Chassis ID** and a description for the switch, and then assign an emergency location.

Ports

Under **Ports**, you can add the switch ports associated with the site.

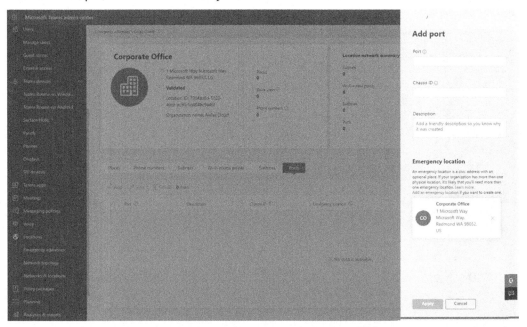

Figure 12.15 – Adding a switch port to an emergency location

On the **Add port** page, enter the port on the switch, the MAC address of the switch under **Chassis ID**, and a description for the switch port. Assign an emergency location.

Testing emergency locations

For organizations using Calling Plans or Operator Connect, you can validate your emergency location configuration by dialing **933**. This special number is routed to a bot that reads back the line's phone number, emergency location details, and whether the call would be automatically routed to the PSAP or be screened first.

For organizations using Direct Routing, contact your **Emergency Service Routing Provider** (**ESRP**) or carrier to validate your emergency routing details.

Dynamic E911 for US Work from Home

In December 2021, as part of compliance with Ray Baum's Act, Microsoft released a feature called *Dynamic E911 for US Work from Home*. This new capability allows a user to either enter location information manually or engage location services on their device to provide more precise location details. This provides first responders with greater detail when responding to emergency calls placed off corporate networks.

Once this feature is enabled, users will be able to configure their own emergency location on the phone dialer in the Microsoft Teams client, as shown in *Figure 12.16*:

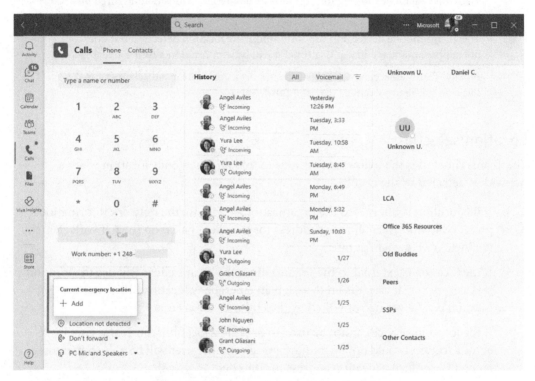

Figure 12.16 – Teams client emergency location

The location will be populated based on the device's location service. If a location cannot be determined, the user will be prompted to allow the Teams client access to location services. If access to location services is restricted, the user can enter the location information manually. Users can continue to manually add dynamic emergency addresses even if location autodetection consent has been turned off.

If a location is already present, you can select **Reset** or **Edit**. **Reset** instructs the client to attempt to redetect the location using the device location services, while **Edit** allows you to enter new data. If location services are not enabled or are unable to determine where the device is, you can click on **Add**, as shown in *Figure 12.16*, which allows you to enter a physical address location. Any address entered will be confirmed against the Azure Maps service.

> **Notes on Dynamic Emergency Locations**
>
> Dynamic emergency calling for non-admin-defined locations is configured *off* by default.
>
> The Teams mobile device app supports automatic location detection but does not support manual entry at this time. It will be supported in a future release.
>
> Finally, Teams emergency policies will support a customizable disclaimer for E911 on the Teams client as part of a future release.

Location selection

The Teams client uses the following methods to find an emergency location when a network is detected by the client:

- If the location is internal to the organization, it will use the network information provided to find an emergency address for the client based on the network element (subnet, WAP, switch, or port).

- If the location is external to the organization, the Teams client will use the location services for the device it is on to assign an emergency location. This emergency location can be verified or edited by the end user for accuracy.

- If the location service cannot be used to provide a location, the Teams client will show a location could not be found message and the user will be able to manually enter and confirm a location address for the client.

- If the location service cannot be used to provide a location and the user does not populate a location address from the client, Teams will use the defined static or registered location address associated with the user for Calling Plans and Operator Connect (or the emergency routing service for Direct Routing).

Next, we'll review how emergency routing works.

PSAP/ECRC routing

To ensure that an address is routed correctly, *Table 12.1* describes what happens when an emergency call is placed:

Type of Emergency Address	Emergency Routing Method
Emergency address defined by administrator	Direct to PSAP
Emergency address derived from geocodes without confirmation for accuracy by the user	ECRC screened and transferred to PSAP
Emergency address derived from geocodes with confirmation for accuracy by the user	Direct to PSAP
Emergency address derived from geocodes and edited and confirmed by the user	ECRC screened and transferred to PSAP
Emergency address edited from scratch and confirmed by the user	ECRC screened and transferred to PSAP
Emergency address edited by map string match and confirmed by the end user	Direct to PSAP
Emergency address statically assigned to the user/number	ECRC screened and transferred to PSAP
No emergency address provided	ECRC screened and transferred to PSAP

Table 12.1 – Emergency routing

As you can see, the level of detail you can provide when configuring emergency locations and policies has a significant impact on how emergency calls get routed. This can have a significant impact on how quickly first responders are dispatched.

Configuring emergency policies

Emergency calling policies define what happens in your organization when a user makes an emergency call. To configure an emergency calling policy, follow these steps:

1. Navigate to the Teams admin center (`https://admin.teams.microsoft.com`) and select **Voice | Emergency policies | Calling policies**.

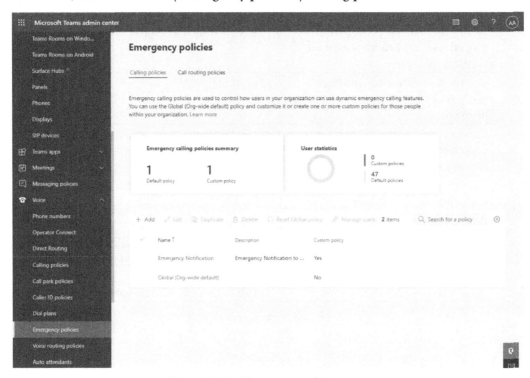

Figure 12.17 – Emergency policies page

2. Click **Add**.

3. On the **Add emergency calling policy** page, add a name and description for the policy. If you want to enable *Dynamic E911 WFH*, enable **External location lookup mode**. Select a notification mode, as shown in *Figure 12.18*:

    -   **Send notification only** will send a Teams message to the assigned notification users or group.

    -   **Conferenced in muted and unable to unmute** will send a Teams message and join the assigned notification users or group into a conference where they can listen (but not participate) in the conversation between the caller and the PSAP operator.

- **Conferenced in muted but are able to unmute** will send a Teams message and join the assigned notification users or group into a conference where they can listen and participate in the conversation between the caller and the PSAP operator.

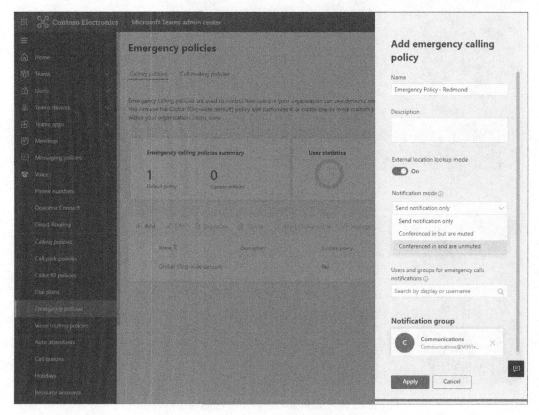

Figure 12.18 – Add emergency calling policy

4. Click **Apply** to save the policy settings.

By selecting either of the conference options, you can enter a PSTN number of a user or group to be called under **Numbers to dial for emergency call notification**.

You can also enter up to 50 email addresses under **Users and groups for emergency calls notifications**. These addresses will receive a message that an emergency call has been placed.

You can create different emergency policies for different locations. You can also apply them to different groups of users by selecting a policy and clicking **Manage users**, as shown in *Figure 12.19*:

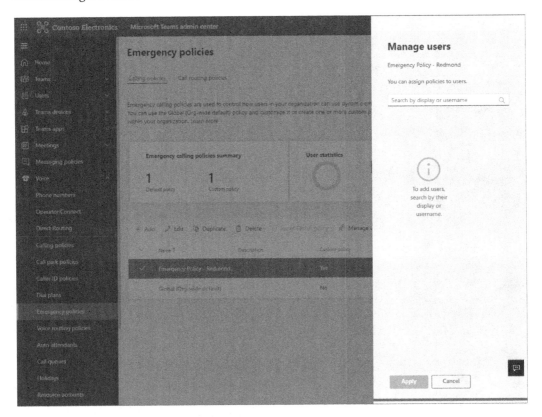

Figure 12.19 – Manage users for an emergency policy

You can also edit the **Global (Org wide default)** policy if you don't have a need to create multiple custom emergency policies.

Configuring emergency information is vital to ensuring first responders can locate callers in the event of an emergency. Completing the configuration of at least one emergency location is required before you can fully assign numbers to Teams users.

In the next section, we'll start configuring calling plans features, such as obtaining and assigning phone numbers.

Configuring Calling Plans

Since Calling Plans-based architectures are fully hosted solutions, there's nothing you need to do from a network or telephony infrastructure perspective to get started. You can simply purchase calling plans and communications credits and begin configuration.

Working with phone numbers

The process for obtaining and assigning phone numbers varies based on what type of architecture you've selected as well as what types of numbers you're requesting or assigning. Since it's possible to use a mix of architectures, we'll lay out the steps for each as follows.

As mentioned earlier in the chapter, a Calling plans architecture means that the phone numbers are wholly managed by Microsoft. You may use numbers provided by Microsoft or choose to transfer your existing numbers (a process known as **porting**) from your existing carrier.

Obtaining phone numbers

In this section, we'll review the two ways in which you can obtain numbers for your calling plans:

- Placing an order with Microsoft

- Porting numbers from a different carrier

Let's start with the easier method—obtaining numbers directly from Microsoft.

Placing an order with Microsoft

Microsoft calling plans include user **Direct Inward Dial** (**DID**) number allowances. These are the phone numbers that can be assigned to users. To obtain numbers, you must first meet the prerequisites:

- Obtain at least one Microsoft 365 license (F3, E1, E3, or E5).

- If a qualifying license does not have Phone System already included (such as F3, E1, or E3), obtain at least one standalone Phone System license.

- Obtain at least one Microsoft Domestic or Domestic and International Calling plan.

- Assign a Teams license and a Phone System license to at least one user.

- Create at least one emergency address.

Once phone numbers are allocated to your tenant, you will be able to assign them in the Teams admin center.

To view or assign phone numbers, follow these steps:

1. Navigate to the Teams admin center (`https://admin.teams.microsoft.com`).

2. Expand **Voice**, and then select **Phone numbers**.

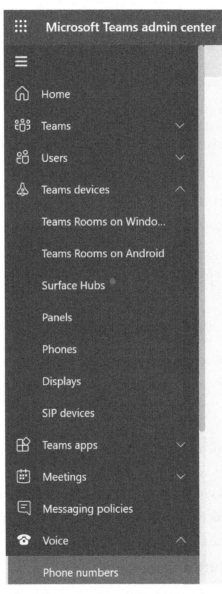

Figure 12.20 – Accessing phone numbers in the Microsoft Teams admin center

3. Under the **Phone numbers** tab, you will be able to acquire numbers from the portal and assign them to license users. If you have no numbers in your tenant, click **Add**, as shown in *Figure 12.21*:

Phone numbers

To set up calling features for users and services in your organization, you can get new numbers or port existing ones from a service provider. You can assign, unassign, and release phone numbers for people or for services, like audio conferencing, auto attendants, or call queues. Learn more

| Numbers | Order history |

+ Add   ↓ Port   ✎ Edit

Figure 12.21 – Obtaining phone numbers

When adding a phone number, you will need to populate the following fields, as shown in *Figure 12.22*:

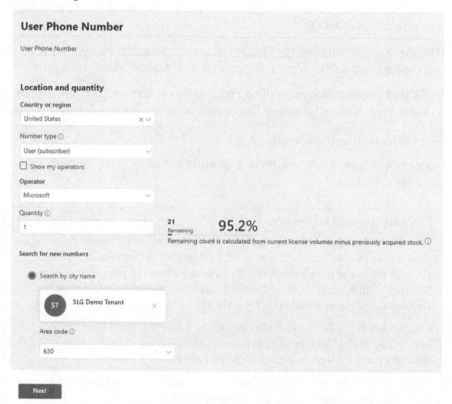

Figure 12.22 – Placing a phone number order

4. Enter a name for the number order.

5. Enter a friendly description for the number order.

6. Select the country or region under **Location and quantity**.

7. Select the number type from the following options:

    *   **User**: Numbers for users in your organization (included with Calling Plans)

    *   **Call Queue (Toll)**: Toll service numbers that are used when creating a call queue with resource accounts (this feature is included with Phone System)

    *   **Auto Attendant (Toll)**: Toll service numbers that are used when creating an auto attendant with resource accounts (this feature is included with Phone System)

    *   **Call Queue (Toll Free)**: Toll-free service numbers that are used when creating a call queue with resource accounts (selecting this option requires communication credits)

    *   **Auto Attendant (Toll Free)**: Toll-free service numbers that are used when creating an auto attendant with resource accounts (selecting this option requires communication credits)

    *   **Dedicated conference bridge (Toll)**: Toll service numbers that are used on conference bridges (this feature is included with Audio Conferencing)

    *   **Dedicated conference bridge (Toll Free)**: Toll-free service numbers that are used on conference bridges (selecting this option requires communication credits)

8. Select **Microsoft** as the operator.

9. Once the operator is selected, enter a quantity of numbers (up to your remaining numbers available).

Calculating Available Numbers

The amount of user numbers is equal to the total number of Domestic Calling plan and/or Domestic and International Calling plan licenses multiplied by 1.1 + 10 additional phone numbers. If you have 25 users in total with either a Domestic Calling plan and/or a Domestic and International Calling plan, you can acquire 38 phone numbers (25 x 1.1 + 10).

The number of service numbers is equal to the total number of Phone System and Audio Conferencing licenses. A complete list of how many numbers you get based on licensing can be found here:

```
https://docs.microsoft.com/en-us/microsoftteams/
how-many-phone-numbers-can-you-get.
```

---

10. You will be able to select a phone number by a predefined emergency location or area code:

- You will need to supply an emergency location for the area code for the number you are looking to obtain. For more information on creating emergency addresses in Teams, refer to the *Configuring E911* section earlier in this chapter.

- If you do not have a location specified, you can add one via the **Add a location** link.

11. You can search for your location by entering the city name used in a configured emergency location. Choose the location and click **Select**.

12. Select an area code for the number from the drop-down menu.

> **Phone Number Support**
>
> If the area code you are looking for is not available, you can select **Get phone number support** located at the top right-hand corner of the page to request the area code from the **Telephone Number Services** (**TNS**) service desk at `https://pstnsd.powerappsportals.com`. For detailed information on submitting a request to the TNS, see `https://docs.microsoft.com/en-us/MicrosoftTeams/manage-phone-numbers-for-your-organization/contact-tns-service-desk`.

13. Click on **Next** to continue. Wait while the service obtains numbers meeting your criteria.

14. Once the numbers are obtained, you will see the selected numbers and have 10 minutes to complete the transaction. At this point, you can select **Place order** to select numbers, **Back** to change the search, or **Cancel** to cancel the number request.

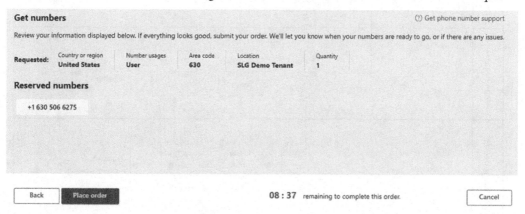

Figure 12.23 – Placing a phone number order

15. If you select **Place order**, you will see a message stating that the inventory is being updated and the number selection is being finalized to your tenant.

16. Click **Finish** to exit the ordering process.

After an order has been completed, you will be able to find the unassigned number listed under **Voice | Phone numbers**.

Number porting

Just like transitioning between traditional or mobile carriers, organizations can port their numbers from their current telephony provider to a Teams calling plan. The following types of numbers can be ported to Microsoft Teams:

- Traditional terrestrial or landline phone numbers
- Mobile device phone numbers
- Toll phone numbers
- Toll-free phone numbers
- Service phone numbers, such as those used for conference bridges and auto attendants
- Fax phone numbers
- VoIP phone numbers from other providers

The following flowchart provides an overview of the porting process:

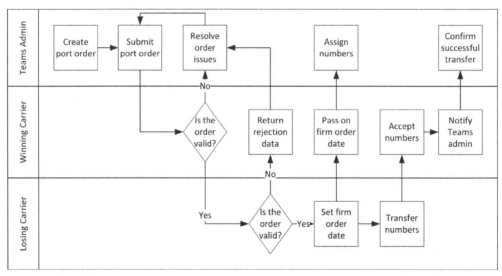

Figure 12.24 – Porting process overview

The porting process begins with a tenant admin submitting a port order. We recommend that a tenant admin requests a **Customer Service Record** (**CSR**) from the losing carrier to make sure that the port order is filled out correctly. Any errors or omissions are likely to cause the port request to be rejected by the losing carrier. It is important to note that at this point, the losing carrier must approve the port before the port can move to the next stage in the porting process.

Porting in

The port request begins with a form. To download the form, follow these steps:

1. Navigate to the Teams admin center (`https://admin.teams.microsoft.com`), select **Voice**, and then select **Phone numbers**.

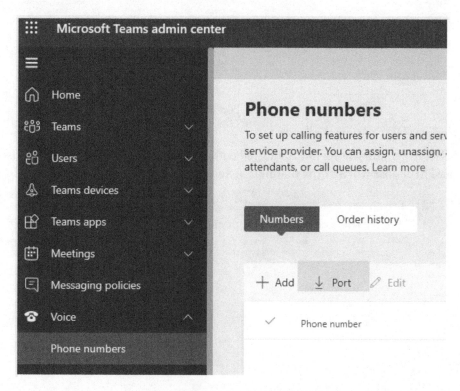

Figure 12.25 – Locating the port order form

2. Click on **Port** to open the port request form. This form is a step-by-step process that will help you generate a signed **Letter of Authorization (LOA)**.

Figure 12.26 – Port order form

3. Click on **Next** to start the request.

4. Select the country or region associated with the numbers to be ported. You'll also need to choose whether the numbers are geographic (local toll number) or toll-free.

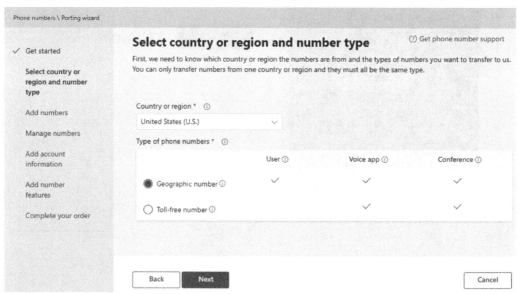

Figure 12.27 – Selecting the region and number type

5. Click on **Next** to continue.

6. Enter the **Billing Telephone Number (BTN)** associated with the numbers to be ported. The BTN can be found on the CSR from the losing carrier. You can click **Check BTN** to verify the number.

7. List the phone numbers to port in a CSV file. The file should be formatted as a single column with no header. Enter one number per row in E.164 format. Upload the CSV file into the form.

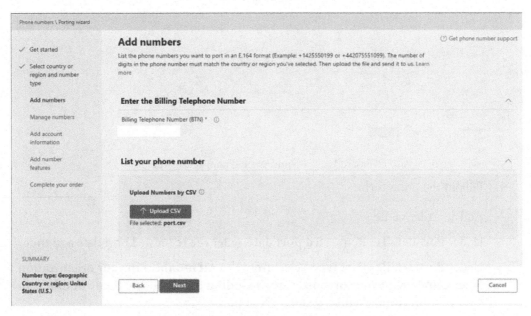

Figure 12.28 – Uploading the numbers to be ported

8. Click on **Next** to continue.

    The wizard will validate the numbers. If successful, you can click on **Next** to continue.

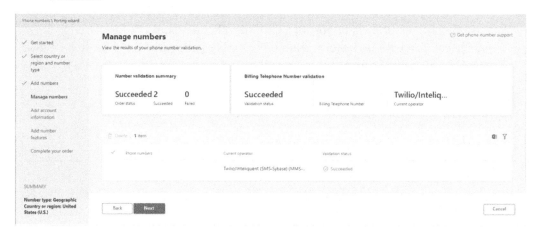

Figure 12.29 – Number validation successful

9. Fill out the order form:

- Add an order name.

- Under **Port details | Requested port date**, enter the requested port date and time.

- Under **Port details | Port type**, select from the **All numbers in your organization**, **Some numbers in your organization, including the BTN**, and **Some numbers in your organization, excluding the BTN** options.

- Under **Organization details | Organization name**, put the organization name associated with the losing carrier CSR.

- Under **Current service provider details | Service provider name**, enter the service provider name associated with the losing carrier.

- Under **Current service provider details | Account number**, enter the account number associated with the losing carrier.

- Under **Current service provider details | Account PIN**, enter the account PIN associated with the losing carrier, as shown in *Figure 12.30*:

Figure 12.30 – Port order details

- Under **Authorized user details | First name**, include the first name of the authorized user for this port.

- Under **Authorized user details | Last name**, include the last name of the authorized user for this port.

- Under **Authorized user details | Title**, include the title of the authorized user for this port.

- Under **Authorized user details | Phone number**, include the phone number of the authorized user for this port.

- Under **Authorized user details | Email address**, include the email address of the authorized user for this port.

- Under **Notifications**, include the notification email addresses for the users who need to be notified about the status of this port.

- Under **Service address**, include the service address associated with the losing carrier (listed on the CSR). If the service address is not listed, click **Add a location** to add the service address.

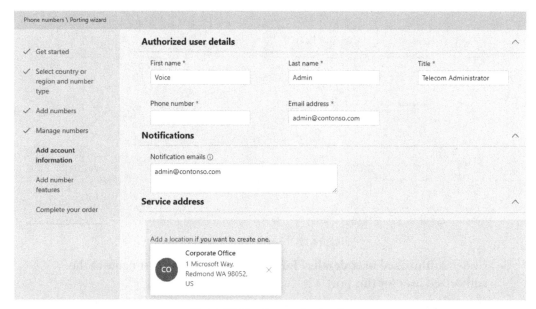

Figure 12.31 – Port order details

- Under **Service address**, select either **Yes, change usages** if you want the number changed to a service or conference number or **No** to keep the number as a user number.

- Click **Next** to continue.

- If you want to port the number as a service of conference number, select the number and select **Update number usage**.

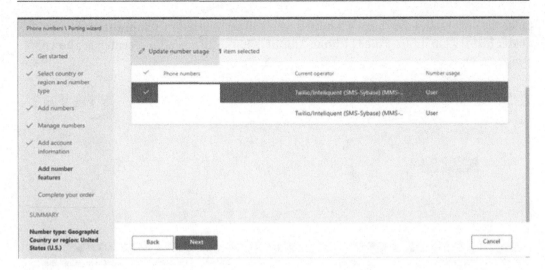

Figure 12.32 – Updating number usage

10. Click **Next** to continue.

11. On the **Complete your order** page, select **Download template** to download the LOA.

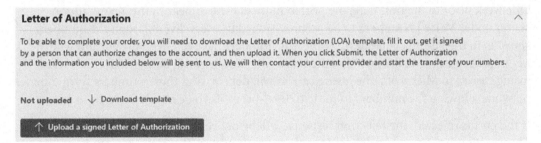

Figure 12.33 – LOA template

12. Print and sign the LOA. Upload a copy of it to the **Complete your order** page.

> **Manually Completing the LOA**
>
> If, for some reason, you are unable to complete the port request form to generate the LOA template, you can download a blank template here:
>
> `https://docs.microsoft.com/en-us/MicrosoftTeams/ phone-number-calling-plans/manually-submit-port- order.`

13. Review the information on the **Complete your order** page. Select **Submit** to send the order or click **Cancel** to cancel the port request.

Once the port request has been submitted, you will see it listed in a **Submitted** state on the **Order history** tab under **Voice | Phone numbers** in the Teams admin center, as shown in *Figure 12.34*:

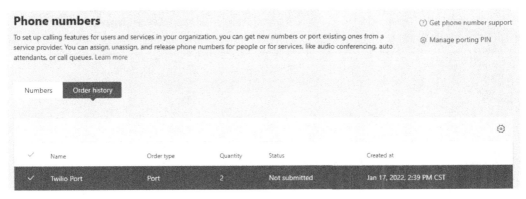

Phone numbers

To set up calling features for users and services in your organization, you can get new numbers or port existing ones from a service provider. You can assign, unassign, and release phone numbers for people or for services, like audio conferencing, auto attendants, or call queues. Learn more

⑦ Get phone number support

⊚ Manage porting PIN

Numbers   **Order history**

	Name	Order type	Quantity	Status	Created at
✓	Twilio Port	Port	2	Not submitted	Jan 17, 2022, 2:39 PM CST

Figure 12.34 – Viewing order status

After submitting your request, it will be routed to the losing carrier for approval. If the losing carrier accepts the request, an approval will be sent to Microsoft with a date to complete the request.

One week prior to the port date, the ported numbers will appear in the Teams admin center under **Voice | Numbers** to be preprovisioned to users. Even though the numbers show up in the admin center at this time, the numbers have *not* been ported and will *not* impact routing. At the port date and time, the numbers will be transferred from the losing carrier to Microsoft. The losing carrier will deprovision those numbers from their network, allowing the numbers to route to the Microsoft voice network.

If the port is rejected, the rejection response will be delivered to Microsoft with a reason. The rejection reason will be delivered to the port requestor. The requestor can remediate the issue and resubmit. If you encounter errors or need assistance during the porting process, you can engage the TNS service desk.

Canceling a port request

If you decide to cancel a port request, you can do so through the Teams admin center. To cancel a request, complete these steps:

1. Navigate to the Teams admin center (`https://admin.teams.microsoft.com`).

2. Expand **Voice** and select **Phone numbers**.

3. On the **Phone numbers** page, select the **Order history** tab.

4. Click on the port request. Under **Actions**, select **Cancel**.

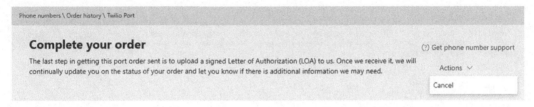

Figure 12.35 – Canceling a port request

5. Confirm the cancelation by clicking **Yes**.

Cancel your order?   ✕

You're about to send a request to cancel your order with your current operator, who'll confirm the cancellation. This action can't be undone. There may be some time between your request and the actual order cancellation confirmation. If you want to port these numbers again, you'll need to wait for this order to be cancelled and start a new port in order. Continue?

Figure 12.36 – Cancel port request confirmation

Once the cancelation has been submitted, the port request will show as **Cancelled** on the **Order history** tab.

Porting out

At any time, you can decide to port your Microsoft Calling Plans numbers to another carrier. As with the porting-in process, a PIN is required to confirm authorization of the port request. To configure a Teams porting PIN, follow these steps:

1. Navigate to the Teams admin center (`https://admin.teams.microsoft.com`).

2. Expand **Voice** and select **Phone numbers**.

3. Click **Manage porting PIN**.

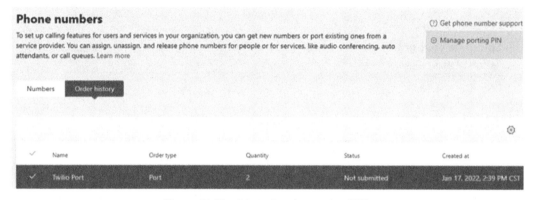

Figure 12.37 – Managing the porting PIN

4. When prompted, enter a 10-digit number and click **Apply** to save. You will need to supply this PIN to the winning carrier during the porting process.

Troubleshooting issues with a porting request

If, at any time, you have an issue with the porting process, you can use the **Get phone number support** link located at the top right-hand corner of the **Phone numbers** page. This will direct you to the TNS service desk.

You can also directly request number porting assistance via the TNS service desk app located here: `https://pstnsd.powerappsportals.com/`.

Instructions on how to submit requests can be found here:

`https://docs.microsoft.com/en-us/MicrosoftTeams/manage-phone-numbers-for-your-organization/contact-tns-service-desk`.

Assigning phone numbers

In order for a user to receive direct PSTN calls, they'll need a phone number assigned. Once you have phone numbers available in your tenant, you can begin the assignment process.

This section will cover assigning phone numbers for both Calling Plans and Operator Connect architectures.

To assign a number to a user, follow these steps:

1. Navigate to the Teams admin center (`https://admin.teams.microsoft.com`). Expand **Voice** and select **Phone numbers**.

2. On the **Numbers** tab, choose the number and click **Edit**.

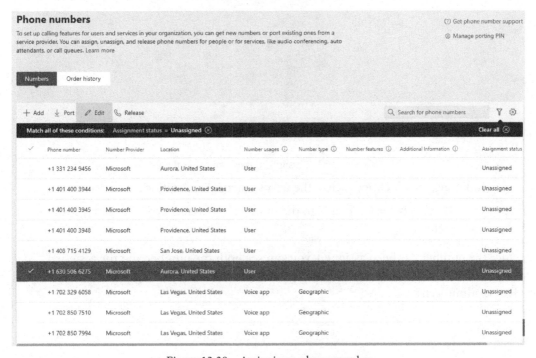

Figure 12.38 – Assigning a phone number

3. On the **Assign/unassign** flyout, enter the first three letters of a user's name. Click the **Select** button to choose that user.

Figure 12.39 – Assign/unassign number flyout

4. In **Emergency location**, select the user's emergency location.

5. Click the **Apply** button to assign the number and associated emergency location to the selected user.

Once the number has been assigned, you can see both the number and the assigned emergency location in the user's Teams profile under **Users | Manage users** in the Teams admin center.

When looking at the properties of a user, you will see the assigned phone number and associated emergency address under the **Account** tab, as shown in *Figure 12.40*:

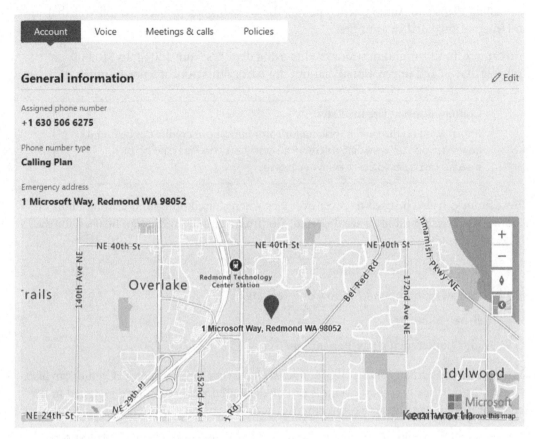

Figure 12.40 – User profile phone number and emergency address information

Now that we've covered obtaining and assigning phone numbers, we'll shift gears to communication credits.

Working with communications credits

Communications credits are used to fund calling services beyond the licensed minutes for Calling Plans and Audio Conferencing. These credits can be used for toll-free dial-in and international dial-out minutes.

You can pre-fund communications credits using deposits from $20 up to $10,000. Toll-free dial-in and international dial-out draw from this pool at a per-minute rate.

> **Communications Credits Rates**
>
> Information on the current pricing for communications credits can be found here: `https://www.microsoft.com/en-us/microsoft-teams/microsoft-teams-phone`.

These funds can also be used to cover overages when shared outbound Calling Plans or Audio Conferencing minutes are depleted. Communications credits can be used for the following purposes:

- Overages on domestic calling plans
- Overages on outbound Audio Conferencing
- Toll-free numbers
- Audio Conferencing pay-per-minute

Communications credit funds roll over and expire 1 year from purchase. Credits can also be set to automatically recharge. Funds can be deposited via a credit card assigned to the tenant or through an enterprise agreement.

Communication credits are pooled at the tenant level and are made available to users by license assignment. Users will not consume communications credits unless they are specifically assigned a Communications Credits license.

To configure a Communications Credits license for a user, follow these steps:

1. Navigate to the Microsoft 365 admin center (`https://admin.microsoft.com`).
2. Select **Users** | **Active users**, and then choose a user from the list.
3. On the **Licenses and apps** flyout, select **Communications Credits** to enable the license, as shown in *Figure 12.41*:

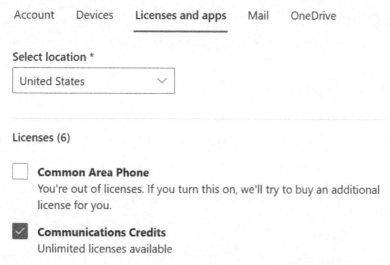

Figure 12.41 – Communications Credits licensing

4. Click **Save**.

To track the utilization of Communications credits, please see *Chapter 19, Reporting in Teams*.

Obtaining and assigning native numbers for calling plans is a relatively straightforward task. As you learned in this section, you can also move numbers from another carrier. The losing carrier (or the carrier you're migrating away from) may decide to put up roadblocks or make the process difficult in order to retain your business.

Next, we'll look at configuring policies that manage the voice features of the platform.

Configuring Teams voice policies

Teams voice policies allow you to control what features are available to users. By default, all users enabled for Teams Phone and Enterprise Voice will be assigned to the built-in global policy.

You can create additional policies and customize end user experiences.

In this section, we'll look at the following policies:

- General calling policies
- Call parking
- Caller ID policies

Calling policies

Teams **calling policies** control a myriad of calling features for Teams users, including the following:

- Ability to make private calls
- Availability of call forwarding
- Ability to enable simultaneous ringing to other Teams users or external phone numbers
- Routing calls to voicemail
- Group calling
- User delegation
- Call recording options
- Busy on busy
- Music on hold
- Web PSTN calling
- Closed-captioning settings
- Autoanswer for meeting invites
- Whether or not SIP devices can be used by Teams users

As you can see, there are quite a few features that can be managed!

Configuring a calling policy

To configure a new calling policy, perform the following steps:

1. Navigate to the Teams admin center (`https://admin.teams.microsoft.com`).
2. Expand **Voice** and select **Calling policies**.
3. Click **Add**.

4. Add a calling policy name and description, as shown in *Figure 12.42*. The following features can be enabled or disabled:

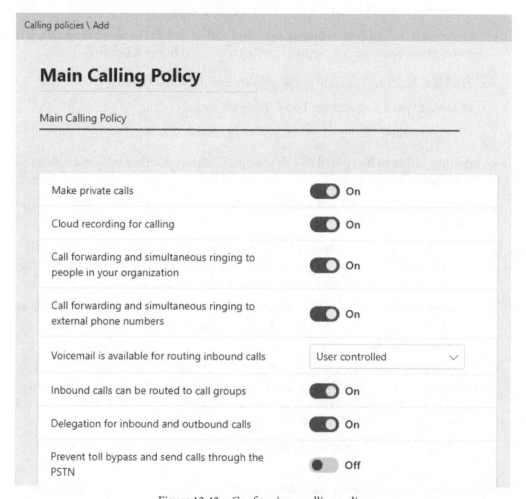

Figure 12.42 – Configuring a calling policy

- **Make private calls**: Controls all calling capabilities in Teams. Turning it off disables all calling functionality in Teams.

- **Cloud recording for calling**: Enables cloud recording for calling.

- **Call forwarding and simultaneous ringing to people in your organization**: Controls whether incoming calls can be forwarded to an internal Teams user or whether an internal Teams user can be added to a simultaneous ring.

- **Call forwarding and simultaneous ringing to external phone numbers**: Controls whether incoming calls can be forwarded to an external number or whether an external number can be added to a simultaneous ring.

- **Voicemail is available for routing inbound calls**: Controls how inbound calls will be routed to voicemail. The setting can be configured to the following:

  - **Enabled**: Voicemail will always be available for inbound calls.

  - **Disabled**: Voicemail will not be available for inbound calls.

  - **User controlled**: Teams users can enable or disable voicemail for inbound calls.

- **Inbound calls can be routed to call groups**: Controls whether inbound calls can be forwarded to a call group.

- **Delegation for inbound and outbound calls**: Controls whether inbound calls can be routed to delegates.

- **Prevent toll bypass and send calls through the PSTN**: When enabled, calls will be sent through the PSTN and may incur telco charges. This is opposed to sending them through the Microsoft network, bypassing toll charges.

- **Music on hold for PSTN callers**: Controls whether music on hold will be on or off when a PSTN caller is placed on hold. It can be set to **Enabled**, **Not Enabled**, or **User Can Control**.

- **Busy on busy when in a call**: Controls how incoming calls are handled when a Teams user is on a call. When enabled, incoming calls can be rejected with a busy signal or, if set to **Unanswered**, redirect based on the Teams user's unanswered call settings. It can be set to **Enabled**, **Not Enabled**, or **Unanswered**.

- **Web PSTN calling**: Controls whether calls can be placed using the Teams web client.

- **Real-time captions in Teams calls**: Controls whether real-time captions can be enabled on a Teams call.

- **Automatically answer incoming meeting invites**: Controls whether an incoming meeting invite will be answered automatically by a Teams client or endpoint.

- **SIP devices can be used for call**: Controls whether a generic SIP device can be used by a Teams user as a Teams calling endpoint.

> **Further Reading**
>
> For more information on the SIP gateway, see the following article: `https://docs.microsoft.com/en-us/microsoftteams/sip-gateway-configure`.

5. Click **Save** to add the policy.

Once a policy has been created, it can be edited, deleted, or assigned to users.

Assigning a calling policy

Calling policies can be assigned to either users or groups.

To assign a policy to an individual, follow these steps:

1. Navigate to the Teams admin center (`https://admin.teams.microsoft.com`).

2. Expand **Voice** and select **Calling policies**.

3. On the **Manage policies** tab, select the policy and click **Manage users**.

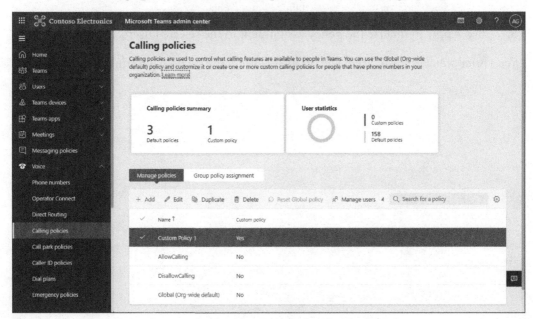

Figure 12.43 – Adding a calling policy to users

4. Use the search bar to find users, and then click **Add** for each user.

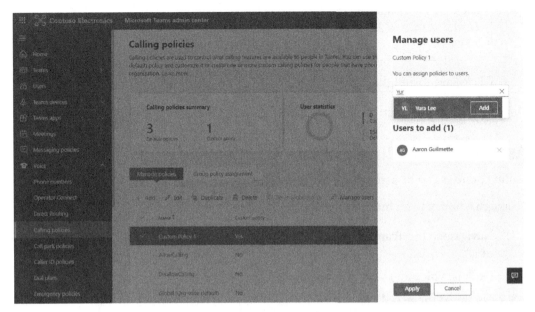

Figure 12.44 – Adding a calling policy for users

5. Click **Apply** to finalize the policy assignment to the selected users.

After a brief policy refresh, users will be subject to their new policy features.

To assign a policy to a group, perform the following steps:

1. Navigate to the Teams admin center (`https://admin.teams.microsoft.com`).

2. Expand **Voice** and select **Calling policies**.

3. On the **Group policy assignment** tab, click **Add**.

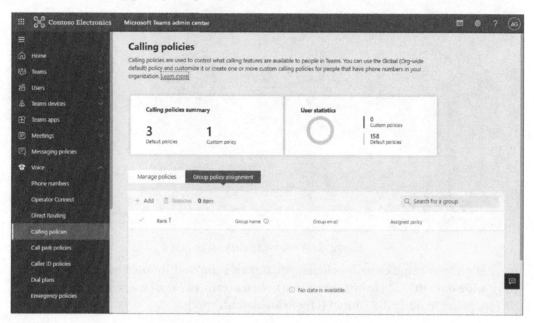

Figure 12.45 – Group policy assignment tab

4. In the search bar, select a Microsoft 365 group that will inherit the policy assignment.

5. Under **Select rank**, choose a numerical ranking for policy inheritance. If users in this group are part of any other groups with a policy assigned, those users will inherit the policy from the group based on the highest rank.

6. Under **Select a policy**, choose the calling policy you want to be assigned to that group. Click **Apply** to assign the policy to that group. See *Figure 12.46*:

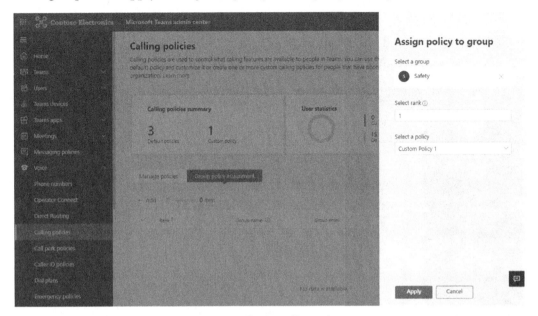

Figure 12.46 – Group policy assignment

In addition to creating custom policies, you can also edit built-in policies, such as **Global (Org-wide default)**. To change the calling policies features for all users not assigned to a custom policy, modify the **Global (Org-wide default)** policy.

Call park policies

Call parking is a feature that allows a Teams user to put a call on hold on one voice endpoint (Teams client, native Teams phone device, or Teams mobile app) and then pick it up on another endpoint. This can be done for a number of reasons, such as transferring from a device whose battery is running out or paging an employee on a shop floor.

A Teams user with a call parking policy applied can perform parking by selecting **More actions** in their calling window during an active call and then selecting **Call Park**. At that point, Teams will display a numeric code that can be entered in the calling app to pick up the call.

You can pick up parked calls by selecting **Parked calls** in the Teams Calls app, as shown in *Figure 12.47*:

Figure 12.47 – Parked calls in the Calls app

After selecting **Parked calls,** the user is prompted to enter the numeric code that was generated when the call was placed on park.

Configuring a call park policy

To configure a call park policy, follow these steps:

1. Navigate to the Teams admin center (`https://admin.teams.microsoft.com`).

2. Expand **Voice** and select **Call park policies**.

3. On the **Manage policies** tab, click **Add**.

4. Configure a name and description for the call park policy.

5. To enable parking, slide the **Call park** toggle to **On**.

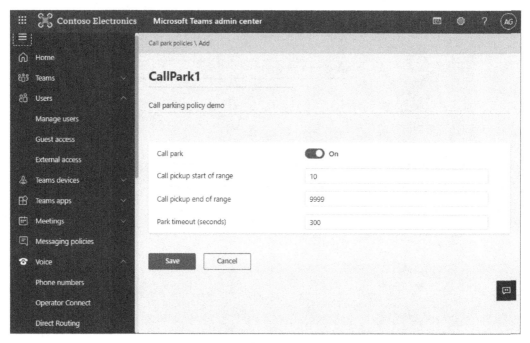

Figure 12.48 – Configuring a call park policy

6. Configure the call park range using the **Call pickup start of range** and **Call pickup end of range** values. The start of range option defines the lowest numeric code that will be generated for a call on park, and the end of range option defines the highest number. The default start of range value is 10; the default end of range value is 99. You can increase the end of range to 9999. Calls placed on park will be assigned a new number (incremented by 1) until they reach the end of the range, at which point the call park ID will reset to the start range value.

7. Configure the **Park timeout (seconds)** value. This value determines how long a call can stay parked before ringing back to the original user who picked up the call. The default value is 300 seconds but can be configured as any value between 120 and 1800 seconds.

8. Click **Save** to create the policy.

You've now created a call park policy that can be applied to users or groups.

Assigning a call park policy

To assign a call park policy, you follow a similar set of steps as you do when assigning a calling policy. Follow these steps:

1. Navigate to the Teams admin center (`https://admin.teams.microsoft.com`).

2. Expand **Voice** and select **Call park policies**.

3. On the **Manage policies** tab, select the policy and click **Manage users**.

4. Use the search bar to find users, and then click **Add** for each user.

5. Click on **Apply** to finalize the policy assignment to the selected users.

After a brief policy refresh, users will be subject to their new policy features.

To assign a policy to a group, perform the following steps:

1. Navigate to the Teams admin center (`https://admin.teams.microsoft.com`).

2. Expand **Voice** and select **Call park policies**.

3. On the **Group policy assignment** tab, click **Add**.

4. In the search bar, select a Microsoft 365 group that will inherit the policy assignment.

5. Under **Select rank**, choose a numerical ranking for policy inheritance. If users in this group are part of any other groups with a policy assigned, those users will inherit the policy from the group based on the highest rank.

6. Under **Select a policy**, choose the call park policy you want to be assigned to that group. Click **Apply** to assign the policy to that group.

In addition to creating custom policies, you can also edit built-in policies, such as **Global (Org-wide default)**. To change the call park policy configured for all users not assigned to a custom policy, modify the **Global (Org-wide default)** policy.

Caller ID policies

Caller ID policies provide management over the caller ID data that is displayed to recipients. Depending on the scenario, it may be beneficial to display a service number or no data as opposed to the actual calling line identity.

Configuring a caller ID policy

To create a custom caller ID policy, follow these steps:

1. Navigate to the Teams admin center (`https://admin.teams.microsoft.com`).

2. Expand **Voice** and select **Caller ID policies**.

3. Click on **Add**.

4. Enter a name and description for the policy.

5. Configure the toggle for **Block incoming caller ID**. Blocking the inbound caller ID will mask the caller ID data for calls received by Teams users.

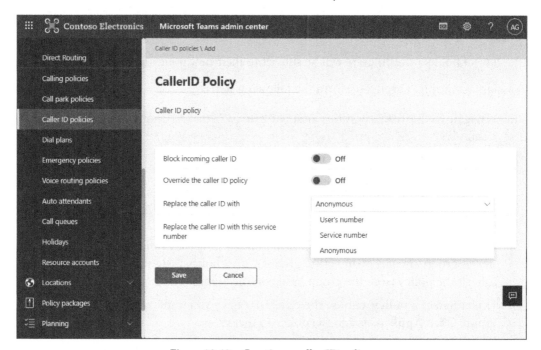

Figure 12.49 – Creating a caller ID policy

6. Configure the **Override the caller ID policy** toggle. Toggling this to **On** will allow the user to override the policy settings.

7. Configure the **Replace the caller ID with** policy dropdown. You can choose to replace the default outbound caller ID value with **Anonymous**, **User's number**, or a configured service number in your tenant.

8. If you choose **Service number** in the **Replace the caller ID with** dropdown, select a service number in the **Replace the caller ID with this service number** dropdown.

9. Click **Save** to create the policy.

After a few moments, the new caller ID policy is available for assignment.

Assigning a caller ID policy

Unlike calling policies or call park policies, caller ID policies are assigned through the **Users** menu.

To assign a caller ID policy, follow these steps:

1. Navigate to the Teams admin center (`https://admin.teams.microsoft.com`).

2. Expand **Users** and select **Manage users**.

3. Select one or more users by clicking the user's row. You can also use filter criteria, such as existing policy assignments or name matches, to help select larger groups of individuals.

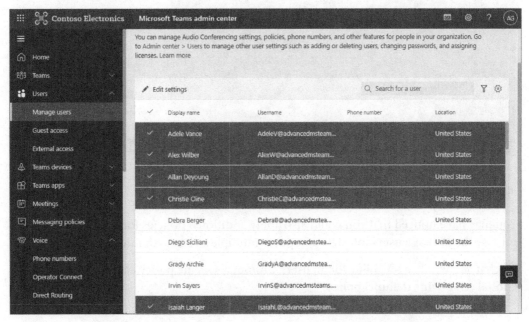

Figure 12.50 – Manage users to configure caller ID policy

4. Click on **Edit settings**.

5. Scroll to the **Caller ID policy** dropdown and select the caller ID policy you wish to apply to the selected users.

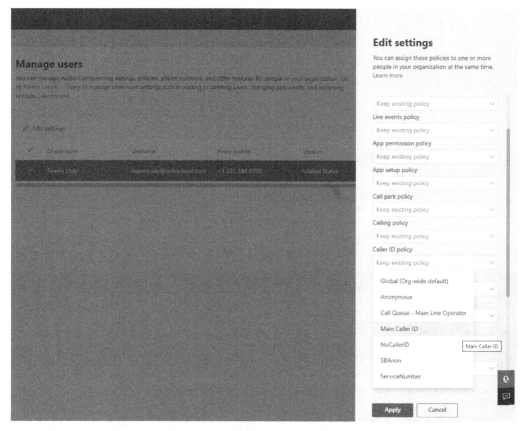

Figure 12.51 – Selecting a caller ID policy

6. Click **Apply**.

You may have noticed that you could also apply additional policies for users as well. You can use the **Manage users** interface to update multiple policy assignments at once.

To change the caller ID policy for all users without a specific policy assigned, modify the **Global (Org-wide default)** policy.

Changing the caller name

When using Teams Calling Plan numbers, organizations may need to change the existing **Caller Name** (**CNAM**) data sent with the caller ID to something more aligned with their organization. To do this, a ticket can be opened with the TNS desk to have the CNAM updated.

The following guidelines must be used when requesting a new CNAM:

- CNAM updates will only reflect on wired called parties as wireless carriers do not have access to the CNAM database to reflect caller ID displays. Each wireless carrier company has its own database that is maintained by them. Requests for CNAM updates must be made directly with those wireless carriers. After an update has been made, you will need to call a landline number with caller ID features activated to verify the change has been successful.

- CNAM updates for toll-free numbers cannot be set.

- CNAM names must have 15 characters or less, including spaces.

After the update request is submitted, it normally takes 24 to 48 hours for the new CNAM value to begin to show up when dialing out with those numbers.

As you've seen in this section, managing and assigning caller ID policies is relatively straightforward. In the next section, we'll look at managing outbound calling features.

Configuring outbound calling

Teams Phone can restrict outbound calling for both the Audio Conferencing and PSTN services. This allows administrators the ability to block calling numbers outside the specified region. Outbound calling restrictions can also be used to disable outbound calling capabilities altogether.

Configuring outbound calling for a user

To configure outbound calling settings for a user, follow these steps:

1. Navigate to the Teams admin center (`https://admin.teams.microsoft.com`).

2. Expand **Users** and select **Manage users**.

3. Select a user to edit by clicking on their display name.

4. On the user's property page, select the **Voice** tab.

5. Under the **Outbound calling** section, click the dropdown for **Dial-out settings for calling**.

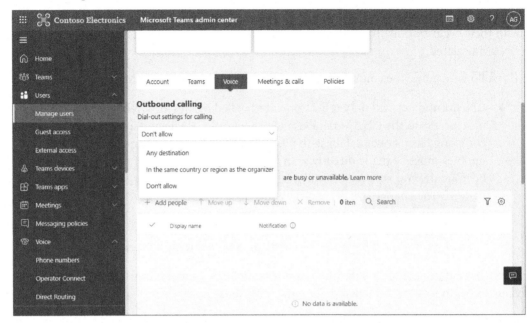

Figure 12.52 – Configuring outbound calling

6. Select from one of the three available options: **Any destination**, **In the same country or region as the organizer**, or **Don't allow**.

As soon as the selection is made, the policy will be applied.

Configuring outbound calling for multiple users

As you saw in the previous example, the Teams admin center user interface only allows configuring a single user's outbound calling policy. In an organization with hundreds or thousands of users, this could become tedious work.

Fortunately, outbound calling policies (as well as many other policies) can also be managed in bulk via the Teams PowerShell module.

To set the policy for a single user, you can use the following command:

```
Grant-CsDialoutPolicy -Identity <username> -PolicyName <policy
name>
```

To configure the default outbound policy tenant-wide, you can run the following command:

```
Grant-CsDialoutPolicy -PolicyName <policy name> -Global
```

You can refer to the following table for valid `PolicyName` values and descriptions:

PowerShell Cmdlet	Description
DialoutCPCandPSTNInternational	User in the conference can dial out to international and domestic numbers, and this user can also make outbound calls to international and domestic numbers.
DialoutCPCDomesticPSTNInternational	User in the conference can only dial out to domestic numbers, and this user can make outbound calls to international and domestic numbers.
DialoutCPCDisabledPSTNInternational	User in the conference cannot dial out. This user can make outbound calls to international and domestic numbers.
DialoutCPCInternationalPSTNDomestic	User in the conference can dial out to international and domestic numbers, and this user can only make outbound calls to domestic PSTN numbers.
DialoutCPCInternationalPSTNDisabled	User in the conference can dial out to international and domestic numbers, and this user cannot make any outbound calls to PSTN numbers besides emergency numbers.
DialoutCPCandPSTNDomestic	User in the conference can only dial out to domestic numbers, and this user can only make outbound calls to domestic PSTN numbers.

`DialoutCPCDomesticPSTNDisabled`	User in the conference can only dial out to domestic numbers, and this user cannot make any outbound calls to PSTN numbers besides emergency numbers.
`DialoutCPCDisabledPSTNDomestic`	User in the conference cannot dial out, and this user can only make outbound calls to domestic PSTN numbers.
`DialoutCPCandPSTNDisabled`	User in the conference cannot dial out, and this user cannot make any outbound calls to PSTN numbers besides emergency numbers.
`DialoutCPCZoneAPSTNInternational`	User in the conference can only dial out to zone A countries and regions, and this user can make outbound calls to international and domestic numbers.
`DialoutCPCZoneAPSTNDomestic`	User in the conference can only dial out to zone A countries and regions, and this user can only make outbound calls to domestic PSTN numbers.
`DialoutCPCZoneAPSTNDisabled`	User in the conference can only dial out to zone A countries and regions, and this user cannot make any outbound calls to PSTN numbers besides emergency numbers.

Table 12.2 – Dialout policy values

For example, to assign the `DialoutCPCDomesticPSTNInternational` policy (which allows for outbound domestic calling from an audio conference or domestic and international calls from a normal call) to all users in the tenant, run the following command:

```
Grant-CsDialoutPolicy -PolicyName
DialoutCPCDomesticPSTNInternational -Global
```

> **Note**
>
> For more information on zone A countries and regions, see the following article: `https://docs.microsoft.com/en-us/microsoftteams/audio-conferencing-zones`.

Summary

In this chapter, you learned about configuring the core platform features, such as E911, calling plans, and voice policies relating to parking, as well as the caller ID and features related to call forwarding and voicemail. Should you want to bring numbers from your existing carrier into the Teams platform, you can use the porting process as well.

With Teams Phone, Microsoft has provided a feature-rich voice platform. The platform is quite flexible. It can be deployed easily using first-party (Microsoft) calling plans as well as be integrated with a carrier through Operator Connect. The Teams platform can also be deployed alongside existing telephony infrastructures using Direct Routing. Direct Routing allows for more complex and integrated voice models. It is important to determine which model (or models) are needed in your organization. All three models can be used together to allow flexibility of services and features.

Teams' voice technology empowers users to extend their collaboration activities with integrated voice features. The Teams platform allows administrators to monitor and manage both voice and collaboration workloads across the organization.

In the next chapter, we'll look at configuring advanced Teams features, such as auto attendants and call queues.

13
Configuring Advanced Teams Phone Features

In *Chapter 12, Deploying Teams Phone*, you learned about the core features of the Teams Phone platform, including configuring E911, managing phone numbers, and deploying voice configuration policies.

Now, it's time to go deeper into advanced features. If you've ever called an organization and navigated a phone tree or menu to reach a specific department or team, you've interacted with some sort of an interactive response or interactive voice response system. When working with Teams Phone, those features and capabilities are handled through auto attendants and call queues.

In this chapter, we're going to cover the following topics:

- Configuring resource accounts
- Configuring holidays
- Configuring auto attendants
- Configuring call queues
- Understanding voice-enabled channels

After reading this chapter, you will be able to explain and set up auto attendants, call queues, and voice-enabled channels.

Let's get to it!

Configuring resource accounts

Resource accounts are used to route calls to two Teams voice applications – **Auto Attendants** and **Call Queues**. Depending on the scenario, a resource account may need a phone number assigned to it.

The flow chart in *Figure 13.1* shows an overview of how to provision a resource account, based on whether it will have a phone number associated with it.

If the resource account requires a phone number, a Phone System Virtual User license needs to be assigned to that resource account. The Phone System Virtual User license is a special no-cost SKU to be used with resource accounts that require a phone number:

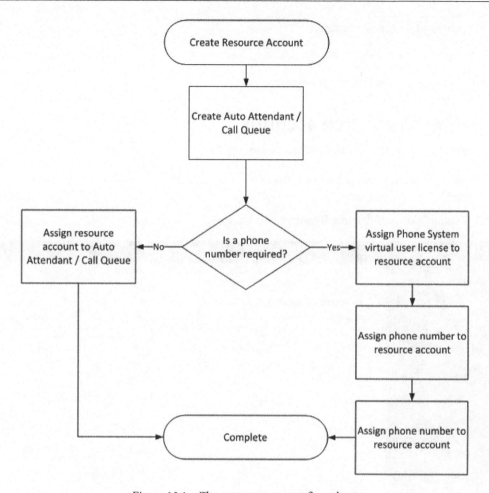

Figure 13.1 – The resource account flow chart

When a Phone System Virtual User license is assigned to a resource account, you can assign a reserved toll or toll-free service number to that resource account. For information on how to reserve service numbers, see the *Obtaining phone numbers* section in this chapter.

If an auto attendant or call queue needs to be external facing, you will need to assign it a phone number.

In the following sections, we'll cover the following:

- Creating a resource account
- Acquiring virtual user licenses
- Assigning licenses to the resource account

- Ordering a service number

- Assigning a service number

Let's take a look at all of these processes.

Creating a resource account

To configure a resource account, follow these steps:

1. Navigate to the Teams admin center (`https://admin.teams.microsoft.com`).

2. Expand **Voice** and select **Resource accounts**:

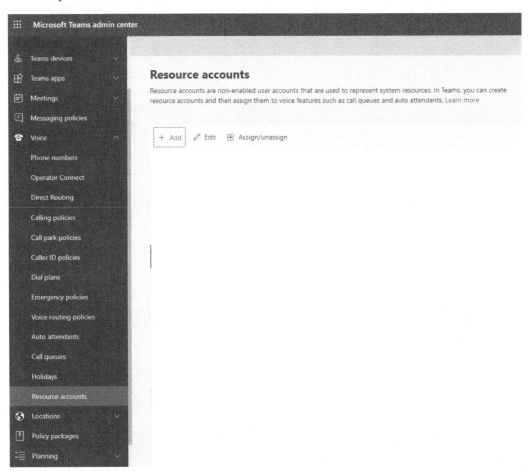

Figure 13.2 – The Resource accounts page

3. To add a resource account, click on **Add**.

4. Configure the resource account properties on the **Add resource account** flyout, as shown in *Figure 13.3*, including the **Display name**, **Username**, and **Resource account type** values:

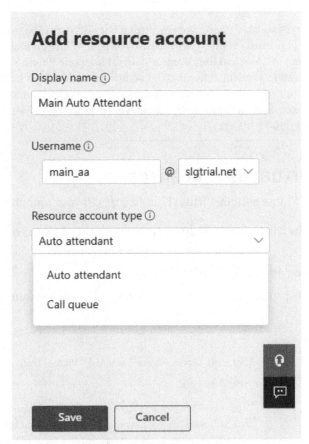

Figure 13.3 – Add a resource account

5. Click **Save** when finished.

As mentioned previously, if the auto attendant or call queue is internal, a phone number is not required. Internal auto attendants or call queues can be dialed directly like a Teams user. If the resource requires a phone number (either now or in the future), you can add the Phone System Virtual User license through the Microsoft 365 admin center (`https://admin.microsoft.com`).

If this resource account will be connected to a toll-free number, you will also need to assign it a communications credit license through the Microsoft 365 admin center as well. You can refer to the *Communications credits* section in this chapter for an example.

> **Virtual User License Allocation**
>
> The number of available Phone System Virtual User licenses is based on the number of normal Phone System licenses owned. Microsoft makes an initial grant of 25 virtual user licenses when at least one Phone System license is added to a tenant. After that, an additional Virtual User license is allocated for every 10 Phone System licenses. For example, if a tenant has 1,000 Phone System licenses, the tenant will be allocated 125 virtual user licenses ((1000/10) + 25).

Acquiring virtual user licenses

To assign allocated Phone System Virtual User licenses to your tenant, follow these steps:

1. Navigate to the Microsoft 365 admin center (`https://admin.microsoft.com`).

2. Expand **Billing** and select **Purchase services**.

3. Click on **View products** and search for **Microsoft Teams Phone Standard - Virtual User**:

Figure 13.4 – A Virtual User license

4. Select **Details**. You will be able to order the allocated number of licenses:

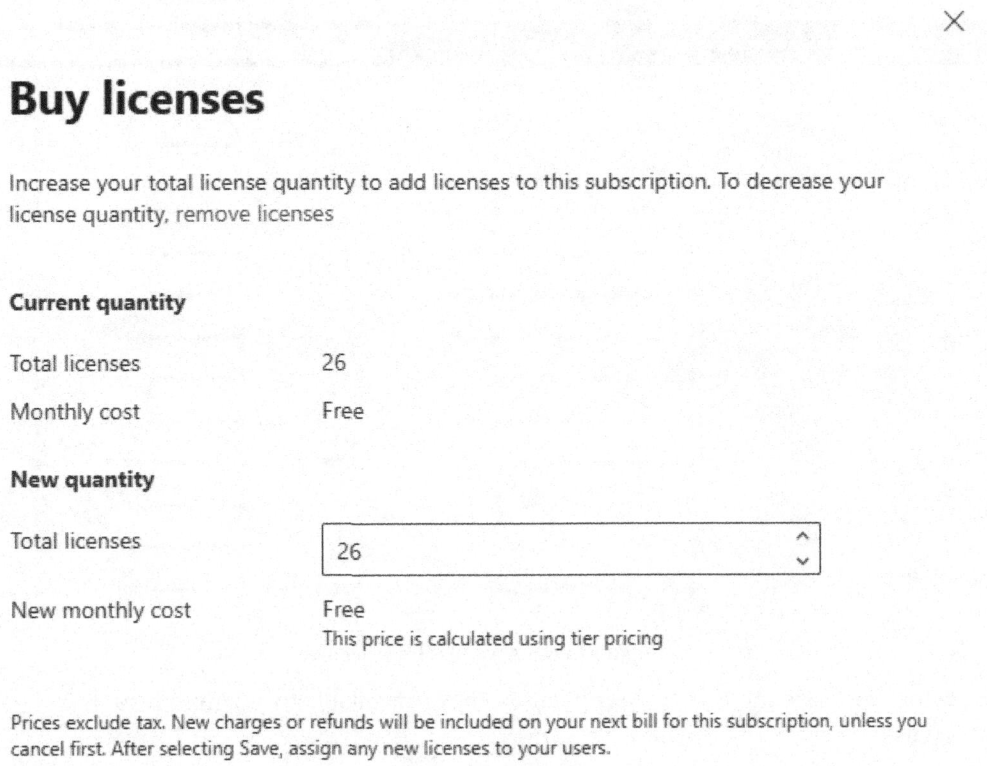

Buy licenses

Increase your total license quantity to add licenses to this subscription. To decrease your license quantity, remove licenses

Current quantity

Total licenses   26

Monthly cost   Free

New quantity

Total licenses

26	

New monthly cost   Free
                      This price is calculated using tier pricing

Prices exclude tax. New charges or refunds will be included on your next bill for this subscription, unless you cancel first. After selecting Save, assign any new licenses to your users.

Figure 13.5 – Allocating Virtual User licenses

5. Click **Buy**.

Once ordered, they will appear in your tenant immediately under the **Billing | Licenses** page, as shown in *Figure 13.6*:

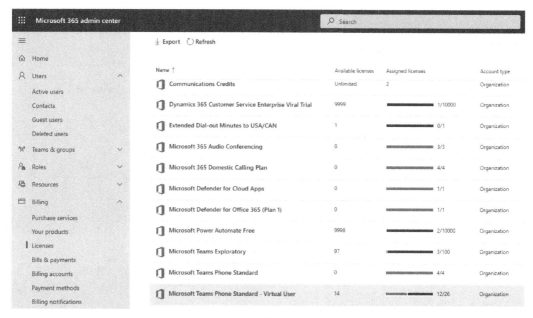

Figure 13.6 – A Virtual User license

Now that you have the Virtual User licenses, they're available to assign to resource accounts.

Assigning licenses to a resource account

To add a Phone System Virtual User license, you'll need to assign it a license through the Microsoft 365 admin center with this process:

1. Navigate to the Microsoft 365 admin center (`https://admin.microsoft.com`).

2. Expand **Users** and select **Active users**.

3. Select the resource account and click on **Manage product licenses**.

4. Select the **Microsoft Teams Phone Standard - Virtual User** license checkbox and click on **Save changes**:

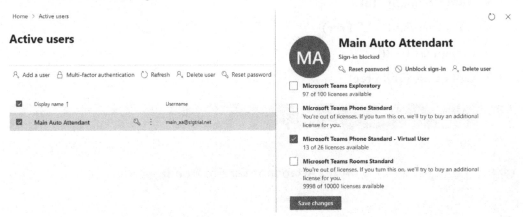

Figure 13.7 – Assigning a Virtual User license

Once the Virtual User license is assigned, you can then assign a service number to the resource account if desired.

Ordering a service number

If you need your call queue or auto attendant to be available externally, you will need to order a service number and then assign it to the resource account. To order a service number for the account, follow these steps:

1. Navigate to the Teams admin center (`https://admin.teams.microsoft.com`).

2. Expand **Voice** and select **Phone numbers**.

3. Click **Add**.

4. Enter a name and description for the number order, and then select **Country or region**.

5. Under **Number type**, select from one of the following, as shown in *Figure 13.8*:

    - **Auto attendant (Toll)**

    - **Auto attendant (Toll Free)**

    - **Call queue (Toll)**

    - **Call queue (Toll Free)**:

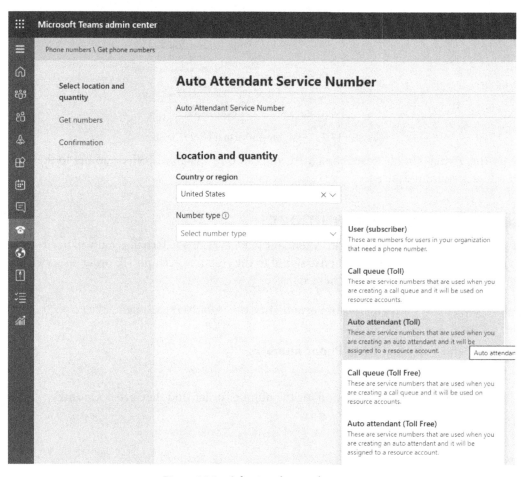

Figure 13.8 – Selecting the number type

6. Select the **Show my operators** checkbox to enumerate connected providers. If you are only using calling plans, Microsoft is the only provider available. If you have configured Operator Connect, you will be able to select a third-party communications provider. For more information on configuring Operator Connect, see *Appendix A*:

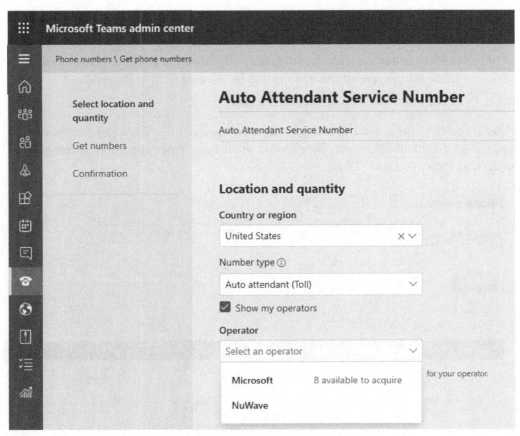

Figure 13.9 – Selecting an operator

7. Select a quantity of service numbers to obtain.

8. Under **Search for new numbers**, select **Search by city name** and enter the city associated with the desired area code. The city value *must* be a defined location in your tenant. If you have not defined locations, please see the *Configuring E911* section in this chapter.

9. After selecting the city, select the desired **Area code** option from the drop-down menu and select **Next** to continue.

10. Click **Place order**. As with obtaining user numbers, you will have 10 minutes to complete the process, or the number will be released back to the pool.

11. Once the order has been placed, click **Finish**.

After completing the order, the number will show up under the **Voice | Phone numbers** page in the Teams admin center. The number will display **Voice app** under **Number usages**, as shown in *Figure 13.10*:

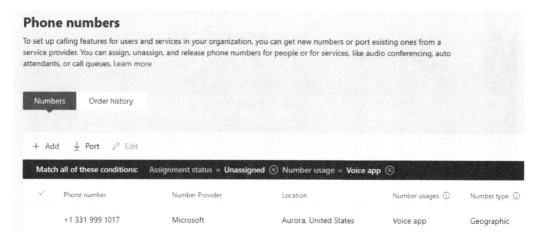

Figure 13.10 – A service number assigned to a tenant

Now that you have a service number available, you can proceed to assign it to a resource account.

Assigning a service number

To assign a service number to a resource account, follow these steps:

1. Navigate to the Teams admin center (`https://admin.teams.microsoft.com`).

2. Expand **Voice** and select **Resource accounts**.

3. On the **Resource accounts** page, select the resource account to which you'll assign a service number:

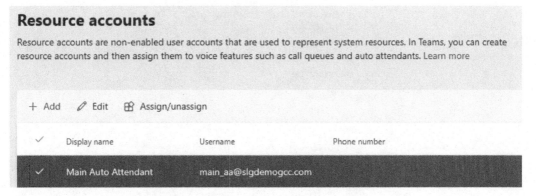

Figure 13.11 – Selecting a resource account

4. Click on **Assign/unassign**.

5. For **Phone number type**, select from one of the following:

   - **Online**: A toll number hosted by Microsoft or an Operator Connect cloud.

   - **Toll-free**: A toll-free number hosted by Microsoft or an Operator Connect cloud. Toll-fre numbers require Communications Credits.

- **On-premises**: A number hosted via Direct Routing on a third-party carrier network, as shown in *Figure 13.12*:

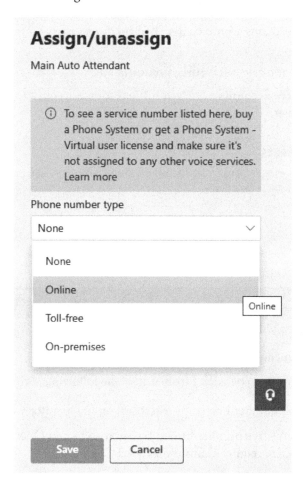

Figure 13.12 – Selecting a phone number type

6. After selecting the provider, select an available service number and click on **Add**:

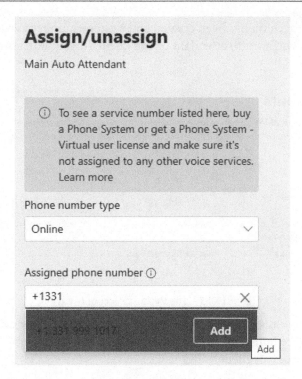

Figure 13.13 – Selecting an available service phone number

7. If the auto attendant or call queue already exists, you can assign this resource account to that voice app, as follows:

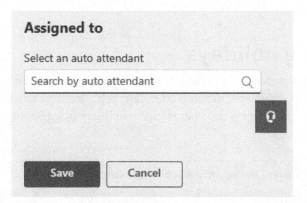

Figure 13.14 – Assigning the phone number to a voice app

8. Click on **Save**.

Now that a resource account has been created and a phone number assigned to it, you can associate it with an auto attendant or call queue (if you didn't do that during the previous steps):

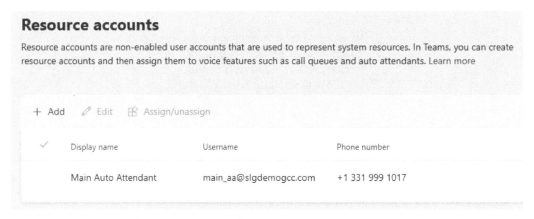

Figure 13.15 – The Resource accounts page

Multiple resource accounts can be added to a single auto attendant or call queue to allow multiple dial-in service numbers. However, a resource account can only be added to a single auto attendant or call queue.

As you can see, resource accounts can be configured and licensed differently, depending on whether the account will have a service phone number associated with it or be available directly to external callers.

Next, we'll examine holiday configurations.

Configuring holidays

Teams Phone allows you to configure a list of holidays that your organization observes. This allows you to configure specific auto attendant behavior on a scheduled basis. It is recommended that you set up your organization's holidays before configuring any auto attendant configurations.

> **Creating Holidays During Auto Attendant Configuration**
>
> While there is the option to add holidays during an auto attendant configuration, doing so will exit the auto attendant setup wizard, and all settings will be lost. If you need to configure an auto attendant that makes use of holidays, we recommend configuring holidays first.
>
> If you discover that you need to reference a holiday configuration during an auto attendant setup, complete the setup without the holiday, create the holiday, and then go back and edit the auto attendant call flow to include the new holiday.

To configure a holiday, follow these steps:

1. Navigate to the Teams admin center (`https://admin.teams.microsoft.com`).

2. Expand **Voice** and select **Holidays**.

3. Click on **New holiday**.

4. Enter a name for the holiday and select **Add new date**.

5. Under **Start time**, click the calendar icon and choose the starting date for the holiday.

6. Use the drop-down list to select the starting time for the holiday.

7. Under **End time**, select the calendar icon and choose the ending date for the holiday.

8. Use the drop-down list to select the ending time for the holiday.

9. If you want to configure additional dates (such as recurring holidays), simply click **Add new date** and specify the start and end times:

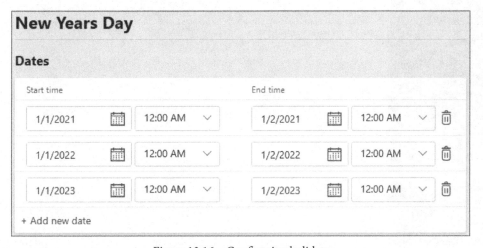

Figure 13.16 – Configuring holidays

Next, we'll begin configuring auto attendants.

Configuring auto attendants

Auto attendants allow for automated call routing in the Teams system based on input from a menu. More specifically, an auto attendant allows an organization to provide callers with the ability to be routed in the Teams voice system without relying on a person to handle incoming calls.

Callers can navigate by either **Dual-Tone Multi-Frequency (DTMF)** digits or **Interactive Voice Response (IVR)**.

When a caller dials a number with an auto attendant configured, the caller may be prompted with a menu option. DTMF allows callers to navigate the menu by pressing a number on the dialpad that maps to an option, while IVR provides the caller with the availability to speak their choice. When paired with call queues, auto attendants can provide automated routing to the appropriate person or department in your organization.

To set up auto attendants, go directly to the Teams admin center:

1. As a Teams administrator or a global administrator, navigate to `https://admin.teams.microsoft.com` and log in.

2. On the left pane, click on **Voice** and then **Auto attendants**:

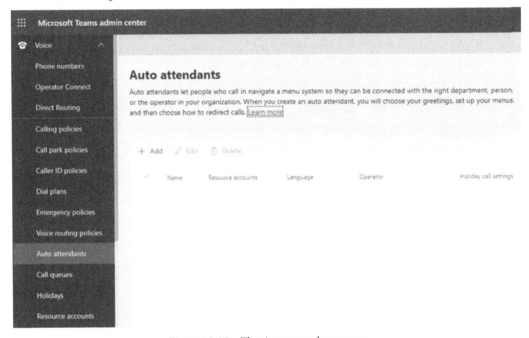

Figure 13.17 – The Auto attendants page

3. Click on **Add**.

4. Enter a **Name** for the auto attendant and then select an operator. An operator is optional but recommended. For an operator, you can select from one the following, as shown in *Figure 13.18*:

   - **No Operator**: The auto attendant will not have an operator option.

   - **Person in organization**: The operator will be a Teams user in your organization.

- **Voice app**: The operator will be another auto attendant or a call queue. If selecting a voice app for the operator, you can search for the resource account associated with the auto attendant or call queue.

- **External phone number**: The operator will be an E.164-formatted PSTN number external to Teams.

> **Routing to an External Phone Number**
>
> If you want to configure an auto attendant to route to an external phone number, you will need to assign a Calling Plan license to the resource account (Calling Plan or Operator Connect architecture) or an online voice routing policy (Direct Routing architecture) for the resource account assigned to this auto attendant.

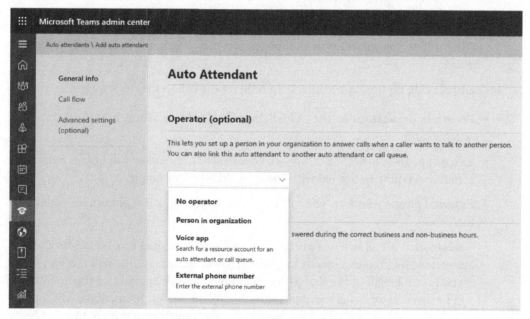

Figure 13.18 – Configuring an operator

5. Select a time zone and language for this auto attendant.

> **Supported Languages for Auto Attendants**
>
> A list of supported languages can be found here: `https://docs.microsoft.com/en-us/microsoftteams/create-a-phone-system-auto-attendant-languages`.

6. Select **Enable voice inputs** if you want to allow callers to use voice navigation.

7. Click on **Next**.

8. On the **Call flows** page, select the welcome greeting for the auto attendant. Under **First play a greeting message**, select an option:

-   **No greeting**: No welcome greeting will be played.

-   **Play an audio file**: An uploaded audio file will be played. Uploaded files must be in .WAV, .MP3, or .WMA formats and must not exceed 5 MB.

-   **Add a greeting message**: Enter a text message of up to 1,000 characters. The message will be converted from text to speech and will be read to the caller.

9. Under **Then route the call**, select the call flow action the auto attendant will take after playing the greeting message:

-   **Disconnect**: The call will be disconnected after playing the greeting message. This setting is ideal for **answer only** mailboxes that play a message and then disconnect the call.

-   **Redirect call**: Options are available to redirect the call to the following:

    -   **Person in organization**: The call will be redirected to a Teams user in your organization.

    -   **Voice app**: The call will be redirected to an auto attendant or call queue. Select the resource account associated with the auto attendant or queue.

    -   **External phone number**: The call will be redirected to a PSTN number external to Teams.

    -   **Voicemail**: The call will be redirected to a shared voicemail box housed in the auto attendant. You can search for the Microsoft 365 group that will receive messages on behalf of the shared voicemail box. The voicemails for this mailbox will be saved as an email message in the Microsoft 365 group mailbox. This option is a good option for playing a message and then transferring the call to a PSTN number. Further, if you want a transcript of the voicemail to be included with the email to the associated Microsoft 365 group mailbox, select **Transcription On**.

10. Under **Set up the greeting and menu options**, you can configure menu options. First, you'll select how you want the caller to be instructed to navigate the menu. To do this, you can select from two options:

-   **Play an audio file**: An uploaded audio file will be played. Uploaded files must be in .WAV, .MP3, or .WMA formats and must not exceed 5 MB.

- **Add a greeting message**: A text to speech message will be played (up to 1,000 characters).

11. Next, click **Assign a dial key** to begin associating dial keys to menu options to route the calls:

- **Dial key** allows you to assign 1–9 for DTMF navigation of the auto attendant menu. 0 is reserved for the operator and # is reserved to go back one menu or replay the menu greeting. **Voice command** will contain a keyword or phrase to select the option if you enable voice routing features. Each destination can be one of the following options, as shown in *Figure 13.19*:

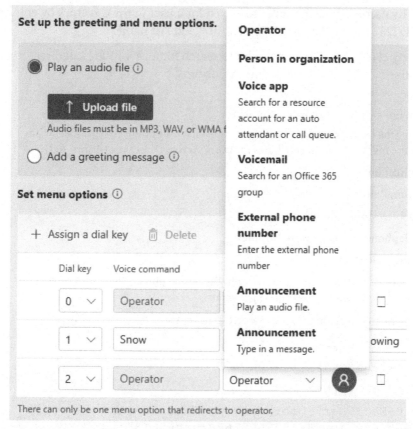

Figure 13.19 – The auto attendant routing destinations

- **Operator**: The assigned operator for the auto attendant.

- **Person in organization**: The call will be redirected to a Teams user in your organization.

- **Voice app**: The call will be redirected to an auto attendant or call queue.

- **Voicemail**: The call will be redirected to a shared voicemail box housed in the auto attendant.

- **External phone number**: The call will be redirected to a PSTN number external to Teams.

- **Announcement**: Play an uploaded audio file.

12. **Directory search** allows you to select from the following:

- **None**: Do not allow a search by name in the auto attendant.

- **Dial by name**: Allow the caller to search for a user in the directory by entering (via DTMF) or saying (via IVR) their first and last name.

- **Dial by extension**: Allow the caller to search for a user in the call directory by entering (via DTMF) their Teams extension.

Assign a User an Extension Number

For **Dial by extension**, call recipients must have an extension specified as one of the following phone attributes in **Azure Active Directory** (**Azure AD**):

OfficePhone

HomePhone

Mobile/MobilePhone

TelephoneNumber/PhoneNumber

OtherTelephone

If populating the extension number in the phone number field in Azure AD, it must be in one of the following formats:

```
+<phone number>;ext=<extension>
```

```
+<phone number>x<extension>
```

```
x<extension>
```

Here is an example:

```
Set-MsolUser -UserPrincipalName usern@domain.com
-Phonenumber "+15555555678;ext=5678"
```

---

13. Click on **Next** to go to **Advanced settings (optional)**.

14. Adjust your desired hours of operations for the auto attendant under **Set business hours**. By default, the auto attendant is set to 24 hours, 7 days a week:

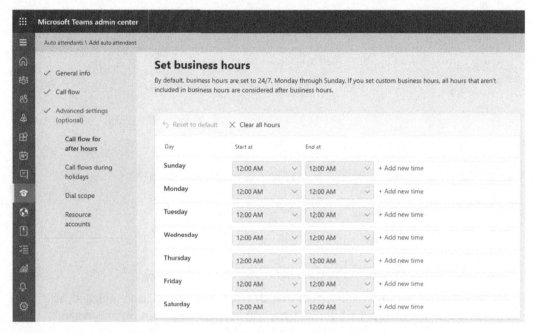

Figure 13.20 – Configuring business hours

- To set the auto attendant to be closed on a day, set the **Start at** and **End at** values to **None**.

- To set the auto attendant to be open on a day from 9AM to 5PM, set **Start at** as **9:00 AM** and **End at** as **5:00 PM**:

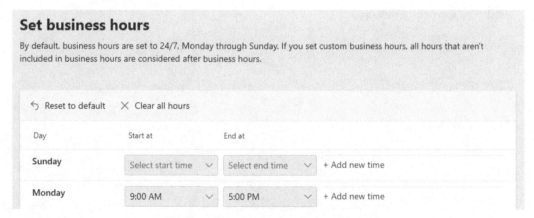

Figure 13.21 – Configuring business hours

- To add a period of closure during the business day – for example, a scheduled lunch break – you can add additional times by clicking **Add new time**:

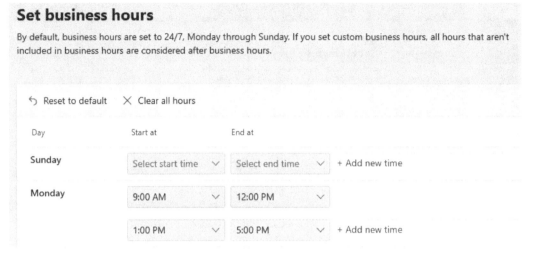

Figure 13.22 – Configuring additional business hours

- You can also define what happens to calls when the organization is closed, also known as **after hours call flows**. Here, you have the same options as presented in the regular call flow. This call flow will be used to route to different options when your organization is in after hours mode:

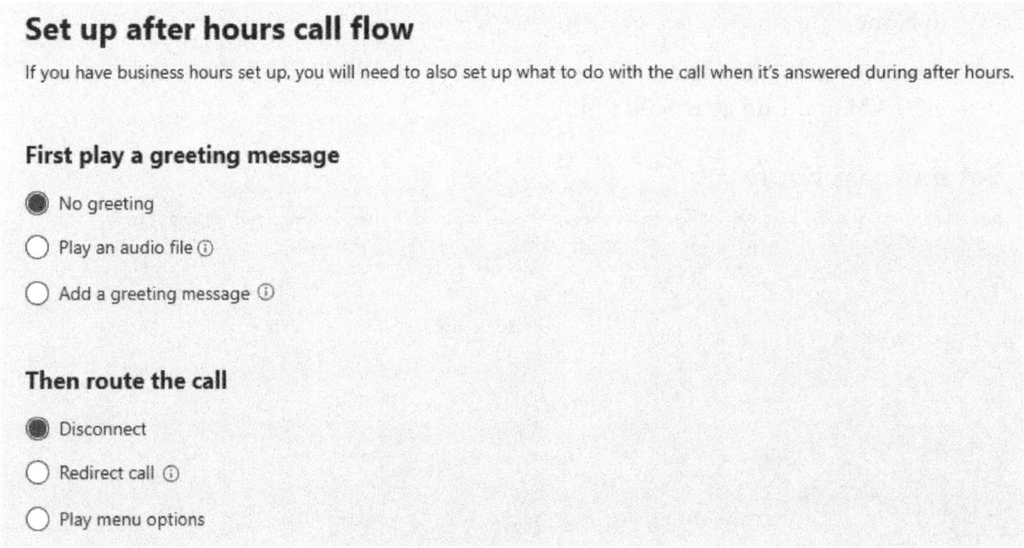

Set up after hours call flow

If you have business hours set up, you will need to also set up what to do with the call when it's answered during after hours.

First play a greeting message

- ● No greeting
- ○ Play an audio file ⓘ
- ○ Add a greeting message ⓘ

Then route the call

- ● Disconnect
- ○ Redirect call ⓘ
- ○ Play menu options

Figure 13.23 – After hours call flow

15. Click on **Next** to go to **Holiday call settings**. This allows special call flows for the auto attendant when the organization is in holiday mode.

16. To add a holiday call setting to this auto attendant, click on **Add**.

17. Select the holiday from the list. If you have not created holidays, see the *Configuring holidays* section in this chapter. Choose the appropriate greeting and call actions and click on **Save**:

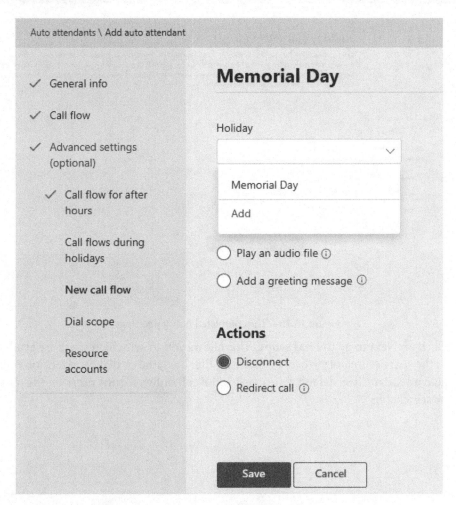

13.24 – Creating a holiday call flow

18. On the **Holiday** page, click on **Add** to create a holiday call flow. Here, you have the same options as presented in the regular call flow.

19. Choose the appropriate options for greetings and call routing.

20. Click on **Save** to add the holiday schedule:

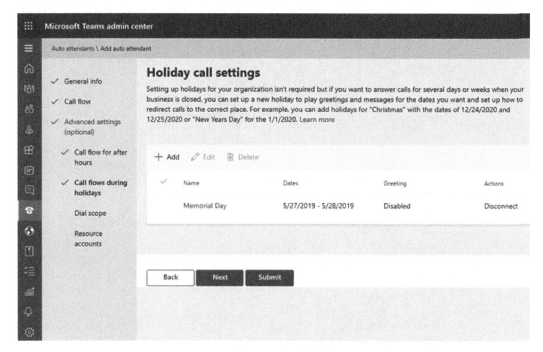

Figure 13.25 – The completed holiday settings

21. Click on **Next** to go to **Dial scope**. This allows you to set which users are available in the search directory when a caller uses dial by name or dial by extension on this auto attendant. The default setting is to allow all online Teams users on the tenant to be searchable:

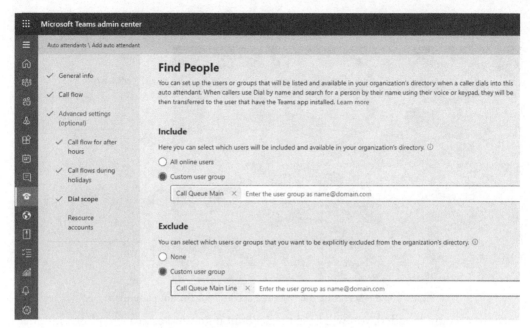

Figure 13.26 – Configuring the dial scope

However, if you wish to limit who can be dialed from the directory, you can use the **Include** and **Exclude** options to filter users. Select **Custom user group** and then choose multiple Microsoft 365 Groups, distribution lists, or security groups to define the dial scope.

22. Click on **Next** to go to **Resource accounts**:

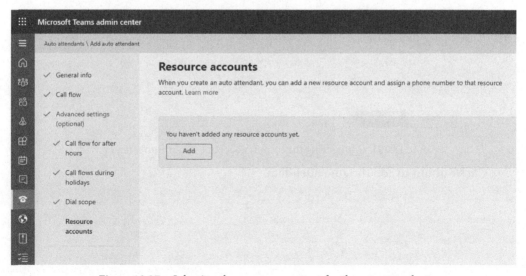

Figure 13.27 – Selecting the resource account for the auto attendant

23. Click on **Add** to add the resource account created for this auto attendant:

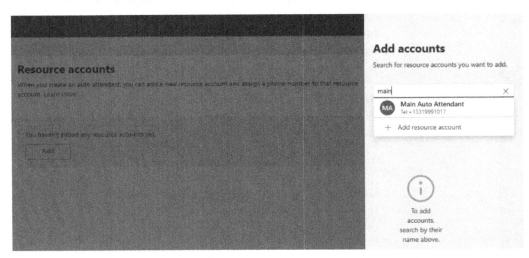

Figure 13.28 – Selecting the resource account for the auto attendant

Once the account is added, you will have the account name and associated phone number added to the auto attendant. Multiple resource accounts can be added to an auto attendant to support multiple dial-in numbers:

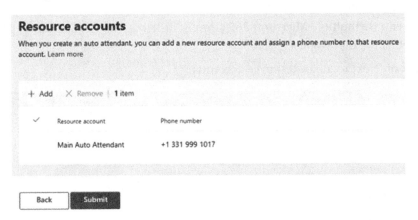

Figure 13.29 – Configuring the resource account for an auto attendant

24. Click **Submit** to add the auto attendant.

Once the auto attendant has been created, you can dial the number or URI of the resource account. The call will be routed to the auto attendant, and you'll experience the call flow you've configured:

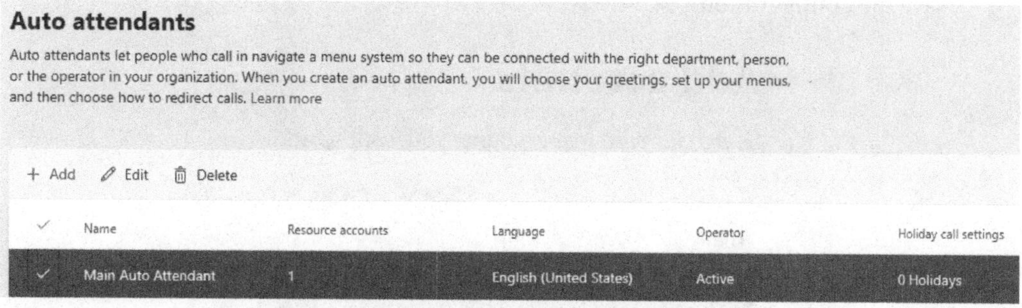

Auto attendants

Auto attendants let people who call in navigate a menu system so they can be connected with the right department, person, or the operator in your organization. When you create an auto attendant, you will choose your greetings, set up your menus, and then choose how to redirect calls. Learn more

+ Add	⬚ Edit	🗑 Delete				
✓	Name	Resource accounts	Language	Operator	Holiday call settings
✓	Main Auto Attendant	1	English (United States)	Active	0 Holidays

Figure 13.30 – Viewing configured auto attendants

Congratulations! You have just created your first auto attendant! You can go back to edit or delete the auto attendant in the Teams admin center.

Next, let's cover call queues.

Configuring call queues

Call queues allow for calls to be distributed to a group of Teams users. When inbound calls are received by a number connected to a call queue, the call will be serviced by a group of Teams users known as **queue agents**. Calls are distributed one at a time to the queue agents.

To set up call queues, you will need to create a resource account using the steps earlier in this chapter under the *Configuring resource accounts section*. Then, follow these steps:

1. Navigate to the Teams admin center (`https://admin.teams.microsoft.com`).

2. On the left pane, expand **Voice** and then select **Call queues**.

3. Click **Add**.

4. Enter a name for your call queue.

5. Under **Resource accounts**, click **Add** to add the resource account you wish to link to this call queue.

6. Search for resource accounts by entering a display or username. Multiple resource accounts can be added to a call queue to support multiple dial-in numbers. Click **Add** for each resource account to add to the queue. When finished, click **Add** to save the configuration:

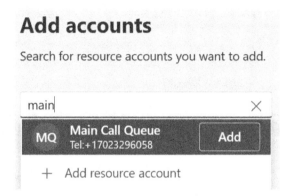

Figure 13.31 – Adding a resource account

7. Under **Assign calling ID**, choose the resource account with the number you would like to use for outbound calls made by agents. Click on **Add** to add the resource account, and then click **Add** at the bottom of the flyout to save the resource configuration, as shown in *Figure 13.32*:

Figure 13.32 – Adding a resource account for a calling line ID

8. Select the language for the call queue:

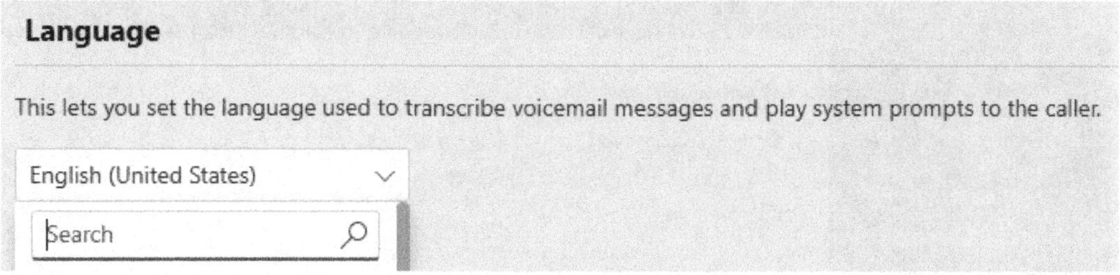

Language

This lets you set the language used to transcribe voicemail messages and play system prompts to the caller.

English (United States)   ∨

Search   🔎

Figure 13.33 – Select the call queue language

9. Select a greeting to be played when a caller enters the call queue. There are two options for greetings:

- **No greeting**: The caller will not hear a welcome greeting and will be placed directly in the queue and start hearing on-hold music.

- **Play an audio file**: A file can be uploaded with a message, tone, or music to be played when a caller enters the queue, and they are then placed in the queue and start hearing on-hold music.

10. Under **Music on hold**, select what callers in the queue will hear. You can choose **Play default music** or **Play an audio file**.

11. Under **Call answering**, select who will receive the calls:

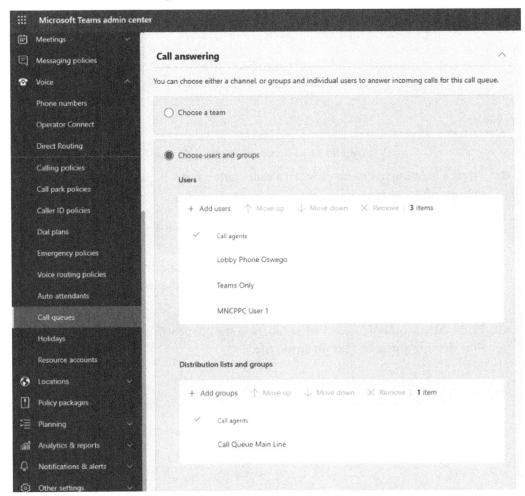

Figure 13.34 – Selecting the Call answering options

You can select **Choose a team** or **Choose users and groups**:

- **Choose a team**: Select an existing team, and then select a channel within that team. The selected channel becomes a **voice-enabled channel**. Up to 200 agents can participate in a Teams-based call queue. Agents will have the ability to collaborate in the channel while taking calls from the queue.

- **Choose users and groups**: Select specific users and/or a group of users to answer incoming calls for this call queue. You can choose both users and groups at the same time. If you select groups, you can choose distribution lists, security groups, and Microsoft 365 groups. Choose your users and/or your groups and click **Add** to save. You can add up to 20 agents individually and up to 200 agents with groups for the call queue.

> **Note**
> Users must be licensed with Phone System to receive calls from a call queue.

12. The **Conference mode** option controls how calls are connected to call agents. You can toggle this setting **On** or **Off**:

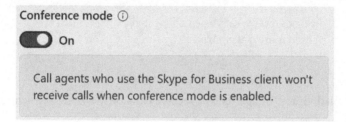

Conference mode ⓘ

🔘 On

Call agents who use the Skype for Business client won't receive calls when conference mode is enabled.

Figure 13.35 – Conference mode

When conference mode is enabled, the call is connected to the call agent via an **ad hoc conference**. When conference mode is disabled, the connection method is a traditional call transfer. The ad hoc conference connection method is faster than the traditional call transfer. If conference mode is enabled, Skype for Business clients and endpoints cannot receive calls from the call queue.

13. Next, choose a routing method. This is the call distribution algorithm that will be used to route the calls to the agents. The following routing methods are available:

- **Attendant routing**: The first call in the queue will ring all the call agents simultaneously. The first call agent to pick up the call gets the call. All other agents will receive a notification that the call has been picked up by an agent.

- **Serial routing**: Incoming calls will ring call agents one by one, starting from the beginning of the call agent list. If the agents are individually added, it will select the agent by how they are ordered in the user list, starting at the top of list and working to the bottom. If the agents are in a group or team, they will be sorted by the last name of the user in the **call queue**.

- **Round robin**: Each call agent will get the same number of calls from the queue.

- **Longest idle**: The next call in the queue will ring the opted-in call agent that has been in an **Available** presence state the longest. When longest idle, **Presence-based routing** will be disabled, since the call will always route to the agent that has been available the longest.

    Presence-based routing can be enabled to take into consideration the agents' presence before routing a call to the agent. Toggle **On** or **Off** for this setting:

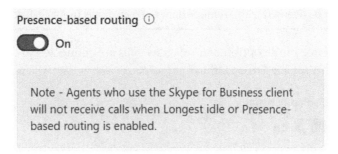

    Figure 13.36 – Presence-based routing

    When enabled, opted-in agents will receive calls only when their presence state is **Available**.

    When disabled, opted-in agents will receive calls regardless of their presence state. This emulates more of a traditional **Automatic Call Distributor** (**ACD**) call distribution. With presence-based routing enabled, an agent can stop receiving calls from the queue by setting their Teams status to **Do Not Disturb** (**DND**).

- **Call agents can opt out of taking calls** can be toggled **On** or **Off**. If enabled, the agent can opt out of the call queue. If disabled, the agent cannot opt out of the call queue.

- **Call agent alert time (seconds)** is used to configure the amount of time the queue will wait for an agent to pick up before moving on to the next agent. You can set this timer as low as 15 seconds and as high as 180 seconds.

- **Call overflow handling** determines how the users in the queue are managed. If a caller is either waiting too long or the maximum calls in the queue (**queue depth**) is reached, callers will be transferred to another resource such as another person, an auto attendant or another call queue, an external phone number, or voicemail. Configure **Maximum calls in queue**, and then choose the **When the maximum number of calls is reached option**, as shown in *Figure 13.36*:

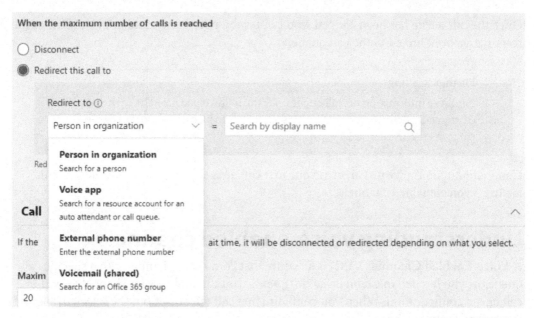

Figure 13.37 – The configuration options for when the maximum number of calls is reached

- **Call timeout handling** is triggered based on how long users are waiting in a queue:

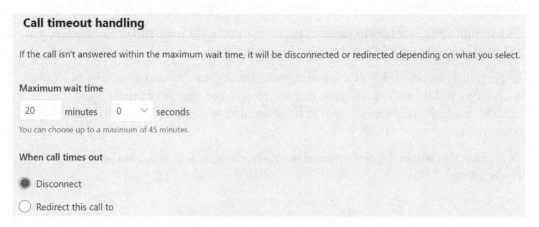

Figure 13.38 – Call timeout handling

To prevent excessive queue wait times, configure the maximum call wait time. The default timeout is 30 minutes but can be configured from 0 to 45 minutes. When this limit is reached, you will be able to configure call disconnect and redirection options.

14. Click on **Save** to add the call queue.

Once the call queue has been created, you can test by calling the number or the URI of the resource account linked to the call queue.

> **Further Reading**
>
> For more information on call queues, see the following article: `https://docs.microsoft.com/en-us/microsoftteams/create-a-phone-system-call-queue`.

Congratulations! You've just created your first call queue! Next, let's look a new Teams feature – voice-enabled channels.

Understanding voice-enabled channels

A **Voice-Enabled Channel** (**VEC**) is a feature that connects a channel with a specific call queue. As you learned in *Configuring call queues*, you can add a Team channel as part of a call queue configuration. When you configure that call queue option, the selected channel is converted into a VEC.

A VEC allows for broader collaboration among the participating queue agents. VECs also allow agents to customize certain settings such as opting out of a call queue, if enabled.

This section will cover how to navigate the VEC interface. By the end of the section, you will be able to explain VECs and navigate the interface.

As previously mentioned, VECs are configured during the creation or editing of a call queue. This will then allow an agent, as a member of the channel, to make a call from the VEC using the resource account's phone number to mask their caller ID with the resource's number.

To see how this works, from the Teams interface, navigate to a VEC, as shown in *Figure 13.39*:

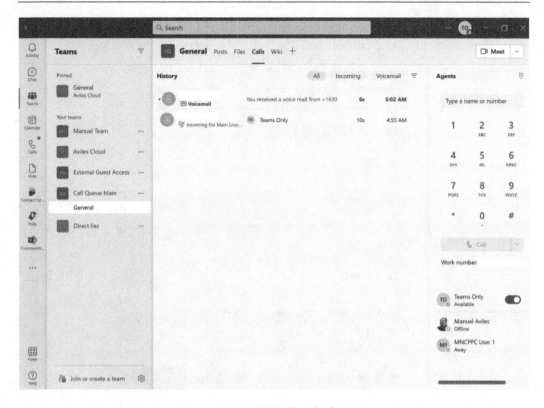

Figure 13.39 – The Calls tab of a VEC

You will notice that a new **Calls** tab appears in in the tab list. This special tab is integrated directly with the call queue. On that tab, you will see **History**, which contains a log of information on your calls. You can filter the log by the following parameters:

- **All**: Displays all the incoming calls answered by the agent signed into the Teams client, as well as all missed calls and voicemails received on the call queue. Selecting a call will give you the option to return the call by clicking the call button.

- **Incoming**: Displays all the incoming calls answered by the agent signed into the Teams client.

- **Voicemail**: Displays the voicemails left in the shared mailboxes built in the call queue. Selecting a certain voicemail will give you details on the message:

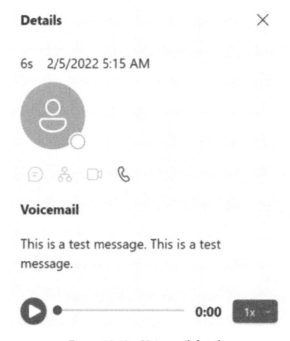

Figure 13.40 – Voicemail details

Voicemail details include the caller ID, timestamp information, and (if enabled), a transcription of the voicemail message.

The dial pad, located at the upper-right side of the interface, allows an agent to place an outbound call from the call queue. Note that the dial pad, as shown in *Figure 13.41*, includes the ability to call out from the queue with either the caller's identity or the identity of the call queue's service number:

Figure 13.41 – A VEC dial pad

The **Agents** list, located at the lower-right-hand portion of the page, shows the agents that are assigned to the call queue with their current presence state. If the call queue allows it, agents can opt in or opt out of the queue by simply sliding the toggle **On** or **Off**, as shown in *Figure 13.42*:

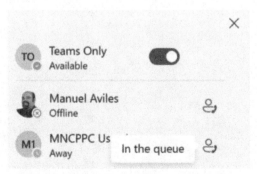

Figure 13.42 – The agent list and opt-in toggle

In addition to seeing an agent's Teams presence, you can also see their queue status by hovering over the call queue icon.

Summary

In this chapter, we learned how to configure important aspects of a resource account, including Virtual User licensing and service numbers. We covered holidays from a Teams voice perspective – and the importance of making sure holiday schedules are configured prior to configuring any auto attendants.

By following the examples in this chapter, you were also able to configure auto attendants and call queues, as well as learn about the new VEC feature of Microsoft Teams.

In the next chapter, we'll look at the wide array of native Microsoft Teams devices.

14
Teams Devices

To get the most out of the Microsoft Teams experience, you should consider using Teams-certified devices. Hardware that has been certified for use with Microsoft Teams is available for every usage scenario, from home, office, and mobile work to executive board rooms.

In this chapter, we're going to learn about the main types of devices that can be used with Microsoft Teams:

- Webcams
- Headsets
- Handsets or desk phones
- Teams Rooms
- Teams displays
- Teams panels
- Surface Hub devices

You'll also learn what to look for when choosing devices. By the end of the chapter, you'll understand the types of devices available and which work best for particular scenarios.

Let's dive in!

Benefits of certified devices

Regardless of the type, one of the most important features to look for in any device is whether it is Microsoft Teams-certified. Certified devices have many advantages over non-certified devices, including the following:

- Rich audio and video quality
- Plug-and-play support
- Integrated call controls
- Advanced indicators and extensibility

Devices that have gone through the Microsoft Teams certification process will provide both the best end user experiences and administrative control.

Let's explore some of the benefits of certified devices.

Rich audio and video quality

The first reason you'll want to look at certified devices is for the quality of the end user experience. Teams-certified audio devices will provide benefits such as echo canceling and distortion-free audio. Video device certification means that devices will meet requirements for video noise and detail, as well as being able to correct jitter and latency.

Plug-and-play support

From an administrative and configuration point of view, plug-and-play support means that you won't need to search for drivers or specialized software for your computer system to recognize your device. It also means no additional provisioning steps are required (though centralized management and provisioning can be configured for some types of devices).

Integrated call controls

Teams-certified devices with audio features include native call controls (such as answer/hang-up, mute/unmute, and volume control) with no additional software necessary. Many devices will feature either dedicated hardware buttons or multipurpose buttons.

Advanced indicators and extensibility

New Teams-certified devices feature a dedicated Teams button and LED indicator lights, as well as integrated notifications for events and alerts from the Teams client. Teams-certified devices can also interact with the Teams client and may include additional functionality to join meetings, activate responses, or access voicemail (based on the type of device). Certification also means that the devices are designed for extensibility, with additional features able to be delivered via software or firmware updates.

Now that you're familiar with the benefits of choosing Teams-certified devices, we can move on to how to select the right device for our needs.

Choosing the right device

Getting the best possible experience for your scenario means selecting the right device. In the following sections, we'll explore some of the common types of devices and their intended uses.

Webcams

Most people's first video or calling experience with Teams will utilize a webcam of some sort—whether it's a native camera integrated into a mobile device or an external webcam.

Integrated devices provide the simplest experience, though they may not provide the same level of high-definition video or audio quality that a third-party or dedicated device may provide. For many scenarios, such as mobile work or infrequent use, they may be acceptable.

External webcams frequently have higher resolution than built-in webcams and can be mounted on top of a monitor or stand upright on a desk. Many third-party webcams also have integrated microphones, allowing you to use a single high-quality device for multiple media inputs.

Regardless of whether you use an integrated or external webcam, we recommend using a hardware lens cover to help ensure total control over your privacy. If you are using an external webcam on a device that supports Windows Hello, be sure to select a cover that doesn't prevent the use of the infrared sensor, even when the cover is engaged.

An extensive list of certified webcams is available at `https://www.microsoft.com/en-us/microsoft-teams/across-devices/devices/category/web-cameras/3`.

Headsets

A Teams-certified **headset** is an audio device that combines one or two earpieces as well as a microphone. In many scenarios, a headset may be the perfect companion to a built-in webcam. Headsets are available in both wired and wireless configurations.

You can have more than one audio input, audio output, or video input device attached to your computer, though you can only use one of each at a time.

Microsoft Teams provides an easy way to select individual audio and video devices, as shown in *Figure 14.1*. If you have more than one audio or video device configured, you can select which one best suits your needs at the time:

Figure 14.1 – Microsoft Teams Device settings panel

Devices can be selected at the beginning of the call and even changed once a call is in progress.

You can choose to use an integrated webcam and third-party headset for travel and a dedicated webcam, a standalone microphone, and integrated speakers for home office use. Just access the device settings and change the audio and video devices for your current situation.

> **More Devices**
>
> You can find a list of Microsoft Teams-certified headsets at `https://www.microsoft.com/en-us/microsoft-teams/across-devices/devices/category/headsets/36`.

Handsets or desk phones

While most Teams users adapt easily to using a webcam, the Teams softphone dialer, and a headset, there are some scenarios where a physical desk phone handset may work best. For example, it may be more user-friendly to place a standard desk phone in a lobby to use as a common area phone. Administrative assistants or operators who route phone calls may also benefit from using a specialized device.

For these situations, traditionally styled handsets with programmable functions and buttons are available from a number of vendors. Desk phones are available in a number of configurations, including high-resolution color displays for video calling and feature-rich soft button features.

Most devices are configured for communications and power via **Power over Ethernet (PoE)**, though several also include wireless communications functionality as well.

> **More Devices**
>
> You can find an extensive list of Microsoft Teams-certified desk phone devices at `https://www.microsoft.com/en-us/microsoft-teams/across-devices/devices/category/desk-phones-teams-displays/34`.

Teams Rooms

While webcams, headsets, and desk phones are devices familiar to most users, **Microsoft Teams Rooms (MTRs)** are a new class of device.

An MTR system, as we discussed in *Chapter 6*, *Microsoft Teams Rooms*, is a group of devices and peripherals designed to turn an ordinary conference room into a collaboration-enabled workspace, complete with audio, video, and content sharing capabilities.

Unlike personal peripheral devices, such as webcams, headsets, and desk phones, MTRs are dedicated systems that require their own resource accounts and licensing.

Most MTRs come with several components:

- A Windows- or Android-based tablet-style control panel interface with features for starting or joining meetings and call controls

- One or more video cameras

- One or more speakers

- One or more remote microphones

MTRs also have the ability to connect via HDMI to an output display, such as a monitor or projector, allowing all participants in the room to see video and other shared content.

While many MTR systems are modular, some are designed for smaller huddles or focus room workspaces. These MTRs may utilize a more compact form factor, integrating microphones, speakers, and video cameras into a single desktop or wall-mounted unit.

Other systems may be configured as a collaboration bar that has integrated cameras, speakers, and microphones coupled with a separate display panel.

When choosing a room system, make sure that the MTR system matches the physical workspace requirements. We recommend working with vendors and partners on larger room environments to ensure the equipment is scaled correctly.

> **More Devices**
>
> For a list of Microsoft Teams-certified rooms systems, see `https://www.microsoft.com/en-us/microsoft-teams/across-devices/devices/category/teams-rooms/20`.

Teams displays

Teams displays are another new entry in the collaboration device category. A Teams display is a glanceable device designed to be used either as a standalone phone or as a peripheral calendar and conferencing device alongside a workstation.

Teams displays have integrated displays, cameras, speakers, and microphones, positioning them between a desk phone and an MTR system.

In addition to supporting the calling and conferencing features of Teams phones, Teams displays also provide access to core Teams functionality (chat, meetings, files, and more), display calendar information at a glance, and allow interaction via Cortana. Teams phones can even be used as a virtual bulletin board for guests who stop by your desk when you're not there, allowing them to leave audio, video, and text notes.

Teams displays are typically configured using the Microsoft Teams user's credentials and can be managed via Intune and the Microsoft Teams admin center.

Teams panels

Microsoft Teams panels are a modern take on room scheduling systems. Designed to be wall-mounted outside of conference rooms, Teams panels are a type of dedicated accessory device.

Teams panels allow for both scheduled and ad hoc meeting reservations and provide colored LED indicators to notify others whether a room is available or scheduled.

Teams panels require an MTR Standard license.

> **More Devices**
>
> You can find Teams panels devices at `https://www.microsoft.com/en-us/microsoft-teams/across-devices/devices/category/room-systems-accessories/73`.

Surface Hub devices

The Microsoft Surface Hub is an all-in-one MTR device that includes a large touch display panel, integrated speaker and microphone devices, and a camera. Like other room systems devices, it features integrated calling and meeting capabilities.

Though the Hub comes with a stylus, it also accepts fingertip input for drawing and interacting with the device.

It also supports Miracast, so users can mirror their device's screen directly to the Hub's screen. The Hub is available in both 50-inch and 85-inch display sizes.

Since it is technically an MTR system, it does require an MTR system Standard license for full Microsoft Teams functionality.

Summary

The Microsoft Teams platform allows people to meet and collaborate in new and exciting ways. Whether you're using integrated cameras and speakers on laptop devices or interactive display panels such as the Surface Hub, Microsoft Teams devices allow users to get the most out of the calling and meeting experiences. In this chapter, you learned about some of the features and benefits of Teams-certified devices and explored the range of devices that can work with Teams.

In the next chapter, we'll shift focus to planning and adoption.

Part 5: Administration

In this part, you will learn to deploy and manage additional Teams features as well as overall adoption, governance, and administration strategies.

This part comprises the following chapters:

- *Chapter 15, Planning and Adoption*
- *Chapter 16, Governance*
- *Chapter 17, Integration with Exchange Server*
- *Chapter 18, Security and Data Protection*
- *Chapter 19, Reporting in Teams*
- *Appendix A, Direct Routing and Operator Connect*

15
Planning and Adoption

In order to get the most value out of any product, you need to have a plan for *adoption*. Successful adoption requires a number of elements, including effective governance, dedicated champions, relevant communication, and the identification of the required business outcomes.

In this chapter, we're going to examine the key pieces of the **Microsoft Adoption Framework** and how they relate to a successful **Microsoft Teams** deployment. These are the areas we're going to tackle in this chapter:

- Introducing the Microsoft Adoption Framework
- Starting your strategy
- Experimenting with early adopters
- Scaling to the rest of your organization
- Planning for change management and support

Microsoft Teams presents many opportunities for aiding collaboration and efficiency. Teams is both an evolutionary and revolutionary product.

It's *evolutionary* in the sense that it continues to leverage the development and architecture of existing **Microsoft 365** products and further extends their capabilities. However, it's also a *revolutionary* product since it has the capability to shift knowledge and collaborative work away from familiar tools (such as **Microsoft Outlook** and discrete web services) and into more chat-based workspaces with integrated applications. While this chapter is primarily about the planning and adoption of Microsoft Teams from a collaboration perspective, the concepts will also be applicable to other aspects of Teams such as **onboarding** and the adoption of the **voice workload** component.

As such, getting users to adopt technology that has the potential to radically change their way of working can also present large cultural and organizational difficulties. Depending on your organization, you may face a wide variety of challenges. The goal of this chapter is to help you overcome them with methodical planning and consistent messaging.

By the end of this chapter, you should be able to start planning a successful Microsoft Teams rollout for your organization or customers.

So, off we go!

Introducing the Microsoft Adoption Framework

The Microsoft Adoption Framework for Teams is a more concise version of its overall **Cloud Adoption Framework** for **Azure** (https://docs.microsoft.com/en-us/azure/cloud-adoption-framework/overview). The Cloud Adoption Framework for Azure focuses on analyzing the business requirements, documenting the desired business outcomes, establishing overall architecture management teams (for example, the strategy, adoption, governance, and operations teams) to work toward these outcomes, and building deployment strategies.

Inside the deployment strategy for a particular product, an organization might have phases such as *plan*, *adopt*, *govern*, *manage*, *secure*, and *organize*.

Microsoft takes these disparate areas and reorganizes them within broad steps to help accelerate Teams adoption. In this chapter, we'll cover the following processes and phases:

- Starting
- Experimenting
- Scaling
- Planning

Let's start working our way through them.

Starting your strategy

Phase 1 of the Microsoft Adoption Framework for Teams is called the *Start* phase. The goal of the Start phase is to ensure organizational readiness. The outcomes of the Start phase include knowing who will play the important roles in the project as well as determining if you need to engage Microsoft or a partner for onboarding assistance.

Identifying your project team members and stakeholders

Once you've decided to embark upon a Teams deployment and adoption project, you'll need to gather a team to help see it through. The project's success largely depends on everyone in the core project team being committed. The core team's roles are outlined in the following list:

- **Executive sponsor**: Most projects require an executive sponsor to help the business understand the relationship between the project and the organization's goals. For a Microsoft Teams deployment, the executive sponsor will be responsible for communicating the business leadership's requirements to the team and helping the leadership understand the importance and value of the project. Executive sponsors are commonly responsible for identifying the need for the project, although sometimes the executive sponsor is brought in later due to the organization requiring a *face* for an ongoing project. The executive sponsor may also help to secure and administer funding, as well as approve the budget items for a project.

- **Success Owner**: The success owner is responsible for making sure that all business goals are realized. The success owner may need to help shape or adjust the deployment plan to make sure the organization's objectives are achieved.

- **Program Manager or Project Manager**: The program manager (or project manager) is responsible for the actual launch and rollout process, including resources and staffing, budgets, and the timeline.

- **Champions**: Champions are department-level liaisons that evangelize the Microsoft Teams deployment, getting users excited about the upcoming project. Champions are also typically involved in some level of end user (or **power user**) training. Champions may conduct lunch-and-learn style events to further build interest within the organization.

- **Training Lead**: The training lead is responsible for managing and communicating training content. A training lead may also procure training materials or classes or participate in train-the-trainer programs to educate champions or other leads on usage and best practices.

- **Department Leads**: The department leads hold a stakeholder role. They identify usage scenarios for how their individual departments will use and benefit from Microsoft Teams. Department leads also can encourage engagement to help ensure adoption.

- **IT Specialists**: IT specialists will be responsible for ensuring the technology prerequisites are met, as well as ensuring the success of technical deployment aspects such as software deployment, authentication, and integration with other applications and devices.

- **Communication Lead**: The responsibility of the communication lead is to oversee the company-wide communications about the Microsoft Teams project. This includes highlighting the timeline and training opportunities and implementing all corporate communications about the project benefits.

As you can see, there are many different roles necessary to have a successful and smooth Microsoft Teams rollout. While larger organizations may have multiple people performing some of these roles, smaller organizations may have a single person performing multiple roles. However, it's important that all of the roles are filled to ensure nothing is missed in the process.

Understanding the product

Since Microsoft Teams is a general collaboration business product, it makes sense for all members of the project team to be familiar with its interface, capabilities, and where it fits into the enterprise architecture of the organization. This will help ensure that team members can communicate using a common vocabulary.

For information on general Microsoft Teams architecture concepts, see *Chapter 1, Taking a Tour of Microsoft Teams*.

Assessing organizational readiness

Organizational readiness, in the minds of most solution designers and IT implementers, is synonymous with *technology*. While it's important to make sure your infrastructure is technically capable of meeting the requirements for any product, when it comes to adoption and change management, organizational readiness is about evaluating its *openness* to new ways of doing business. Organizational readiness has more to do with the *cultural mindset* of an organization than anything else.

Your organization may already follow an established change management methodology such as **Awareness**, **Desire**, **Knowledge**, **Ability**, and **Reinforcement** (**ADKAR**), the **Accelerating Implementation Methodology** (**AIM**), or the **Kubler-Ross Change Curve**, which will make implementing change in an organization much easier. Your organization may even have certified change management practitioners or an **Adoption and Change Management** (**ACM**) practice/group. If so, we recommend that you leverage these individuals to help your adoption efforts take hold within the organization.

Most change management frameworks or methodologies involve concepts of rationalizing change and overcoming change aversion within a given setting, both of which are important to helping individuals internalize the need for adoption.

You may find it beneficial to research effective change management methodologies to help you along your journey. You can refer to the *Further reading* section of this chapter for additional resources.

Change management isn't a one-person job. While this book is targeted at IT professionals, the role of change management will require others within the business.

Assessing your organization's readiness will involve evaluating three types of people: *stakeholders*, *early adopters*, and *all users*.

Stakeholders

Stakeholders are the key business representatives and leaders in your organization. For each stakeholder identified, you'll want to ask yourself several questions:

- Is this individual friendly or open to new technology?

- Is this individual satisfied with the current state of the organization's technology?

- Is this individual willing to try new things to accelerate results or move the business goals forward?

- What kind of pressure is this individual under to deliver results?

- Will this individual be willing to be a champion or evangelize on behalf of the project?

- Does this individual have good relationships with members of the project team?

- What motivates this individual? Key motivators may include financial benefits, being viewed positively by leadership, and being seen as a change agent or visionary.

As part of the project team, you'll want to identify individuals who want to be seen as change agents, who are friendly to technology and change, and who express some level of dissatisfaction with the current tools. These individuals can act as advisors to the team to help you with adoption efforts.

Early adopters

Identifying *early adopters* is a key task in the Start phase—you need to find individuals who are interested in change and are excited to try new things. Gathering early adopters from a broad cross-section of the company is important to make sure the project team understands how Microsoft Teams will work with different parts of the business. These key insights will help the project team deliver effective messaging.

You can poll your organization with a questionnaire to help users express an interest in taking part in an *early adopter* program.

Users

The *users* group is comprised of everyone else in the organization. Knowing the culture of your organization is key to understanding how to put together effective adoption strategies. If the organization's culture is generally adverse to change, you'll want to start early on your messaging campaign and drive home the importance of how Microsoft Teams will benefit both the business and individual users.

The Start phase is focused on building the project team and the business case, as well as assessing the organizational readiness. After selecting the project team and identifying the different stakeholders in the business, you're ready to begin the *Experiment* phase.

Experimenting with early adopters

The *Experiment* phase is really about implementing a small-scale deployment of Microsoft Teams for real-world scenarios. In this phase, we recommend that you look for a project, task, or business process with these characteristics:

- It should be led by one of the business stakeholders that is IT-friendly and has a good relationship with the project team.

- It should have a willingness and ability to involve early adopters.

Choosing one or two projects, tasks, or business processes that can incorporate these individuals will really help you learn more about how your organization can benefit from Microsoft Teams and also provide feedback for various aspects of the project, including its technical readiness and communication strategies.

Finding your champions

Champions are an essential part of both the *evangelism* and *feedback loop* processes for a project. Champions will help get other employees and users excited about the technology and processes as well as communicate back to the project team any successes and challenges they encountered along the way. Champions are primarily motivated by helping others and working toward the overall organizational success of the deployment.

To increase their effectiveness, champions should be formally trained in the Microsoft Teams product so that they can answer questions from users and potentially deliver ad-hoc training such as brown bag meetings or lunch-and-learn sessions.

You may also want to encourage champions to join a broader community. Microsoft provides a free monthly Champions community call as part of their worldwide **Champions Program** (available at `https://aka.ms/O365Champions`). Here, individuals can learn tips and tricks to improve their effectiveness, gain deeper insights into how Microsoft Teams works, find out more about evangelism, and learn about getting the most out of the platform.

A good internal champions program can really help excite your organization and help adoption efforts gain traction.

Developing a governance strategy

Governance refers to the broad strategy for how an organization will manage its **data estate**. Governance plans will dictate the life cycle of different aspects of the adoption, such as how users will be onboarded into the system, how their data will be secured, and what will happen to their data after they leave the organization.

Governance planning is one of the most often-overlooked pieces of a project. It's also one of the most difficult things to go back and apply later (for example, after people have developed bad habits or processes that don't line up with the business goals). Lack of governance can also expose organizations to risk, so it's important to be as prescriptive as possible with it early on.

We will take a deeper dive into governance in *Chapter 16, Governance*.

Identifying usage scenarios and telling user stories

Helping individuals understand how a new product or service will benefit them is key to many change management methodologies, for example, the **ADKAR (Awareness, Desire, Knowledge, Ability, Reinforcement)** model. Human nature frequently drives people to choose the known over the unknown and to favor the status quo over change. You can help overcome this change aversion by helping people internalize the answer to a simple question: *What's in it for me?*

This is where usage scenarios and user stories become important. Microsoft provides several templates and ideas around this, as shown in *Figure 15.1*:

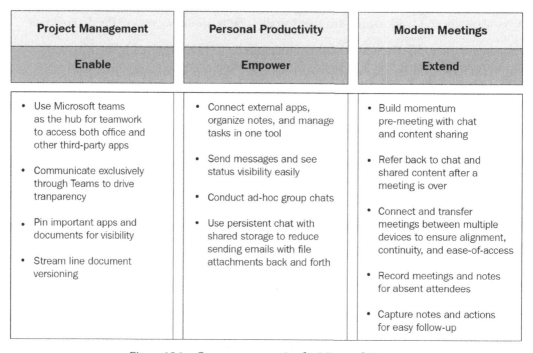

Figure 15.1 – Core usage scenarios for Microsoft Teams

Building these user stories is essential to helping users understand their own set of advantages in using a new product. Once these benefits are internalized, users will be more likely to approach adoption with an open mindset.

You can use the template in *Figure 15.2* to help build your own user stories or usage scenarios:

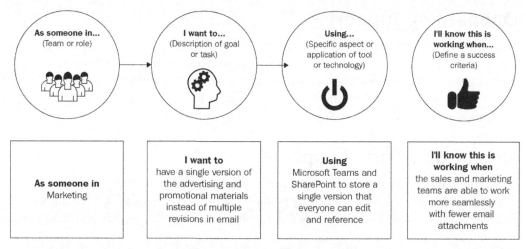

Figure 15.2 – Usage scenario template

Building relatable and realistic user stories and usage scenarios will be beneficial to your overall project effort. With these, you'll be able to focus on what applications you need to integrate and how the business will derive an overall benefit from the project. You can work with your champions and business stakeholders to identify key scenarios to help build buy-in and momentum for your adoption process.

Interviewing business stakeholders

At the beginning of the Experiment phase, we recommended that you select a project, task, or business process that you can manage with Microsoft Teams. With this project, task, or process in mind, interview the relevant business stakeholders. You'll want to ask several questions to help develop success criteria and tailor how you'll use Teams:

- What are some of the challenges or pain points as they relate to communications or collaboration that you've experienced in previous projects or tasks, or that you are currently experiencing in this business process?

- What are some areas you'd like to see improve?

- What methods of communication or collaboration generally seem to work best for your team?

- How is information typically created and shared within your team?

You may already think you know the answers to some of these questions, but part of the change process is allowing others to participate and feel like they are both being heard and providing value. Listening to concerns and recommendations is a key part of consensus building and will help stakeholders take ownership of the success of the project.

Onboarding Support

Since Microsoft Teams may be new for many people, it's important to bring your support teams up-to-date with training materials. In addition to the early adopter and champion communities, you'll want to make sure your support teams are fully equipped to support user requests—specifically relating to technical issues such as installation, access, and authentication, as well as device and network requirements.

Onboarding Early Adopters

Once you've identified projects, tasks, or processes that you'll use to pilot Microsoft Teams, you can start building your early adopter community. This may involve things such as a dedicated **Yammer** group or a new Microsoft Team for early adopters and champions.

After you've decided how to host the resources for your early adopters, follow these steps to begin engagement:

1. Send an invitation email to invite them to the early adopter program or community. This email might include pre-requisite tasks such as downloading and installing Microsoft Teams and accepting a meeting invitation for a kick-off call.

2. Host a kick-off call to explain the goals of the early adoption program. You may wish to introduce the core project team and explain some of the user scenarios you've already identified.

3. Ensure everyone has access to the relevant tools (for example, Yammer groups, Microsoft Teams groups, SharePoint sites, or other resources) for support and feedback.

4. Schedule community meetings or surveys to gather feedback from early adopters.

Be sure to take advantage of the feedback of early adopters—this will help identify any issues (technical or cultural) that could impact a broader Microsoft Teams deployment and adoption effort.

Once the Experiment phase is underway, it's time to begin planning for the Scale phase.

Scaling to the rest of your organization

The *Scale* phase involves revisiting the feedback your project has received so far (both positive and critical) and adjusting your delivery methodology to overcome any technical and organizational challenges. Where the Experiment phase may have focused on a few particular projects, tasks, or business processes, the Scale phase will likely expand to see Teams used in ways you didn't anticipate. It's important to maintain support and flexibility to ensure the broadest adoption of the platform—good ideas can come from anywhere and are not limited to only the project team.

In this section, we'll explore the best practices for ensuring you complete a successful Microsoft Teams rollout and adoption.

Defining success

In the Start and Experiment phases, you likely identified key projects, tasks, or processes that could benefit from Microsoft Teams. You probably also worked on building user stories and usage scenarios to support investment, ownership, and adoption.

As you prepare to move into the Scale phase, it's important to revisit and expand all of these to cover as many aspects of your organization as possible.

Successful outcomes can generally be divided into four categories:

- **Organizational**: These include employee retention, talent acquisition, cultural transformation, and operational agility.

- **Cultural**: These include employee morale or sentiment, customer feedback, openness to innovation, and improved attitudes toward new technologies and processes.

- **Tangible**: These include financial success (for example, cost reduction, revenue generation, improved margins), operational efficiency, improved net promoter scores from interactions (for example, customers or human resources), security, and the simplification of access.

- **Individual**: These include employee engagement and morale, productivity, and innovation.

You can reuse the scenario template provided in *Figure 15.2* to help map out success criteria for the business outcomes.

Selecting a service enablement strategy

As you begin to build your plan for broad rollout and adoption, you'll need to select a *service enablement strategy*. The strategy behind the Scale phase will largely depend on a few core metrics:

- How broadly Microsoft Teams is already deployed in your organization
- What competitive products are in place that could cause disruption to your timeline
- If **Skype for Business** (either on-premises or online) is deployed
- Executive/management commitments or organizational politics

Microsoft has identified five core enablement strategies and what might lead an organization to choose one of them:

- **Teams First**: This strategy works best for teams that have new or low usage or engagement of Microsoft 365 customers. This approach builds on the Experiment phase directly by highlighting core usage scenarios and user stories to drive adoption.
- **Teams Core**: This strategy is focused on enabling Teams with **Microsoft SharePoint** and **OneDrive** components and drawing strong integration between the components. It focuses on enabling multiple collaboration tools together such as Teams, Yammer, **Planner**, and SharePoint.
- **Teams Go Big**: This strategy is recommended for organizations with less than 5,000 users. It relies on the creation of company-wide teams that everyone is automatically added to. The *Teams Go Big* strategy is an immersive strategy that focuses on getting everyone to use Microsoft Teams as quickly as possible by providing new ways to accomplish tasks through integrated apps (such as vacation request), surveys, company-wide meetings, and executive engagement.
- **Skype Side by Side**: This strategy is also sometimes referred to as *Meetings First*. It is intended for organizations that have deployed Skype for Business or **Skype For Business Online** calling features. *Skype Side by Side* is a coexistence mode where the enterprise calling features still utilize the existing Skype client and infrastructure but use the *Teams Core* strategy collaboration and chat tools.
- **Migration**: This coexistence strategy leverages both *Skype Side by Side* and *Teams Core*, with a focus on transitioning enterprise voice and calling features from Skype for Business to Microsoft Teams.

Expanding your deployment in the Scale phase may also require you to go back and re-evaluate your governance strategy if you didn't map it out or implement it fully.

If you have a large or geographically distributed organization, you may also find it beneficial to revisit the Experiment phase for piloting and onboarding. Recognize that there may be organizational and cultural differences that require flexibility in the timing and approaches used to achieve the best result.

As with the initial Experiment phase, you'll want to be sure to involve key influencers, decision-makers, and other stakeholders.

Optimizing feedback

One challenge that organizations face when migrating and adopting any new technology (particularly a disruptive or transformative technology that changes how users engage in their daily roles) is deciding when to use the new (versus the old) tool. In the Experiment phase, you began collecting feedback about how Microsoft Teams was working across the organization. Undoubtedly, the question of when to use Teams came up.

Some other questions you might encounter are as follows:

- How do I choose when to use Microsoft Teams or email?
- Can I share confidential or sensitive information within Teams?
- What business scenarios are approved for use with Teams? What scenarios aren't?
- How do I develop new applications on this platform?

Based on the feedback you received, you may wish to develop some sort of **Frequently Asked Questions** (**FAQs**) resource to help users find answers to these common queries. Share this information through multiple channels (for example, Teams, email, community calls, champions, and so on) to help users locate the information they need.

Driving awareness

Part of your broad adoption program is going to be telling users that a new, useful tool is available to them. You can do this with an *awareness program*, which is really a marketing campaign targeting your users.

Along the adoption journey, you'll want to hold events (for example, town hall-style question-and-answer sessions, meetings, and calls) to help employees understand the importance of the change and how they will benefit from it. You'll also want to provide links to training materials to help users learn on their own. It may be beneficial to hold regularly scheduled end user meetings (in addition to your champion and early adopter meetings) to continue to drive awareness and generate a buzz about your project.

You can use the self-help video series at `https://aka.ms/teamstraining` to start building your own library of end user training materials.

Delivering a training program

To really get the most out of any platform (including Microsoft Teams), you may also want to deliver more formal training for both end users and administrators. There are currently a number of resources available for both, including webinars, instructor-led training, and certification courses.

For more information on training and certification options, see `https://docs.microsoft.com/en-us/microsoftteams/instructor-led-training-teams-landing-page`.

Establishing checkpoints and reviews

At some point, your deployment will shift from *onboarding* to *operations*. Once you reach an operational phase, the management tasks of the Microsoft Teams infrastructure will shift away from the project team to an operational support team responsible for service delivery.

Before that happens, though, you will want to plan how to share information from the project team with the operations team. There will be some sort of transition period between the project and the support teams, and this is a good time to help bring the support team up-to-speed on how Microsoft Teams works, as well as to share any usage, capability, health, or operational insights you may have.

Plan to establish a periodic cadence meeting between the project team and the operations team during the Scale phase to discuss the following areas:

- **Service usage**: This may include active Microsoft Teams usage data or other reporting metrics from within the Microsoft 365 platform. You may also choose to highlight how Teams onboarding and adoption have impacted other tools in your environment (such as decreased usage or the retirement of other tools).

- **Service health**: Use this area to discuss things such as network connectivity and bandwidth, call quality (if calling features are part of the deployment), service ticketing procedures, and support incidents.

- **Roadmap**: This topic can be used to discuss the current project status, such as onboarding or adoption percentages, as well as how the Microsoft Teams project could be impacting other collaboration projects throughout the organization.

You should work toward building a good relationship between the core project team and any operational teams during this project. Depending on your role in the organization, you may find yourself working with those individuals closely again. Establishing a good, mutually respectful relationship will help this individual project, improve operational efficiency for the organization, and positively influence future projects.

Planning for change management and support

Especially in larger organizations, a Microsoft Teams adoption program will involve a lot of moving parts. The change management and communication teams will likely be made up of several non-technical individuals, so it's important that everyone from the project or implementation team work together to build a coherent plan and strategy.

In this section, we'll briefly outline the various roles, and we'll lay out a sample task list that can be used in planning.

Using a roles matrix

Every project has a number of defined roles. In smaller organizations, one individual may perform several of the roles. While people may have multiple roles assigned to them, each role has certain responsibilities. While some roles were identified earlier in this chapter, the following table lists common roles associated with a project.

Role	Description
Executive sponsor	The executive sponsor (sometimes called the project sponsor) is generally a member of an organization's leadership who is responsible to the business for the success or outcome of a project.
Success owner	The success owner is responsible for making sure business goals are realized. The success owner may need to help shape or adjust the deployment plan to make sure the organization's objectives are achieved.
Program manager	The program manager is an individual authorized by an organization to lead one or more teams responsible for completing projects.
Communications team	The communications team can comprise individuals from internal corporate communications staff.

Role	Description
IT leadership team	This contains leaders of various IT teams in an organization (such as the project services, service desk, and IT operations teams).
Subject matter expert	Subject matter experts will be responsible for ensuring the technology prerequisites are met, as well as ensuring the success of technical deployment aspects such as software deployment, authentication, and integration with other applications and devices.
Vendor	Vendors may include hardware or software vendors for Microsoft Teams phones, room systems hardware and devices, add-ins, or other collaborative features.
Microsoft team	The Microsoft team comprises support resources from Microsoft, including Microsoft FastTrack, Microsoft consulting services, and Microsoft Premier Support for Partners.
Champion program	An organization-wide team that identifies champion teams for particular programs or projects.
Champion team	Champions are department-level liaisons that evangelize the Teams deployment, getting users excited about the upcoming project. Champions are also typically involved in some level of end user (or power user) training. Champions may conduct lunch-and-learn style events to further build interest in the organization.
Training lead	The training lead is responsible for managing and communicating training content. A training lead may also procure training materials or classes or participate in train-the-trainer programs to educate champions or other leads on usage and best practices.
Adoption and change management specialist	Adoption and change management specialists are trained individuals that can help overcome both individual and organizational biases against change.

Role	Description
Implementation team	The broad team of IT generalists and specialists that will be enabling features, devices, and users.
Collaboration improvement team	The broad project team tasked with improving collaboration processes and technology across the organization.
Business leads or stakeholders	Business leads or stakeholders are organization leaders whose interests are represented or impacted by a project.
Human resources	The human resources representative, team, or department of an organization.
Legal	The legal representative, team, or department of an organization.

Table 15.1 – A project roles matrix

It's important not just to build a *deployment* plan but also to build an *adoption* plan. Adoption plans seek to transform the business rather than just install a new piece of software for everyone. Building a project team focused on adoption will help make your project a success.

A sample adoption plan

It's important to have a list of tasks that can be incorporated into a larger change management plan. Your organization may have an existing template or blueprint for building projects. You can use this sample task breakdown as a starting point for your own project plan or to help flesh out an existing template.

Role	Description
Implementation team	The broad team of IT generalists and specialists that will be enabling features, devices, and users.
Collaboration improvement team	The broad project team tasked with improving collaboration processes and technology across the organization.
Business leads or stakeholders	Business leads or stakeholders are organization leaders whose interests are represented or impacted by a project.
Human resources	The human resources representative, team, or department of an organization.
Legal	The legal representative, team, or department of an organization.

Set up a Microsoft Teams team for project collaboration.	IT team
Conduct stakeholder and service communications.	Program or project manager
Schedule a regular meeting and communication cadence.	Communications team
Align on the stakeholder key messages, reporting milestones, and formats.	IT leadership, success owner, communications team
Conduct monthly reviews with key stakeholders.	Program or project manager
Identify the communications channels for key updates, including stakeholder reporting, service adoption updates, and helpdesk/support communications.	Communications team
Review the strategy and business scenarios.	Success owner, business leads, implementation team
Review the service strategy template.	Success owner
Complete the draft service strategy template.	Success owner, business leads, implementation team
Review the default persona templates.	Success owner, business leads
Identify and document the business scenarios.	Success owner, business leads
Receive any feedback from key user populations.	Implementation team, communications team
Receive any feedback from select business leads.	Implementation team, communications team
Draft per-scenario service onboarding and adoption plans.	Implementation team
Review all deployment plans with the stakeholders.	Success owner, implementation team
Define success criteria.	Success owner
Set baselines for usage and process data.	Implementation team
Usage reporting	IT team
Crowdsourced success stories	Communications team
Campaign reach	Communications team

Task	Owner or responsible party
Training participation and satisfaction	Training team
Complete technical readiness checks.	IT Team
Request FastTrack assistance, if desired.	Implementation team, success owner, IT team
Complete all legal and security reviews, including the service capability review, guest access, and provisioning processes.	Implementation team, IT team
Complete any network assessments for voice and video services (if necessary).	IT team
Complete client requirements assessments.	IT team
Ensure that there is proper network communication with Microsoft 365 data center resources.	IT team
Enable services (licensing).	IT team
Implement enterprise policies, including governance, guest access, and security policies.	IT team
Assign any required additional support and security roles (such as report readers and Teams supporting service roles).	IT team
Onboard the support organization.	IT team
Identify any champion/training leads.	Champion program
Conduct a service overview with the support and champion leads.	IT team
Update the service desk systems.	IT team
Train the support organization.	IT team, training lead
Define the support processes for the early adopter program (EAP).	IT team
Create a Yammer community for any EAP feedback.	IT team
Develop and launch the champion program.	Champion program
Recruit the champions.	Champion program
Define the feedback systems.	Success owner, implementation team

Task	Owner or responsible party
Develop training materials.	IT team, training lead
Champion onboarding and training.	Champion program, training lead
Define and launch the EAP.	Champion program
Recruit the early adopters.	Champion team
Develop and circulate baseline surveys to capture sentiment about existing collaboration tools in the organization and what participants are hoping to see from Microsoft Teams.	Communications team
Develop the feedback systems.	Champion team
Develop training materials.	Champion team, training lead
Conduct the EAP kickoff and training.	Champion team, implementation team
Monitor all feedback.	Champion team
Define and hold office hours.	Champion team
Send final surveys to capture any further sentiment.	Champion team, communications team, implementation team
Incorporate EAP feedback into the broad deployment plan.	Implementation team
Develop and launch an awareness campaign plan.	Communications team
Create key messages and calls to action.	Communications team
Identify key audiences.	Communications team
Validate feedback systems.	Implementation team
Review the current Microsoft Teams Customer Success Kit materials and adapt if desired.	Communications team
Develop awareness campaign success metrics.	Communications team
Develop communication plans (for example, a welcome kit, 30/60/90 day user communications).	Champion team, communications team, adoption and change management specialist
Implement stakeholder reviews and sign-off.	Success owner, implementation team
Make the launch announcement.	Executive sponsor, communications team

Task	Owner or responsible party
Organize measurements and reporting.	Success owner
Onboard core teams to the Microsoft 365 service and usage reporting.	IT team
Develop broad training plans.	Training team
Identify internal training requirements, including the feedback from the EAP and key business scenarios.	Training team
Develop internal training programs.	Training team
Set up an ongoing training schedule and resources.	Training team
Implement stakeholder reviews and sign-off.	Success owner, Training lead
Launch the training programs.	Training team
Manage feedback and listening.	Training team, communications team, implementation team
Standardize the reporting methods for feedback systems, such as surveys and reports.	Training team, communications team, IT team, implementation team, adoption and change management specialist
Manage onboarding and continuous improvement.	Success owner
Manage the ongoing prioritization of key issues.	Success owner
Make periodic updates regarding usage trends, business scenario updates, and technical issues.	IT team
Identify further business scenarios for adoption and/or improvements.	Success owner
Provide ongoing guidance and education for the user community.	Champion team, communications team, training team

Table 15.2 – A sample adoption plan

It's important to note that the adoption plan has a lot of places to collect feedback. Feedback is an important part of the change management process, as it both identifies potential issues and gives users a way to feel as though their voice is being heard. Allowing for feedback and participation ultimately leads to better organization-wide adoption.

Summary

In this chapter, you learned about how to use the Microsoft Adoption Framework to organize and drive a deployment program for Microsoft Teams. A Microsoft Teams project involves more than just technology—it also involves a significant change management component. You learned about some change management methodologies and how to get buy-in and engagement across the organization.

The Microsoft Adoption Framework for Teams includes three core phases: Start, Experiment, and Scale. You learned about the tasks inside each of these phases and how to best prepare your organization for successful deployment.

In the next chapter, we'll examine governance in the context of Microsoft Teams.

Further Reading

Successful project and program management are broad topics, as are the different change management methodologies. In fact, many individuals devote their entire careers to researching and writing about these areas.

In this section, you'll find information about various resources – including books, websites, and certifications – to help you along in your Microsoft Teams adoption process and change management education:

- *What is the Microsoft Cloud Adoption Framework for Azure?* (`https://docs.microsoft.com/en-us/azure/cloud-adoption-framework/overview`).

- *ADKAR: A Model for Change in Business, Government and Our Community*, *J. M Hiatt, Prosci Learning Center*.

- *Organizational Change as a Process of Death, Dying, and Rebirth, Deone Zell*, *Journal of Applied Behavioral Science*.

- *Prosci Methodology* (`https://www.prosci.com/resources/articles/prosci-methodology`).

- *Itil® Foundation, Itil 4 edition, Axelos The Stationery Office (TSO)*.

- *Learn More About AIM* (`https://www.imaworldwide.com/resources-aim-methodology`).

16
Governance

What is **governance**? It's essentially a policy framework that dictates how your organization will conduct its business. In this context, we're specifically looking at how to address security requirements, industry regulations and standards, and day-to-day operational tasks related to your Microsoft 365 environment.

Many organizations choose to ignore governance topics until they encounter problems – such as regulatory issues, legal discovery matters, or a sprawling cloud infrastructure that has become too hard to manage.

The Microsoft 365 platform provides a wide array of governance tools and processes to help you lay a strong foundation for management and compliance.

In this chapter, we're going to explore several areas of governance, including the following:

- Security
- Compliance
- Life cycle management
- Building a governance team
- Governance questionnaire

Security and compliance will cover the core topics around securing the Microsoft 365 environment, classifying content, and how to use the tools provided by the platform to comply with industry guidelines and regulations. Life cycle management will cover the strategies that are used to create, manage, and deprovision identities and teams in the Microsoft 365 ecosystem. Finally, the governance questionnaire will help guide you through the types of business and technical questions to ask your organization when setting your governance and compliance goals.

By the end of this chapter, you should be equipped with the necessary knowledge to guide your organization through governance policy-setting discussions.

Let's dig in!

Security

From a security standpoint, governance may dictate several things, such as procedures for assigning or removing permissions to/from resources, types of approved authentication protocols, or how content is secured outside of an organization. In this section, we're going to look at the governance surrounding the following topics:

- Identity and authentication
- Sharing and access controls
- Classification
- Approved apps

Let's dive deeper into these areas.

Identity and authentication

As you're well aware, Azure AD identity is the security foundation for everything in the Microsoft 365 ecosystem. The Azure AD identity platform has five general identity models that govern how your organization's users are provisioned and authenticated. They are as follows:

- **Cloud-only identity**: User identities for Microsoft 365 services exist only in Azure AD. Users may have on-premises identities as well, but they are maintained separately. Organizations may select this method if they have no existing on-premises Active Directory or if they are deploying a tenant for testing purposes. Otherwise, organizations do not typically choose this option.

- **Identity synchronization**: User identity details have been synchronized from an on-premises Active Directory; however, no single sign-on capabilities exist. User passwords are maintained separately for each system. Organizations do not typically choose this option.

- **Identity synchronization with Password Hash Synchronization**: Both user identity details and Active Directory password hashes have been synchronized to Azure AD. If a user changes their password in their local Active Directory, the change is reflected in Azure AD.

- **Identity synchronization with pass-through authentication**: User identities have been synchronized from an on-premises Active Directory to Azure AD. However, when a user needs to authenticate, the request is sent to one or more listening agents in the on-premises environment and the password is validated against the local Active Directory. No passwords or password hashes are stored in Azure AD by default. If the on-premises Active Directory environment is unavailable or misconfigured, users will be unable to log on.

- **Identity synchronization with Federation**: User identities have been synchronized from an on-premises Active Directory to Azure AD. All authentication screens and password validations are redirected to and performed against the on-premises Active Directory environment. If the on-premises Active Directory or federation environments are unavailable or misconfigured, users will be unable to log on.

Microsoft freely provides Azure Active Directory Connect (also stylized as Azure AD Connect or AAD Connect) to synchronize identity from an on-premises Active Directory to Azure AD. With this software deployed, Microsoft generally recommends using Identity synchronization with Password Hash Synchronization for the simplest and quickest deployment.

Most customers select one of the last three options when configuring their Microsoft 365 environments. The following table lists many of the considerations and features of the three most common identity architectures:

Feature	Password hash synchronization	Pass-through authentication	Federation with AD FS
Authentication location	In the cloud	In the cloud after password validation on-premises	On-premises
Server requirements	AAD Connect server	AAD Connect server plus one additional server per redundant authentication agent	Minimum of four servers for high availability (two web application proxies in addition to farm servers)
Internet access requirements	Outbound only on port 443	Outbound only on port 443	Inbound internet access on port 443 from the internet
TLS/SSL certificate requirement?	No	No	Yes
Monitoring capability	Synchronization status in Azure AD admin center	Synchronization and pass-through agent status in Azure AD admin center	Azure AD Connect Health service
Single sign-on capability?	Yes, with Seamless SSO	Yes, with Seamless SSO	Yes
Supported sign-in types	UserPrincipalName + password; Windows-integrated authentication; Alternate ID	UserPrincipalName + password; Windows-integrated authentication; Alternate ID	UserPrincipalName + password; Windows-integrated authentication; certificate and smartcard authentication; Alternate ID

Feature	Password hash synchronization	Pass-through authentication	Federation with AD FS
Windows Hello for Business support	Yes, Key trust model	Yes, Key trust model	Yes, Key Trust model or Certificate Trust model
Multi-factor authentication options	Azure AD MFA; custom controls with Conditional Access	Azure AD MFA; custom controls with Conditional Access	Azure AD MFA; Azure MFA server; supported third-party MFA, custom controls with Conditional Access
User account state support or recognition	Disabled accounts	Disabled accounts; account locked out; account expired; password expired; Active Directory sign-in hours	Disabled accounts; account locked out; account expired; password expired; Active Directory sign-in hours
Access filtering options	Azure AD Premium Conditional Access	Azure AD Premium Conditional Access	Azure AD Premium Conditional Access; AD FS claims rules
Ability to block legacy protocols	Yes	Yes	Yes
Sign-in page customization	Yes, with Azure AD Premium	Yes, with Azure AD Premium	Yes
Advanced options	Smart password lockout; leaked credential reporting	Smart password lockout	Multisite low-latency authentication; AD FS extranet lockout; integration with Third-party identity systems

Table 16.1 – Authentication options comparison

As part of your governance plan, you will need to evaluate each of those options with the following categories (at a minimum) in mind:

- Security features and capabilities offered

- Redundancy and availability

- Implementation and support costs

- Compliance with industry regulations (for example, organizations that need to comply with IRS 1075 requirements may need to provide compensating controls for authentication methods other than AD FS or have additional log retention requirements)

While any of the authentication methods may meet your needs from a technical perspective, you'll ultimately need to make this decision as guided by business requirements.

Sharing and access controls

Microsoft Teams offers an array of sharing and access controls to limit (or enable) content collaboration and sharing between users – whether those users are internal or external (referred to as **guests**) to the Microsoft 365 tenant.

These sharing security controls are generally managed in three places:

- **Microsoft 365 admin center**: The admin center (`https://admin.microsoft.com`) provides the coarsest controls for allowing external sharing with guests. These settings are located under **Settings | Org Settings | Services | Microsoft 365 Groups**, **Settings | Org settings | Services | Microsoft Teams**, and **Settings | Org settings | Security & privacy | Sharing**, and they are used to govern whether users can add guests to the Microsoft 365 environment, whether Microsoft Teams can contain external guests, and whether guests are allowed to access SharePoint content, respectively.

- **Microsoft Teams admin center**: The Teams admin center (`https://admin.teams.microsoft.com`) contains additional settings for how guests can interact in chat sessions, meetings, and teams. Guest access must be enabled for these settings to take effect. Guest settings are managed via **Org-wide settings | Guest access** in the Microsoft Teams admin center.

- **SharePoint Online admin center**: The SharePoint Online admin center (`https://admin.microsoft.com` | **Admin centers** | **SharePoint**) governs the scope of guest sharing, such as whether content can be shared with new guests (not previously invited to your Microsoft 365 environment or limited only to currently invited external users).

From a governance perspective, it's important to qualify how data should be shared. Some common questions you may ask are as follows:

- What type of data can or will be shared?

- Will this data include information that requires compliance controls (sensitive information, such as trade secrets or personally identifiable information)?

- Will you allow guests from outside the organization to access the data? If so, under what circumstances?

- Will external sharing requests need to be approved or tracked?

These critical data security questions may reveal a need for identifying data or teams that are good (or poor) candidates for external collaboration and sharing. Fortunately, this task can be performed using tools native to Azure AD, such as labels.

Classification with sensitivity labels

Classification is the process by which data is identified by its characteristics (such as content, importance to the organization, or relationship to a product or service). Organizations may choose to classify content in a variety of ways. For example, you may decide to create content classifications with names such as the following:

- Low Impact

- Medium Impact

- High Impact

- General

- Public

- Confidential

These broad classifications can be applied to groups and, in turn, used to drive automation, allowing or preventing certain types of sharing scenarios. Sensitivity labels are the mechanisms by which you can create and assign classification and protection settings for Microsoft Teams content. For a deeper look at configuring classifications and sensitivity labels in Microsoft Teams, see `https://docs.microsoft.com/en-us/microsoft-365/compliance/sensitivity-labels-teams-groups-sites?view=o365-worldwide`.

Approved apps

Applications play a large role in the Microsoft Teams ecosystem. Whether they are first-party or third-party, apps can be used to create, interact with, and view data inside the boundaries of the Teams experience.

A governance process should include an approval process for apps, including an understanding of how those apps can interact with organization data, where that data is stored, and what provisions may need to be made for content protection.

App controls are located inside the Microsoft Teams admin center at `https://admin.teams.microsoft.com`, under **Teams apps**:

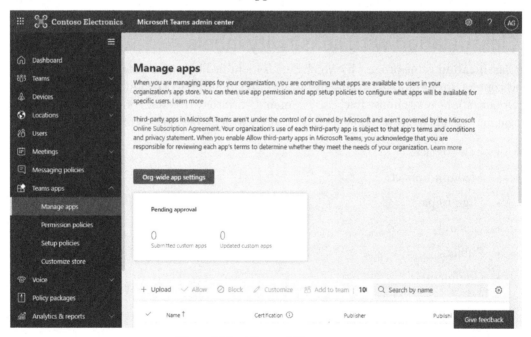

Figure 16.1 – Microsoft Teams apps

There, you can control what apps are allowed in your organization (a coarse control), as well as what users are allowed to access those applications (a fine control). As we noted previously, Microsoft clearly states that third-party apps and the data stored in them aren't covered by your Microsoft Online Subscription Agreement, so your governance process should include a review of any third-party application's security and data management practices.

Whether it's identity and authentication technologies, sharing controls, or content classification, identity and data security concepts play an important role in the governance of the Microsoft 365 platform.

In the next section, we'll review compliance governance topics.

Compliance

Compliance is a broad topic that generally refers to the legal obligations an organization has surrounding its data management practices. There are several security requirements, compliance, or other regulatory laws that your organization may need to follow, depending on your industry (the public sector, financial, energy, education, and health industries commonly have their own reporting and compliance frameworks).

In this section, we'll cover the following topics:

- Frameworks and documentation
- Retention and disposal
- Information barriers and Supervised Chat
- Compliance filters, boundaries, and eDiscovery

Let's examine each of these areas in more detail.

Frameworks and documentation

Microsoft Compliance Manager is a tool that can be used to validate adherence to various compliance and control frameworks. You can use Microsoft 365 Compliance Manager to help monitor your progress against more than 300 pre-configured templates, including the following:

- European Union General Data Protection Regulation
- CAN-SPAM Act
- COBIT-5

- ISO/IEC 27001:2013

- NIST 800-53

- **California Privacy Rights Act (CPRA)**

Compliance Manager allows you to track and document the controls and actions that are recommended for your environment, including the controls attested to by Microsoft. You can access Microsoft 365 Compliance Manager at `https://compliance.microsoft.com/compliancemanager`. The **Assessment templates** dashboard is displayed in the following screenshot:

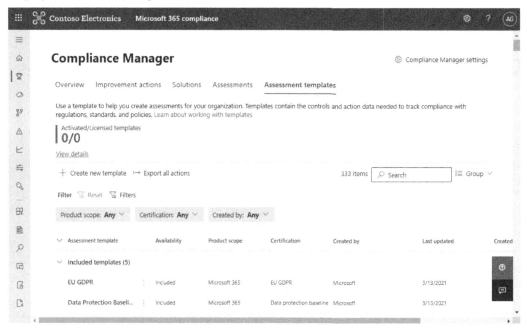

Figure 16.2 – Compliance Manager – Assessment templates

Different templates and assessments are available based on your organization's subscription licenses. Commercial cloud customers have access to the Microsoft Data Protection Baseline, GDPR, ISO 27001:2013, and NIST 800-53 templates by default; Government Community Cloud customers (including GCC Moderate, GCC High, and Department of Defense) customers also have **Cybersecurity Maturity Model Certification (CMMC)** templates included.

Compliance Manager also includes testing automation options to verify that the improvement actions were completed successfully. Finally, Compliance Manager can also serve as a repository to upload supporting documentation linked to individual controls, as shown in the following screenshot:

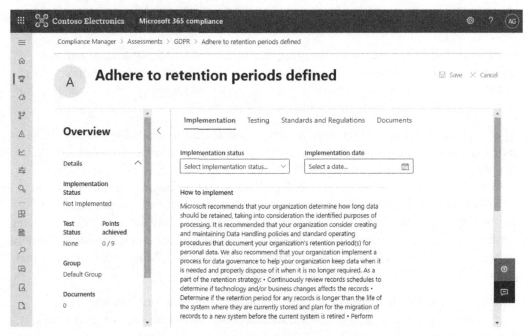

Figure 16.3 – Compliance Manager controls details

If your organization needs (or wants) to prove compliance against several standards and controls, Compliance Manager is an effective tool to use as part of your governance strategy.

Retention and Disposal

Many organizations, as part of their governance, need to plan for both retention and disposal of data at the end of a retention period. While identity, security, and provisioning tasks usually take the spotlight, the life cycle of data is a critical and often-overlooked governance component. Unfortunately, this governance topic frequently only gets addressed once a problem has occurred.

If your organization is in a regulated industry (such as the public sector, health, financial, legal, energy, or education), you may have to comply with very specific regulations surrounding the retention and disposal of data. Failure to do so may result in lawsuits or fines, so the first step in governance is to understand your organization's legal obligations. This usually means working with your organization's legal and records management teams.

From a data life cycle governance perspective, the Microsoft 365 platform provides a robust capability to retain data – including retention length minimums and maximums and how to handle data at the end of a retention period (do nothing, trigger a disposition review with a data custodian, or permanently delete it).

As with other Microsoft 365 services, retention policies can be scoped as broadly as the entire tenant or as narrowly as a single object. It's important to note that separate policies can be created to govern communication within a team (conversations stored within the Microsoft Teams team object), as well as chat (instant messaging) communication between two or more users (conversations stored in individual user mailboxes). Your organization's governance and records management policies may dictate different policies for different types of content, so you'll need to be sure to capture and differentiate the data content types and storage locations (Microsoft Teams 1:x chats, Microsoft Teams channel conversations, and Microsoft Teams channel files).

Microsoft recommends creating and implementing appropriate policies *before* you start consuming the service to ensure maximum compliance with your organization's internal policies.

Next, we'll look at a few different ways to ensure compliant communication and discovery.

Information barriers and Supervised chat

If your organization is in a highly regulated industry (such as the banking, trading, or legal professions), you may need to separate different groups of individuals from being able to communicate with each other. If this is the case, the information barriers capability is worth exploring in your governance model.

Information barriers allow you to introduce the concept of ethical walls to prevent certain parts of the organization from communicating with each other (for example, a financial services firm might need to prevent investment personnel from communicating with banking personnel). For more information on configuring information barriers for Microsoft Teams, see `https://docs.microsoft.com/en-us/microsoftteams/information-barriers-in-teams`.

Supervised chat is a feature targeted toward educational institutions. Supervised chat allows administrators to configure roles for users, which, in turn, dictates who users can chat with. Educational organizations may find this useful, for example, to allow 1:1 chat between students and educators, but not between students without an educator present. If your organization requires this type of governance, be sure to include it in your governance plan and technical requirements. To learn more about Microsoft Teams Supervised chat, see `https://docs.microsoft.com/en-US/microsoftteams/supervise-chats-edu`.

Information barriers and supervised chat cover compliance boundaries from a communications perspective; in the next section, we'll look at compliance boundaries from an eDiscovery perspective.

Compliance filters, boundaries, and eDiscovery

By default, the Microsoft 365 tenant is the security boundary, and individuals performing eDiscovery can locate content anywhere in the tenant. While some organizations need to establish communications boundaries (using things such as information barriers), many organizations need to establish discovery boundaries.

For example, a business may have several divisions sharing a single Microsoft 365 tenant or a regional government may have several disparate agencies consolidated into a single Microsoft 365 tenant.

In these circumstances, the individual divisions or agencies may be fully autonomous organizations and need to prevent the users from one organization from inadvertently (or purposefully) using the eDiscovery process to access content belonging to another organization. **Compliance filters** or **compliance boundaries** can be used to effectively segment discovery between different parts of the tenant.

Compliance filters can be constructed using a wide variety of filters, such as department, office, domain, or even values stored in mailbox attributes or SharePoint site paths. The governance strategy surrounding discovery may influence the design or architecture of Microsoft 365 services in your organization, so it's important to work with other business units to determine what eDiscovery boundaries may be necessary, as well as what filter properties will work best.

Compliance filters or boundaries must be configured via PowerShell using the `New-ComplianceFilter` cmdlet. It's important to remember that teams have mailbox and SharePoint site components, so you'll need to configure both appropriately if you need to restrict the scope of an eDiscovery search. It may be best to use some sort of naming standard or policy to make it easier to construct filters.

> **More on Compliance Boundaries**
>
> For more information on configuring compliance boundaries for
> Microsoft 365, see `https://docs.microsoft.com/en-us/`
> `microsoft-365/compliance/set-up-compliance-`
> `boundaries?view=o365-worldwide`.

Compliance is a broad topic, as you've seen so far while discussing the implementation
of policy frameworks and ethical boundaries. Many organizations have individuals
(or even teams) dedicated to addressing the concepts we've addressed, such as retention
and adherence to frameworks and regulations.

In the next section, we'll review Microsoft Teams life cycle concepts.

Life cycle management

Life cycle management describes how you're going to manage the core Microsoft Teams
team object (and its underlying Microsoft 365 group), from its inception through to the
end of its useful life, when the organization has decided the team is no longer needed.

In this section, we'll discuss managing the entire course of a team object's life cycle, from
creation and naming through retirement.

Provisioning and retirement

The life cycle of a team begins with its creation. While Microsoft's broad intention for
Microsoft Teams is that users can create teams when their business needs justify it, there
may be times when it's necessary (or beneficial) to put some controls around how and
when teams are created (and what they're named).

As you learned back in *Chapter 1*, *Taking a Tour of Microsoft Teams*, a team is built upon
the foundation of a Microsoft 365 group. The Azure AD Premium P1 and P2 subscription
plans offer several life cycle management tools and features. If you're designing a
governance strategy, you should review and incorporate these capabilities:

- Group creation permissions
- Expiration
- Naming policies

We'll dig deeper into what each of these means and their governance capabilities in the following sections.

Group creation permissions

By default, every user in the Microsoft 365 environment can create up to 250 groups (administrators, however, are not bound by this limitation). If you have a large organization, this can mean tens of thousands of objects cluttering the directory – introducing administration complexity as well as the potential for data duplication and security misses.

By utilizing the group creation permissions capabilities (`https://docs.microsoft.com/en-us/microsoft-365/solutions/manage-creation-of-groups?view=o365-worldwide`), you can limit the individuals that can create Microsoft 365 groups (and, by extension, Microsoft Teams objects). As part of your governance plan, you may choose to restrict this to a certain team of administrators or even implement a Power App-based automation solution, such as this template: `https://docs.microsoft.com/en-us/microsoftteams/platform/samples/app-templates#request-a-team`.

Expiration

Humans, by nature, are forgetful. If you've spent any time administering technology systems, you've undoubtedly encountered distribution or security groups that have gone out of use.

Part of a security and governance policy or framework should include identifying objects that are no longer being used, as they can pose a security risk to the organization.

Microsoft 365 group expiration policies allow you to build automated renewal options for groups. You can configure groups to prompt owners to renew at a specified interval. If the owner doesn't renew, the group is flagged for deprovisioning. Microsoft also provides a mechanism for archiving teams, making them read-only: `https://docs.microsoft.com/en-us/microsoftteams/archive-or-delete-a-team`.

Naming policies

Governance surrounding naming standards and policies becomes increasingly important in larger organizations. You can use the naming policies features to allow prefixes and suffixes based on strings or attributes to help you easily identify what part of the business created or owns a group:

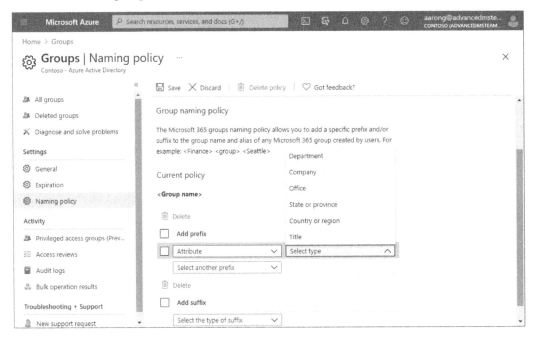

Figure 16.4 – Microsoft 365 group naming policy

A naming policy can contain multiple prefixes and suffixes. You can also specify a list of up to 5,000 words that are prohibited from being part of a group name.

Finally, we'll look at life cycle management techniques that can be applied to security across your organization – whether it's internal users or even guests.

Access packages

As we mentioned earlier in this chapter, organizations frequently end up with unused objects in their directory – this can be security groups, users, external guests, or teams. We've addressed how to handle some things such as unused groups and teams through expiration policies. Access packages help your governance strategy by providing mechanisms for you to automate the life cycle of access to resources in your environment.

An **access package** is a collection of settings, resources, and policies that can be used to manage access to a service, application, or another resource in your tenant. The general architecture of how access packages can work between organizations is shown in the following diagram:

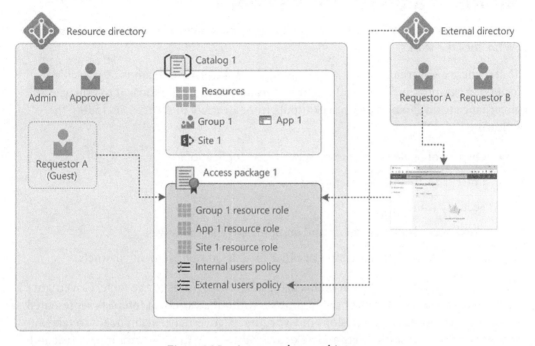

Figure 16.5 – Access package architecture

Access packages are comprised of resources, roles, and policies. Policies can be used to dictate periodic access reviews to ensure users who don't continue to need access are removed in a timely fashion. Like many of the advanced governance features of Microsoft 365, access packages require an Azure AD Premium subscription.

As shown in the preceding diagram, an access package contains resources. Requestors (whether they are internal or external) can request access to the package, which starts an approval process. Approvals can happen automatically or through an approver. At the end of an access period, individuals can be assigned to review the access assignments to make sure the list is current.

You can learn more about the technical details regarding configuring access packages at https://docs.microsoft.com/en-us/azure/active-directory/ governance/entitlement-management-organization and see a step-by-step implementation at https://www.undocumented-features.com/series/ connected-organizations/.

Managing their creation by retiring team and group objects (as well as access to resources) is an important piece of the governance picture.

Building a governance team

Now that we've reviewed the core things that governance covers, you may be wondering, "Who does the work?"

That's where a governance team comes into play. A governance team is responsible for taking business and technical requirements and formulating those into policy. A governance team should look to seek inputs from a variety of sources, including the following:

- Owners of business processes, services, or applications
- Enterprise architecture, service desk, and operations teams
- Security team
- Legal, records management, and compliance representatives
- Microsoft 365 message center or other product announcement channels

Each of these different groups or teams brings their own needs to the table. Governance needs to cover all the aspects of the business – without a variety of interests represented, IT runs the risk of making decisions in a vacuum. A governance team needs to take into account an organization's assets and risks to produce guidance that minimizes risk and promotes operational efficiency and productivity.

A governance team should meet regularly to review new business drivers, technology developments, or other business influences to make sure the guidance they're providing is current and reflects the current opportunity and risk landscape.

Finally, let's look at a structured method for having governance conversations with stakeholders.

Governance questionnaire

Now that you have a handle on the areas of governance, we'll provide a questionnaire to help guide your governance discussions with business stakeholders. Many of these questions may result in deeper meetings – don't be discouraged if it takes a while to decide on some items:

Area	Questions/Decisions
Identity and authentication	What identity and authentication model will your Microsoft 365 tenant use?
	What, if any, types of conditional access controls will be used in the following scenarios? • Users on trusted networks with trusted devices • Users on trusted networks with untrusted devices • Users on untrusted networks with trusted devices • Users on untrusted networks with untrusted devices
Guest and external access	Will you allow guests in your tenant?
	Will guests be allowed in some teams, all teams, or no teams?
	What types of limitations will guests have for participating in teams, meetings, and chats?
	Will you need to enable or disable guest access on a per-team basis?
Content classification	Do you need to create classifications or labels to identify the scope, content, data sharing restrictions, or other risks and constraints of teams?
Compliance	What regulations or policy frameworks does your organization need to follow?
	What retention requirements do you have for Teams content? • 1:x chat (instant messages) • Team channel conversations • Team shared files
	Do you need to plan for Teams archival?
	Does your organization need to implement some form of supervised chat?
	Does your organization need to deploy information barriers (ethical walls) between departments, agencies, or business units?
	Does your organization need to employ eDiscovery search filters (boundaries) between departments, agencies, or business units?

Area	Questions/Decisions
Life cycle management	Are restrictions necessary to manage the creation of Microsoft 365 groups and teams?
	Is automation necessary (or desired) to manage the creation of Microsoft 365 groups and teams?
	Do you require a naming policy? If so, what types of properties or attributes should a naming policy include?
	Should groups expire? If so, what time frames do you want to use for renewal?
	Will you use access packages to manage entitlements for resources?

Table 16.2 – Governance questionnaire

The discussion points in the preceding table will help you build a strong governance plan for Microsoft Teams features. The good part about a governance discussion is it allows the business to understand the features of the tools and bring alignment between the business goals and the technical capabilities.

Summary

In this chapter, we explored several areas of governance from the Microsoft 365 and Microsoft Teams perspectives, ranging from identity and authentication to eDiscovery and some of the controls that are available for securing data. We looked at the Microsoft Compliance Manager offering and how your organization can use its templates to track your compliance against industry standards. Finally, we examined some of the life cycle concerns around provisioning identity and access to Microsoft 365 resources.

In the next chapter, we'll look at connecting the cloud-based Microsoft Teams environment with an on-premises Exchange Server deployment.

17
Integration with Exchange Server

While services such as Microsoft Teams and **Exchange Online** have reached significant maturity milestones (for example, since Business Productivity Online Services, the precursor to Office 365, which was launched in 2008), many organizations are still in the beginning stages of exploring **Software-as-a-Service** (**SaaS**) applications. These organizations still have significant investments in on-premises technology (such as Microsoft Active Directory, Exchange, and SharePoint). Fortunately, there are many options available to help these organizations begin to adopt cloud technologies such as Microsoft Teams.

As you've already seen in previous chapters, Microsoft Teams offers a rich set of collaborative technologies such as instant messaging, a calendar, file storage and editing, and dashboards. Organizations can use hybrid technologies to connect Microsoft Teams to an Exchange server environment, thereby gaining instant access to Teams features.

In this chapter, we're going to learn how to configure Teams and Exchange in a hybrid manner so that Teams users can view the free/busy information for on-premises Exchange users from within the application.

We'll look at the following areas:

- Overview of Teams and Exchange Server hybrid

- Understanding environment requirements

- Enabling hybrid features

Let's go!

Technical requirements

To take advantage of the Teams features in an Exchange hybrid environment, you'll need to meet a few requirements:

- On-premises identities need to be synchronized to Azure Active Directory with **Azure Active Directory Connect (AAD Connect)**.

- Azure Active Directory identities for corresponding on-premises users must have both an Exchange and Teams license assigned.

- Azure AD Connect needs to be configured with the **Exchange Hybrid Deployment** feature.

- On-premises Autodiscover and **Exchange Web Services (EWS)** resources must be published externally (for example, a CNAME record such as `autodiscover.contoso.com` published in DNS and `https://autodiscover.contoso.com/EWS/Exchange.asmx` available externally).

- The on-premises environment must be Exchange Server 2016 with **Cumulative Update (CU)** 3 or later.

- OAuth authentication must be enabled (typically configured while running the Exchange Hybrid Configuration Wizard).

For most organizations, so long as Autodiscover and EWS are published externally and the messaging environment is Exchange Server 2016 CU3 or later, simply deploying AAD Connect with the Express option and running the Exchange Hybrid Configuration Wizard should successfully configure all of the organization-wide settings.

Overview of the Teams and Exchange Server hybrid

With Exchange hybrid features enabled, on-premises Exchange users have access to all the Teams features, such as creating and joining teams, configuring tabs and bots, and using calling and instant messaging. Exchange Hybrid features will allow both cloud and on-premises Exchange mailbox users to be able to successfully access on-premises Exchange calendars (for themselves and other organization users) through the Teams interface using the standard Exchange Autodiscover process.

In the next section, we'll briefly walk through the Exchange Hybrid Configuration Wizard and explore some of the manual configurations if you're unable to use the Exchange Hybrid Configuration Wizard in your environment.

Enabling hybrid features

In this section, we're going to review the key settings to ensure the environment is prepared. Specifically, we will cover the following topics:

- Verifying your domains
- Updating your on-premises user principal names
- Configuring Azure Active Directory Connect
- Running the Exchange Hybrid Configuration Wizard
- Verifying Teams integration
- Assigning licenses
- Reviewing manual configuration steps

After performing these steps, an on-premises mailbox user should be able to use the Teams application to query on-premises free/busy times and schedule a meeting.

Verifying your domains

To enable a hybrid experience, you'll need to configure your Microsoft 365 tenant to use the same **Domain Name System** (**DNS**) namespace as your on-premises email domains. To do this, you must add your domain to Microsoft 365. Microsoft 365 generates a code that you add as a text (TXT) record to your organization's public DNS. This proves that you control the domain. A domain can only be associated with one Microsoft 365 tenant at a time.

There are many ways to complete this task. You've most likely already completed this before, so we won't spend a lot of time on this topic (but we will address it from a completeness perspective). In the interest of expediency, we'll only discuss the most straightforward way:

1. Using Global Administrator credentials, log into the Microsoft 365 admin center at `https://admin.microsoft.com` and select **Settings | Domains**.

2. Click **Add domain**.

3. Enter the name of the domain to add, and then click **Next**.

4. Choose how you want to verify ownership of the domain:

   - If the domain registrar uses **Domain Connect** (`https://docs.microsoft.com/en-us/microsoft-365/admin/setup/add-domain?view=o365-worldwide#registrars-with-domain-connect`), you can provide your credentials through the Microsoft 365 admin center and Microsoft will configure the DNS records automatically.

   - Select the **TXT** record option for Microsoft to provide you with the value that you will add to your public DNS. Each domain hosting system is different; you may need to check with your hosting provider, registrar, or network administrator if you're unsure about the specifics of adding this record.

   - You can also add a text file to your domain's public website. Microsoft will provide you with a text file to place on a website that matches the domain name and then check to make sure you have placed it correctly.

5. If you choose either of the first two options, DNS changes will need to be made:

   - If you select **Add the DNS records for me**, provide credentials for the Domain Connect process.

   - If you choose **I'll add the DNS records myself**, Microsoft will provide you with general information for the types of records and values. It will be up to you to enter that data on behalf of your organization.

6. After using either option, click **Finish**.

Once you've done this, your environment is technically ready to start deploying Azure AD Connect and set up Exchange hybrid. However, there is an additional step that Microsoft recommends to get the most out of your experience: ensuring alignment between **User Principal Names (UPNs)**, **email SMTP addresses**, and the domains you've verified in Office 365.

Updating your on-premises user principal names

You'll have the best single sign-on experience if you verify your email address domains in your Microsoft 365 tenant before proceeding.

With adoption and change management in mind, remember that new technologies will be more quickly and easily adopted if the end user process is straightforward.

As we mentioned previously, Microsoft recommends ensuring your users' primary SMTP address matches their UPN, and that the domain suffix for that address is verified in your Microsoft 365 tenant. There are several reasons for this, including the following:

- Simplicity for the end user sign-on process

- Autodiscover and sign-on for Microsoft Teams

- Autodiscover and sign-on for Microsoft Outlook

Many organizations have fully qualified Active Directory forest or domain names that do not match the organization's public email address domains. For example, an organization may have configured an Active Directory domain name such as `fabrikam.local`, while the email domain for its users is `contoso.com`.

About User Principal Names

While changing a user principal name or user principal name suffix is generally a trivial task, you will want to ensure that you don't have internal dependencies, such as single-sign-on integration with a proxy server, an internal Certificate Authority that issues user certificates, or claims-based authentication using the UPN as a claim.

There may be additional technical details to take into consideration for your organization, which are outside the scope of this book. Some of these may include mergers and acquisitions, implications of UPN suffix routing in multi-forest environments, and how other federated applications integrate with your directory. For more advanced information on the UPN architecture and preparation for Azure Active Directory, please refer to `https://docs.microsoft.com/en-us/microsoft-365/enterprise/prepare-a-non-routable-domain-for-directory-synchronization?view=o365-worldwide` and `https://docs.microsoft.com/en-us/previous-versions/windows/it-pro/windows-server-2003/cc784334(v=ws.10)`.

To change a user principal name suffix, you can use the Active Directory Users and Computers snap-in or PowerShell. If you use the Active Directory Users and Computers snap-in, the UPN suffix will have to exist in your forest before you can use it:

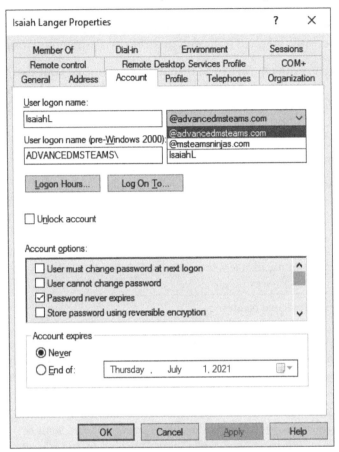

Figure 17.1 – Active Directory Users and Computers

You can set any suffix you like through PowerShell, regardless of whether it's been added to your forest.

For bulk updates for your Active Directory users, you can consider using a tool such as **Set-UpnToMailAddress**, which is available via the PowerShell Gallery: `http://aka.ms/SetUpnToMailAddress`.

Once your UPNs have been updated, you can start configuring Azure Active Directory Connect.

Configuring Azure Active Directory Connect

To successfully locate on-premises users in the **Global Address List** view that Microsoft Teams uses, you'll need to synchronize your local Active Directory environment to Azure.

Azure Active Directory Connect supports several different authentication methods. For this example, we're going to use a default **Express Settings** installation of Azure Active Directory Connect, which selects all the objects in Active Directory and then enables Password Hash Synchronization.

To do that, follow these steps:

1. On a new physical or virtual server, navigate to `https://aka.ms/aadconnect` and download the current version of Azure Active Directory Connect.

2. Launch the downloaded application; that is, **AzureADConnect.msi**.

3. On the **Welcome** page, check the box to agree to the license terms and click **Continue**.

4. On the **Express Settings** screen, click the **Use express settings** button:

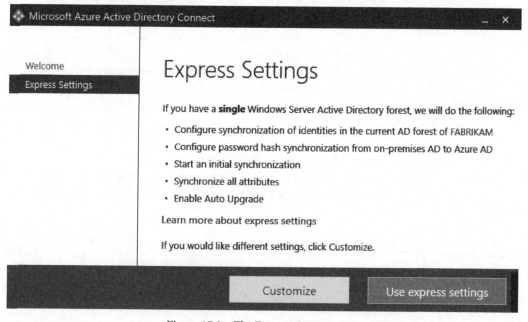

Figure 17.2 – The Express Settings page

5. On the **Connect to Azure AD** screen, enter credentials for a Global Administrator in Office 365 and click **Next**:

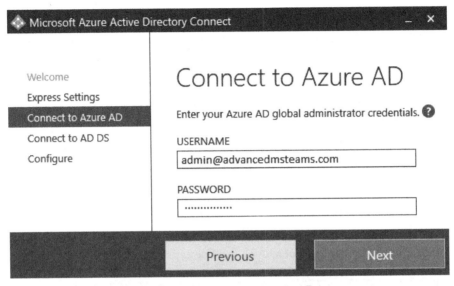

Figure 17.3 – The Connect to Azure AD page

> **Troubleshooting Azure AD Connect Setup**
>
> If you encounter errors when configuring Azure AD Connect, you can try the Azure AD Connect Communications Test script, located at `https://aka.ms/aadnetwork`, to ensure your server meets the minimum software and communication requirements.

6. Next, on the **Connect to AD DS** page, enter the credentials for an enterprise admin account either in NetBIOS or FQDN domain name format (`contoso\administrator` or `contoso.com\administrator`), and then click **Next**:

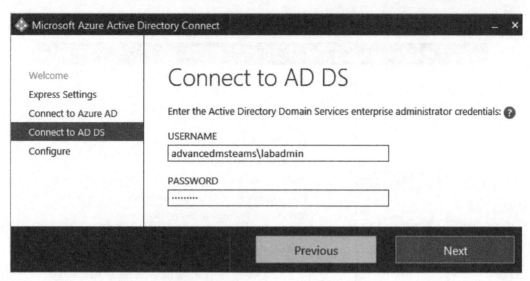

Figure 17.4 – The Connect to AD DS page

7.   If the Azure AD sign-in configuration page is displayed, it is because you didn't verify all your forest or domain UPN suffix domains in Microsoft 365. You can select the **Continue without matching all UPN suffixes to verified domains** checkbox to continue without adding and verifying all forest UPN suffixes in Azure AD, or go back and verify the additional domains in your tenant by following the steps provided in the previous section. Then, click **Next**:

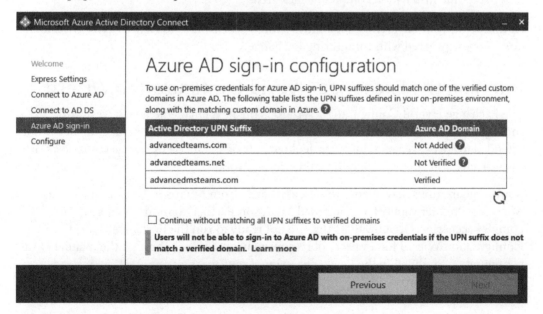

Figure 17.5 – The Azure AD sign-in configuration page

8. Select the **Exchange hybrid deployment** checkbox and then click **Install**:

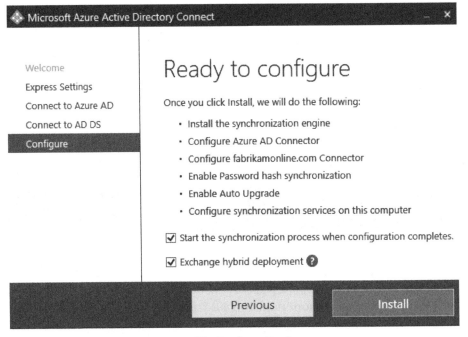

Figure 17.6 – The Ready to Configure page

9. After the installation completes, click **Exit**.

At this point, your on-premises identities should synchronize to Azure Active Directory. You can now proceed with configuring Exchange Hybrid.

Running the Exchange Hybrid Configuration Wizard

The Exchange Hybrid Configuration Wizard is the next enablement step we'll work through. Microsoft Exchange organizations may vary in size; this general guidance is not intended to cover scenarios for large deployments or advanced Exchange scenarios, but instead, give you an overview of how the process works.

Many organizations may choose to seek assistance from Microsoft Consulting Services, Microsoft Premier support, or the broad Microsoft Partner community to assist in complex scenarios. Organizations that are not ready to run the Exchange Hybrid Configuration Wizard for a variety of reasons may opt to work through the manual OAuth configuration, outlined in the *Reviewing manual configuration steps* section, instead.

To run the Exchange Hybrid Configuration Wizard, follow these steps:

1. Log into an Exchange server with an account that is a member of the local Administrators group on the server, as well as a member of the Exchange Organization Management group.

2. Launch the Microsoft Edge browser and navigate to `https://aka.ms/hybridwizard`.

3. When prompted to open the runtime application, choose `Microsoft.Online.CSE.Hybrid.Client.application` and select **Open**:

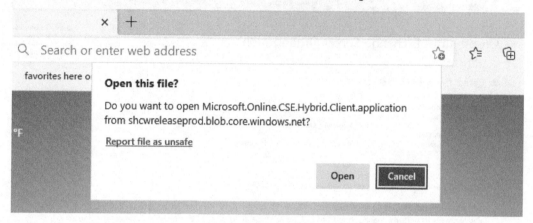

Figure 17.7 – The Microsoft.Online.CSE.Hybrid.Client.Application dialog

4. Then, click **Install**:

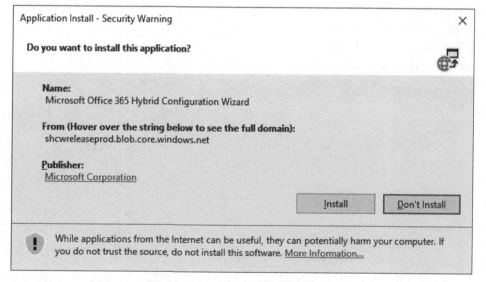

Figure 17.8 – Exchange Hybrid Wizard

5. Wait while the most recent version of the application is downloaded. When the **Open File – Security Warning** dialog box appears, confirm that the publisher is **Microsoft** and click **Run**.

6. On the introductory page of the Hybrid Configuration Wizard, click **Next**.

7. Select an Exchange server in your organization and select an Office 365 Exchange Online organization (for most customers, this will be Office 365 Worldwide). Then, click **Next**:

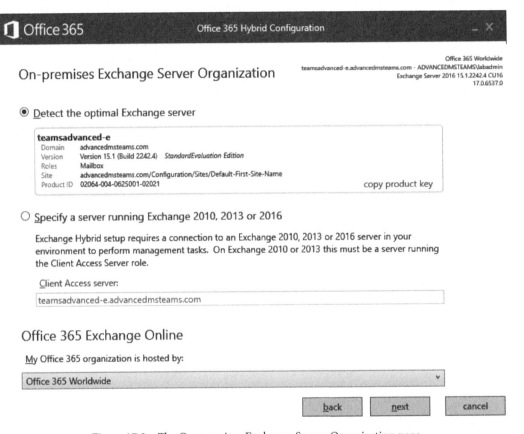

Figure 17.9 – The On-premises Exchange Server Organization page

> **Required Exchange Server Versions**
>
> While the Hybrid Configuration Wizard indicates that you can select any server running Exchange 2010 or newer, remember that only mailboxes hosted on Exchange Server 2016 CU3 or later will be accessible from Microsoft Teams.

8. If necessary, enter different credentials for the on-premises Exchange administrator. The account you select must be a member of **Organization Management** for you to create a federation trust with Microsoft 365.

9. Add your Microsoft 365 Global Administrator account under **Office 365 Exchange Online Account**. When you're finished, click **next**:

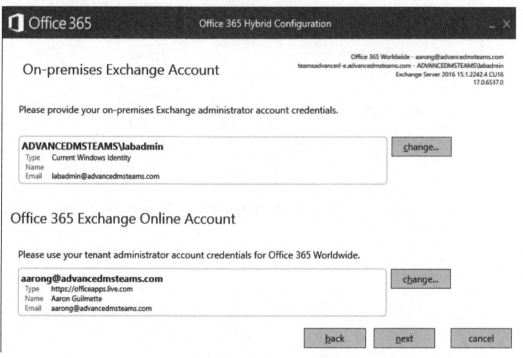

Figure 17.10 – Th Hybrid Configuration Wizard credentials page

10. Wait while the Hybrid Configuration Wizard verifies your credentials and retrieves both the on-premises and Office 365 organization configurations. When you're ready, click **Next**:

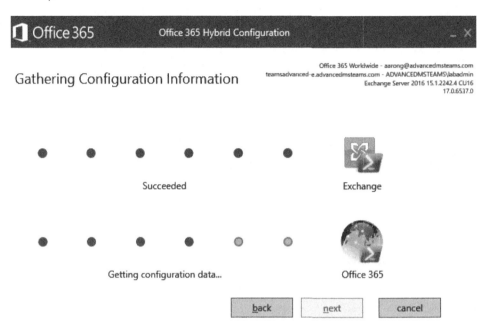

Figure 17.11 – The Gathering Configuration Information page

11. Select the radio button for the **Full Hybrid Configuration** option and click **next**:

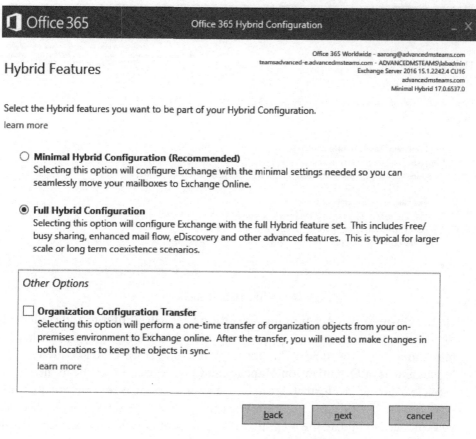

Figure 17.12 – The Hybrid Features page

12. Select the **Use Exchange Classic Hybrid Topology** radio button and click **next**:

Figure 17.13 – The Hybrid Topology page

13. On the **On-premises Account for Migration** page, click **Enter** to add credentials for an on-premises account. This process creates a migration endpoint for later migrations to Microsoft 365. This account must have at least the **Recipient Management** or **Organization Management** privilege and must be in the DOMAIN\Username format. It can be the same account as the one you are using to complete the Hybrid Configuration Wizard. If you change this account's password, you will need to update the migration endpoint configuration in Exchange Online. Click **Next** when the credential has been added.

14. Select the **Configure my Client Access and Mailbox Servers for secure mail transport (typical)** radio button. Most organizations don't deploy Edge Transport servers with Microsoft 365, but if you are planning to do so, you will need to complete that configuration separately. You can also rerun the configuration and change this option later. Click **next** when you're ready:

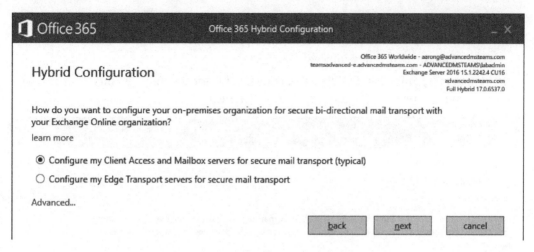

Figure 17.14 – The Hybrid Configuration page

15. On the **Receive Connector Configuration** page, select one or more Exchange
    Servers to receive inbound mail from Exchange Online. These servers will need
    to be configured to allow inbound port 25 access from the Exchange Online IP
    address ranges (see `http://aka.ms/o365endpoints` for the complete list).
    Click **next** when you're finished:

Figure 17.15 – The Receive Connector Configuration page

16. On the **Send Connector Configuration** page, select one or more Exchange Servers
    to be configured to send mail or relay to Exchange Online. After one or more
    servers have been selected, click **Next**.

17. On the **Transport Certificate** page, select a certificate to use with hybrid mail transport. This certificate must be from a publicly trusted Certificate Authority. Select **next** when you're finished.

18. On the **Organization FQDN** page, enter a value for the fully qualified domain name for your on-premises organization and click **next**:

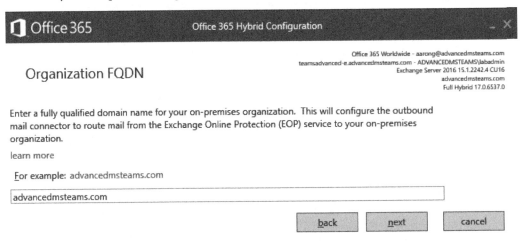

Figure 17.16 – The Organization FQDN page

19. On the **Ready to Update** page, click **Update**.

20. On the **Congratulations** page, click **Close**.

If you need to rerun the Hybrid Configuration Wizard at any point, you can relaunch the wizard from the shortcut left behind on the desktop. If you can run the Hybrid Configuration Wizard successfully, you can skip the next section and proceed with *Assigning licenses*.

For organizations that are unable to run the Exchange Hybrid Configuration Wizard, you can also perform the OAuth configuration steps manually. This *will not* enable the full integration (such as mail delivery components between cloud and on-premises users), but it will allow you to perform hybrid free/busy lookups.

Reviewing manual configuration steps

For Microsoft Teams to interact with on-premises mailboxes, you must configure OAuth authentication between the Microsoft 365 platform and the on-premises Exchange organization. This is automatically configured when you run the Hybrid Configuration Wizard; however, there may be business and technical factors that prevent you from running the Hybrid Configuration Wizard.

In that event, you can manually configure the OAuth settings. Before you begin, you'll need a few pieces of information and prerequisites to be met:

- A verified domain in your Microsoft 365 tenant (such as `contoso.com`).

- The value for your coexistence domain, in the form of `tenant.mail.onmicrosoft.com`; for example, `contoso.mail.onmicrosoft.com`.

- Access to a machine with the Azure AD PowerShell cmdlets. They can be installed using `Install-Module MSonline` from an elevated PowerShell console session.

- Your external Autodiscover service endpoint. It's most likely similar to `https://docs.microsoft.com/en-us/exchange/architecture/client-access/autodiscover?view=exchserver-2019`.

- List of publicly available endpoints for your Exchange organization. You can return a list of external endpoints by running the following commands:

```
Get-MapiVirtualDirectory | FL server, ExternalUrl
Get-WebServicesVirtualDirectory | FL server, ExternalUrl
Get-OABVirtualDirectory | FL server, ExternalUrl
```

Once you have gathered the required information, follow these steps to complete the configuration:

1. Launch an Exchange Management Shell in your on-premises Exchange organization.

2. First, you will need to create the authorization objects for Exchange Online. Copy and paste the following commands, replacing `<your tenant coexistence domain>` with the correct value for your tenant:

```
New-AuthServer -Name "WindowsAzureACS" -AuthMetadataUrl
"https://accounts.accesscontrol.windows.net/<your tenant
coexistence domain>/metadata/json/1"

New-AuthServer -Name "evoSTS" -Type AzureAD
-AuthMetadataUrl https://login.windows.net/<your
tenant coexistence domain>/federationmetadata/2007-06/
federationmetadata.xml
```

3. Next, you will need to enable the Exchange Online partner application:

```
Get-PartnerApplication | ?{$_.ApplicationIdentifier -eq
"00000002-0000-0ff1-ce00-000000000000" -and $_.Realm -eq
""} | Set-PartnerApplication -Enabled $true
```

4. Once the partner application has been enabled, copy and paste the following script to export the on-premises authorization certificate:

```
$thumbprint = (Get-AuthConfig).
CurrentCertificateThumbprint
if((test-path $env:SYSTEMDRIVE\OAuthConfig) -eq $false)
{
    md $env:SYSTEMDRIVE\OAuthConfig
}
cd $env:SYSTEMDRIVE\OAuthConfig
$oAuthCert = (dir Cert:\LocalMachine\My) | where {$_.
Thumbprint -match $thumbprint}
$certType = [System.Security.Cryptography.
X509Certificates.X509ContentType]::Cert
$certBytes = $oAuthCert.Export($certType)
$CertFile = "$env:SYSTEMDRIVE\OAuthConfig\OAuthCert.cer"
[System.IO.File]::WriteAllBytes($CertFile, $certBytes)
```

5. Copy the exported `OauthCert.cer` file to the computer that has the Azure AD module installed (or install it on the Exchange Server where you exported the certificate).

6. On the computer where the Azure AD module is installed, launch a PowerShell console and change directories to the location where you saved the `OauthCert.cer` file.

7. Copy and paste the following script into the PowerShell console session to import the authorization certificate to Exchange Online. When prompted, provide a Global Admin credential for your tenant:

```
Connect-MsolService
$CertFile = (pwd).Path+"\OAuthConfig\OAuthCert.cer"
$objFSO = New-Object -ComObject Scripting.
FileSystemObject
$CertFile = $objFSO.GetAbsolutePathName($CertFile)
$cer = New-Object System.Security.Cryptography.
X509Certificates.X509Certificate
$cer.Import($CertFile)
$binCert = $cer.GetRawCertData()
```

```
$credValue = [System.Convert]::ToBase64String($binCert)
```

```
$ServiceName = "00000002-0000-0ff1-ce00-000000000000"
```

```
$p = Get-MsolServicePrincipal -ServicePrincipalName
$ServiceName
```

```
New-MsolServicePrincipalCredential -AppPrincipalId
$p.AppPrincipalId -Type asymmetric -Usage Verify -Value
$credValue
```

8. Using the external endpoints you gathered in the prerequisite area, add them to the following script, replacing <ExternalUrl#>. You can add as many entries as you have endpoints:

```
$ServiceName = "00000002-0000-0ff1-ce00-000000000000";
```

```
$x = Get-MsolServicePrincipal -AppPrincipalId
$ServiceName;
```

```
$x.ServicePrincipalnames.Add("<ExternalUrl1>");
```

```
$x.ServicePrincipalnames.Add("<ExternalUrl2>");
```

```
Set-MSOLServicePrincipal -AppPrincipalId $ServiceName
-ServicePrincipalNames $x.ServicePrincipalNames;
```

9. Next, you'll need to go back to the Exchange Management Shell session and run the following commands to create an **IntraOrganizationConnector** from your Exchange organization to Office 365:

```
$ServiceDomain = Get-AcceptedDomain | where {$_.
DomainName -like "*.mail.onmicrosoft.com"} | select
-ExpandProperty Name
```

```
New-IntraOrganizationConnector -name
ExchangeHybridOnPremisesToOnline -DiscoveryEndpoint
https://outlook.office365.com/autodiscover/autodiscover.
svc -TargetAddressDomains $ServiceDomain
```

About the Service Domain

If $ServiceDomain is empty in your environment because you haven't begun preparing for an Exchange hybrid deployment, you can set $ServiceDomain equal to your tenant mail routing domain, such as contoso.mail.onmicrosoft.com.

---

10. The final step is to configure an **IntraOrganizationConnector** from Office 365 to your on-premises organization. You'll need the Autodiscover endpoint you identified in the prerequisites section, as well as your primary SMTP domain namespace (such as contoso.com). Once you have that, edit the following script with your values and then paste it into a PowerShell console session:

```
$Credential = Get-Credential
```

```
$Session = New-PSSession -ConfigurationName Microsoft.
Exchange -ConnectionUri https://outlook.office365.
com/powershell-liveid/ -Credential $Credential
-Authentication Basic -AllowRedirection
```

```
Import-PSSession $Session
```

```
New-IntraOrganizationConnector -name
ExchangeHybridOnlineToOnPremises -DiscoveryEndpoint <your
on-premises Autodiscover endpoint> -TargetAddressDomains
<your on-premises SMTP domain>
```

Once you've completed these steps, you can verify that your OAuth connectivity works from Office 365 to your on-premises organization. To do this, you'll need the following:

- A cloud-based mailbox

- An on-premises endpoint that is exposed to the internet

You can test this by connecting to Exchange Online PowerShell and running the following command:

```
Test-OAuthConnectivity -Service EWS -TargetUri https://<on-
premises endpoint>/metadata/json/1 -Mailbox <cloud mailbox> |
Select ResultType,Identity
```

The following screenshot displays an example of a successful test and the resulting output. You can use this and compare it with your configuration:

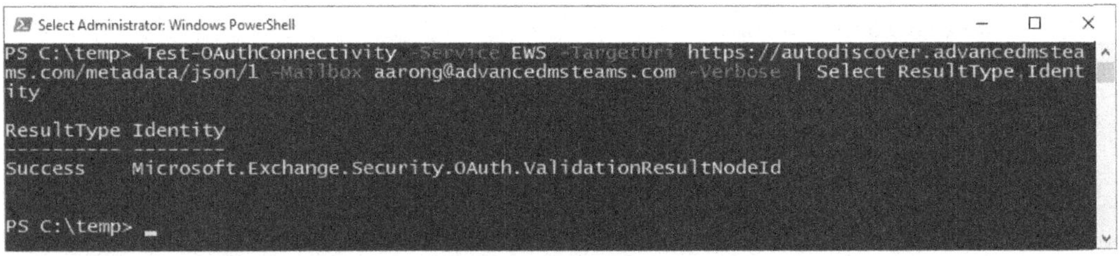

Figure 17.17 – Test-OAuthConnectivity example

After a successful test, you can begin assigning licenses.

Assigning licenses

Users, whether they have on-premises or cloud-based mailboxes, will need both a Microsoft Teams license as well as an Exchange Online license to access the Teams calendar features.

To assign licenses to a user, follow these steps:

1. Navigate to the Microsoft 365 admin center at `https://admin.microsoft.com` and select **Users | Active users**.

2. Select the ellipsis next to a user and then select **Manage product licenses**:

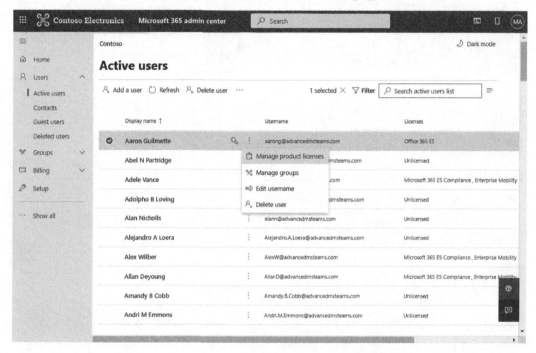

Figure 17.18 – Microsoft 365 Admin Center – Active users

3. On the licenses flyout, select either suite or individual licenses for Exchange Online and Microsoft Teams and click **Save changes**. You can also bulk-assign licenses through Azure Group-Based Licensing (`https://docs.microsoft.com/en-us/azure/active-directory/fundamentals/active-directory-licensing-whatis-azure-portal`) or PowerShell (`https://docs.microsoft.com/en-us/microsoft-365/enterprise/assign-licenses-to-user-accounts-with-microsoft-365-powershell?view=o365-worldwide`):

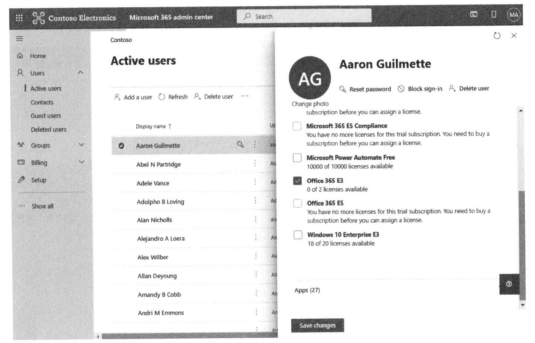

Figure 17.19 – Microsoft 365 Admin Center – License flyout

After a few minutes, licenses should be assigned to your users and you can begin testing.

Verifying your Teams integration

Once the licenses have been assigned to your on-premises Exchange users, you can verify that everything is working by simply launching Teams.

After Microsoft Teams launches and you have signed in as a user with an on-premises mailbox, look at the user interface. If you see the calendar icon displayed on the left rail, that means Teams knows about your Exchange license:

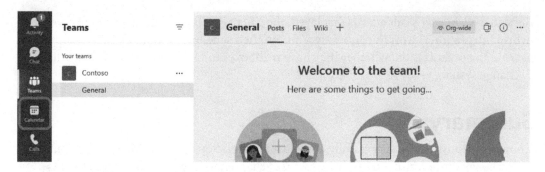

Figure 17.20 – Microsoft Teams Calendar

If the calendar icon is not displayed after a few minutes, you may need to verify that you have an Exchange Autodiscover record pointing to your on-premises Exchange environment. You can use the tools at `http://www.testconnectivity.microsoft.com` and select the Outlook Connectivity tool. If that is successful, you can then try the **Teams Calendar Tab Test** at `https://www.testconnectivity.microsoft.com/tests/TeamsCalendarMissing/Input`.

Once the calendar icon is displayed, you can try selecting it. This is the result:

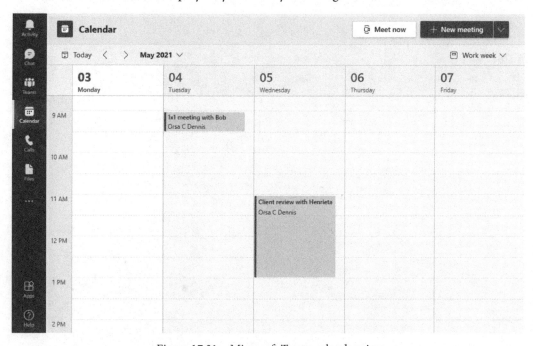

Figure 17.21 – Microsoft Teams calendar view

If the logged-in user's calendar is displayed, the Microsoft Teams and Exchange Server hybrid integration is working correctly. You can then schedule meetings with other users in the organization, whether they have mailboxes in Office 365 or the on-premises Exchange system.

Summary

Congratulations! You've successfully configured integration between Microsoft Teams and an Exchange on-premises environment. In this chapter, we reviewed the requirements for configuring Teams and Exchange integration and learned about the steps necessary to enable free/busy searches between the platforms.

In the next chapter, we'll address security and data protection strategies.

18
Security and Data Protection

Like other corporate resources, such as Exchange and SharePoint, the Microsoft Teams experience may need to be protected against data loss or risky access scenarios.

Using native products in the Microsoft 365 platform, you can secure both access to the platform as well as how data is shared. These factors are especially important if you're dealing with **Personally Identifiable Information** (**PII**), financial data, or trade secrets.

In this chapter, we're going to explore two core technologies that can be used to enhance the security posture of your Teams environment:

- Conditional Access
- Data Loss Prevention

By the end of this chapter, you should understand how to configure policies to help further reduce risk to your organization.

Technical requirements

In order to complete some of the activities and configurations in this chapter, you'll need a Microsoft 365 tenant with the following licenses activated (either in trial or paid subscriptions):

- Azure Active Directory Premium P1 or P2 (for Conditional Access)
- Microsoft 365 35 Compliance (for Microsoft Teams Data Loss Prevention)

You can obtain trial versions of these products through the Microsoft 365 Admin Center.

Conditional Access

Through the years, many organizations have implemented policies that determine how and from where users can access applications and data. The most common policies and restrictions have focused on using **network location** as the primary criterion to determine whether a user or device was allowed to access a resource.

In traditional security trust models, organizations generally trust users, devices, applications, and data on networks that they either directly own or manage. In Azure AD, these "known" networks are referred to as network locations.

This model worked well when most of the applications and resources that a company used were inside its own network boundaries. However, as more organizations have adopted cloud technology, allowed users to work remotely, or permitted the use of personal devices, this constraint doesn't always align with business goals.

That's where Conditional Access fits in. **Conditional Access** is a set of rules that allows organizations to evaluate whether a particular user or device is permitted to access a resource, based on meeting a set of predetermined criteria. If the criteria are met, the user is allowed to access the data or application. If the platform determines there is a risk, then the user may be challenged to provide additional authentication measures, restricted to be able to only use a subset of features, or denied completely.

This identity-based security concept is part of a broader security philosophy called a **zero trust model**. With zero trust security models, organizations pivot from a model of inherently trusting users and devices on their network to recognizing that threat actors can be anywhere – including inside a corporate network on a compromised device.

Conditional Access reflects one way that Microsoft addresses zero trust principles. By validating who a user is based on multiple factors of authentication and verifying that a machine meets a compliance specification, organizations can have assurances that the individuals accessing a system are who they say they are and are accessing the resources legitimately. Compliance requirements might include network location, approved client applications, enforced domain, Azure Active Directory membership, or enrollment in the Intune managed device platform.

What does that mean for organizations wanting to protect data transmitted through Microsoft Teams? Deploying the most common set of Conditional Access policies requires an Azure Active Directory Premium P1 license, though some advanced features require a P2 license.

While Azure Active Directory Premium includes many features, we're going to focus on the features directly related to **Conditional Access** and **Identity Protection**:

Conditional Access	Premium P1	Premium P2
Conditional Access based on group, location, and device status	✓	✓
Azure Information Protection integration	✓	✓
SharePoint limited access	✓	✓
Terms of use (set up terms of use for specific access)	✓	✓
Multi-factor authentication with Conditional Access	✓	✓
Microsoft Cloud App Security integration	✓	✓
Third-party Identity Governance partners integration	✓	✓
Identity Protection		
Vulnerabilities and risky accounts detection		✓
Risk events investigation		✓
Risk-based Conditional Access policies		✓

Table 18.1 – Features of Conditional Access and Identity Protection

You can review the entire feature comparison between Azure AD editions at `https://azure.microsoft.com/en-us/pricing/details/active-directory/`.

One of the most common challenge methods is confirming a user is indeed who they say they are by performing a secondary authentication, such as using the Microsoft Authenticator app on their mobile device.

In this section, we're going to look at configuring a common Conditional Access scenario that requires multi-factor authentication for all users not on trusted networks.

Let's dig in!

Requiring multi-factor authentication for all users not on trusted networks

This policy enforces a multi-factor authentication prompt for all users who are not on one of the configured trusted networks. It's similar to legacy (pre-cloud) policies that only allow access if a user is on a trusted network but with the additional capability to allow a user to prove themselves.

To configure this policy, follow these steps:

1. Navigate to the Azure portal (`https://portal.azure.com`) and log in as a user with Global Administrator privileges.

2. In the search bar, enter `named locations` and select **Azure AD Named locations**:

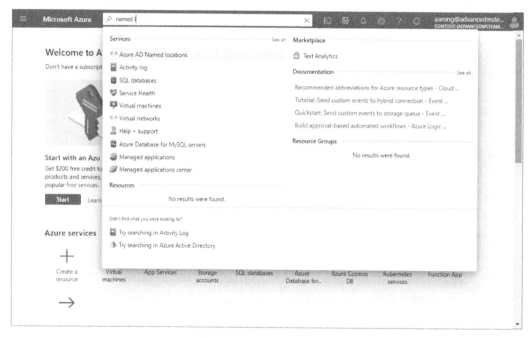

Figure 18.1 – Azure portal

3. Click + **New location**.

4. Enter a value for the name, select the checkbox to **Mark as trusted location**, and then add one or more of your organization's external address ranges in the **IP ranges** area. When finished, click **Create**:

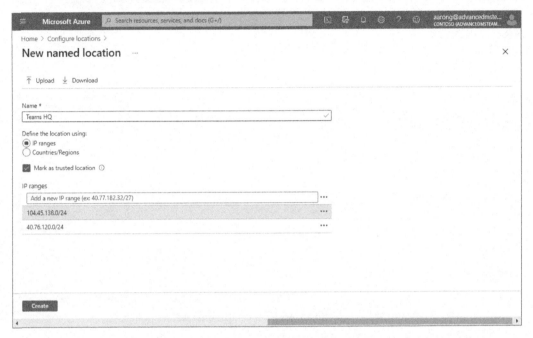

Figure 18.2 – Configuring a trusted location

5. In the search bar, type `Conditional` and select **Azure AD Conditional Access**.

6. Select + **New policy**.

7. Enter a value for the name of the policy.

8. Under **Assignments | Users and groups**, select **All users** (or a subset, if you wish to try it out first). You may also want to add an exclusion for a **break-glass** account (an administrative account used for emergency administration):

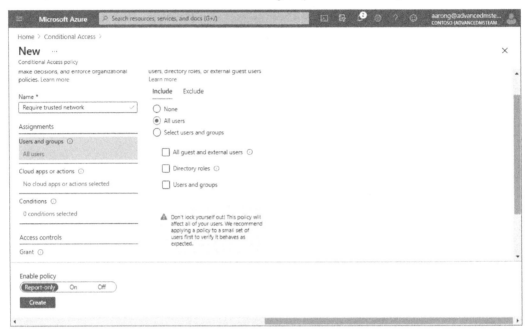

Figure 18.3 – Selecting users for a Conditional Access policy

9. Under **Assignments | Cloud apps or actions**, choose the **Select apps** radio button, and then select Microsoft Teams from the application list. Since Microsoft Teams builds on additional Microsoft 365 services, such as SharePoint, you may also want to include that application.

10. Under **Assignments | Conditions**, click **Not configured** under **Locations**:

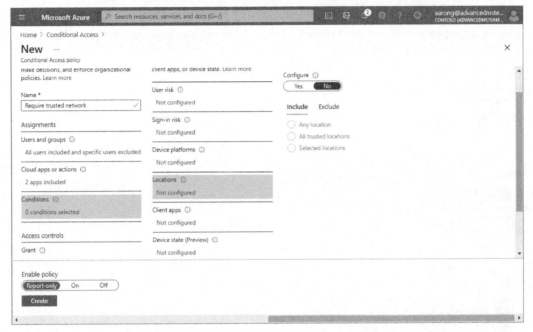

Figure 18.4 – Configuring the Conditional Access policy location settings

11. Move the toggle under **Configure** to **Yes**, and then select the **Exclude** option.

12. Under **Exclude**, select the **All trusted locations** radio button to exclude the previously configured locations from the multi-factor authentication policy:

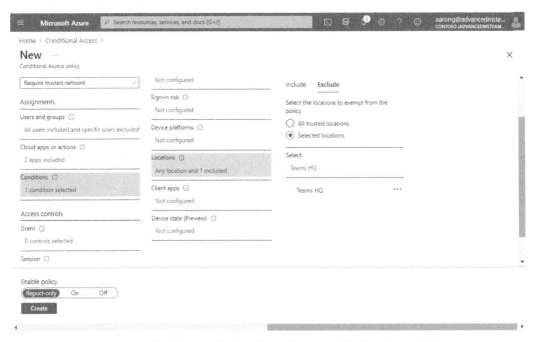

Figure 18.5 – Configuring the Conditional Access policy location exclusion

13. Under **Access controls | Grant**, select the **Grant access** radio button, and then select the **Require multi-factor authentication** checkbox. Click the **Select** button to confirm your choices:

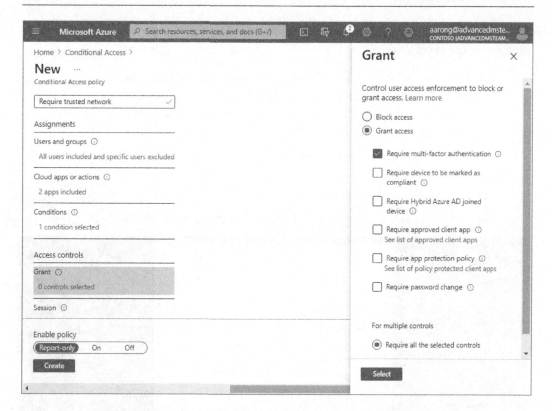

Figure 18.6 – Configuring the Conditional Access policy grant action

14. Under **Enable policy**, select the **On** toggle, and then click **Create**.

Once the policy has been created, you can move on to testing it.

Testing the Conditional Access policy

In order to validate that your new Conditional Access policy for trusted locations behaves as you intend, you'll need to log in from two different locations (both a trusted IP address and an untrusted IP address). You should already be familiar with the logon process prior to implementing your Conditional Access policy (that is, no multi-factor authentication prompt). You'll want to verify that the same experience persists when logging on with a device that was listed as a trusted location.

Then, you'll want to test from an untrusted location. You can use the following process to help verify the experience:

1. Select a device whose external IP address is not in your trusted locations configuration. If you need help determining this, you can use a function such as `Check-ExternalIP` (`https://www.powershellgallery.com/packages/Check-ExternalIP`) from the PowerShell gallery.

2. Launch a browser, such as Microsoft Edge, and navigate to `https://teams.microsoft.com`.

3. Enter your credentials (if prompted).

4. You should receive a prompt asking you to confirm multi-factor authentication:

Figure 18.7 – Multi-factor authentication prompt

5. Confirm your login using the Microsoft Authenticator (or another authentication app, depending on how your organization has configured multi-factor authentication).

As you can see from the user interface flow, the Conditional Access policy is triggered and requires secondary authentication before allowing you to log in.

> **Extending the Time between Authentication Prompts**
>
> As shown in *Figure 18.8*, users can choose to not be prompted again for authentication for 90 days by default. To configure additional multi-factor authentication settings (including changing the timeout period for reauthentication), see `https://docs.microsoft.com/en-us/` `azure/active-directory/authentication/howto-mfa-` `mfasettings`.

Next, we'll shift gears by looking at how to prevent sensitive data from being transmitted using data loss prevention features.

Data Loss Prevention

Data Loss Prevention (DLP) is a feature that is designed to allow organizations to prevent mishandling of sensitive data. DLP policies can be applied to content in Microsoft 365 to identify and protect certain types of data. Building on the features of Microsoft 365 DLP, you can now implement DLP policies in Microsoft Teams. DLP can be used to protect content in both messages and file attachments.

DLP policies in the Microsoft 365 platform rely on **sensitive information types** (stylized as **sensitive info types** in the user interface). A sensitive information type is a complex definition of what constitutes sensitive information to your organization. A sensitive information-type definition can include a mixture of simple keywords, large keyword dictionaries, and regular expressions. To help refine the definition, a sensitive information type can also include having supporting (or corroborating) evidence, which increases the confidence of a match based on the supporting element's proximity to the primary match information.

Let's say you want to identify US-based phone numbers in documents. You can create a sensitive information type or a DLP rule that looks for instances of 10 numerals in a row. That can be expressed with a very simple regular expression, such as `(\d{10})`. This also, unfortunately, may catch a lot of things that are *not* phone numbers as well. You can keep building and adding complexity to your regular expression until it meets your requirements. In this example case, I'm going to use a more advanced expression that identifies validly formatted numbers, with (or without) parentheses, periods, or dashes, as well as an optional country code field: `(?:\+?(\d{1,3}))?[-. (]*(\d{3})` `[-. )]*(\d{3})[-. ]*(\d{4})`.

> **Regular Expressions**
>
> While learning how to craft regular expressions is outside the scope
> of this particular book, it's an incredibly useful skill to develop
> (or at least remember that it exists so that you can go search for help later on).
> Some of our favorite resources for learning and testing regular expressions
> include *RegexOne* (`https://www.regexone.com`), *RegEx Pal*
> (`https://www.regexpal.com`), and *Regular Expressions 101*
> (`https://www.regex101.com`).

Figure 18.9 shows creating a regular expression pattern:

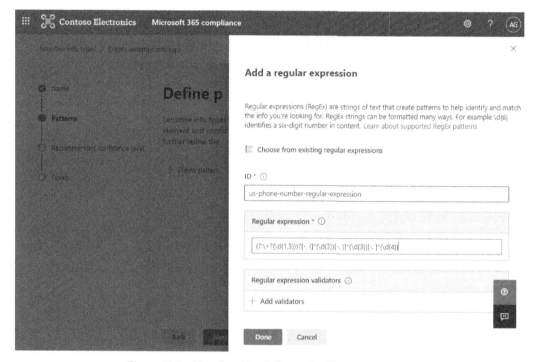

Figure 18.8 – New Sensitive Information Type parameters

To further tighten the requirements (and more accurately identify content matching your sensitive information type), you can configure the **proximity** and **supporting elements** conditions.

Supporting elements are pieces of data whose presence (or lack thereof) can be used to more accurately identify when content is likely to be a match for your policy. We can take the example of the phone number regular expression and then search for keywords such as "tel," "telephone," "fon," "number," or "phone" nearby. With both the presence of a character string that matches our regular expression and one or more of those supporting keywords, we can increase our confidence that the content matches a phone number.

Proximity refers to the distance between the identified primary and supporting elements. For example, a 10-digit number may be a US phone number, but it may also be a numerical representation of a financial transaction, an account number, or some other type of record identifier. If it's relatively close to the supporting elements ("tel," "telephone," "fon," "number," or "phone"), we can be more confident that the pattern matched was a telephone number. If they're separated by a lot of text, then maybe they're not related – and that information can be used to decrease the match confidence. *Figure 18.10* shows both the confidence level and proximity settings configured:

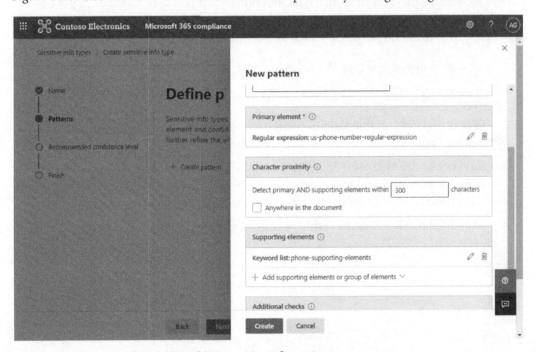

Figure 18.9 – New sensitive information type parameters

DLP policies can be built by applying a sensitive information type to a location, such as Microsoft Teams. You can apply a policy to chat or storage locations (such as OneDrive and SharePoint). DLP policies, when applied to Microsoft Teams, can be used to block content when shared in the Teams application with users who have either guest access in teams or channels, or external access in meetings and chat sessions.

One caveat, however, is that DLP for external chat sessions only works when *both* the sender and receiver are in Teams Only mode.

Now that you have an understanding of how sensitive information types and DLP work, let's go ahead and create a sensitive information type and test it. Then, we'll create a data loss prevention policy and test it.

Creating a Sensitive Information Type

In this example, we'll create a simple data loss prevention policy to target a US phone number and test it. You've already seen some of the customizations in the previous examples, so you should be familiar with doing this now:

1. Launch Notepad and type the following text:

    ```
    John Q. Test, phone: 425-555-1212
    ```

2. Save the text file on the desktop (we'll be using it later to test the sensitive info type that we create).

3. Navigate to the Microsoft 365 Security and Compliance Center (`https://compliance.microsoft.com`). You'll need administrative rights to perform this action (typically, Global Administrator or Compliance Administrator).

4. Expand **Data classification** and select **Sensitive info types**.

5. Click **+ Create sensitive info type**:

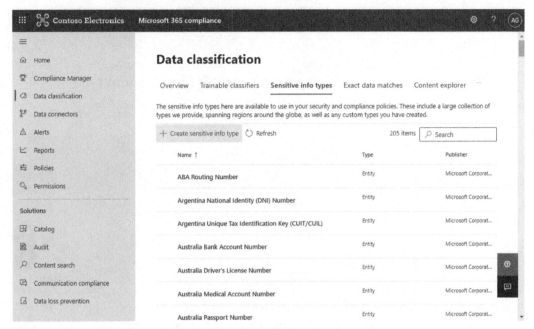

Figure 18.10 – Creating a sensitive info type

6. Enter a name (such as a US phone number) and a description, and then click **Next**.

7. On the **Define patterns for this sensitive info type** page, click **+ Create pattern**:

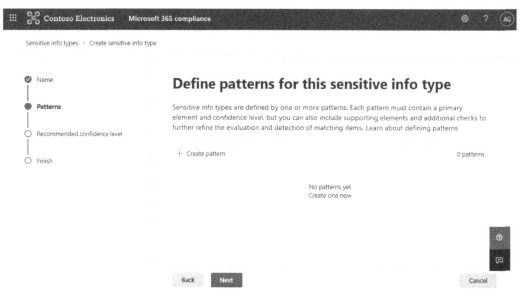

Figure 18.11 – Requirements for matching

8. In the **Primary element** area, click the **Add primary element** dropdown and select **Regular expression**.

9. In the **ID** section, enter a name for the element (this element can be reused later as part of another sensitive info type).

10. In the **Regular expression** textbox, enter a regular expression value to identify phone numbers. We'll use the previous example of `(?:\+?(\d{1,3}))?[-.(]*(\d{3})[-.)]*(\d{3})[-. ]*(\d{4})`.

11. Click **Done**.

12. In the **Supporting elements** area, click **+ Add supporting elements or groups of elements**, and then select **Keyword list**:

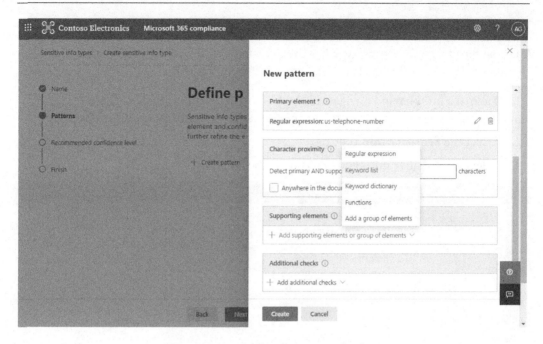

Figure 18.12 – Adding supporting elements

13. In the **ID** box, enter a name for the keyword list (this element can be reused in other sensitive info types, such as the regular expression element created earlier).

14. In the **Keyword group #1** box, place your cursor inside the case insensitive textbox. Enter the values `tel`, `telephone`, `fon`, `number`, `phone`, `cell`, `call`, and `mobile` values, each on separate lines. Click **Done** when finished.

15. Under **Confidence Level**, set the value to **High confidence**.

16. Under **Character proximity**, set a new value such as `100` (if desired – the default is `300`).

17. Review the settings and click **Create**.

18. Click **Next** to proceed to the **Choose the recommended confidence level to show in compliance policies** page. Select **High confidence level** and click **Next**.

19. Click **Create**.

20. Click **Done**.

Testing a Sensitive Information Type

After the sensitive information type has been created, you'll want to test it to make sure it identifies data. To test the newly created type, follow these steps.

1. Launch a browser and navigate to the **Microsoft 365 compliance center** (`https://compliance.microsoft.com`). Select **Data classification**.

2. Select the **Sensitive info type** tab.

3. Select the sensitive info type to test from the list, and then click **Test**:

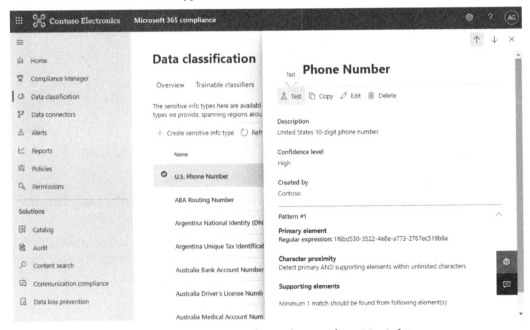

Figure 18.13 – Prompt to test the newly created sensitive info type

4. On the **Upload file to test** page, click **Upload file**, and choose the test file you saved in *step 2* of the *Creating a sensitive information type* exercise:

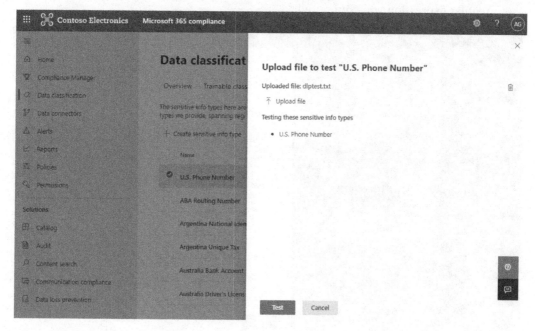

Figure 18.14 – Testing the sensitive info type

5. Click **Test**.

6.   Verify that your submitted document generates a DLP match. If no match is found, verify your source document has the right content and review the syntax of the regular expression you configured:

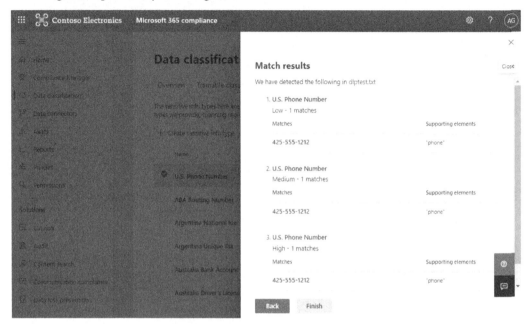

Figure 18.15 – Sensitive info type match results

7.   Click **Finish**.

You should now have a new sensitive info type available that can be used when creating a DLP policy, which we'll cover next.

Creating a Data Loss Prevention Policy

Now that you've got a working sensitive info type to test with, we can create a DLP policy and apply it to Microsoft Teams. If you are going to apply a DLP policy to Microsoft Teams chat messages, you will need to apply the Advanced Compliance license to all members whose content will be protected.

To create and apply the DLP policy, follow these steps:

1. Navigate to the Microsoft 365 Compliance Center (`https://compliance.microsoft.com`). You'll need administrative rights to perform this action (typically, global administrator or compliance administrator).

2. Select **Policies**, expand **Data**, and then select **Data loss prevention**.

3. Select the **Policies** tab.

4. Click **+ Create policy**:

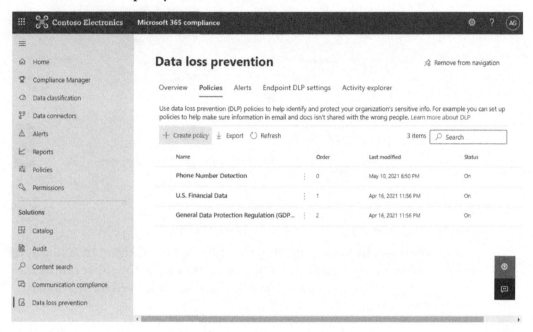

Figure 18.16 – Creating a DLP policy

5. Select the **Custom** template and **Custom policy** type options, and then click **Next**:

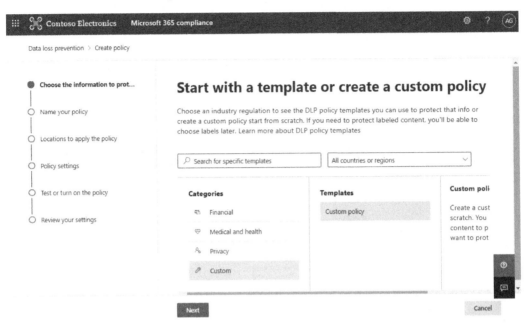

Figure 18.17 – Custom policy selection

6. Enter a policy name and description and then click **Next**.

7. On the **Choose locations to apply the policy** page, shown in *Figure 18.19*, toggle off all of the options except **Teams chat and channel messages**. To further restrict the scope of the policy, you can limit it to only include or exclude certain individuals. Click **Next** when complete:

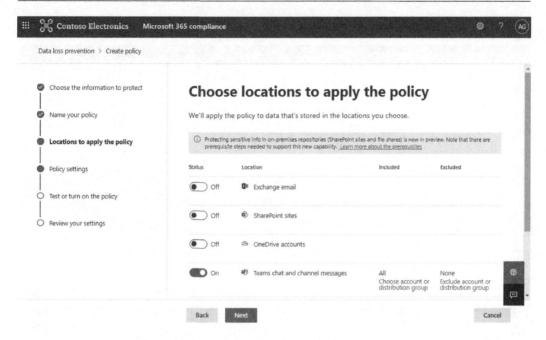

Figure 18.18 – Selection locations to apply DLP policy

8. On the **Define policy settings** page, the **Create or customize advanced DLP rules** radio button is already selected. Click **Next**.

9. Select either **with people outside my organization** or **only with people inside my organization** from the **Detect when this content is shared** option to further refine how you want to scope the policy. In this instance, set it to detect content with people inside the organization. Click **Next** to continue.

10. On the **Customize Advanced DLP rules** page, click **+ Create rule**.

11. On the **Create rule page**, enter **Name** and **Description** values for the rule.

12. In the **Conditions** section, click **+ Add condition** and select **Content contains**.

13. Click the **Add** dropdown and select **Sensitive info types**, as shown in *Figure 18.20*:

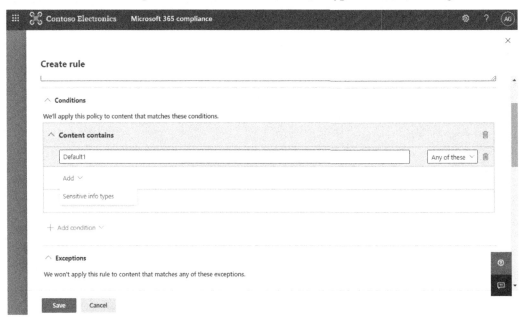

Figure 18.19 – Add a sensitive info type

14. From the list of sensitive info types, select the US phone number sensitive info type that you created and tested in the previous exercise. Click **Add**.

15. Scroll to the **Actions** area. Select **+ Add an action**, and then select **Restrict access or encrypt the content in Microsoft 365 locations**. Then, select the **Restrict access or encrypt the content in Microsoft 365 locations** checkbox:

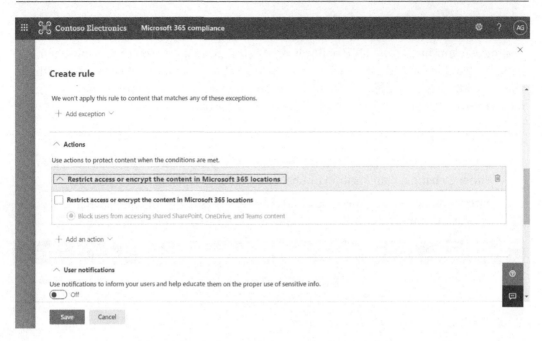

Figure 18.20 – Restricting access to DLP-protected content

16. Scroll to **User notifications**. Turn the toggle to **On**.

17. You can further edit the policy by adding notification text customization or by allowing certain individuals to override the policy. For this exercise, we're just going to accept the defaults and click **Save**.

18. After the rule shows up in the policy, click **Next**.

19. The last configuration page allows you to set the policy to be enabled right away, set it to test mode (default), or just save the policy for later enablement. Select **Turn it on right away** and click **Next**.

20. Confirm the settings and click **Submit**.

The policy will be enabled but will not begin actively monitoring and processing content until up to 24 hours have passed.

Testing the Data Loss Prevention Policy

Testing a Teams messaging DLP policy is pretty straightforward. You can simply enter data that would violate the policy in a chat message. We'd recommend not testing with *real* data but instead synthetic or manufactured data that is designed to mimic real-life data to ensure the privacy and confidentiality of the system.

To test a policy, follow these steps:

1. Log into Microsoft Teams (either the desktop app or the web app) and navigate to either a channel conversation or chat conversation.

2. Either edit an existing message or create a new message with content that will trigger the policy:

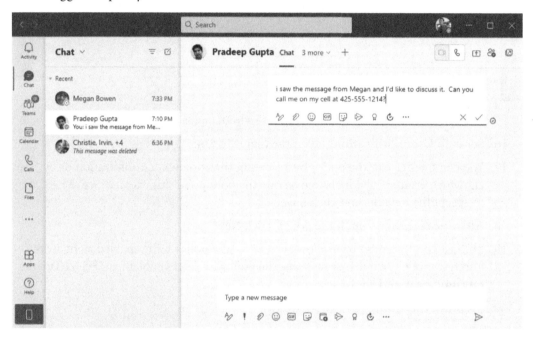

Figure 18.21 – Editing a chat message to include policy-violating content

3. After sending the message, notice that the message box has turned red, and a notification indicating that the message was blocked appears:

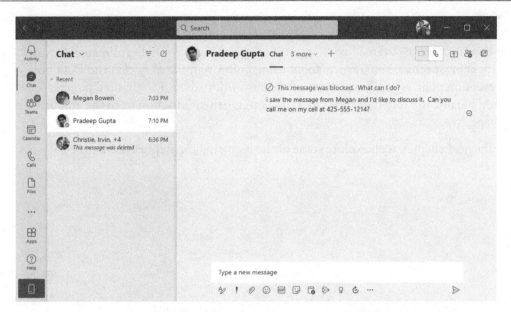

Figure 18.22 – Sender's view indicating that a policy violation has occurred

4.   The recipient sees a similar message indicating that content was blocked due to the organizational policy:

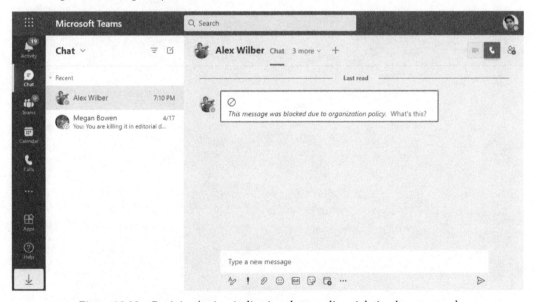

Figure 18.23 – Recipient's view indicating that a policy violation has occurred

As you can see, the policy effectively prevents content matching the DLP policy from being shared.

Summary

In this chapter, we covered how to protect Microsoft Teams – both from an access and content perspective. You learned about using both Conditional Access and Data Loss Prevention policies to secure Microsoft Teams workloads and configured policies for both. Finally, you tested the policies and got to see them in action from the end user's perspective.

In the next chapter, we'll explore some of the reporting capabilities of Microsoft Teams.

19
Reporting in Teams

IT admins regularly rely on **reporting** and **analytics** to gain insights into end users' experience with online services. This is critical to operations in any environment of any size because reporting and analytics can help paint a picture of how deployments are going, as well as how much of a service is being accessed, consumed, or otherwise engaged with in any way – or not at all. For Microsoft 365, different reports are available for different services. For example, mail flow-related reports are available in the Exchange Admin Center.

In this chapter, we will cover all the Teams activity-related reporting that's available to IT admins in the Teams Admin Center. This includes usage reports, activity reports, and call quality analytics.

Specifically, in this chapter, we will cover the following topics:

- Teams usage reports
- Teams app usage reports
- Live events usage reports
- User-based call reports
- PSTN-based reports
- Call Quality Dashboard

We will also cover the Teams activity report, which is located in the Microsoft 365 admin center. By the end of this chapter, you will be familiar with all the types of reports that are available to you as an IT administrator. Let's get started!

Technical requirements

Before we get started, while we will not be creating anything in this chapter, you must have the right permissions to *access* the Teams Admin Center and the Microsoft 365 Admin Center. To do so, you must be assigned to one of the following roles:

- Global admin
- Global reader (*no access to Call Quality Dashboard*)
- Teams service admin
- Teams communications admin
- Teams communications support engineer
- Teams communications support specialist

With one of these roles assigned to you, you can access the relevant reports.

For certain Teams activities, such as PSTN calling, one of the following licenses is required to see some data:

- Phone System
- Calling Plan
- Direct Routing
- Audio Conferencing
- Communication Credits

These licenses will populate data for the PSTN-based reports.

To use Power BI to analyze reports, you will also need a Power BI license.

Teams usage report

The **Teams usage report** will give you analytics and insights about overall Teams usage within your organization. The objective of this section is to help familiarize you with accessing this report and understand the different data points provided.

The **Teams usage report** can be found in the Teams Admin Center. This report will give you a high-level overview of the number of active users, channels, messages, reactions, and meetings that have been scheduled in your organization's Teams environment. To access this report, follow these steps:

1. Navigate to `https://admin.teams.microsoft.com` and sign in.
2. On the left, click on **Analytics & reports**, then **Usage reports**.
3. Under the **View reports** tab, locate **Report** and select a **report** from the dropdown.
4. Choose **Teams usage**.
5. Locate **Date range** and select a **date range** from the dropdown.
6. In this example, we will choose **Last 30 days**.
7. Click **Run report**.

You can pull 7-, 30- or 90-days' worth of usage data, and the report will state the date range that was specified. The Teams usage report will display data from the last 30 days, as shown in the following screenshot:

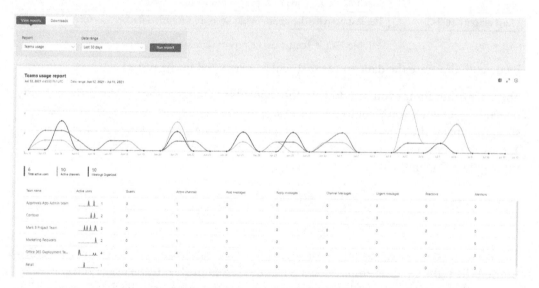

Figure 19.1 – Teams usage report

If you scroll horizontally to the right, you will see other metrics, such as **Meetings organized**, **Privacy**, and **Last activity (UTC)**.

It is important to understand the metrics that are provided out of the box. The following table shows a list of data points that are provided, a short description, and the value of each:

Data Points	Description and Value
Team name	Name of team, during the specified time.
Active Users	Active users in a team, during the specified time, populated in digits.
Guests	Active guests in a team, during the specified time, populated in digits.
Active Channels	Active channels in a team, during the specified time, populated in digits.
Post messages	Posted messages in a channel, during the specified time, populated in digits.
Reply messages	Reply messages in a channel, during the specified time, populated in digits.
Channel messages	Channel messages during the specified time, populated in digits.
Urgent messages	Urgent messages posted in a channel during the specified time, populated in digits.
Reactions	Reactions to a post in a channel during the specified time, populated in digits.
Mentions	Mentions in a channel during the specified time, populated in digits.
Meetings organized	Scheduled or ad hoc meetings during the specified time, populated in digits.
Privacy	Specifies team's privacy setting – public or private.
Last activity (UTC)	The last activity the channel has seen, in month, date, or year format.

Table 19.1 – Teams usage report data points

By default, these are the data points that will be presented in the report.

There are other things you can do with the report by clicking on one of the three options, depending on what you want to do. For example, you can export the report to an Excel sheet or expand the report to full screen to get a better view by clicking on the arrows. You can also customize the data points shown. These three options can be found at the top-right section of the report, respectively.

Figure 19.2 – Report options

You can edit columns to customize the data metric that's shown by clicking on the settings gear on the right. If, for example, you are not interested in **Reactions** usage across the organization, you can customize your report to hide **Reaction** data. Each column can be toggled off, depending on what you need. When you click on the **Edit columns** icon, you will see the following on the right-hand side of the screen:

Figure 19.3 – The Edit columns view

If you click the **Excel** icon shown in *Figure 19.2*, you will be taken to the **Downloads** tab. There, you will be shown the progress of the export. You can retrieve the file in a **CSV (Comma-Delimited Formation)** format once it has been generated.

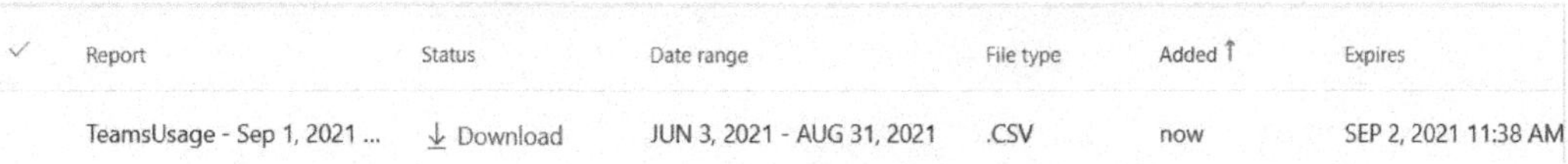

	Report	Status	Date range	File type	Added ↑	Expires
✓	TeamsUsage - Sep 1, 2021 ...	↓ Download	JUN 3, 2021 - AUG 31, 2021	.CSV	now	SEP 2, 2021 11:38 AM

Figure 19.4 – The Downloads tab

If you open the CSV file, you will see data similar to what's in the report in the Teams Admin Center.

Id	DisplayName	Privacy	ActiveUsers	ActiveCh	Guests	ReplyMe	PostMess	Meetings	UrgentM	Reactions	Mentions	Channel	LastActivity (UTC Time)
d8c38ab2-3466-4ed4-b804-0438aa33f1ec	Approvals App Admin team	Private	1	1	0	0	0	0	0	0	0	0	2021-07-05T15:25:19Z
377014cd-8d76-492b-9f8e-459753f3906a	Contoso	Public	2	1	0	0	0	0	0	0	0	0	2021-07-06T17:34:34Z
47ba2f84-814e-4500-8879-de62cc38ee67	Mark 8 Project Team	Public	2	1	0	0	0	1	0	0	0	0	2021-07-08T21:56:32Z
d738b50a-54a0-4da2-ac5c-c10954941da6	Marketing Requests	Public	2	1	0	0	0	0	0	0	0	0	2021-07-08T20:47:19Z
550105f9-6df5-405f-835f-501bcccebdb1	Office 365 Deployment Team	Private	4	4	0	0	0	0	0	0	0	0	2021-07-08T16:32:42Z
51b8911c-be9c-4a49-a77f-2e47396e0a46	Retail	Private	1	1	0	0	0	0	0	0	0	0	2021-06-21T17:44:00Z
a1d2c9a3-17ac-4fb5-8bf8-e957b1674d95	Sales and Marketing	Public	1	1	0	0	0	0	0	0	0	0	2021-06-21T14:52:55Z

Figure 19.5 – Example of a CSV file

Id refers to the **Teams ID** value. Each Team has a unique string of values for identification and management purposes. You can see the **DisplayName** property associated with the Team to differentiate it. Otherwise, the data points are the same as the ones in the Teams Admin Center report.

There is another Teams usage report that's located in **Microsoft 365 admin center**. These reports differ slightly and can also help capture high-level Microsoft Teams activity within the organization. This report will provide data from the past 30, 60, 90, or 120 days.

To access this report, follow these steps:

1. Navigate to `https://admin.microsoft.com` and sign in.

2. On the left, locate **Reports** and click the dropdown.

3. Choose **Usage**.

4. Notice that the chart on this page shows the number of active users for all the available services in your organization. Scroll down until you find **Microsoft Teams activity**. Click on **View more**.

5. First, note the two tabs:

Figure 19.6 – Teams activity tabs

Under **User activity**, you will see Teams activity data concerning licensed users:

Figure 19.7 – Licensed activity user report

You will see this data in a table format if you scroll down to the bottom of the page.

Under **Device usage**, you will see Teams activity data concerning the types of devices licensed users are engaged in:

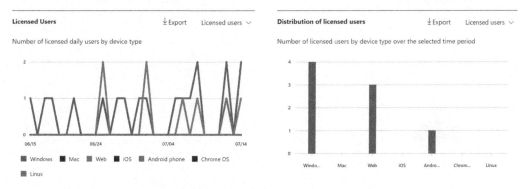

Figure 19.8 – Licensed activity device report

6. You can also view this data in a table format if you scroll down to the bottom of the page.

As with all reports, you can filter data according to certain conditions, export this into a CSV file, and view it from there.

This concludes the Teams usage report. We covered two different types – the Teams usage report in the Teams Admin Center and Teams usage based on licensed users and devices in the Microsoft 365 Admin Center. You also learned how to navigate to each specific report, the data points that are logged out of the box, and the available customization and download options. Next, we will cover the Teams app usage report.

Teams apps usage report

Microsoft Teams is a collaboration hub. It is quite common for IT admins or users to add apps to their Teams environment. For example, a department may favor using the Planner app to organize a happy hour or a colleague's retirement celebration. As an IT admin, you want a clear picture of how often these apps are used, the app's type, versioning, and more to maintain a secure, productive Teams environment. Accessing this report is very similar to that of the Teams usage report:

1. Navigate to `https://admin.teams.microsoft.com` and sign in.
2. On the left, click on **Analytics & reports**, then **Usage reports**.
3. Under the **View reports** tab, locate **Report** and select **report** from the dropdown.
4. Choose **Apps usage**.
5. Locate **Date range** and select **date range** from the dropdown.
6. In this example, we will choose **Last 90 days**.
7. Click **Run report**.

The report should look something like this:

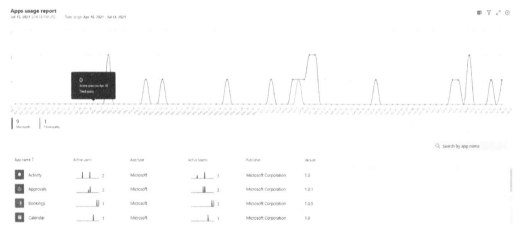

Figure 19.9 – Apps usage report

The report that's generated should show data from the time specified. The data will contain the following information:

Data Point	Description and Value
App name	Name of the app, populated as the display name.
Active users	Users that opened the app, from the specified time, populated in numbers.
App type	Either a first-party Microsoft app or a third party, populated in either Microsoft or Third party, respectively.
Active teams	Teams that have users in the team that opened the app, during the specified time, populated in digits.
Publisher	The app's software publisher, populated by the publisher.
Version	The app's software version, populated in digits.

Table 19.2 – Teams apps usage report

Like the Teams usage report, you can export to Excel, filter by specific conditions, expand to full screen, and customize the data points for this report:

Figure 19.10 – Usage report options

8. To filter, click on the **Filter** icon next to the Excel icon:

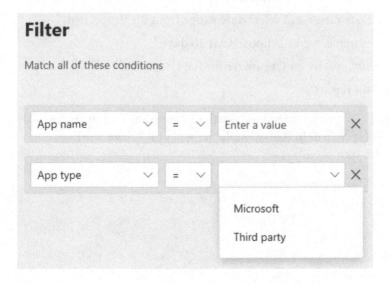

Figure 19.11 – App report filter

You can filter by **App name** and enter a specific value. The other filter is for **App type**, so you can target either **Microsoft** or **Third party** apps.

This concludes the Teams apps usage report. We covered how to navigate to this specific report, the data points that are logged out of the box, and the available customization and download options. Next, we will cover the live event usage report.

Live event usage report

Microsoft live events are a great way to host group, organizational-wide, or even public events virtually. The **live event usage report** will give you analytics and insights about overall Live event usage within your organization. In this section, you will become familiar with accessing this report and understand the different data points provided.

Like the **Teams usage report**, the live event usage report can be found in the Teams Admin Center. This report will give you a high-level overview of Live event usage in your organization. You can access this report by following these steps:

1. Navigate to `https://admin.teams.microsoft.com` and sign in.
2. On the left, click on **Analytics & reports**, then **Usage reports**.
3. Under the **View reports** tab, locate **Report** and select **report** from the dropdown.
4. Choose **Teams live event usage**.
5. Locate **Date range** and select **date range** from the dropdown.
6. In this example, we will choose **Last 30 days**.
7. Optionally, specify an **Organizer** for the Live event.
8. Click **Run report**.

You can pull 7, 28, or a custom days' worth of usage data and the report will state the date range that was specified. In this example, we will pull 7 days' worth of data. This may look something like this:

Figure 19.12 – Live event usage report

The report that's generated should show data from the time specified.

It is important to understand the metrics that are provided out of the box. The following table shows a list of data points provided, a short description, and the value for each:

Value	Description
Event	Name of the Live event
Start time (UTC)	Timestamp for the Live event's start time
Event status	Status of the event
Organizer	Name of the Live event's organizer
Presenters	Number and name of the presenter(s)
Producers	Number and name of the producer(s)
Views	Number of attendee views
Recording	On if the recording setting is turned on, Off if the recording setting is turned off
Production Type	Team or external application or device type of Live event

Table 19.3 – Live event usage report

When you click on the meeting itself, the Teams Admin Center will populate Live event resources associated with the event. The available resources include a **Q & A report** (if applicable), an **Attendee engagement report**, and two copies of **Recording** (if applicable). For example, you can click on **Q & A report** to download it directly:

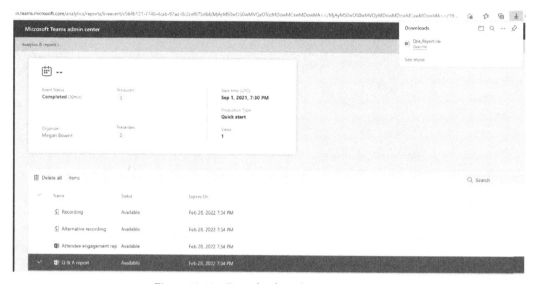

Figure 19.13 – Downloading the Q & A report

You can see the same information on this page via the report. In addition to downloading these resources, you can delete them.

This concludes the Live events usage report. We covered how to navigate to this specific report, the data points that are logged out of the box, and how to download the available resources. Next, we will cover user-based call reports.

User-based call reports

In this section, we will cover two different types of reporting. First, we will cover the Teams user activity report, which is very similar to the Teams usage and apps usage reports. Then, we will cover **Call Analytics**, where you can gain more insight into a user's specific call or meeting quality.

The **Teams user activity** report can be found under the **Usage reports** section of the Teams Admin Center. To get there, follow these steps:

1. Navigate to `https://admin.teams.microsoft.com` and sign in.

2. On the left, click on **Analytics & reports**, then **Usage reports**.

3. Under the **View reports** tab, locate **Report** and select **report** from the dropdown.

4. Choose **Teams user activity**.

5. Locate **Date range** and select **date range** from the dropdown.

6. In this example, we will choose **Last 90 days**.

7. Click **Run report**.

The Teams user activity report may look something like this:

Figure 19.14 – Teams user activity report

The report that's generated should show data from the time specified. The data will contain the following information:

Data Point	Description and Value
Display name	Name of the user.
Channel message	Unique Teams channel messages the user posted, during the specified time, populated in digits.
Reply message	Unique Teams channel reply messages the user posted, during the specified time, populated in digits.
Post message	Unique Teams channel post messages the user wrote, during the specified time, populated in digits.
Chat message	Unique messages in private chats, during the specified time, populated in digits.
Urgent message	Unique urgent messages the user posted, during the specified time, populated in digits.
Meetings organized and scheduled on one occasion	One-time meetings the user scheduled during the specified time, populated in digits.
Meetings organized and scheduled on a recurring basis	Recurring meetings the user scheduled during the specified time, populated in digits.
Ad hoc meetings organized	Ad hoc (unplanned) meetings the user scheduled during the specified time, populated in digits.
Total meetings organized	Total meetings the user scheduled during the specified time, populated in digits.
Meetings participated in and scheduled on one occasion	One-time meetings the user participated in during the specified time, populated in digits.
Meetings participated in and scheduled on a recurring basis	Recurring meetings the user participated in during the specified time, populated in digits.
Ad hoc meetings participated in	Ad hoc (unplanned) meetings the user participated in during the specified time, populated in digits.
Total meetings participated in	Total meetings the user participated in during the specified time, populated in digits.
1:1 calls	1:1 calls the user participated in during the specified time, populated in digits.
Audio time	Audio time the user participated in during the specified time, populated in digits, measured in minutes.
Video time	Video time the user participated in during the specified time, populated in digits, measured in minutes.
Screen sharing time	Screen sharing time the user participated in during the specified time, populated in digits, measured in minutes.
Last activity (UTC)	Timestamp of when the user participated in Teams last.
Other activity	Activities in which user is considered active in Teams; for example, reading a notification, populated in digits.

Table 19.4 – User-based call reports

From this report, an IT admin can see how active a Teams user is or was. Just like the previous two reports, some of these data points can be hidden. The report can also be exported to a CSV file and viewed full screen.

If, as an IT admin, you want to investigate a specific user in more depth, you can investigate that user's meeting and call history in the Teams Admin Center. This is called **Call Analytics**. To navigate to a specific user, follow these steps:

1. Navigate to `https://admin.teams.microsoft.com` and sign in.

2. On the left, click on **Users**. You will be taken to a list of licensed Teams users and resource accounts.

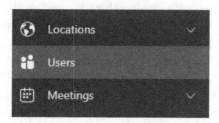

Figure 19.15 – The Users page

3. Choose a user and click on their **Display Name**. In this example, we will look at Megan Bowen.

4. Go to the **Meetings & calls** tab, which is located between the **Voice** and **Policies** tabs.

Figure 19.16 – The Meetings & calls tab

5. Click on the **Meetings & calls** tab to see the user's meetings and call history.

Here, you will see user-specific call analytics listed and organized per meeting or call. In this report, the data points that are provided are a good starting point to understand how the user leverage Teams as a conferencing platform and the quality of these interactions.

First, let's discuss the first high-level dashboard, which is located at the top of the page:

Figure 19.17 – Call analytics user information

This dashboard contains basic information that's located on the left and center of the dashboard, such as the user's location, **Email**, and **Directory status**. There is also the option to contact the user directly. You can see these icons next to their profile picture. By clicking on the chat icon on the left or the email icon on the right, you can either chat with the user on Teams or start an email directly, respectively. On the right-hand side, there's a **7-DAY QUALITY** graph, which shows the user's meetings and/or calls. Purple indicates good quality, maroon indicates poor, and white means unknown. The last section on the right, **7-DAY ACTIVITY**, specifies the user's meeting and calls activity for the past 7 days.

Now, let's look at the past meeting information on the second half of the page:

Meeting or call ID	Start time ↓	When	Participants	Duration	Activity type	Client	Audio quality
915d9134-98a9-4cb0-a60b-fba378ff09a3	**Aug 31, 2021** 7:03 PM	17 hours ago	2 Participants	00:11:19	Conference	Multiple	Good
50bef2eb-60ee-4129-af36-e639762946a8	**Aug 31, 2021** 6:37 PM	18 hours ago	2 Participants	00:22:56	Conference	Multiple	Poor

Account   Voice   Meetings & calls   Policies

Past meetings 51 meetings & calls ⓘ

Figure 19.18 – Meetings and calls

The following screenshot shows the history for a user's call and the call analytics for those calls:

Meeting or call ID	Start time ↓	When	Participants	Duration	Activity type	Client	Audio quality
366f2c00-3f60-4627-b21...	Jul 12, 2021, 5:04 PM EDT	17 hours ago	2 Participants	00:04:40	Call	Microsoft Teams	Good
624ba376-1d7c-4696-b6...	Jul 7, 2021, 10:50 AM EDT	6 days ago	1 Participant	01:51:45	Conference	Microsoft Teams	Good

Account   Voice   Meetings & calls   Policies

Past meetings 14 meetings & calls ⓘ

Figure 19.19 – Call analytics user history

This report will show the past meetings and calls the user started or participated in for the last 30 days. Each meeting or call will contain the following data:

Value	Description
Meeting or call ID	A string value that identifies the Teams session
Start time	The meeting's or call's start time
When	Days in respect to the day you are checking
Participants	Number of participants in the meeting or call
Duration	Duration of the meeting or call
Activity Type	Conference or call
Client	Client the user used for the Teams meeting or call
Audio Quality	Quality of the meeting's or call's audio

Table 19.5 – Call analytics

If you have a specific event you would like to investigate, you can click on the meeting's ID. This will take you to a different page within the Teams Admin Center. Investigating a specific meeting between a specific user or users through the dashboard that's provided is called **Call Analytics**. This can help you identify and troubleshoot any issues for specific users. For example, if an executive informs you that the latest Teams meeting had device issues, a **Teams Communications Support Specialist** or **Teams Communications Support Engineer** can go into the history and troubleshoot.

Let's dive into a specific meeting. If your report has a **meeting ID** that is considered a **Conference**, click on the one you'd like to explore. Clicking on **meeting ID** will take you to a landing page that should look like this:

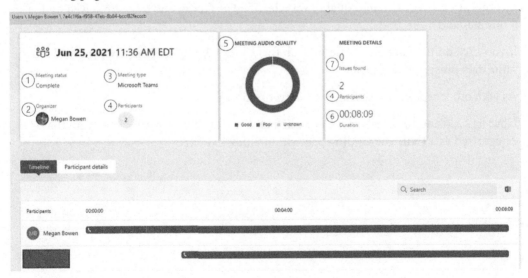

Figure 19.20 – Call analytics meeting report

From the dashboard, starting from the left, you can see the following details:

1. **Meeting status**: Displays the status of the meeting
2. **Organizer**: Displays the organizer of the meeting
3. **Meeting type**: Displays the type of meeting
4. **Participants**: Displays the number of participants in the meeting
5. **MEETING AUDIO QUALITY**: Displays the audio quality of the meeting
6. **Duration**: Displays the duration of the meeting
7. **Issues found**: Displays any audio quality issues that were found during the meeting

Then, there is a **Timeline** chart that shows, visually, when participants entered and exited the meeting, with a timestamp. If you choose a participant and hover over the purple line associated with that user, you will see more details specific to that user:

Figure 19.21 – Timeline view

For example, in the preceding screenshot, you can see that Megan Bowen joined the meeting at 11:37 A.M., audio quality was classified as **Good**, and that she stayed on for 6 minutes and 44 seconds.

If you click on the **Participant details** tab that's located next to **Timeline**, you will see the same data presented as a table.

As with other reports, these can also be exported to Excel.

Now, let's look at the details of a **Call**. Click on the **Call ID** property of an event that is categorized as a **Call**. The landing page should look like this:

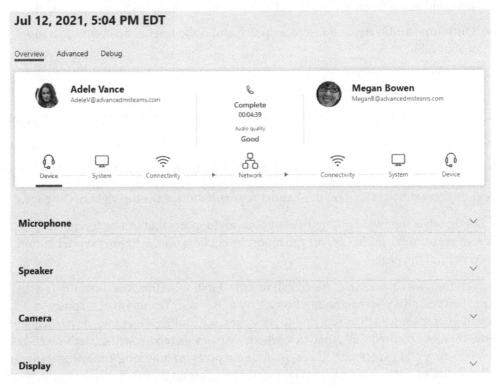

Figure 19.22 – The Overview tab

Notice the three tabs on top – **Overview**, **Advanced**, and **Debug**. Let's start with the insights in the **Overview** tab.

In the **Overview** tab, you will see **device**, **system**, **connectivity**, and **network** information for each participant. You will see that **Device** under Adele Vance is highlighted. If you stay on **Device** under Adele Vance, you can find more information on Adele's specific devices if you expand the tabs for **Microphone**, **Speaker**, **Camera**, and **Display**. Similarly, if you click on **System** under Adele Vance, you can get information on her client. Under **Connectivity**, you can get some insight into her internet connection. You can find data on the other participants by clicking the **Device**, **System**, and **Connectivity** icons under the other user. **Connectivity** will provide network stream insight between the two participants.

In the **Advanced** tab, you will see a table of information organized by each participant. For each participant, you will find the following data:

- **Microphone**: Lists the microphone device's name, if applicable.
- **Speaker**: Lists the device's name and driver, if applicable.

- **Inbound audio stream**: Lists the ratio of non-functioning render events, if applicable.

- **Outbound audio stream**: Lists the speech and noise level, echo events, and more, if applicable.

- **System**: Lists the system's name, operating system, IP address, CPU speeds and cores, and virtualization platform, if applicable.

- **Connectivity**: Lists the network connection information and Wi-Fi data, if applicable.

- **Inbound network**: Lists inbound jitter, the packet loss rate, and more, if applicable.

- **Outbound network**: Lists outbound jitter, the packet loss rate, and more, if applicable.

Export this report by clicking on the **Export report** button at the top right of the page.

The **Debug** tab will provide multiple data points and reports that can be leveraged to debug an event. You can also export the report by clicking on the **Export report** button at the top right of the page.

In this section, we covered user-based call reports. First, we visited the Teams user activity report. This will give you insight into how active a user is in Teams when it comes to different interactions, such as replying to messages, scheduling a meeting, or participating in one. Then, we covered Call Analytics, where we investigated a specific user's meetings and call history and experience. There, we found reports on how long a meeting went on for, the device's information, internet connectivity data, and data to debug an event, if applicable. Now, let's look at PSTN-based reports.

PSTN-based reports

In this section, we will cover the three different PSTN-related reports. When you use Teams to make calls or hold meetings with PSTN numbers and users, you will need a report that provides insights into your organizational use, such as users and total minutes. By the end of this section, you will be able to navigate to and understand the PSTN-based reports in the Teams Admin Center.

In the Teams Admin Center, there are three PSTN-related reports:

- **PSTN blocked users**: This report contains users who are disabled from making PSTN calls.

- **PSTN minute and SMS (preview) pools**: This report specifies the total minutes used based on licensing capacities.

- **PSTN and SMS (preview) usage**: This report specifies users who are leveraging PSTN calling capabilities through Calling Plan, Direct Routing, or Audio Conferencing.

To refresh, a **PSTN**, or a **Public Switched Telephone Network**, call is when you connect to another phone through a network of underground copper wires. You can use phones or landlines to accomplish this. Microsoft Teams allows PSTN calls with Phone System licensing and Calling Plan, Direct Routing, and Audio Conferencing (with limited capabilities). These three reports can provide insight into the types of domestic and/or international calls your users are making, their minutes consumed and left, licenses used, and more.

First, we have the **PSTN blocked users** report. To get to this report, follow these steps:

1. Navigate to `https://admin.teams.microsoft.com` and sign in.
2. On the left, click on **Analytics & reports**, then **Usage reports**.
3. Under the **View reports** tab, locate **Report** and select **report** from the dropdown.
4. Choose **PSTN blocked users**.
5. Click **Run report**.

The purpose of this report is for IT admins to generate, keep track of, and manage those users who are blocked from dialing out to a specific capacity. For example, with both the Audio Conferencing and Calling Plan/Direct Routing licenses, there are dial-out plans that can dictate the type of outbound PSTN calls. Depending on how you want to manage your users' dial-out capabilities, you can dictate whether a user can dial out from a conference call (this assumes they have Audio Conferencing capabilities) or if a user can make outbound calls internationally, domestically, or tied to specific zones.

> **Outbound Calling Restriction**
>
> To understand more of the different types of PSTN calls available to your users and how to restrict certain outbound calls, go to `https://docs.microsoft.com/en-us/microsoftteams/outbound-calling-restriction-policies`.

Next, let's look at the **PSTN minutes and SMS (preview) pool** report. To get there, follow these steps:

1. Navigate to `https://admin.teams.microsoft.com` and sign in.
2. On the left, click on **Analytics & reports**, then **Usage reports**.
3. Under the **View reports** tab, locate **Report** and select **report** from the dropdown.
4. Choose **PSTN minutes and SMS (preview) pool**.
5. Click **Run report**.

Depending on the licenses that have been assigned to your tenant, you will see a chart, a tab, and a table.

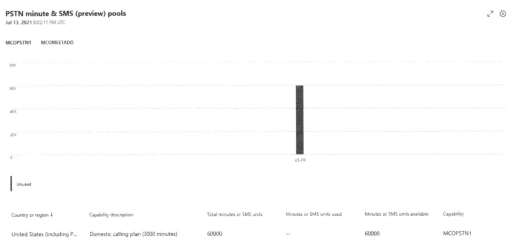

Figure 19.23 – PSTN minutes and SMS report

If you have multiple Calling Plan, Direct Routing, and Audio Conferencing licenses assigned to your tenant, you will have multiple tabs. For example, in the preceding screenshot, we have a **Domestic calling plan** and an **Audio Conferencing** plan.

MCOPSTN1   MCOMEETADD

Figure 19.24 – The calling plan tab

Under these tabs, you will see the following data:

- **Country or region**: This identifies the usage location.
- **Capability description**: This identifies the capability – "domestic" and/or "international."
- **Total minutes or SMS units**: This shows the total minutes available for the month.
- **Minutes or SMS units used**: This shows the used minutes for the month.
- **Minutes or SMS units available**: This shows the available minutes left for the month.
- **Capability**: This identifies the license that was used.

As with other reports, you can export this as a CSV file and make it full screen. For more information on the different capabilities available and this report, go to https://docs.microsoft.com/en-us/microsoftteams/teams-analytics-and-reports/pstn-minute-pools-report.

Next, we will look at the **PSTN and SMS (preview) usage** report. This report differs from the minutes usage because you get to see who makes calls at a specific time. The date range for this report is **7 days**, **28 days**, or **custom**. To see this, follow these steps:

1. Navigate to `https://admin.teams.microsoft.com` and sign in.

2. On the left, click on **Analytics & reports**, then **Usage reports**.

3. Under the **View reports** tab, locate **Report** and select **report** from the dropdown.

4. Choose **PSTN and SMS (preview) usage**.

5. Locate **Date range** and select **date range** from the dropdown.

6. In this example, we will choose **Last 28 days**.

7. Click **Run report**.

Depending on the licensing you want to look at, you can choose the tab that's available to you.

CALLING PLANS/SMS (PREVIEW)   <u>DIRECT ROUTING</u>

Figure 19.25 – The PSTN and SMS usage calling plan tab

The report should display usage like this:

Figure 19.26 – The PSTN & SMS usage report view

This report will contain the following details:

Data Points	Description and Value
Start time (UTC)	The time the call started, in UTC.
Display name	Displays the name of the user.
Username	Username of the user, in email address format.
Phone number	The number that received an incoming call or the number that was dialed for an outbound call.
Caller ID	ID for the incoming call or the outbound call.
Operator	The operator of the service.
Call/SMS type	Inbound or outbound PSTN call performed by a user or a bot or using an Audio Conferencing bridge.
Destination dialed	Country or region that the user dialed.
Charge	Amount of money associated with the call.
Currency	The currency that was used to charge a certain cost.
Duration	Duration of the call.
Source of call duration	Based on the telecommunication provider.
Domestic/international	Specifies whether the call was either within a country or region or across countries or regions.
Call ID	Call identifier.
Number type	Call made from a service or subscriber (user).
User's location	Country or region that a user is located in.
Conference ID	Conference ID of the Audio Conference meeting.
Capability	The license that was used for the call.

Table 19.6 – The PSTN and SMS usage report

For more information and details on the interpretation of this report, please go to `https://docs.microsoft.com/en-us/microsoftteams/teams-analytics-and-reports/pstn-usage-report`.

To export this report, you can click on the **Excel** icon in the top-right corner of the report. The status of the export job will be displayed under the **Downloads** tab. To view the report in full screen, click on the **full screen** icon.

Like the other reports, you can also filter the data and customize the metrics provided out of the box by choosing the **Filter** and **Edit column** icons, respectively.

This concludes the PSTN usage report. We covered how to navigate to this specific report, the data points that are logged out of the box, and the available customization and download options. Next, we will cover the Call Quality Dashboard.

Call Quality Dashboard and Quality of Service

The **Call Quality Dashboard (CQD)** is a **near-real-time** data feed that shows the quality of Teams calls and meetings at an org-wide level. Near-real-time means that data will populate within 30 minutes after a meeting or call ends. This dashboard, because it reports from a tenant-wide level, will provide valuable insight for IT admins and network engineers to help them make decisions on optimizing their network to provide the best meeting or call quality possible. We will also quickly cover **Quality of Service (QoS)**. QoS is used to identify and prioritize important network traffic. Once your network has been prepared and optimized, you can use the CQD dashboard to understand the health of a Teams meeting and the call quality in your network.

In this section, we will cover best practices for leveraging the CQD. This includes instructions on where to set up the CQD, interpreting the reports, and recommendations on how to leverage **Power BI** to create a comprehensive dashboard.

Setting up the CQD

As a best practice, Microsoft recommends that you assign specific users Office 365 admin roles to access the CQD. For example, you can assign a user the **Global reader** role so that they can read the available reports in the CQD. For specific information on the permissions that each administrator role has, go to `https://docs.microsoft.com/en-us/microsoftteams/turning-on-and-using-call-quality-dashboard`.

Uploading information about the physical network in your office building(s) and endpoints will drastically improve the accuracy of the CQD reports.

If you are accessing the CQD for the first time, you want to make sure you sign in as a **Global Administrator**. To access CQD, follow these steps:

1.   Navigate to `https://admin.teams.microsoft.com` and sign in.

2.   Locate the **Call quality dashboard** link on the left-hand side, on the bottom.

Figure 19.27 – Locating the Call quality dashboard

3.   Click on it; it should open a new browser tab.

4.   The page will ask you to log in again. Click on the **Sign In** link at the top right of the page.

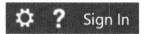

Figure 19.28 – Sign In

5.   Because this is the first time you've logged in, you should see a banner that looks like this:

Microsoft Call Quality Dashboard   Summary Reports ⌄

For the best experience, try uploading your building data.   Upload now ➜

Figure 19.29 – Call Quality Dashboard view

6.   Click **Upload now** to upload your building data.

7.   Fill in the wizard provided.

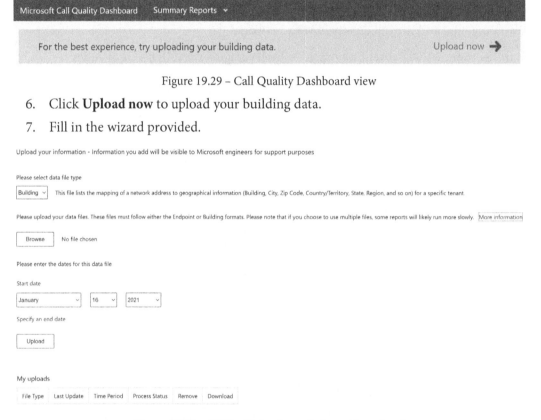

Figure 19.30 – CQD – Upload your information wizard

There are templates that you can use to provide the necessary information and deliver a full picture. The template package can be found at `https://github.com/MicrosoftDocs/OfficeDocs-SkypeForBusiness/blob/live/Teams/downloads/locations-template.zip`.

When you look at the template provided, it should look like this:

	A	B	C	D	E	F	G	H	I	J	K	L	M	N
1	10.0.128.0	SVC-1	32	USCAMTVC	Contoso Leased RE&F	Office	RE&F	Mountain \	94043	US	CA	US	1	1
2	10.0.130.0	SVC-1	32	USCAMTVC	Contoso Leased RE&F	Office	RE&F	Mountain \	94043	US	CA	US	1	1
3	10.0.131.0	SVC-1	32	USCAMTVC	Contoso Leased RE&F	Office	RE&F	Mountain \	94043	US	CA	US	1	1
4	10.0.132.0	SVC-1	32	USCAMTVC	Contoso Leased RE&F	Office	RE&F	Mountain \	94043	US	CA	US	1	1

Figure 19.31 – Template example view

More details on the information that's required for the building, endpoint, and networking mapping can be found at `https://docs.microsoft.com/en-us/microsoftteams/cqd-upload-tenant-building-data`.

Analyzing the CQD

Once you have everything set up, you can use the default dashboards and reports that are provided in the CQD to analyze data.

Let's start by looking at **Summary reports**, which is the default page when you first open CQD. This page includes four tabs – **Overall Call Quality**, **Server – Client**, **Client – Client**, and **Voice Quality SLA**.

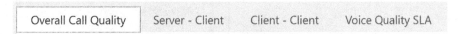

Figure 19.32 – The CQD tabs view

The first tab, **Overall call quality**, will display snapshots of **audio streams monthly** and **daily trends**, **server to client monthly** and **daily trends**, and **client to client monthly** and **daily trends**. The following screenshot shows an example of the **Audio Streams Monthly Trend** report on the left, and **Daily Trend** on the right:

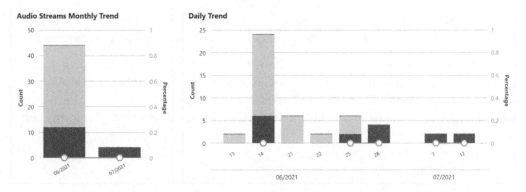

Figure 19.33 – The Audio Streams Monthly Trend view

The other tabs – **Server – Client, Client – Client,** and **Voice Quality SLA** – will contain helpful data as it pertains to server and client endpoints within your network and Skype for Business voice quality if it exists in your environment.

Other detailed reports can be found at the top of the page.

Figure 19.34 – Reports available in CQD

An explanation of each report can be found at `https://docs.microsoft.com/en-us/microsoftteams/cqd-data-and-reports#detailed-reports`.

Another way to analyze the data is to use **Power BI**. Power BI is a Microsoft data visualization tool that's part of the Microsoft 365 suite. You may want to use this if you want to distribute these reports to more users and allow them to access this information without requiring them to go directly into the CQD. The appropriate CQD roles are still required for these users.

Microsoft has published a template to help you organize queries and dashboards. It can be found at `https://docs.microsoft.com/en-us/microsoftteams/cqd-power-bi-query-templates`.

Auto-attendant and call queue reporting

To be able to monitor and report on auto-attendant and call queue activity, you will need the Power BI report template provided by Microsoft. To obtain the latest template, go to `https://docs.microsoft.com/en-us/microsoftteams/cqd-teams-aa-cq-historical-report`.

This report requires the Power BI desktop application, which can be installed from the Microsoft Windows Store or downloaded from `https://powerbi.microsoft.com/`.

These historical reports provide some insight into the performance of the Auto Attendant and Call Queue. Data will be available for the report within 30 minutes. The report will need to be manually refreshed in the Power BI Desktop app to display the new data.

The following three reports are available:

- Cloud Auto Attendant Analytics
- Call Queue Analytics
- Cloud Call Queue Agent Timeline

Let's start by looking at Cloud Auto Attendant Analytics.

Cloud Auto Attendant Analytics

This report shows the performance and call handling of the auto attendants. You can sort and filter data in the report by several fields, including **Date**, **Time**, **Auto Attendants**, and **Resource Accounts**.

The report shows the last 28 days of data on the Auto Attendants

Figure 19.35 – The Cloud Auto Attendant Analytics report

1. The Cloud Auto Attendant Analytics report shows the following metrics:

*   **Incoming call source**: Whether the calls were internal or external, along with the total call volume

*   **Directory search methods**: DTMF (touch keys) or **Speech**

*   **Caller actions**: Whether the caller hung up, was transferred to an Auto Attendant or Call Queue, was transferred externally to a PSTN number, or was transferred to a Teams user

*   **Average Seconds in AA**: Average length of time callers spent in the Auto Attendant

*   **Average Caller Actions**: Average actions performed by callers in the Auto Attendant

- **Call results**: Whether callers in Auto Attendants were transferred to a Teams user, terminated the call at the Auto Attendant, terminated the call because of automatic selection, or is currently in the process of transferring from the Auto Attendant

- **Caller actions count**: The total count of what options the callers selected in the Auto Attendant

The bottom of the report shows the latest caller actions in the auto attendant. This report provides high-level statistics on the auto attendants to give administrators a view of how they are being used by callers.

Call Queue Analytics

The **Call Queue Analytics** report shows the performance and call handling of the Call Queues. You can sort and filter data in the report by **Date**, **Time**, **Call Queues**, or specific **Resource Accounts**. This report shows the last 28 days of data on the Call Queues:

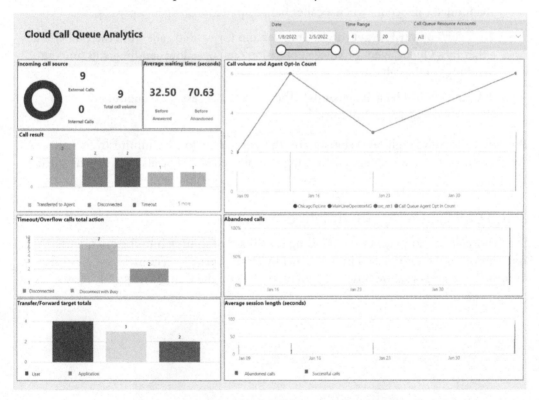

Figure 19.36 – The Cloud Call Queue Analytics report

The Cloud Call Queue Analytics report shows the following metrics:

- **Incoming call source**: Whether the calls were internal or external, along with the total call counts.

- **Average waiting time (seconds)**: The average call length in seconds a caller waited in the queue before the call was answered by an agent or abandoned (the caller hung up).

- **Call volume and Agent Opt-In Count**: The average call volume for the call queues and the agent opt-in count for the call queues.

- **Call result**: The count of the call results for the calls coming into the call queues.

- **Timeout/Overflow calls total action**: The count of overflow actions where a call overflowed because of congestion in the call queue.

- **Abandoned calls**: The total number of abandoned calls in the Call Queue. An abandoned call occurs when a caller hangs up before an agent answers.

- **Transfer/Forward target totals**: Transfer and forwarded calls from the Call Queue either by a Queue agent or voice application (call overflow handling/call timeout handling) in the call queue.

- **Average session length (seconds)**: The average call session's length in terms of abandoned and successful calls.

This report provides high-level statistics on the call queues to give administrators an overview of how call queues are performing and how effectively calls are being handled by agents.

Cloud Call Queue Agent Timeline

This report shows how agents are handling calls that are coming into the call queues. You can sort and filter the data in the report by **Date**, **Agent Usernames**, and **Resource Accounts**. This report shows the last 28 days of data on the Call Queues and Agents:

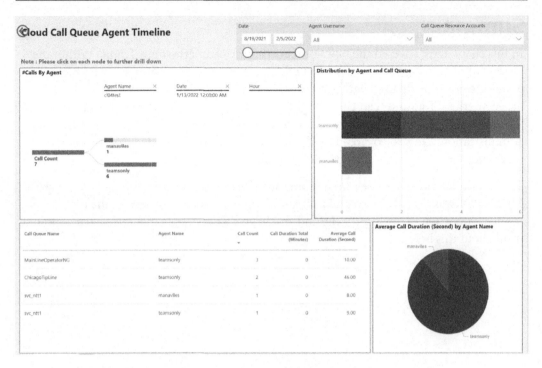

Figure 19.37 – The Cloud Call Queue Agent Timeline report

The **Cloud Call Queue Agent Timeline** report shows the following metrics:

- **#Calls by Agent**: This shows the total Call Counts coming into the queues and how those calls are being answered by the agents that have been assigned to those Call Queues.

- **Distribution by Agent and Call Queue**: This shows the distribution of agent calls to agents by the Call Queue.

- **Average Call Duration (Second) by Agent Name**: This shows the average call duration by the agent.

The bottom of the report shows the latest agent activity by Call Queue. This report provides high-level statistics on the agents servicing Call Queues to give administrators a view of how agents are handling calls from the Call Queues.

Summary

In this chapter, we covered the types of reporting we can perform in Teams. Within the Teams Admin Center, there is a myriad of reports that can give admins a solid picture of how Teams is being used within an organization. From Call analytics to Teams app usage metrics, IT admins can gain insights into these reports, gather data, and make intelligent decisions to help improve and maximize user productivity, collaboration, and administration. We also covered how to access each of these reports, how to customize them, and the specific information they provide.

This concludes our deep dive into the Microsoft Teams architecture and how to integrate Microsoft Teams for advanced end user and administration functions. In the next chapter, you will find answers to the end-of-chapter assessments that have been scattered throughout this book.

Appendix A
Direct Routing and Operator Connect

In this appendix, we're going to go into additional detail for other voice connectivity architecture options, such as **Direct Routing** and **Operator Connect**. While we briefly discussed these architectures in *Chapter 11, Planning for Teams Phone*, and *Chapter 12, Deploying Teams Phone*, we wanted to present additional content, should you choose one of these architectures.

In this chapter, we'll cover the following topics:

- Planning considerations for Direct Routing

- Enabling Operator Connect

Let's jump in!

Planning considerations for Direct Routing

Enabling **Direct Routing** is one of the most flexible (albeit complex) integration options for Teams voice. It involves not only understanding the Teams ecosystem, but also the downstream infrastructure you are connecting to. This includes understanding the **session border controller** (**SBC**) that will bridge between Teams, your existing infrastructure, and the SIP provider.

The following are examples of SIP-based providers:

- An SIP-based PBX
- An SIP-based service provider that offers an SBC as a service
- A direct SIP trunking service
- An SIP gateway
- An analog telephone adapter

The information in this appendix has been indented to provide general guidance and recommendations for enabling Direct Routing. It is *not* intended to be a complete configuration guide, since Direct Routing implementations vary widely, depending on the regional service providers, different brands of session border controllers, or other components you plan to integrate with Teams.

Direct Routing can be broken down into three distinct enablement areas:

- The Microsoft 365 service
- The session border controller
- Downstream SIP-based systems

For our discussion, we will focus on the Microsoft 365 service's preparation and enablement tasks.

Verifying the prerequisites

To use Direct Routing with Microsoft 365, your environment must meet the necessary prerequisites. Some prerequisites will be simple (such as provisioning a tenant), while others will be more difficult.

In this section, we'll cover the following high-level requirements:

- Microsoft 365 tenant prerequisites
- User prerequisites
- Session border controllers
- Networking

Let's briefly examine each of these in the following sections.

Microsoft 365 tenant prerequisites

First, you must have a valid Microsoft 365 tenant with enterprise voice enablement capabilities. To get the enterprise voice capabilities, you must obtain either an Office 365 E5 or Microsoft 365 E5 subscription. You can also use other SKUs such as E1, E3, or F3, but you must also purchase a standalone Phone System SKU. The Phone System SKU is what will give you the entitlements necessary to establish direct route peering with a third-party provider.

By default, tenants are established with an **initial domain** in the form of *tenant.onmicrosoft. com*. To enable enterprise voice features, you must add a vanity domain to the service. To add a domain, you'll need access to your organization's DNS. Microsoft requires customers to insert specially-crafted TXT records to prove public domain ownership. You can go to `https://docs.microsoft.com/en-us/microsoft-365/admin/setup/add-domain?view=o365-worldwide` for the exact steps.

User prerequisites

After adding a vanity or custom domain to your tenant, you'll need to configure users with an address using that new domain. Any user who wishes to use Direct Routing must be assigned to use a vanity domain associated with the tenant – Direct Routing will *not* work with the initial domain.

Session border controllers

Once the tenant's basic configuration has been performed, you will need to set up a **session border controller** (**SBC**). SBCs were discussed in *Chapter 11*, *Planning for Teams Phone*. Depending on your existing phone system, you may already have a device that includes this capability. If not, you will need to acquire a new device (either physical or virtual). The SBC is the device that will peer the tenant to the SIP provider and enable you to route calls.

> **Choosing a Session Border Controller**
>
> Please review the *Session border controllers* section of *Chapter 11*, *Planning for Teams Phone*, for a list of supported SBCs.

Each SBC must have a public IP address assigned to it, as well as a **fully qualified domain name** (**FQDN**). The SBC will also require a third-party public certificate with the SBC's FQDN. You'll use this certificate to create secure SSL peering. Each vendor's configuration steps will be different, so you'll need to use the provided documentation.

Networking

The firewall interfaces between the internal network, the SBCs, and Microsoft Teams should have the following addresses and ports open to allow for successful peering between the SBC and Teams service:

Traffic	From	To	Source Port	Destination Port
SIP/TLS	SIP Proxy	SBC	1024 – 65535	Defined on the SBC (for Office 365 GCC High/DoD only, port 5061 must be used)
SIP/TLS	SBC	SIP Proxy	Defined on the SBC	5061
UDP/SRTP	Media Processor	SBC	3478 – 3481 and 49152 – 53247	Defined on the SBC
UDP/SRTP	SBC	Media Processor	Defined on the SBC	3478 – 3481 and 49152 – 53247

Table A.1 – Required ports

In addition, the SBC will need to be able to resolve the following endpoints:

DNS Name	FQDN Description
`sip.pstnhub.microsoft.com`	A global FQDN that's used to resolve to the primary Azure data center that's hosting Direct Routing based on the tenant's location.
`sip2.pstnhub.microsoft.com`	Secondary FQDN that maps to the second priority region.
`sip3.pstnhub.microsoft.com`	Tertiary FQDN that maps to the third priority region.

Table A.2 – DNS resolution endpoint

Once these infrastructure requirements are in place, you can begin configuring Direct Routing's features.

> **Supporting Documentation**
>
> Detailed planning information can be found here: `https://docs.microsoft.com/en-us/MicrosoftTeams/direct-routing-plan`.
>
> In addition, detailed Direct Routing configuration guidance can be found on the Direct Routing configuration landing page: `https://docs.microsoft.com/en-us/microsoftteams/direct-routing-configure`.

Next, we'll look at some specific guidance and recommendations for configuring E911.

Direct Routing and dynamic E911 considerations

When you're working with Direct Routing, some additional considerations need to be addressed so that the Dynamic Routing information can flow to the SBC and the **Emergency Routing Service (ERS)**. This Dynamic Routing information, known as a **Presence Information Data Format Location Object (PIDF-LO)**, is an XML tag that includes the location data.

In addition to the E911 information provided in *Chapter 11, Planning for Teams Phone*, and *Chapter 12, Deploying Teams Phone*, some key requirements and settings are necessary for E911 when it's being configured with Direct Routing:

- The Teams emergency call routing policy that's assigned to Direct Routing users should have the `AllowEnhancedEmergencyServices` option set to `$true`.

- The **PSTN Gateway** that's been configured for Direct Routing should have the `PidfloSupported` option set to `$true`.

Direct Routing also requires the configuration of additional Emergency Routing Service. With Calling Plans and Operator Connect architectures, the ERS is included. As of this writing, here are the certified Emergency Routing Services (ERS) that can be used with Teams:

Vendor	Site
Bandwidth Dynamic Location Routing	`https://www.bandwidth.com/partners/microsoft-teams-direct-routing/`
Intrado Emergency Routing Service (ERS)	`https://www.intrado.com/en/life-safety/home-business-safety/enterprise-e911-solutions/emergency-routing-service`
Intrado Emergency Gateway (EGW)	`https://www.intrado.com/en/safety-services/public-safety/e911-large-enterprise`
Inteliquent	`https://www.inteliquent.com/services/emergency-services/E911`

Table A.3 – Emergency routing services for Teams

> **Further Reading**
>
> For more information on certified ERS providers for Teams, see the following article: `https://docs.microsoft.com/en-us/microsoftteams/emergency-calling-dispatchable-location`.

Next, we'll look at a managed carrier integration solution: **Operator Connect**.

Enabling Operator Connect

Before you configure Operator Connect, you will want to confirm your eligibility with your carrier and ensure you have the correct hardware requirements. To begin with, you'll need to add your carrier as the operator and then fill out the carrier-specific sign-up form.

To configure Operator Connect, follow these steps.

1. Launch the Teams admin center (`https://admin.teams.microsoft.com`).
2. Navigate to **Voice | Operator Connect**.

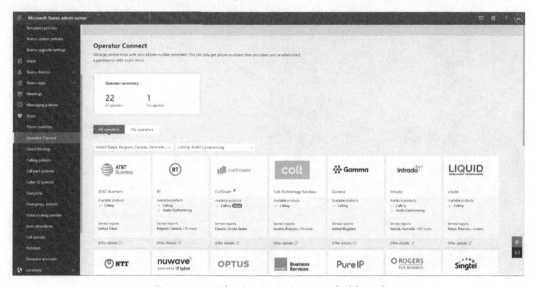

Figure A.1 – The Operator Connect dashboard

3. This site will show all the available operators. You can also sort by regional availability and available capabilities (**Calling**, **Audio Conferencing**, or both).

4. To select a carrier, click on the carrier you want to use from the list. Each carrier will have terms. If prompted, acknowledge any forms or agreements, and click **I accept**:

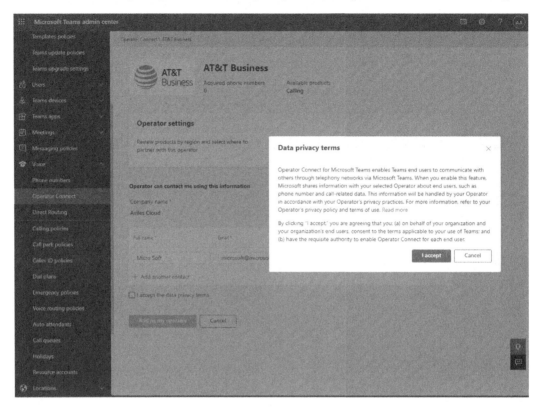

Figure A.2 – Operator Connect – Data privacy terms

5.   Click on **Add as my operator** to add the operator to your tenant:

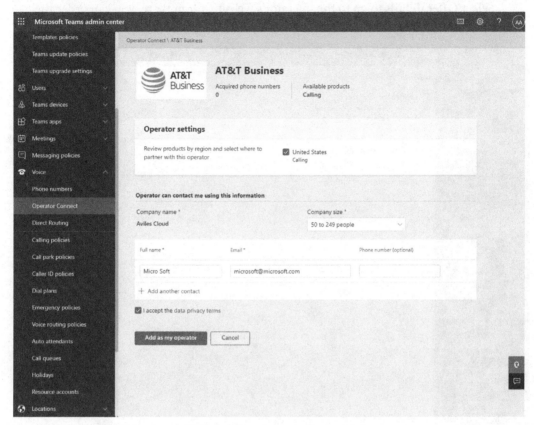

Figure A.3 – Operator Connect – The Operator settings page

6. Once the provider has been added, they will show up under the **My Operators** tab. Select **Offer details** to go to the operator's website. From there, you can order the service from them.

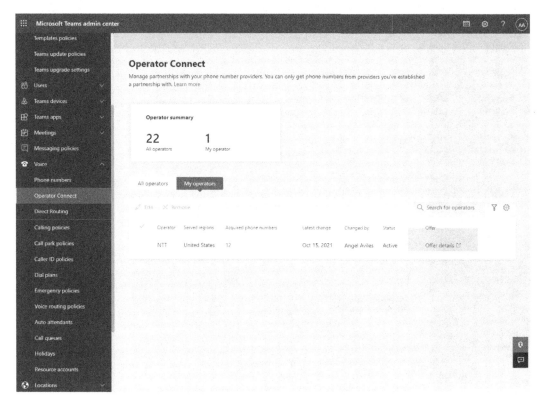

Figure A.4 – The My operators page

7. Complete any necessary operator order forms:

Figure A.5 – Operator-specific sign-up page

8. Once the order has been fulfilled by the operator, you can assign those numbers to users and services under **Voice | Phone numbers** in the Teams admin center.

Figure A.6 – Phone numbers assignment page

All ordered numbers will appear in the tenant. If additional numbers are required, another order request will need to be processed through the operator carrier.

In addition to user and service numbers, you can also request conferencing numbers for the Teams Audio Conferencing service. These numbers are requested in the same way as we described previously, but they can be assigned to the Teams bridge service, allowing you to use an operator's dial-in conferencing numbers versus Microsoft's conferencing numbers. One advantage of using this service is that if your conferencing numbers are already tied to the operator, you do not have to go through the additional step of porting the numbers to the M365 tenant to assign them to the Audio Conferencing service.

Operator Connect Conferencing

For specific instructions on how to configure Operator Connect Conferencing for your organization and users, go to `https://docs.microsoft.com/en-us/microsoftteams/operator-connect-conferencing-configure`.

Once you have enabled Operator Connect in your environment, please revisit *Chapter 12, Deploying Teams Phone*, and *Chapter 13, Configuring Advanced Teams Phone Features*, to configure features such as calling policies, auto attendants, and call queues.

Summary

In this appendix, you learned about additional guidance for configuring Direct Routing with Microsoft Teams, including specific requirements for E911 services. You also learned how to configure Operator Connect.

We hope you've enjoyed reading our book on Microsoft Teams and we look forward to hearing about your successful deployments!

Index

B

Packt>

Subscribe to our online digital library for full access to over 7,000 books and videos, as well as industry leading tools to help you plan your personal development and advance your career. For more information, please visit our website.

Why subscribe?

- Spend less time learning and more time coding with practical eBooks and Videos from over 4,000 industry professionals

- Improve your learning with Skill Plans built especially for you

- Get a free eBook or video every month

- Fully searchable for easy access to vital information

- Copy and paste, print, and bookmark content

Did you know that Packt offers eBook versions of every book published, with PDF and ePub files available? You can upgrade to the eBook version at packt.com and as a print book customer, you are entitled to a discount on the eBook copy. Get in touch with us at customercare@packtpub.com for more details.

At www.packt.com, you can also read a collection of free technical articles, sign up for a range of free newsletters, and receive exclusive discounts and offers on Packt books and eBooks.

Other Books You May Enjoy

If you enjoyed this book, you may be interested in these other books by Packt:

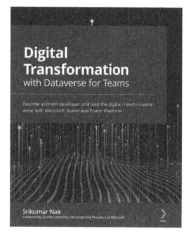

Digital Transformation with Dataverse for Teams

Srikumar Nair

ISBN: 978-1-80056-648-4

- Gain a deeper understanding of Microsoft Dataverse for Teams by exploring various business scenarios
- Design, build, and deploy enterprise-grade applications for Teams
- Develop Power Automate flows and PVA bots using Dataverse for Teams
- Discover administration and security best practices

- Understand the licensing requirements and advanced features of Microsoft Dataverse

- Identify scenarios in your organizations where your citizen development skills can be leveraged

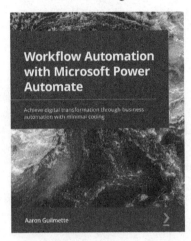

Workflow Automation with Microsoft Power Automate

Aaron Guilmette

ISBN: 978-1-83921-379-3

- Get to grips with the building blocks of Power Automate, its services, and core capabilities

- Explore connectors in Power Automate to automate email workflows

- Discover how to create a flow for copying files between two cloud services

- Understand the business process, connectors, and actions for creating approval flows

- Use flows to save responses submitted to a database through Microsoft Forms

- Find out how to integrate Power Automate with Microsoft Teams

Packt is searching for authors like you

If you're interested in becoming an author for Packt, please visit `authors.packtpub.com` and apply today. We have worked with thousands of developers and tech professionals, just like you, to help them share their insight with the global tech community. You can make a general application, apply for a specific hot topic that we are recruiting an author for, or submit your own idea.

Share Your Thoughts

Now you've finished *Expert Microsoft Teams Solutions*, we'd love to hear your thoughts! Scan the QR code below to go straight to the Amazon review page for this book and share your feedback or leave a review on the site that you purchased it from.

https://packt.link/r/1-801-07555-7

Your review is important to us and the tech community and will help us make sure we're delivering excellent quality content.

Made in the USA
Middletown, DE
28 December 2023

46896300R00349